"Therefore those who were scattered
went everywhere preaching the word."

Acts 8:4 (NIV)

Office of the President
of the Philippines
Malacañan Palace

MESSAGE

⎯⎯⎯⎯

The case of Angelo dela Cruz exemplifies the sad plight that our countrymen experience in their desire to have a job abroad. His experience, together with numerous cases of exploitation and maltreatment of our Overseas Filipino Workers represents the negative aspect of the Filipino diaspora which our government has been seriously addressing through the years. It is in this context that our decision to pull out our humanitarian mission to Iraq must be considered. By deciding as we have, we reaffirm the overriding principle in our foreign policy – that is to uphold the welfare of millions of Filipinos overseas.

On the other side of the equation, we recognize the tremendous contribution of overseas Filipinos especially their sacrifices and perseverance which have kept our economy afloat in not a few instances. We continue to reform our policies, improve the delivery of services and strengthen bilateral relations so that we may effectively protect and serve the overseas Filipinos. In my interactions with Filipino communities during state visits as well as day to day correspondences from Filipino communities, I can see that they are making our nation proud in so many ways. They have been contributors in their adopted communities, have been active in charity work here and have actively preserved our culture and traditions. Let me mention at this juncture that an important parcel of this cultural heritage has been the sustenance and propagation of our deep faith in God.

It is in this respect that this book, "Scattered: The Filipino Global Presence" acquires significance as a source of information and inspiration for our countrymen abroad. Indeed, in a strange land where the opportunities are intertwined with the risks and to seek one's fortune entails embracing the hazards, sound spiritual relationship with God is a perfect source of strength from which one can draw in facing life's challenges.

I thus invite our overseas Filipinos to share the perspectives that the book enunciates and derive inspiration from it. I also enjoin everyone back home to acquire a deeper appreciation of the situation of our countrymen overseas through this book. I am confident that the rich experiences relayed herein will be a valuable reference in showing how God's love transcends the distance and the tribulations that we may encounter in our daily lives.

Gloria Arroyo

Her Excellency GLORIA MACAPAGAL-ARROYO
President
Republic of the Philippines

LEADERS SPEAK OF THE SIGNIFICANCE OF
FILIPINO DIASPORA

"In the book of Acts and at the time of the outpouring of the Holy Spirit we see the plan of God unfolding to reach people from all over the world outside their homeland. Today, this plan continues especially with the Filipinos in the diaspora. SCATTERED is a great resource for strategic outreach in the Arab world."

Henri Aoun
Director of Affairs, North Africa, Middle East
Campus Crusade for Christ International

"The Filipino Diaspora is one of the strategic means of God (in these needy but exciting days) to minister the Gospel and compassionate care to the millions of Filipinos scattered throughout the world, as well as the masses of unreached peoples. May God be pleased to use this book SCATTERED in encouraging and motivating many for His glory!"

Doug Nichols
International Director
Action International Ministries (ACTION)

"SCATTERED is theologically sound, historically and biblically insightful; strategically transferable and inspiring ethnographic reports. Urban and rural pastors must lead their congregations into 'Glocal-missions' in order to impact the world for Jesus Christ."

Vergil Schmidt
Senior Pastor, Deer Park Alliance Church
Red Deer, Alberta, Canada

"SCATTERED is an inclusive chronicle of a diaspora missionary movement flourishing with intentionality, innovation and impact. Compiled by theologians, missiologists, strategists, and practitioners this volume is invaluable for missions in general but imperative for diaspora movements around the world."

Dr. T.V. Thomas
Co-Chair, International Network of
South Asian Diaspora Leaders

"What many may view as a consequence of a national economic tragedy, God graciously transformed into an amazing global strategy for mission. SCATTERED is the untold saga of Filipino Christians in the diaspora. They did not only advance the frontiers of the Gospel but contributed to the renewal and revitalization of declining churches at home and overseas. It is a must reading for the 21st Century church and mission leader."

Dr. Agustin "Jun" Vencer, Jr.
Executive Director, Leadership Development
DAWN Ministries International
Former International Director, World Evangelical Alliance

"We have seen how the dispersed Jewish synagogues throughout the Roman Empire served the apostle Paul and his colleagues in their ministries. Recently, we are beginning to see the meaning of the scattering of the Chinese and the 10,000 churches they have built around the world. Now we are seeing the significance of the Filipino Diaspora and their great potentials for the advancement of the Kingdom. God the Great Strategist for global missions has done it again!"

Dr. Thomas Wang
President, Great Commission Center International
Chairman, AD 2000 & Beyond Movement

SCATTERED:

THE FILIPINO GLOBAL PRESENCE

꘏꘏

Luis Pantoja Jr., Th.D.
Sadiri Joy B. Tira, D.Min.
Enoch Wan, Ph.D.

EDITORS

LIFECHANGE
Publishing, Inc.

SCATTERED: The Filipino Global Presence

Published in Manila, Philippines
By
LifeChange Publishing, Inc.
Copyright © 2004 by Filipino International Network (FIN)

Luis Pantoja Jr., Sadiri Joy Tira, Enoch Wan
Editors

ISBN: 971-92796-9-9

Cover Design and Book Layout: Megatone Printhauz, Inc.
Arnaldo G. Santos, Creative Artist

Printed in the Philippines

Updated Edition
PBK 09 10 11 12 MPH 04 05 06

SCATTERED:

THE FILIPINO GLOBAL PRESENCE

The National Library of the Philippines CIP Data

Recommended entry:

Scattered: the Filipino global presence / Luis
Pantoja, Jr., Sadiri Joy Tira, Enoch Wan,
Editors. – Manila: Lifechange Pub., 2004
1 v

1. Emigration and immigration – Religious
aspects – Christianity. 2. Missions, Filipino. 3.
Church work with immigrants. I. Pantoja, Luis.
II. Tira, Sadiri Joy. III. Wan, Enoch.

BV2695.E4 266.023 2004 P043000627
ISBN 971-92796-9-9

Dedicated to give glory to God,

To fulfill the mission of the Church

And to salute our modern day heroes—

The Overseas Filipino Workers and our Expatriate Kababayans

Honorably represented by

Dr. Rebecca A. Benzon

CONTENTS

Contents

FOREWORD

I find it a great pleasure to write the foreword for this book, "SCATTERED: The Filipino Global Presence." In the pages of this book the Filipino "diaspora" as in its etymological meaning of "scattering" across the globe, is narrated and considered from varied thematic threads each connected to the overriding theme of global missions.

The phenomenon of diaspora can be traced back to biblical times, carrying with it significant implications and compelling challenges for God's people. Today, we are witness to the emergence and development of the Filipino diaspora. This said diaspora, owing to the extent it has affected our national life, merits serious consideration. It demands both a meaningful and relevant response from the Church and the Philippine government. A better understanding of the dispersion of millions of Filipinos in over 180 countries all over the world may in actuality provide us with insightful ways as we participate in the fulfillment of the Great Commission.

This book comes as an exciting effort to open our minds to a candid consideration of the Filipino dispersion across the globe and how it significantly relates to a relevant and meaningful response in our obedience to the Great Commission.

The various contributors to this book inform us of the historical demography, biblical theology, missiological methodology and global strategy in order to provide a clear context towards our understanding of the Filipino diaspora and its implications in our mission work around the world.

And in these pages you will find personal stories that narrate the lived-experiences of the "scattered" Filipinos who are making impact for Christ as Overseas Foreign Workers. Their stories give us useful strategies and inspire ways for our work in global missions. The lives of these OFWs pay tribute to the resilience and enduring spirit of the Filipino work ethic.

"Scattered: The Filipino Global Presence" is a must read not only for the Filipinos who inevitably feel the pride of their compatriots' powerful witness for Christ; rather this book also inspires and suggests that the phenomenon of the Filipino diaspora suggests several innovative ways of doing missions work across cultures. The authors of these articles deserve our heartfelt thanks for putting this theme of the Filipino diaspora in the forefront today.

BISHOP EFRAIM M. TENDERO
National Director
Philippine Council of Evangelical Churches

ACKNOWLEDGMENTS

⸺⊷⸺

To the tireless work and countless hours of special individuals behind the scenes, who took care of the tiny yet all-important details of physically putting a book together, we salute and thank Nilo Marcos & Susan Sosmeña of LifeChange Publishing, Inc., Lorajoy & Dennis Dimangondayao & Cheryl Zamora of FIN.

We also thank the members of First Filipino Alliance Church and the friends and partners of the Filipino International Network for their collaboration, prayer support and sacrificial gifts.

Special thanks go to the contributors and to those who gave their thoughtful critique of the articles. We are grateful to the Christian leaders and Philippine Government officials who endorsed this publication. Thank you to the men and women of the Filipino Diaspora who shared their lives and stories with us.

Our very special thanks, too, to the two Valencia sisters, Mervil and Mea, who accorded our editorial team and project consultant, Dr. Idrenne Lim-Alparaque, with their gracious Filipino hospitality unrivaled this side of the Canadian prairies.

And of course we are truly grateful to our loving wives, Liwayway, Lulu and Mary, who didn't mind those many hours that kept us away from home to work on this project.

Luis Pantoja Jr., Th.D.
Sadiri Joy B. Tira, D. Min.
Enoch Wan, Ph.D.

THE FILIPINO
INTERNATIONAL NETWORK
Seoul Consultation

O n April 12-15, 2004 we convened the Filipino Diaspora and Missions Consultation held at the campus of TORCH Trinity Graduate School of Theology (TTGST) in Seoul, Korea. At this historic consultation, a select group of Filipino scholars, theologians, and practitioners were invited to present papers on the Filipino Diaspora and discuss the implications of this "scattering" of a nation for global missions. Like the children of Isachar, we gathered to read and understand our times. Every morning, before breakfast we sought together the face of God and prayed together for our countrymen in the dispersion. Many of them are hurting, lonely, and isolated. We read papers and listened to reports. It impressed upon us the uniqueness of the Filipino nation and their role in helping fulfill the Great Commission of our Master Jesus Christ.

As we grappled with many issues affecting the Filipinos in the diaspora, we encouraged ourselves to see beyond the statistics. Consequently, before leaving Seoul, all the participants were convinced that the dispersion or scattering of our nation is being used by God to gather other nations before His throne. We longed to see the nations and tribes gather to worship the King of Kings.

This book emerges from "Seoul Consultation" in time for the Lausanne Congress on World Evangelization (LCWE) Forum 2004 to be held in Pattaya, Thailand from September 28-October 5. One of the issues to be addressed at Forum 2004 is the Diaspora Movements, including the Filipino Diaspora, as well as very important national issues affecting the Filipino global church.

The FIN Global Committee, therefore, has committed to share this book with the delegates of Forum 2004 for a couple of reasons: (1) to enhance awareness of the Diaspora Movements and its implications for global missions, (2) to solicit prayers in particular for the Filipinos as they live their faith in Jesus Christ in their adopted nations. Ultimately, this book is for the Filipinos themselves. As they read these pages, may they celebrate their dispersion as divinely ordained and may they be affirmed in their labor.

We are ever thankful to the presenters at the Consultation and for those who did not make it but submitted their respective articles. Three recognized missiologists and evangelism strategists who are non-Filipinos were invited as critics. They are Dr. Elias Medieros dos Santos originally from Brazil and now the Chair of Missions Department at the Reformed Theological Seminary (Jackson, Mississippi); Dr. Enoch Wan originally from Hong Kong and now directing the Doctor of Missiology Program at the Western Seminary (Portland, Oregon); and Dr. T.V. Thomas originally from Malaysia and now directing the Centre for Evangelism and World Missions (Regina, Saskatchewan). Their insights during the consultation and reactions to the papers were invaluable in shaping this volume of readings. Dr. Jonathan Eximo, President of the Alliance Biblical Seminary (Manila, Philippines) also served as critic and responder. Mr. Doug Nichols, International Director of Action International Ministries (AIM) and "adopted Filipino" having spent many years as missionary in the Philippines led the group in morning devotions. He challenged us to move on beyond papers and to "do good works!"

The Seoul Consultation would have not taken place if not for the gracious hospitality of the TTGST and the Filipino Ministerial Association in Korea. Our special thanks to the Network of Filipino Evangelical Missionaries in Korea (NFEMK) represented by Dr. Tereso Casiño of the International Baptist Church in Seoul, Rev. Jessie C. Arce of the Soo Jung International Ministry, Rev. Ronald Chamos of the Touch International Christian Church, Rev. Jose Mariano with Bread of Life in Korea, and Pastor Allan Gadon of Word for the World Christian Fellowship. We also appreciate the support of our Korean partners: Mr. Chang-Joo Kim, Dr. Kwang-Soo Lee, and the International Church of Sae Joong-Ang Presbyterian Church. Our deep gratitude also goes to Dr. Kenneth Meyer, and to Dr. Glenn Jent, President and Vice-President for Academic Affairs respectively of TTGST.

And there is one other group of people who, through their prayers and generous financial support, made the Seoul Consultation a reality. Our heartfelt thanks to: the Dr. Benzon Professional Corporation, Mr. Dave Chung and Associates Inc., the Christian and Missionary Alliance in Canada, and the members of First Filipino Alliance Church (Edmonton, Alberta).

Blessings to you all!

SADIRI JOY B. TIRA, D.Min.
International Coordinator
Filipino International Network
Edmonton, Alberta, Canada

SEOUL CONSULTATION PARTICIPANTS

- **Ronald Adhikari**, SEND International (Taiwan)
- **Jessie Arce**, Soo Jung International Ministry, Seoul, South Korea
- **Rosalinda Dimapilis-Baldoz**, Philippine Overseas Employment Administration
- **Tereso Casiño**, Torch Trinity Graduate School of Theology, Seoul, South Korea
- **Ronald Chamos**, Touch International Christian Church, Seoul, South Korea
- **Lorajoy Tira Dimangondayao**, Filipino International Network, Edmonton, Alberta, Canada
- **Jonathan Exiomo**, Alliance Biblical Seminary, Philippines
- **Rodrigo Felomino**, Kowloon Tong International Congregation, Hong Kong
- **Allan Gadon**, Word for the World Christian Fellowship, Seoul, South Korea
- **Maria Chona Jomilla**, Asian Center for English Studies, Philippines
- **Bob Lopez**, Philippine Missions Association, Philippines
- **Carol Mack**, Fulbright Fellow, Korean-American Educational Commission
- **Charlie H. Mance**, River of Life Alliance Church, Calgary, Alberta, Canada
- **Jose Mariano**, Bread of Life, Seoul, South Korea
- **Elias Medeiros**, Reformed Theological Seminary, Jackson, Mississippi, USA
- **Doug Nichols**, Action International Ministries, Washington, USA
- **Luis Pantoja Jr.**, Greenhills Christian Fellowship, Philippines
- **Narry F. Santos**, Greenhills Christian Fellowship, Philippines
- **Raul Santos**, Christian & Missionary Alliance in Canada, (Limited Access Nation)
- **Amador A. Remigio, Jr.**, Trinity Western University, British Columbia, Canada
- **Reynaldo Solano**, Kapatiran ng mga Simbahang Pilipino sa Singapore/ Victory Family Centre, Singapore
- **Nilo Marcos Sosmeña**, Lifechange Publishing, Inc., Philippines
- **TV Thomas**, Centre for Evangelism & World Missions, Regina, Saskatchewan, Canada
- **Sadiri Joy B. Tira**, Filipino International Network, Edmonton, Alberta, Canada
- **Enoch Wan**, Western Seminary, Portland, Oregon, USA
- **Cheryl Zamora**, Filipino International Network, Edmonton, Alberta, Canada

INTRODUCTION

⚜

T he history of the formation of FIN (Filipino International Network) is a testimony to God's sovereign grace – serving His divine (Kingdom) purpose through the suffering of scattered Filipinos everywhere and the sacrificial servanthood of Filipino individuals abroad; even in dire circumstances and remote areas. The purpose of this volume is four-fold:

- to create awareness of where the Filipino believers are strategically located;

- to encourage the Filipino churches in the homeland and in diaspora to maximize their participation for the acceleration and fulfillment of the Great Commission;

- to encourage partnerships among like-minded organizations and individuals in evangelism, discipleship, and ministry by means of cooperation in producing manuals, providing training, etc.;

- to strategically cooperate with other diaspora groups in global outreach.

The stories of how a local Filipino congregation in mid-Western Canada under the pastoral ministry of a lowly seminary graduate emerging gradually into "glocal missions" and global movement of FIN are detailed in Chapter 7. The strategy of FIN and the planning of the Seoul Consultation were part of Sadiri Joy Tira's doctoral research and dissertation at Reformed Theological Seminary (Jackson) under the mentorship of Enoch Wan. The partnership in editing this volume is built on the decades-long personal friendship and ministerial comradeship of the above two and Luis L. Pantoja, Jr.

For the sake of clarity, definition of several key terms are provided below:

Etymologically, **diaspora** (from Greek διασπορα) means scattering. Originally the term refers to the Jewish dispersion, i.e., to the scattering of Jews outside Palestine and technically used of Jews whom for one reason or another, lived or lives outside Palestine. However, in this volume, the term **diaspora** is used with neither quotation marks nor italicization, in a non-technical and generic English style referring to the phenomenon of "dispersion of any ethnic group." Therefore, "Filipino Diaspora" is a descriptive term in reference to the reality of "people from the Philippines being dispersed into foreign lands."

The term **migration** is used to describe the movement of people from one location to another with no reference to home country; whereas **emigration** is leaving one's own country for another, while **immigration** is just moving to another country.

The term "OCW" or "OFW" means "overseas contract/foreign worker" and in the context of this volume is used in reference to ethnic Filipino, unless noted to be otherwise.

The timing of the Seoul Consultation and the resultant publication of this volume, both preceding the LCWE Forum 2004 in Thailand, is by no means accidental. The partnership of FIN with several organizations, the sponsorship and the endorsements of many key-leaders and Christian organizations are all providential.

All the contributors were invited to first conduct research separately then gathered together to report their findings to the Seoul Consultation on April 12-15, 2004.

By design, presenters at the Seoul Consultation were invited on the basis of their expertise in research and ministry covering various aspects of Filipino diaspora and Christian missions. Their research findings are organized into five parts and each part begins with a simple "introduction."

In order to provide a diachronic perspective for the readers, the volume begins with Part I on "Historical Demography" with two chapters: Chapter 1 is a general survey of the background and demographic reality of Filipino diaspora and Chapter 2 is the descriptive study of the OFW phenomenon.

The two chapters in Part II "Biblical Theology" complement each other and together provide the biblical and theological foundation for the entire undertaking of Filipino diaspora for Christian missions. Chapter 3 is a biblical survey on diaspora of Jews and gentile in the Bible, and Chapter 4 is an attempt to formulate an evangelical theology for Filipino diaspora. The theological insights from this chapter may have significance for Christian missions of other ethnic diaspora groups.

Part III "Missiological Methodology" begins with a general missiological study of the phenomenon of diaspora for Christian missions (Chapter 5), followed by a vigorous attempt (Chapter 6) to answer the question: Is diaspora missions of Filipino valid? This exercise is missiologically informative for all those who are interested/engaged in diaspora Christian missions regardless of ethnic origin or ministry context.

The eight chapters (Chapters 7 to 15) form Part IV "Global Strategy," ranging from the overview of "Glocal Missions" as a paradigm (Chapter 7), general issues related to training (Chapters 8, 9), and various case studies in different continents and various contexts (Chapters 10 to 15). Readers interested in the missiological study of "Glocal Missions" may consult Sadiri (Joy) Emmanuel B. Tira's doctoral dissertation (Reformed Theological Seminary, Jackson, Mississippi, USA) and those interested in FIN may visit the website: http://www.fin-online.org for further details.

Several true stories (Chapters 16-23) are included in Part V "Personal Stories" as ethnographic illustrations of hardship, suffering, injustice, joy and triumph for rejoicing and intercession. For security reasons, names of individuals and places of some stories have been altered; yet readers can still glean from them information and insights to become more sympathetic to the problems and plight of frontline Filipino diaspora faithful workers engaged in Kingdom ministry in unfavorable circumstances.

Part I

HISTORICAL DEMOGRAPHY

PART I

INTRODUCTION

We begin by examining the "who," "when," "why," and "where" of the Filipino Diaspora, i.e., the historical demography of the Filipino dispersion.

"Globalization" has become a buzzword in recent years. Economists, bankers, travel agents, sociologists, anthropologists, educators, missiologists, and theologians have been using this term in different ways. The impact of globalization is pervasive; affecting the way we think, travel, communicate, and conduct business in our "global village." Indeed, we live in the so-called "global village" and have been ushered into a "borderless world."

The Filipinos have become integral members of the global village. In all four corners of the globe we find Filipinos. Definitely, globalization has impacted the Philippine society, particularly the Philippine labor industry. Today, Filipinos are represented in every industry. There are nurses in the hospitals of New York, engineers with Boeing in Seattle-Tacoma, doctors in Libya, architects in Dubai, bar tenders in Milan, laborers in the oilfields of Saudi Arabia, entertainers in Tokyo, maids in Singapore and Hong Kong. Filipino seamen are working in cruise ships and oil tankers. There are also hundreds of Filipino scholars studying in universities around the world.

In recent decades, the Philippine government has encouraged its people to find jobs overseas. Thus, we now have millions of migrant workers criss-crossing the globe. The Philippine government calls them the Overseas Filipino Workers (OFWs).

In this chapter, Dr. Amador A. Remigio who teaches Human Geography at Trinity Western University in Langley, British Columbia (Canada), analyzes the historical and global demographic distribution of the Filipino diaspora. The administrator of the Philippine Overseas Employment Administration (POEA), Hon. Rosalinda Dimapilis-Baldoz, examines the OFW phenomenon from the Philippine government perspective. Their respective findings complement each other to give the reader a background to the flight and plight of Filipinos scattered outside their homeland.

A DEMOGRAPHIC SURVEY OF THE FILIPINO DIASPORA

Amador A. Remigio, Jr.

INTRODUCTION

This chapter provides a brief historico-demographic survey and analysis of the Filipino Diaspora across the geographical dimensions of time and space in the last hundred years. It also inquires into the historical factors and events that have been largely contributory to this peculiar demographic phenomenon that has resulted in a substantial segment of the Philippine population being geographically dispersed to so many countries around the world. Some policy implications and questions are outlined as a result of this survey.

HISTORICAL BACKGROUND

The Philippines is a nation-state located in the western Pacific off the coast of Southeast Asia with Taiwan to the north and Borneo in the south. It has a land area of 298,170 square kilometers distributed among its 7,100 islands.

Until about 3,000 years ago, the islands operated almost completely in isolation. Among the first inhabitants of the islands were the "aetas," a small negroid race, followed later by waves of Indonesian and Malay migrants. Most people lived in small villages at the mouths of rivers, subsisting on fish and rice. Traders from various parts of Asia visited the islands long before the Europeans came. With this growth of intra-regional trade, however, Chinese,

Indian, Arab, and Indonesian travelers brought a pan-Asian influence upon the islands. Islam was introduced to the southern part of the islands during the 15th century.

In 1493, Spain and Portugal as maritime powers decided bilaterally to divide up the unexplored portions of the earth. By 1521, Ferdinand Magellan landed in what is now Cebu. The islanders killed him later, but these did not prevent the Spaniards from further colonizing the 7,100-island country for more than 300 years. As Spanish explorer Ferdinand Magellan claimed the islands for Spain in 1521, Magellan's claim marked the genesis of Spanish colonial history in the Philippines that ended in an indigenous political revolution that ushered in Philippine independence on June 12, 1898. When Spain capitulated to the US, however, in the Spanish-American War, the Philippines fell under America's authority when the United States occupied the country and claimed it as its territory after the Treaty of Paris was signed to end the Spanish-Cuban-American War in 1898. American military authorities, supplanted later by a civilian government, governed the Philippines until the creation of the ten-year Philippine Commonwealth in 1935. American rule in the islands was interrupted in 1941 by the Japanese invasion and occupation associated with the Second World War. The US and its allies recaptured the islands, which were a major battleground in World War II, in 1945, with the Philippines officially gaining again its independence from the US on July 4, 1946.

Some historians have mentioned that a unique dimension of Philippine history has been the emergence of a nation whose cultural matrix has been considerably influenced by Asian, Spanish and American influences. The colonial experience of the Philippines with Spain left a heavy imprint of folk Roman Catholicism in the islands. Likewise, Carino mentioned that Spain's other legacy was the Filipinos' subordination to the dominant economic and political interests of the colonizers which purportedly helps to explain the Filipino-American's acceptance of similarly dominant interests in the United States."(Carino 1996: 294).

It was, however, the colonial experience of the Philippines with the United States that had a profound impact on Philippine immigration. It was this colonial nexus between these two countries that virtually assured the overwhelming economic, political and social influence of America over all aspects of Philippine life. Instrumental in the propagation of this influence has been the patterning of the Philippine educational system after the United States and the widespread use of English as the sole medium of instruction in the school system. To the American colonizer, the use of English became a very useful tool for communication given the extant linguistic diversity of the islands. Also, such similarity of the Philippine and American educational systems enabled Filipino professionals to integrate themselves later insofar as the United States employment mainstream was concerned.

It was American colonization of the Philippines then that laid the seminal groundwork for an exodus of Filipinos to the United States. There were two types of Filipinos who went to the United States. One type was comprised of the educated and typically middle class Filipinos who came as *pensionados*, or government scholars, for the purpose of furthering their education and training in the U.S. The second type was the economically disenfranchised Filipinos who came as a source of cheap migrant labor for Hawaiian plantations, California farms, and the Alaska fishing industry.

Beyond California and Hawaii, migrant-worker Filipinos had also spread to other parts of the United States in search of jobs. Based on agricultural crops and seasons, Filipino farm workers found their way to Arizona, Utah, Colorado, Montana, North Dakota, and even as far as New York. In summer, thousands of Filipinos journeyed to Alaska to work in the fishing and fish canning industries.

While most of the *pensionados* went home after several years of schooling, most of the Filipino migrant workers eventually adopted the U.S. as their new homeland. Some of these migrant workers who came to the United States (without the benefit of scholarships) eventually completed their education by supporting themselves (Posadas 999). Such collective experiences of the *pensionados* and migrant workers were contributory to the early history of the Filipino Americans in the US, and prefigured what would become later as more large-scale demographic movements in the history of the Filipino Diaspora.

Meanwhile, during the colonial and post-colonial period, the United States maintained large military naval and air bases in the country (considered the largest in the Asian Pacific region) that facilitated marriages between American military personnel and Filipino women and eventually the migration of their families to the United States. In addition, there was also a vast recruitment of Filipinos into the United States navy that at one point "there were more Filipinos serving in the U.S. navy than in the entire Philippine navy" (Carino 1996:294). See Appendix I where a timeline of Filipino immigration to the US is presented.

While Filipino fruit pickers began streaming into the US as early as the end of the 18th century, it was not until the 1950s and 1960s that Filipino professionals such as dentists, engineers, doctors, nurses, scholars began streaming in to North America in larger numbers.

With the end of organized Filipino labor importation in 1946, the increase in the number of Filipinos migrating to the U.S. in the 1950s was the result of spouses and children petitioned under American immigration rules. Later, the U.S. Immigration and Nationality Act of 1965 allowed for a new and different wave of Filipino migration. The law allowed for a "dual chain" system of immigration consisting of the "relative-selective" and "occupational" migration. Under "relative-selective immigration," Filipinos came as petitioned relatives of previous migrants who have become U.S. citizens.

On the other hand, the "occupational immigration" clause in the 1965 immigration law was in response to the need for more professionals, specifically in the medical field, in the U.S. Thousands of Filipino professionals, mostly doctors and nurses, arrived in the U.S. as complete families, (i.e., with their spouses and children). Most of them ended up in the east coast, thus creating an occupational distinction between Filipino communities in the east coast and those that were in the west coast, including Alaska and Hawaii.

As a result of this dual chain of immigration, the number of Filipinos in the U.S. multiplied. Steffi San Buenaventura (1995: 439-453) claims that in 1970 there were 343,060 Filipinos in the U.S; in 1980, it rose to 782,895; and in 1990, it was 1,406,770. She notes that this post-1965 immigration had few links with the pre-1965 immigration experience. In the 1990s, California and Hawaii continued to host the largest number of Filipinos in the U.S. Both these states were followed by Illinois, New York, and New Jersey that absorbed much of the post-1965 immigration. Currently, however, Filipinos can be found all over the fifty states of the U.S., signaling the fact of their being one of the fastest growing Asian communities in the U.S.

Equipped with folk Christianity that was part and parcel of the Spanish colonial legacy, as well as English that they had learned as a second language from the Americans, they slowly began arriving on other shores, too. They became dancers and musicians in nearby Malaysia and other Southeast Asian countries. They went to Nigeria and New Guinea as professors and bank tellers. In the 1970s, Middle Eastern nations in search of workers to sustain the exploding oil industry hired Filipino construction workers, excavators, and hotel and medical help.

In the '70s, the exodus of Filipinos to other countries became very pronounced because of the economic boom in the Middle East as petrodollars gushed in huge amounts to the Gulf States, with many Filipino men and women employed in the oil-based economies of these Middle Eastern countries.

The '80s was the coming of age of the newly industrialized countries (NICs): the dragon economies of Singapore, South Korea, Hong Kong and Taiwan, with migrant workers flocking to these areas in the early 1980s. High economic growth implied that the women of these countries had to be liberated from their homes and mobilized accordingly into the mainstream labor force. This explains largely why the pattern of the importation of foreign labor into these countries in the '80s leaned heavily on the procurement of domestic help workers and their services. In both the '80s and '90s, in other nations like Italy, Filipinas began taking care of the home front, enabling local women to avail of domestic work opportunities.

After the eighties came the period of consolidation in the 1990s – with the concomitant economic restructuring of these migrant-worker-importing countries. This period involved the painful process that resulted in the termination of some of the workers' jobs, because after the import of many foreign workers, the time came when their services were no longer needed by these host countries.

This was also the period when many migrant–worker "receiving "countries in Asia formulated tougher rules for migration because they had this realization that while migrants were good as cheap labor, they were not prepared to kowtow to the increasingly militant assertion of human rights by some of these migrant workers.

This brief historical survey shows the tragic divide between the concepts of migration in the West, compared to that prevailing in Asia. In Europe and America, countries eventually provide residency arrangements to their migrant workers, where the migrants, after a certain number of years working in their countries, will be able to live as citizens. In Asia, there is hardly any country that offers similar arrangements. Thus, migrant workers in Asia are just viewed as tools imported to ensure that their foreign-labor dependent economies thrive. Such workers were readily discarded once they have outlived their usefulness. Thus, migrant workers in Asia never had a real chance to be really integrated into the society of their host countries.

THE CURRENT SITUATION

An article in the Los Angeles Times (Schoenberger 1994) described overseas Filipinos as follows:

"Distinctive among the huddled masses of global economic migrants, overseas Filipinos represent the elite, high end of the labor market. They are generally well-educated and usually accomplished speakers of English. But like other itinerant workers, they lack opportunities in the dysfunctional Philippine economy. So women with college degrees serve as maids in Tokyo and Hong Kong. Semi-skilled laborers toil in Kuwait while Filipino seamen ply the oceans on the world's ships. Filipino business graduates dominate the mid-level management ranks of many multinational corporations in Southeast Asia, earning wages they couldn't dream of at home."

During the '70s, the Philippine government under the Marcos administration formed the Overseas Employment Development Board (OEDB), an agency that supported overseas employment of Filipinos. The government's objectives were to address domestic unemployment pressures and to stimulate economic growth. The program was widely accepted with the assumption that individual families with members working overseas would benefit from higher incomes and that the workers would stimulate savings and invest their money in productive enterprises. It was hoped that these investments would in turn bring new employment opportunities and higher wages to the migrant-worker-sending communities. The program was also thought to be temporary and tightly monitored. Indeed, since the inception of this policy, the Philippines became one of the leading sources of international labor migration first in construction jobs in Africa, the Middle East and Europe and then later to service-oriented jobs in Europe, the United States and the developed countries in Asia. In fact, Philippine officials reported U.S.$800 million overseas earnings remitted back into the Philippine economy during the peak years of the seventies (Lindquist, Asian Pacific Migration Journal, Vol. 2, 1993:78).

Recent studies have shown however, that although some migrant workers returned home and started recruiting kin to follow them, most of these workers stayed after their contracts expired and worked illegally or moved on to another developed country and entered as tourists. During this time, the most preferred country of destination for these workers was the United States. An interesting finding in these studies shows that little of the earnings of migrant workers were directed toward productive enterprise. Instead, the earnings were used as "debt repayments, subsistence living, land purchase, house construction, and consumption of imported items." (Lindquist 1993:78). Some observers speculate that remittances fueled inflation instead and just exacerbated the already glaring disparities between the wealthy and those that were economically marginalized.

During the '80s when the Philippines was in deep economic and political crisis due to the politically turbulent years of the Marcos regime and the politically unstable Aquino administration, there was a massive exodus of Filipinos abroad. Although the initial destination may not have been the United States (pre-departure immigrants to the U.S. will usually take a "lifetime" to wait for a visa without an immediate family member who is a citizen or a resident; also, obtaining non-immigrant visas became a very tedious and costly process), joining the ranks of migrant workers was an intermediate step to reaching the premium final destination – the United States (Pessar 1995:6-10). Most workers, however, departed without legal work contracts and the quickest way to leave the country would be to travel under a tourist visa. Since there was no scarcity of workers willing to go abroad, recruiters began to extract fees from these aspiring contract workers. These recruiters-cum-gatekeepers took advantage of those willing to pay large sums of money for the opportunity to go abroad. Many new graduate nurses and other health service professionals who are now residing in the United States were victimized under these conditions. There were also numerous Filipino professionals in the middle class sector with stable jobs such as teachers, bank employees, government employees who left as tourists. Many of these professionals ended taking up menial jobs in their host countries.

Nonetheless, the diversity of Filipinos in the United States today cannot be overemphasized. They may be grouped as the "old timers" or plantation-based Filipinos and their second- or third-generation descendants; the pre-World War II Filipino immigrants of mostly single men; the war brides who came immediately after the war and those that came after independence; the professional Filipinos and their families in the post-1965 period; the Filipino-American military personnel and their families; the spouses of American military personnel and their families; and the current flow of pre-departure immigrants with different visa categories. They include the immediate families of U.S. citizens and residents; and occupational based immigrants. There are also non-immigrant category admissions that include students, tourists, delegates to conventions, Filipino war veterans, household members of the diplomatic corps, businessmen, contract workers, fiancées of U.S. citizens and others. The latter category of non-immigrant admissions that chose to stay in the United States eventually found ways to adjust their status to other visa categories.

In view of the fact that the Filipino immigrating population contains a higher proportion of professionals (Carino 1996:297), "they tend to be less clustered" and "visible." Their integration is not problematic due to the fact that they have the English proficiency to interact with the host society. Carino adds that Filipino Americans have high levels of educational attainment relative to both the U.S. and Philippine population. Interestingly, the socio-economic position of these Filipino Americans tends to be varied. Those who were born in the Philippines and raised in the United States and have attained higher education receive higher incomes compared to Filipinos who were not raised in the US. This may be attributed to the fact that having been reared in the American culture, they are more familiar with the finer details of coping with the pressures of living and surviving in American society.

There are also socio-economic disparities between recent Filipino immigrants to the US. Those who come on the basis of occupational skills are women in their prime working age, with a more professional background marked by higher educational attainment. The family-based immigrant groups, on the other hand, are much older, less professional in occupational background and less likely to be absorbed in the American labor market. If ever they get jobs, they end up in sweat shops, jobs without benefits, domestic services, or any odd jobs with internal arrangements for wages that do not require deductions for income taxes. Also, this is the group that most often would claim government welfare assistance.

Social interaction between and among these Filipinos in North America usually takes place in Filipino-American ethnic associations. These associations celebrate Philippine holidays including religious holidays. Social interaction also takes place frequently among those who share hometown origins. Hometown ties become important because one's townmate is a peer whom one can trust and depend on. It is not surprising to see two newly acquainted Filipinos who inevitably ask the question of where they come from in the Philippines. Families usually maintain clan networks on both maternal and paternal sides. These are usually kept separate from other social networks such as friends, church associates and work associates. These families are also involved in celebrations of family anniversaries, birthdays, graduations and weddings. Notwithstanding these, Filipinos are not exempt from racism in the United States. Just like other minorities, direct or indirect forms of racial discrimination have affected the economic success of Filipinos in the US.

Okamura (1998) views Filipino migration to the United States from a diasporic perspective. Instead of focusing on an ethnic Filipino minority and its host society in the U.S., he contends that a diasporic perspective usefully emphasizes the transnational relations and ties involving the movement of people, money, consumer goods, information, and ideas that are created and maintained among that minority, its homeland, and other diasporic Filipino communities. He argues that such transnational relations and practices will continue to be an increasingly important dimension of the Filipino American community because of the ongoing family-based immigration from the Philippines, further technological advances in communication and transportation, the expansion of transnational capital, and continuing racism and discrimination. All these factors can be viewed as historico-geographic forces that impel Filipinos in the United States, the Philippines and throughout the world to create and maintain diasporic lives and cultures.

As of December 1999, the Commission of Filipinos Overseas reported that there were an estimated total of 7.29 million Filipinos that were away from the Philippine homeland. Of these 7.29 million Filipinos, 2.98 million are temporary workers in host countries; 2.37 million are permanent residents of other countries, while 1.94 million reside illegally (Estrella, 2001). Among the host countries for temporary workers and illegal residents cited in the report were Saudi Arabia, Hong Kong, Japan, United Arab Emirates, Taiwan, Singapore, Italy, Kuwait, Brunei, United Kingdom, Iran, Lebanon, Israel, India, Iraq and Pakistan (Estrella, 2001).

The latest stock estimates on overseas Filipino workers (as of December 2001) show an estimated total of 7.4 million Filipinos overseas. Of these 7.4 million, 3.1 million are temporary workers; 2.74 million are permanent residents of other countries, while 1.57 million are irregulars or illegal residents (Commission on Filipinos Overseas, 2001). See Appendix II (Stock Estimates on Overseas Filipino Workers, as of December 2001).

The official Philippine policy of aggressively promoting the export of its manpower resources and human capital through international labor migration has therefore been a powerful impetus for why Filipinos can be currently found in over 130 countries throughout the world (Okamura 1998).

HISTORICO-DEMOGRAPHIC ASPECTS IN ASIAN-BASED ETHNIC DIASPORAS

Graeme (1998) notes that there has been an unprecedented increase in international population movements in the Asia-Pacific region in the last decade. While the causes for such demographic shifts are complex and are associated with rapid economic and social change in the region, the forces of globalization, improvements in transport and communication and the proliferation of migration networks, he nonetheless foresees that work force age groups will continue to grow rapidly in Asia over the medium-term even with overall population growth in the region decelerating. Thus, he concludes that such increased numbers in these peak mobility work-force age groups will be a significant element that will be contributory to increased levels of international migration both within and beyond the Asia-Pacific region. Thus, what has been happening to the Philippines as a labor-exporting country can be usefully viewed against the larger canvas of this regional demographic forecast.

From the seventies onward, various demand factors have been identified by Varona (2001) as an explanatory variable that accounts for the job types as well as employment destinations of Filipino migrant workers.

Period	Demand Factors	Destination	Origin	Job Types	Gender
Mid-'70s	Petrodollars	Middle East countries, India, Pakistan, Philippines	Arab	Construction	Men
Early-'80s	High economic growth; high cost of local labor	Middle East	India, Pakistan, Philippines, Korea	Semi-skilled	Men
		Japan	Philippines, Thailand	Entertainers	Women
		Hong Kong	Philippines, Thailand, India, Bangladesh	Domestic workers	Women
		Singapore	Indonesia, Philippines	Domestic	Women
		Malaysia	Indonesia	Plantations	Men

		Middle East	*India, Philippines	*Semi-skilled *Skilled	*M *M/W
			*India, Philippines, Thailand	*Domestic workers *Professionals	*W *M/W
		Japan	*Philippines, Thailand, Korea, China	*Entertainers	*W
Mid- to late-'80s	High economic growth; high cost of local labor		*Philippines, Korea, China	*Trainees	*M/W
		Malaysia	Indonesia, Philippines	*Plantation *Domestic workers	*M *W
		Singapore	Malaysia, Philippines	Manufacturing	M/W
		Hong Kong	China	Construction	M
		Macau	China	Manufacturing	M/W
1990's	Economic restructuring	Middle East	Philippines, Indonesia, India, Vietnam	Construction, maintenance	M
			Bangladesh, Sri Lanka, Thailand, Pakistan, Nepal	Domestic workers	W
			(various countries; see above)	Manufacturing, services (incl. military), medical, professionals	M/W
		Japan	Philippines, Korea, Iran, Bangladesh, Pakistan, India, Indonesia, Peru, Brazil, China	Construction, manufacturing, services	*M *M/W
			Philippines, Thailand, China, Korea, Russia	Entertainers	W

1990's		Malaysia	Indonesia, Philippines	Domestic workers	W
			Bangladesh, Indonesia	Plantations	M
			Indonesia, Philippines	Construction	M
			Indonesia, Philippines	Manufacturing	M/W
			Indonesia, Philippines	Other services	M/W
		Singapore	Philippines, Sri Lanka, Indonesia, India, Malaysia	Domestic workers	W
			Malaysia	Manufacturing	M/W
		Korea	China, Bangladesh, Indonesia, Philippines, L. America, Sri Lanka, Africa, Vietnam, Uzbekistan	Manufacturing	M/W
		Hong Kong SAR	Philippines, Indonesia, Thailand, Sri Lanka, India	Domestic workers	W
			China	Construction	M
		Thailand	Myanmar, China, Bangladesh, Laos	Construction	M
			Myanmar, Laos	Manufacturing	M/W
			Myanmar	Fishing	M
			Myanmar, China	Entertainers	W

1990's		Brunei	Philippines	Domestic workers, teachers	W
		Papua New Guinea	Philippines	Teachers, other professionals	M/W
		Australia	*Philippines, Vietnam	*Professionals	M/W
			*Various countries	*Students	M/W

GEOGRAPHIC DIMENSIONS OF THE FILIPINO DIASPORA

While Filipinos have had a long history of migration, it is clear from the preceding diagram that it was only in the last thirty years that a massive demographic movement of its workers to other parts of the world transpired because of these various demand factors.

Also, structural economic and demographic factors (a weak economy with high rates of unemployment and rapid population growth) combined with an inward-looking industrialization policy have sustained such a strong labor outflow from the Philippines, in contrast to the Asian newly industri-alizing economies (e.g., Hong Kong, Singapore, South Korea, Taiwan) that have become net importers of labor (Abella, 1993). In a similar vein, Alburo (1993) identifies the government's heavy reliance on import substitution and protectionism as well as weaknesses in the domestic economy as variables that propel Filipino workers to go overseas, with an economy that has become heavily reliant and dependent on workers' remittances as a valuable source of foreign exchange currencies.

There are two terms for classifying these migrant workers from the Phil-ippines: *balíkbayan*, or immigrant Filipinos primarily from North America who periodically visit the motherland, and OCWs (overseas contract workers), who are employed on a contractual basis in such places as the Middle East, Europe, East and Southeast Asia.

Indeed, the Marcos regime's interest in overseas Filipinos was part of its plan to spur the tourist industry both as a generator of foreign exchange and a showcase for its putative accomplishments. Offering a combination of bargain airfares, tax breaks and other incentives, the Philippine government then in the seventies and early eighties encouraged dollar-earning Filipinos, especially from North America, to visit the country and see for themselves the claimed success of Martial Law-based governance. Living in close proximity to sources of foreign capital, balikbayans were treated like tourists in their land of origin. As preferred consumers, balikbayans, like other foreign visitors, were also accorded deference and generously accommodated by local officials.

By the early 1980s, changes in the global economy increased the demand for skilled and semi-skilled Filipino workers in many parts of the Middle East, Asia and Western Europe (Rafael 1997). Unlike the earlier groups of Filipino-Americans, this later group of workers was bound by temporary contracts to foreign employers in international locales. They came to be known in the Philippines by a particular description as OCWs for overseas contract workers or as OFWs for overseas Filipino workers.

Unlike Filipinos in the U.S. who generally tended to assimilate either as professional middle class suburbanites or, as in the case of second generation Filipino-Americans as ethnicized, hyphenated Americans (Espiritu 1994), OCWs rarely ever expect to remain permanently in their host country. Occupying positions of relative subservience and marginality because of their contractual terms of work and their effective exclusion from meaningful participation in their host societies, OCWs are viewed as just temporarily expedient labor resources that nonetheless perform useful functional roles in the communities of their host countries. Rather than batting for the rights of citizenship, as Filipino immigrants in North America are inclined to do, OCWs tended instead to optimize their earnings capability in environments that guarantee their safety and maximizes their welfare. Thus, they are not very keen in influencing legislation or engaging in political lobbying in the country where they work, oftentimes depending on human rights and worker welfare organizations to represent their interests.

It is perhaps for this reason that OCWs often refer to their travels as a kind of "adventure," or in Tagalog as *pakikipagsapalaran* and *pagbabakasakali* (Constantino 1966). To go abroad is to find one's fortune (palad), as well as to take risks (magbakasakali). Through the availment of foreign work opportunities, they intend "to convert the products of their labor into "gifts" with which to endow one's kin at home and thereby gain their respect and recognition." This does not, however, detract from the recognition of the concomitant risks involved in the conditions under which these workers labor in terms of uncertain futures and hazardous employment conditions (e.g., as exemplified by the recent July 2004 experience of Angelo de la Cruz who was taken hostage in Iraq).

It was precisely during this moment in Philippine history that OCWs, increasingly made up by the mid-1980s of women going abroad as domestic helpers, "mail order" brides and sex workers, came to be known as "the new heroes."

By labeling OCWs as "national heroes," President Aquino and her successor, Fidel Ramos, have sought to contain the anxieties attendant upon the flow of migrant labor, including the emotional distress over the separation of families and the everyday exploitation of migrants by job contractors, travel agents and foreign employers. The prevalence of such conditions apparently pointed to the inability of the Philippine state to provide enough economic opportunities for its people.

Thus, Filipinos working abroad "simultaneously signify the failure of the nation-state to contain its excess population and the success of global capitalism in absorbing and accommodating this failure. They can best be regarded as both the product and producers of surplus: sheer labor power immediately translatable into the universally understood form of value—money." (San Juan 1998)

As Filipino-American newspaper publisher Alex Esclamado put it, "Remittances by overseas Filipinos [estimated in 1995 to be about $6 billion annually] to their families are now considered direct foreign aid... that can have a radical effect on people's lives—building houses in depressed rural villages, paying off medical bills, sending little brothers and sisters and cousins to school."

Currently, there are more than 8 million overseas Filipinos today, according to unofficial estimates; the majority of these are workers toiling in over

130 countries worldwide. Each day, around 2,000 overseas Filipino workers (OFWs) fly out of the Philippines as exported labor. Official Philippine statistics from the Philippine Overseas Employment Administration display these migrant labor placements in greater detail, for a five-year period from 1998 to 2002 (See Appendix III). Each day, an average of two OFWs are sent home in coffins. An undetermined number, meanwhile, also go back home each day after they have completed their contracts, lost their jobs, or been forcibly sent home due to various reasons.

Stories abound about the difficulties many OFWs experience when they finally decide to go home for good. The primary problem is joblessness back home and the lack of economic opportunities for the returning migrant and his/her family. Many of the OFWs opt to stay abroad, in harsh "3D" (dirty, dangerous, disdained) jobs, or as undocumented migrants, because oftentimes this is better than going home without jobs, as a source of decent livelihood, and an uncertain future. This is the irony of working abroad – being jobless, displaced and uprooted when the migrant workers finally returns home. Indeed, packing one's bags and going home for good after being an OCW/OFW is much easier to say but the actual reality at the ground level makes it difficult to cope operationally for those OCWs / OFWs who are contemplating on this option.

While the economy is unable to absorb OFW returnees into the workforce, "there is also no comprehensive, coherent and sustained reintegration program by the government." And while OFWs remit over US$7 billion a year to keep the Philippine economy, the peso and the national budget afloat, there have been very little, and oftentimes unreliable, channels for OFW reintegration, social enterprises, and meaningful participation in national economic policy-making and development planning. Every December, the red carpet is rolled out at our airports to honor and welcome the "new economic heroes." We have always said that this gesture is more symbolic of the blood and suffering of OFWs as there are still prevalent abuses, deaths and violations of OFWs' rights abroad. This gesture is also hollow because of the absence of viable reintegration and economic empowerment options for returning OFWs." (Joint Statement On Overseas Filipino Workers Day, 22 June 2003, Hong Kong, Forum Of Filipino Reintegration & Savings Groups

(FFRSG), Coalition For Migrants' Rights (CMR), Asian Domestic Workers Union, Asian Migrant Theater Company & Asian Migrant Centre).

While the Filipino Diaspora has definitely generated positive economic impacts for most overseas Filipino workers and the Philippine economy, one wonders whether the negatives in terms of the social costs has been seriously reckoned with in terms of its short-term as well as long term-impacts on Philippine polity, society and economy. It does not take much imagination to delineate the devastating social costs that the Filipino Diaspora has entailed for the families of overseas workers. It can probably be gauged in terms of children that have been seasonally "orphaned" and families that have broken up because of the tremendous psycho-sociological pressures and strains arising from spouses that have been geographically separated and dispersed (Cruz 1987).

Subject to the daily pressures and exploitative demands of an alien working environment and taxed by their efforts to negotiate with or, more commonly, evade the apparatus of a state hostile to (illegal resident foreign workers) or indifferent to their situation, Filipino overseas contract workers often relate lives of loneliness, deprivation, abuse (Ballescas, 1992; Ventura, 1992; Dormiendo, 1995; Margold in Ong and Peletz, eds., 1995; Rafael, 1997; Constable, 1997) and quiet desperation (see book appendices on some ethnographic stories of the Filipino Diaspora).

Also, Tan (1993) argues that in four major occupational groupings (seamen, production/ construction workers, domestic helpers and entertainers), there has been little transmission of value-added human capital acquired from overseas deployments to the domestic economy. She posits the view that the homeward transmission of value-added human capital that can be useful to the domestic economy when Filipino overseas workers return will be largely dependent on whether these workers' skills acquired from these overseas jobs are readily applicable and transferable to domestic economic activities.

SOME POLICY QUESTIONS

Thus, from a macro-policy perspective, the Filipino diasporic experience raises profoundly haunting and deeply disturbing questions. Was it really worthwhile for the Philippine government to have intentionally encouraged an aggressive policy of labor and manpower export, considering both the positives and the negatives? Or was the policy a desperate but convenient political safety valve that was opened in order to relieve the Philippine nation-state from rising political temperatures (that could have ignited a political upheaval) in the seventies and eighties? Sadly, a dominant feature of the Philippine nation state from the seventies to the present has been its spectacular failure to provide enough economic opportunities for its people as a result of its relatively dismal economic performance vis-à-vis its more economically progressive Asian neighbors. Such failure as it interfaced with emerging and subsequently dominant endogenous-cum-exogenous factors eventually constituted the main driving force behind the Filipino Diaspora from the seventies onwards. On the other hand, could it be that Divine Providence has allowed all these to happen for Filipinos to be Gospel missionaries for the Great Commission as Christ's witnesses to the furthest corners of the Earth?

CONCLUSION

From this brief survey of the Filipino Diaspora, the historical factors and events that propelled this demographic movement of Filipinos worldwide to seek better economic opportunities elsewhere were identified and examined. It seems likely that as long as these endogenous as well as exogenous factors continue to be operative at the local, regional, national and international levels, the continuing dispersion of Filipinos worldwide to distant shores will not abate in the foreseeable future even as the impacts of globalization is further heightened in the international labor market. It is a development that bears watching in the years ahead just as the spatial, temporal and spiritual ramifications and implications of the Filipino Diaspora can be far-reaching indeed.

REFERENCES

Abella, Manolo (1993) "Labor Mobility, Trade and Structural Change: The Philippine experience" in *Asian and Pacific Migration Journal.* Vol.2, No. 3, 249-268.

Alburo, Florian (1993) "Remittances, Trade and the Philippine Economy" in *Asian and Pacific Migration Journal.* Vol.2, No. 3, 269-284.

Ballescas, Maria Rosario, P. (1992) *Filipino Entertainers in Japan: an Introduction.* Quezon City: The Foundation for Nationalist Studies.

Carino, Benjamin V. "Filipino Americans: Many and Varied" in Silvia Pedraza and Ruben Rumbaut, eds. (1996), *Origins and Destinies: Immigration, Race and Ethnicity in America.* Belmont, California: Wadsworth Press.

Catalan, Daisy C.S.(1996)"The Diversity of Filipinos in the United States" at http:// www.yale.edu /ynhti /curriculum / units /1996/4/96.04.05.x.html

Catholic Institute for International Relations (1987). *The Labor Trade: Filipino Migrant Workers Around the World.* London: Catholic Institute for International Relations.

Cheng, Grace Jadyn, SINGAPORE: Seen Everywhere, but Little Heard "at (http:// www.ips.org/migration/1003_8.html)

Commission on Filipinos Overseas – COF (2001). Annual Report. Manila: Department of Foreign Affairs, Republic of the Philippines.

Constable, Nicole (1997). *Maid to Order in Hong Kong: Stories of Filipina Workers.* Ithaca, New York: Cornell University Press.

Constantino, Renato (1966). The Miseducation of the Filipino. Manila.

Cruz, Victoria Paz (1987). *Seasonal Orphans and Solo Parents: The Impact of Overseas Migration.* Manila: Scalabrini Migration Center and CBCP Commission on Migration and Tourism; Normine Printing House.

Diamond, David (June 2002) "One Nation, Overseas" in *Wired,* Issue 10.06.

Dormiendo, Justino (1995) *Nagmamahal, Flor: Mga Liham Mula sa Mga OCW.* Pasig: Anvil Publishing.

Espiritu, Yen (1994) "The Intersection of Race Ethnicity, and Class: The Multiple Identities of Second Generation Filipinos" in *Identities,* Vol. 1, No. 2)

Estrella, Dulce (November 2001) " Globalization and Asian Women: The Philippine Caser," *Asian-Pacific Newsletter on Occupational Health and Safety,* Vol. 8, No.3, 66-70.

Forum of Filipino Reintegration & Savings Groups (FFRSG), Coalition for Migrants' Rights (CMR), Asian Domestic Workers Union (ADWU), Asian Migrant Theater Company (AMTC) & Asian Migrant Centre (AMC), *Joint Statement on Overseas Filipino Workers' Day*, 22 June 2003, Hong Kong.

Graeme, Hugo (1998) "The Demographic Underpinnings of Current and Future International Migration in Asia" in *Asian and Pacific Migration Journal*, Vol. 7, No.1, 1-25.

Grassi, Ricardo "ITALY: Migrants Embrace Second Culture" at (http://www.ips.org /migration/1003_3.html)

Jeong, Yunsik SOUTH KOREA: More Income, but Split Families at (http://www. ips.org/migration/1003_7.html)

Lindquist, Bruce (1993) "Migration Networks: A Case Study in the Philippines" *Asian and Pacific Migration Journal*, Volume 2, No.1. Manila: Scalabrini Migration Center.

Mandap, Daisy C.L. HONG KONG : The Call of the Sea (and its Men) at (http:// www.ips.org/migration/1003_4.html)

Margold, Jane "Narratives of Masculinity and Transnational Migration: Filipino Workers in the Middle East" in Aihwa Ong and Michael Peletz, eds. (1995) *Bewitching Women, Pious Men: Gender and Body Politics in Southeast Asia*. Berkeley: University of California Press, 274-298.

McCoy, Alfred W., ed. (2000) Lives at the Margin: Biography of Filipinos, Obscure, Ordinary, and Heroic. Quezon City: ADMU Press.

Micaller, Cookie. "HONG KONG: Crossing the Line" at (http://www.ips.org/ migration/1003_2.html)

Mi-Young Ahn. "SEOUL: Dreams for a High Price" at http://www.ips.org/ migration/1003_6.html

Moran, Kathy "PHILIPPINES: Children of Migrant Workers Feel Lost at Home" at (http://www.ips.org/migration/1003_5.html)

Anil Netto "MALAYSIA: Fishing for a Better Deal" at (http://www.ips.org/ migration/1803_1.html)

Okamura, Jonathan Y. (1998). *Imagining the Filipino American Diaspora: Transnational Relations, Identities, and Communities*. New York and London: Garland Publishing.

Pedraza, Silvia and Rumbaut, Robert (1996) Origins and Destinies: Immigration, Race and Ethnicity in American History (Belmont, California: Wadsworth Publishing Co.

Pessar, Patricia (1995). *A Visa for a Dream.* Needham Heights, Massachusetts: Allyn and Bacon.

Pido, Antonio J. A (1985). *The Filipinos in America: Macro/Micro Dimensions of Immigration and Integration.* New York: Center for Migration Studies of New York.

Posadas, Barbara (1999). The Filipino Americans. Westport, Conn: Greenwood Press), 14-25.

Rafael, Vicente L. " Ugly Balikbayans and Heroic OCWs" in Hector Santos, ed. Philippine History and Culture Series; at http://www.bibingka.com/phg/balikbayan/. US, 19 June 1997)

San Buenaventura, Steffi (1995). "Filipino Immigration to the United States," *The Asian American Encyclopedia.* New York: Marshall Cavendish, pp. 439-453.

Schoenberger, Karl (1994), 'Living Off Expatriate Labor," *Los Angeles Times,* August 1, 1994, 1.

San Juan, Jr, E. (1998). *From Exile to Diaspora: Versions of the Filipino Experience in the United States.* Boulder, Colorado: Westview Press.

Takaki, Ronald (1995). *In the Heart of America: Immigrants from the Pacific Isles.* Adapted by Rebecca Stefoff with Carol Takaki. New York and Philadelphia: Chelsea Book Publishers.

Teodoro, Luis V. Jr. ed. (1981) Out of this Struggle: The Filipinos in Hawaii. Honolulu: The University of Hawaii Press.

Varona, Rex (February 2001). Excerpted from remarks delivered at the seminar *"On the Philippine Migration Trail: Some Migration and Reproductive Health Aspects",* Bangkok, Thailand.

Ventura, Rey (1992) *Underground in Japan.* London: Jonathan Cape.

Zabriskie, Phil "IRAQ: Life in the Danger Zone" at (http://www.time.com/time/asia/2004/ peace_troops/iraq_phil.html)

APPENDIX I

Timeline of Filipino Immigration to the United States (adapted from Daisy C.S. Catalan, 1996)

1898 Commodore Dewey sailed to Manila as war broke out between United States and Spain. Spain ceded the Philippines to the United States at the Treaty of Paris on December 10th.

1900-1945 First Phase of Filipino Immigration to the United States

1900 First Filipino immigrants came to the mainland United States. They were made up of students called *"pensionados."* They were sons and daughters of rich influential Filipinos who were friends of United States officials. They were sent to study at the expense of the United States government. They were often "mestizos," a mixture of Spanish and Filipino blood. They were also volunteers for services in the U.S. army, navy, and merchant marines during World War I. Most of these Filipinos stayed in the United States after the war.

1906 First group of 15 Filipino men arrived in Hawaii to work in the sugar plantations. They were recruited by the Hawaiian Sugar Planters Association from rural areas in Northern and Central Philippines. They were called *"sacadas."* Several years earlier the Chinese, Japanese, Koreans, Portuguese and others had already started working in the plantations.

1922 Filipino laborers in Hawaii were recruited to work for higher wages in the United States mainland as canners in Alaska, fruit and vegetable farmers in the state of Washington and California. Some laborers whose contracts had expired in Hawaii opted to go to the mainland rather than returning home. Likewise, Filipino students came to the mainland United States with plans to complete their education. Most of these students were on their teens or early twenties. Many had only a few dollars in their pockets having used most of the money from the mortgage of their parents' lands or sale of their animals to pay their fares. Although they were eager to continue their education they discovered that they could not earn enough money to support themselves and go to school at the same time. Many of these Filipinos had limited job opportunities that were oftentimes confined to the lowest paying menial occupations.

1930 Approximately 150,000 (Pedraza and Rumbaut,1996:296) became con-tract workers in the sugar and pineapple plantations in Hawaii. After their contracts expired, more than 50,000 (Teodoro, 1981:4) either returned to the Philippines or went on to the mainland. At this time, in the wake of the Great Depression, 7,300 Filipinos (Teodoro,1981:4) were repatriated to the Philippines because of lack of work.

1934 U.S. Congress passed the Tydings-McDuffie Independence Act which established the Commonwealth of the Philippines. It set a ten-year transition period for which the United States would withdraw all rights of possession over the Philippines.

1934-1945 Post-depression and World War II years. A quota of 50 Filipinos a year could emigrate to the United States as permanent residents.

1946 Philippine Independence from the United States.

1946-1965 Second Phase of Filipino Immigration

The majority of immigrants at this time were war brides or wives of Filipino service men. Immigration quota was raised to 100 Filipinos per year immediately after independence. President Truman signed the Immigration and Nationality Act which enabled many Asian residents in the United States to apply for citizenship. Filipinos who had served honorably for three years in the United States Armed Forces were eligible for naturalization as U.S. citizens. The law likewise gave the Filipinos the opportunity to request or petition members of their family who were entitled to non-quota or high preference status to join them. The recruitment of plantation workers to Hawaii continued. Some established workers requested recruitment of younger male relatives. During the two decades from 1946 to 1965 over 34,000 Filipinos (Pedraza-Rumbaut, 1996:295) came to the United States.

1965 -Present Third Phase of Filipino Immigration

1965 Liberalization of immigration laws. This increased the Filipino immigration to the United States. The guiding philosophy behind the new policy was the admission of relatives, the reunification of families and the recruitment of needed skilled professional workers. The number of immigrants allowed to enter by quota in each country from the eastern hemisphere was 20,000. Those allowed to enter were classified under preference categories. Exempted from the quota were minor children, spouses and parents of adult U.S. citizens. Also exempted from the quota was the admission of refugees. The influx of Filipino immigrant professionals such as doctors, nurses, medical technologist, teachers etc. began.

1980s More than half of the Filipino American population in the United States were foreign born.

1990s The Immigration and Naturalization Service (INS) reported 1 million (Pedraza-Rumbaut,1996:295) Filipino admissions to the United States.

APPENDIX II

STOCK ESTIMATES ON OVERSEAS FILIPINO WORKERS
As of December 2001

COUNTRY	PERMANENT	TEMPORARY	IRREGULAR	TOTAL
WORLD TOTAL	**2,736,528**	**3,099,940**	**1,566,426**	**7,402,894**
AFRICA	271	31,530	10,103	41,904
EGYPT	53	1,018	1,400	2,471
LIBYA	75	4,350	485	4,910
NIGERIA	18	10,500	1,500	12,018
OTHERS	125	15,662	6,718	22,505
ASIA (East and South)	**70,349**	**826,782**	**360,527**	**1,257,658**
BRUNEI	26	20,240	1,500	21,766
HONG KONG	404	171,485	2,000	173,889
JAPAN	65,647	138,522	36,379	240,548
KOREA	1,510	12,018	13,000	26,528
MALAYSIA	310	58,233	167,936	226,479
SINGAPORE	152	56,377	71,917	128,446
TAIWAN	1,901	116,480	4,300	122,681
OTHERS	399	253,427	63,495	317,321
ASIA (West)	**1,546**	**1,233,325**	**123,332**	**1,358,203**
BAHRAIN	61	26,356	5,000	31,417
ISRAEL	41	9,058	21,136	30,235
KUWAIT	92	53,067	10,000	63,159
LEBANON	19	19,825	5,500	25,344
OMAN	18	18,551	1,500	20,069
QATAR	13	37,626	1,000	38,639
SAUDI ARABIA	239	897,000	18,000	915,239
UAE	373	128,604	38,000	166,977
OTHERS	690	43,238	23,196	67,124
EUROPE	**152,851**	**420,232**	**203,249**	**776,332**
AUSTRIA	3,205	1,191	2,000	6,396
FRANCE	925	4,804	26,121	31,850
GERMANY	41,321	7,005	4,392	52,718
GREECE	84	7,514	17,500	25,098
ITALY	2,431	69,998	78,000	150,429
NETHERLANDS	7,632	2,351	700	10,683
SPAIN	33,643	5,687	4,000	43,330
SWITZERLAND	605	5,953	9,300	15,858
UNITED KINGDOM	45,889	15,767	8,344	70,000
OTHERS	17,116	299,962	52,892	369,970
AMERICAS / TRUST	**2,291,311**	**286,793**	**848,879**	**3,426,983**
CANADA	338,561	21,146	4,000	363,707
UNITED STATES	1,910,844	60,373	532,200	2,503,417
CNMI	80	16,205	3,705	19,990
GUAM	41,541	434	2,025	44,000
OTHERS	285	188,635	306,949	495,869
OCEANIA	**220,200**	**46,009**	**20,336**	**286,545**
AUSTRALIA	204,075	687	2,041	206,803
NEW ZEALAND	16,045	236	100	16,381
PAPUA NEW GUINEA	63	1,661	7,339	9,063
OTHERS	17	43,425	10,856	54,298
SEABASED TOTAL		**255,269**		**255,269**

Prepared by: Commission on Filipinos Overseas, Department of Foreign Affairs
Stock estimates on overseas Filipino workers (as of December 2001)

APPENDIX III

Relevant demography-related statistics (1998-2003) of Filipino migrant labor placements, Philippine Overseas Employment Administration

PHILIPPINE OVERSEAS EMPLOYMENT ADMINISTRATION
Deployed Landbased Overseas Filipino Workers by Destination (New hires and Rehires) *

	1998	1999	2000	2001	2002	2003	Percentage Change
MIDDLE EAST	**279,767**	**287,076**	**283,291**	**297,533**	**306,939**	**285,564**	**-7.0%**
Bahrain	5,180	5,592	5,498	5,861	6,034	6,406	6.2%
Egypt	358	334	487	539	421	490	16.4%
Iran	18	24	132	641	112	240	114.3%
Iraq	10	23	42	86	50	1,490	2880.0%
Israel	2,022	3,488	4,429	5,562	5,049	5,094	0.9%
Jordan	551	456	541	560	701	812	15.8%
Kuwait	17,372	17,628	21,490	21,956	25,894	26,225	1.3%
Lebanon	1,342	1,674	2,783	3,350	3,046	2,786	-8.5%
Libya	7,084	5,937	5,962	5,489	6,114	5,083	-16.9%
Oman	5,199	5,089	4,739	4,512	3,303	3,652	10.6%
Qatar	10,734	7,950	8,679	10,769	11,516	14,344	24.6%
Saudi Arabia	193,698	198,556	184,724	190,732	193,157	169,011	-12.5%
Syria	99	109	151	1,705	193	138	-28.5%
United Arab Emirates	35,485	39,633	43,045	44,631	50,796	49,164	-3.2%
Yemen	591	582	589	1,140	553	629	13.7%
Middle East (unsp.)	24	1	-	-	-	-	0.0%
ASIA	**307,261**	**299,521**	**292,067**	**285,051**	**288,481**	**254,520**	**-11.8%**
Afghanistan	-	16	1	-	2	19	850.0%
Bangladesh	501	220	190	230	182	416	128.6%
Bhutan	-	5	1	-	1	-	-100.0%
Brunei	16,264	12,978	13,649	13,068	11,564	9,829	-15.0%
Cambodia	179	224	355	524	629	719	14.3%
China	1,280	1,858	2,348	1,979	2,046	2,168	6.0%
East Timor	-	-	-	24	812	439	-45.9%
Hong Kong	122,337	114,779	121,762	113,583	105,036	84,633	-19.4%
India	191	165	185	454	249	408	63.9%
Indonesia	2,471	1,706	1,507	1,411	1,492	1,534	2.8%
Japan	38,930	46,851	63,041	74,093	77,870	62,539	-19.7%
Kazakhstan	3	4	32	311	548	1,580	188.3%
Kirgiztan	-	2	1	2	-	-	0.0%
Korea	2,337	4,302	4,743	2,555	3,594	7,136	98.6%
Laos	63	82	118	174	71	181	154.9%
Macau	2,021	1,983	2,208	1,860	1,963	2,335	19.0%
Malaysia	7,132	5,978	5,450	6,228	5,721	7,124	24.5%
Maldives	82	147	117	123	105	186	77.1%
Mongolia	72	31	47	28	15	9	-40.0%

Myanmar	153	96	153	215	187	221	18.2%
Nepal	3	7	7	13	4	5	25.0%
Pakistan	186	136	107	180	65	58	-10.8%
Singapore	23,175	21,812	22,873	26,305	27,648	24,737	-10.5%
Sri Lanka	230	290	396	629	502	309	-38.4%
Tadzhikistan	3	3	-	3	3	4	33.3%
Taiwan	87,360	84,186	51,145	38,311	46,371	45,186	-2.6%
Thailand	1,384	1,014	1,015	2,056	1,162	2,139	84.1%
Turkmenistan	98	35	94	126	33	2	-93.9%
Uzbekistan	4	80	28	17	18	8	-55.6%
Vietnam	802	531	494	549	588	596	1.4%

PHILIPPINE OVERSEAS EMPLOYMENT ADMINISTRATION
Deployed Landbased Overseas Filipino Workers by Destination (New hires and Rehires) *

	1998	1999	2000	2001	2002	2003	Percentage Change
EUROPE	**26,422**	**30,707**	**39,296**	**43,019**	**45,363**	**37,981**	**-16.3%**
Albania	-	1	-	-	-	-	0.0%
Andorra	48	64	49	92	68	180	164.7%
Austria	468	363	334	206	165	152	-7.9%
Azerbaijan	53	88	76	87	113	190	68.1%
Belgium	183	168	160	159	148	189	27.7%
Belorussia	1	2	-	-	-	-	0.0%
Bosnia and Hercegovina	2	2	-	-	-	-	0.0%
Bulgaria	1	1	1	1	2	8	300.0%
Channel Islands	-	-	1	-	-	-	0.0%
Croatia	2	1	2	-	-	-	0.0%
Cyprus	941	1,168	1,500	1,548	1,836	1,637	-10.8%
Czech Republic	3	10	9	3	8	13	62.5%
Denmark	78	55	28	27	25	30	20.0%
Faeroe Island	-	-	-	-	-	-	0.0%
Finland	16	16	12	13	8	15	87.5%
France	122	130	297	149	129	92	-28.7%
Georgia	-	-	-	-	-	14	0.0%
Germany	156	131	120	134	89	75	-15.7%
Gibraltar	1	-	2	42	1	-	-100.0%
Greece	593	2,145	1,618	1,402	1,819	1,880	3.4%
Hungary	6	5	2	4	11	-	-100.0%
Iceland	1	3	4	17	25	35	40.0%
Ireland	18	126	793	3,734	4,507	5,642	25.2%
Isle of Man	-	-	10	13	-	7	0.0%
Italy	20,233	21,673	26,386	21,641	20,034	12,175	-39.2%
Luxembourg	7	6	2	-	1	-	-100.0%
Macedonia	-	1	1	-	-	-	0.0%
Malta	11	9	15	30	13	15	15.4%
Moldova	1	-	-	-	-	1	0.0%
Monaco	6	14	7	-	-	-	0.0%
Netherlands	473	326	292	432	213	228	7.0%
Norway	108	252	180	139	125	126	0.8%
Poland	7	10	7	23	12	6	-50.0%

Portugal	12	26	40	44	55	38	-30.9%
Romania	8	2	-	-	3	1	-66.7%
Russia	31	56	112	77	57	67	17.5%
Slovenia Republic	-	1	-	-	-	1	0.0%
Spain	1,940	1,557	1,913	1,783	1,751	1,258	-28.2%
Sweden	35	26	29	59	29	21	-27.6%
Switzerland	312	312	298	239	324	238	-26.5%
Turkey	41	39	129	201	137	49	-64.2%
United Kingdom	502	1,918	4,867	10,720	13,655	13,598	-0.4%
- England	491	1,896	4,834	10,695	13,633	13,558	-0.6%
- Northern Ireland	7	22	21	-	-	3	0.0%
- Scotland	4	-	12	25	22	37	68.2%
Yugoslavia	2	-	-	-	-	-	0.0%

PHILIPPINE OVERSEAS EMPLOYMENT ADMINISTRATION
Deployed Landbased Overseas Filipino Workers by Destination (New hires and Rehires) *

	1998	1999	2000	2001	2002	2003	Percentage Change
AMERICAS	**9,152**	**9,045**	**7,624**	**10,679**	**11532**	**11,049**	**-4.2%**
Antigua	9	-	-	2	17	16	-5.9%
Argentina	23	41	40	34	6	18	200.0%
Armenia	-	1	-	-	-	1	0.0%
Aruba	792	1,428	168	119	121	230	90.1%
Bahamas	22	32	41	128	219	161	-26.5%
Barbados	-	-	50	36	-	-	0.0%
Belize	-	56	-	-	-	9	0.0%
Bermuda	177	128	239	196	272	118	-56.6%
Brazil	19	35	61	41	32	69	115.6%
Canada	1,957	2,020	1,915	3,132	3,535	4,006	13.3%
Caribbean (unsp.)	-	-	2	19	-	-	0.0%
Cayman Is.	200	278	352	645	798	613	-23.2%
Chile	34	5	1	1	41	11	-73.2%
Colombia	3	1	7	1	83	90	8.4%
Costa Rica	2	11	1	26	4	3	-25.0%
Cuba	314	299	319	216	652	495	-24.1%
Diego Garcia	1,444	673	306	726	1,281	1,042	-18.7%
Dominica	1	-	-	-	3	-	-100.0%
Dominican Republic	7	4	1	7	12	11	-8.3%
Ecuador	-	4	1	-	2	2	0.0%
El Salvador	1	-	4	4	4	2	-50.0%
Grenada	8	9	-	-	6	4	-33.3%
Guam	812	370	209	195	100	269	169.0%
Guatemala	1	11	1	28	11	11	0.0%
Guyana	4	5	-	-	2	14	600.0%
Haiti	11	20	24	37	48	43	-10.4%
Hawaii	-	-	1	41	1	-	-100.0%
Honduras	11	12	4	7	7	4	-42.9%
Jamaica	27	26	13	8	34	14	-58.8%
Mexico	33	90	241	242	78	50	-35.9%
Midway Is.	23	21	25	27	7	-	-100.0%

Netherlands Antilles	-	1	15	20	32	4	-87.5%
Nicaragua	-	2	4	-	4	1	-75.0%
Panama	2	3	3	13	26	4	-84.6%
Peru	2	3	2	1	-	-	0.0%
St. Nevis - Anguilla	-	1	-	-	-	-	0.0%
St. Kitts Nevis	1	-	-	1	3	-	-100.0%
St. Vincent	1	2	-	-	-	1	0.0%
South America (unsp.)	3	1	-	-	-	5	0.0%
Surinam	2	8	2	-	-	-	0.0%
Trinidad and Tobago	-	11	7	1	10	6	-40.0%
United States of America	3,173	3,405	3,529	4,689	4,058	3,666	-9.7%
Uruguay	17	5	3	-	-	14	0.0%
Venezuela	14	15	13	21	12	23	91.7%
Virgin Is.	2	3	14	13	8	12	50.0%
West Indies (unsp.)	-	5	6	2	3	7	133.3%

PHILIPPINE OVERSEAS EMPLOYMENT ADMINISTRATION
Deployed Landbased Overseas Filipino Workers by Destination (New hires and Rehires) *

	1998	1999	2000	2001	2002	2003	Percentage Change
AFRICA	**5,538**	**4,936**	**4,298**	**4,943**	**6,919**	**8,750**	**26.5%**
Afars and Issas	-	-	-	12	-	1	0.0%
Algeria	1,258	705	280	393	742	1,076	45.0%
Angola	681	772	788	1,119	950	922	-2.9%
Botswana	26	24	27	50	72	21	-70.8%
Burundi	-	1	-	-	-	-	0.0%
Cameroon	12	19	4	30	77	102	32.5%
Cape Verde	-	15	7	-	2	2	0.0%
Central African Republic	1	1	2	6	11	92	736.4%
Chad	1	-	-	77	2,010	1,895	-5.7%
Congo	66	35	43	69	181	105	-42.0%
Djibouti	11	-	2	2	3	2	-33.3%
East Africa (unsp.)	4	-	-	-	-	3	0.0%
Equatorial Guinea	40	732	865	773	544	961	76.7%
Eritrea	44	8	2	9	19	14	-26.3%
Ethiopia	15	9	19	10	12	12	0.0%
Gabon	53	66	63	81	74	138	86.5%
Ghana	18	42	70	37	44	64	45.5%
Guinea	125	121	-	-	-	1	0.0%
Ivory Coast	7	4	22	25	35	7	-80.0%
Kenya	37	57	47	48	48	41	-14.6%
Lesotho	-	3	6	29	29	10	-65.5%
Liberia	-	5	1	1	1	1	0.0%
Madagascar	1	1	6	9	5	5	0.0%
Malawi	4	22	17	19	16	12	-25.0%
Mali	61	50	52	27	10	11	10.0%
Mauritania	-	3	19	2	5	2	-60.0%
Mauritius	2	1	-	1	2	1	-50.0%
Morocco	42	37	38	37	48	51	6.3%
Mozambique	9	3	7	7	9	7	-22.2%

Namibia	14	5	4	14	42	586	1295.2%
Nigeria	1,496	1,110	833	1,039	1,061	1,472	38.7%
Rwanda	2	2	-	-	-	2	0.0%
Sao Tome & Principe	14	7	1	-	2	3	50.0%
Senegal	-	5	-	3	-	6	0.0%
Seychelles	547	191	125	242	238	112	-52.9%
South Africa	123	182	106	112	76	42	-44.7%
Sudan	317	420	236	329	308	362	17.5%
Swaziland	3	1	8	4	4	11	175.0%
Tanzania	30	30	37	59	57	42	-26.3%
Togo	-	1	2	1	-	-	0.0%
Transkei	1	-	-	-	-	1	0.0%
Tunisia	14	21	13	8	4	3	-25.0%
Upper Volta	-	1	-	1	-	9	0.0%
Uganda	34	27	26	24	16	13	-18.8%
West Africa (unsp.)	357	149	366	98	60	42	-30.0%
Zambia	16	24	33	20	15	15	0.0%
Zimbabwe	4	5	14	4	5	1	-80.0%
Africa (unsp.)	48	19	107	112	82	469	472.0%

PHILIPPINE OVERSEAS EMPLOYMENT ADMINISTRATION
Deployed Landbased Overseas Filipino Workers by Destination (New hires and Rehires) *

	1998	1999	2000	2001	2002	2003	Percentage Change
TRUST TERRITORIES	**7,677**	**6,622**	**7,421**	**6823**	**6,075**	**5,023**	**-17.3%**
Commonwealth of Northern Mariana Islands	5,982	4,837	5,215	4,681	4,163	3,562	-14.4%
- Rota	162	106	146	127	63	55	-12.7%
- Saipan	5,139	2,270	3,760	2,288	1,830	1,539	-15.9%
- Tinian	94	89	95	160	94	74	-21.3%
- Marianas	587	2,372	1,214	2,106	2,176	1,894	-13.0%
Federated States of Micronesia	429	554	494	431	451	358	-20.6%
- Chuuk (Truk)	9	34	2	6	8	6	-25.0%
- Pohnpei (Ponape)	60	61	69	138	58	54	-6.9%
- Yap	9	22	11	4	2	-	-100.0%
- Micronesia (unsp.)	351	437	412	283	383	298	-22.2%
Republic of Marshall Is.	65	71	109	107	86	86	0.0%
- Majuro	9	11	3	1	3	-	-100.0%
- Marshall Is. (unsp.)	56	60	106	106	83	86	3.6%
Republic of Belau	1,084	1,010	1,480	1,420	1,233	923	-25.1%
Melanesia	111	127	111	162	117	77	-34.2%

- Cook Is.	-	2	-	-	4	5	25.0%
- Fiji Is.	31	58	36	101	51	28	-45.1%
- Solomon Is.	72	58	69	57	59	40	-32.2%
- Vanuatu	8	9	6	4	3	4	33.3%
- Melanesia	-	-	-	-	-	-	0.0%
							0.0%
Polynesia	6	23	11	7	25	17	-32.0%
- Samoa	6	23	11	7	19	9	-52.6%
- Tonga					6	8	0.0%
Trust Territories (unsp.)	-	-	1	15	-	-	0.0%

PHILIPPINE OVERSEAS EMPLOYMENT ADMINISTRATION
Deployed Overseas Filipino Workers by Destination *

	1998	1999	2000	2001	2002	2003	Percentage Change
OCEANIA	**2,524**	**2,424**	**2,386**	**2,061**	**1,917**	**1,698**	**-11.4%**
Australia	182	184	234	148	138	156	13.0%
Nauru	38	37	47	20	42	7	-83.3%
New Caledonia	3	4	8	-	10	8	-20.0%
New Zealand	75	102	110	150	185	64	-65.4%
Papua New Guinea	2,226	2,097	1,987	1,743	1,542	1,463	-5.1%
UNSPECIFIED	**2**	**-**	**6,921**	**11,530**	**10,882**	**46,279**	**325.3%**
Deployed Landbased Total	**638,343**	**640,331**	**643,304**	**662,648**	**682,315**	**651,938**	**-4.5%**
Deployed Seabased Total	**193,300**	**196,689**	**198,324**	**204,951**	**209,593**	**216,031**	**3.1%**
LAC NAIA	192,799	196,367	196,916	204,088	209,135	215,260	2.9%
POEA Reg'l Ctrs./Ext. Units	501	322	1,408	863	458	255	-44.3%
Phil. Waterports & Seaports	-	-	-	-	-	516	0.0%
GRAND TOTAL	**831,643**	**837,020**	**841,628**	**867,599**	**891,908**	**867,969**	**-2.7%**

Processed by: Policies and Programs Division
       : PLANNING BRANCH

*   Based on the report of POEA's Labor Assistance Center on the actual departures of OFWs at the international airports;

**   Ceased operation since October 1999

***   Number of Deportees from Malaysia based on the report of POEA Zamboanga

**** Number of workers with Special Exit Clearance Issued by Employment Regulation Branch, POEA

THE OVERSEAS FILIPINO WORKERS (OFW) PHENOMENON

Rosalinda Dimapilis-Baldoz

‹‹‹•›››

There are many questions surrounding the OFW phenomenon. I will do my best to answer the following questions from the perspective of the Philippine government: Who is the OFW? Why call it the OFW phenomenon? Where are the OFWs? What are they doing? What is the profile of OFWs in general? Why do they leave their homeland? What do their employers say about them? How are they treated back home? What has the Philippine government have to say about them?

Who Is An OFW?

OFW means Overseas Filipino Worker. He used to be called OCW which means Overseas Contract Worker. Whether we call them OFWs or OCWs, our country hails them as our "modern day heroes." Very recently, no less than our President Gloria Macapagal-Arroyo called them OFIs, or Overseas Filipino Investors. Economist as she is, her emphasis is clearly on the billions of dollars of remittances that they pour into the Philippine economy.

To the host country or their employer, our OFWs are more often referred to as "guest workers," "expatriates" or "temporary workers." They work in their country (OFWs) because their immigration and labor laws allow them to accept the entry of foreign nationals either to meet shortages in certain labor market supply of specific skills, jobs or professions. They work on a temporary basis usually defined in contracts of employment of one, two or three years duration (OCWs). They leave the Philippines with intention to return after completion of contracts. Statistics show that on the average, an

OFW or OCW would normally return five times to work with the same employer in the same country or with other employers in the same country or move elsewhere in another country. If it is a 2-year contract, the average duration is equivalent to a ten-year period with breaks of one or two months vacation leave in the Philippines after every completion of the contract.

Technically and strictly speaking, therefore, OCWs as properly referred to by employers as guest or temporary worker, do not include immigrants or those who have acquired permanent resident status in their host country. Apparently, OFWs or OFIs are more encompassing. It can include permanent residents who also send dollar remittances to their families.

An inter-agency committee, tasked to monitor the Stock Estimate of Overseas Filipinos annually, gives the world total of 7,582,504 as of December 2002. It consists of 2,807,356 permanent residents, 3,167,978 temporary workers (OCWs) and 1,607,170 irregular workers. Apparently, the biggest bulk of Overseas Filipinos are the temporary workers or the OCWs.

By world groupings, Americas and Trust territories is the biggest with 3,334,297. Second is Asia, East and South, with 1,453,296. Third is Middle East or Asia, West with 1,371.621. Fourth is Europe with 803,169. Fifth is Oceania with 298,609. And sixth is Africa with 66,243 Overseas Filipinos.

Specifically, for temporary workers or OCWs, the top 10 countries of destination in 2003 are: 1) Saudi Arabia, 2) Hong Kong, 3) Japan, 4) United Arab Emirates, 5) Taiwan, 6) Kuwait, 7) Singapore, 8) Qatar, 9) United Kingdom, and, 10) Italy.

WHY CALL IT THE "OFW PHENOMENON?"

History tells us that labor migration in the Philippines is an old phenomenon. It begun at the turn of the century when Filipinos, mostly Ilocanos, started leaving the country to work as sugar plantation workers in Hawaii. Later, they migrated to California to pick crops, then to Alaska to work in canneries, and the East Coast to toil in the service industry. The presence of Filipinos in the United States multiplied as demand for foreign labor grew, brought about by the easing of the recruitment for the US Navy through the

RP-US Military Treaty, the 4-H program, the exchange visitors program, the severe nursing shortage in the 1980s, and the demand for physical therapists to take care of America's graying population.

The phenomenon expanded dramatically in the 1970s when the Philippine government started setting up an organized system of overseas employment program and aggressively promoted Filipino skills abroad, particularly in the Middle East, initially as a response to the world oil crises. The program continues even today, helping ease unemployment problems and generating billions of dollars in remittances that have propped up our economy.

The continuous "exodus" or "diaspora" of Filipinos has been described as a phenomenon that far exceeded "biblical proportion" of two million Israelites who fled from Egypt. Even the documented OCWs have far exceeded their numbers. At any given point in time, there are 2.9 million temporary workers overseas or OCWs. At the Philippine Overseas Employment Administration, we serve a daily average of 3,000 Filipinos looking for jobs abroad at a "low" day and 5,000 Filipinos at a "peak" day. Daily, we record an actual deployment of 2,748 OCWs. In 2001, deployment was 867,599 and 981,908 in 2002. Despite the Iraq War and the SARS epidemic, deployment in 2003 was 867,969 or a decline of only 2.7% from 2002.

The 1st Quarter 2002 *Ulat ng Bayan*, Pulse Asia Survey findings say that one out of five Filipinos want to leave the country and stay abroad, indicating that there will be no let up in the mass exodus of Filipinos that we have seen in the past few decades.

WHERE ARE THE OFWS? WHAT ARE THEY DOING?

OFWs, numbering over 2.9 million, have penetrated almost all industry sectors in over 180 countries all over the globe. We have the professionals consisting of information technologists, business and management experts, engineers and planners, teaching personnel, arts and science experts and creative artists. They are found in the United States, Japan, and Europe working in multinational technology firms like Trend Micro, America Online, Fujitsu Software, NEC, Toshiba, ACER, Intel and Motorola, among others.

Another major occupational grouping is the medical workers consisting of nurses, doctors, physical therapists, medical technologists, pharmacists and midwives. We have deployed over 100,000 medical professionals to more than 120 countries specifically in the Middle East, Americas, Asia and Europe.

Under the category of operations and maintenance workers, we have electronics technicians and specialists, civil work technicians and specialists, automotive transport technicians and specialists, electrical, mechanical technicians and specialists. Their concentration is mostly in Middle East countries especially the Kingdom of Saudi Arabia.

Construction workers consist of large pool of manpower in fields of specialization ranging from professional engineers, architects and skilled workers. Filipinos were involved in the construction of the Mina Abdullah Refinery Modernization Project in Kuwait, one of the largest of its kind; the 4,500 capacity Philsinports, Jeddah Housing Complex, the Mecca Sewerage and Drainage Project and the Riyadh Outer Ring Road, all in the Kingdom of Saudi Arabia; the Ishtar Sheraton Hotel and Samawa General Hospital in Iraq; the Malang Highway, one of Indonesia's major highways in the Surabaya, and the Wadaslingtan Dam also in Indonesia; the Yuen Long Industrial Estate Development in Hong Kong; the Palau Compact Road in Palau, the Ship Repair and Maintenance of Varna Shipyard in Bulgaria; and the Gynia/Gdansk Shipyards in Poland, among others.

Other occupational groupings are hotel workers specializing in food service, food production and hotel and restaurant management. They are found serving the world's most prestigious and internationally-famous chains of hotels.

Indicative percentages of deployed workers in 2003 based on skill categories as may be gathered from the data on newly-hired workers show that the highest share goes to service workers; professional and technical workers, second; production workers, third, and the rest are clerical, sales, agricultural and other workers.

Seafarers comprise 20% of the total 1.23 million seafarers worldwide, making the Philippines the leading supplier and the manning capital of the world. They man ocean-going tankers, passenger vessels, reefer vessels, bulk and chemical carriers of about 116 flags of registry that include Norway, Germany, Singapore, Cyprus, Greece, Panama, Liberia, Bahamas, Jamaica and Malta, among others.

Deployment trends show increasing trends from only 36,035 in 1975 to 214,590 in 1980 to 598,769 in 1990 to 866,885 in 2002 and 867,969 in 2003. A very significant increase in trend is the deployment of women based on 2003 data on newly-hired workers: from 12% in 1975 to 47% in 1985 to 61% in 1998 to 64% in 1999 to 70% in 2000, 72% in 2001, and 73% in 2002 and 2003.

The POEA regularly releases official statistical data on deployed workers based on world groupings, country of destination, occupational groups and gender disaggregation. The scattering of Filipinos across the globe is reflected in the various countries of destination appearing in said official statistical data.

WHAT IS THE PROFILE OF OFWs IN GENERAL?

Based on the Census 2000, there were 992,397 Filipino overseas workers, accounting for 1.3% of the total population. Almost half of the overseas workers came from Southern Tagalog, the National Capital Region, and from Central Luzon combined.

There were 101 male overseas workers for every 100 of their female counterparts. Half of the OFWs were below 32 years old. One out of every ten overseas workers was less than 15 years old. There were more women in the younger age groups, while men dominated the older age groups. More than half of the overseas workers were married.

More than half of male overseas workers were heads of their households; more than half of the female overseas workers were either daughters or spouses of their household heads. Eight out of every ten overseas workers were Roman Catholics. One out of every three belonged to the prominent ethnic group of Tagalog. Half of the workers had attended/finished high school. Almost all were literate.

There were 800,051 households with at least one Filipino overseas worker. Households with overseas workers were larger than those without overseas workers. Housing characteristics of overseas workers revealed that they were economically better off than the average household with no overseas worker. This was manifested in the bigger houses (median floor area of housing units of overseas workers was 39.40 square meters while the median floor area of non-overseas workers was 28.56 square meters), stronger materials of roofs and walls of the housing units of overseas workers, and higher proportion of owner-ship of major household amenities like radio, television set, and refrigerator.

WHY DO THEY LEAVE THEIR HOMELAND?

Migration in the Philippines is largely induced by high levels of unemploy-ment and underemployment and high incidence of poverty. This is further reinforced by severe labor shortages experienced by developed countries due to the aging of their workforce, and acceleration in globalization of trade which puts in place less stricter immigration rules.

Incidence of poverty in the Philippines is 40%, meaning 31 million Fili-pinos or 1/3 of the population is poor. In the case of unemployment and under-employment, 1 out of 3 Filipinos who should be working is either jobless or underemployed or whose work and compensation is way below the workers' qualifications. The 13.9% unemployment rate means 4.86 million of the 35 million labor force are jobless. The 19.6% underemployment rate means an additional 6 million Filipinos are wanting of more jobs.

More Filipinos have actually found jobs overseas compared to those added to the number of employed locally, indicating that without the overseas jobs, unemployment would have been worse. The problem could be more serious if we consider the fact that even the so-called own account and unpaid family workers are included in the job accounting system of government. We have a reported 4.1 million unpaid family workers and 11.4 million own account workers.

Referring again to the Asia Pulse Survey findings, the push factors other than poverty and joblessness include rampant urban crime, corruption at every level of government, bungling political leaders and some of the world's worst pollution. A better future and a safer place for their children are the main reasons for wanting to leave.

While many are leaving, a few migrants are also coming home. The returnees who lived in a culture not their own for many years, have realized that there is no place like home – the land of their birth.

WHAT DO THEIR EMPLOYERS SAY ABOUT THEM?

Findings of various studies and surveys made on Filipino workers and managers show the following:

1. Most multinational managers in the Asia-Pacific region rate their Filipino workers highly – both management and staff – in terms of skill, capabilities and sheer creativity and cheerfulness.

2. In the United States, Filipino-Americans have been rated as having the highest per capita income among all Asian-American groups. One major reason is that a good number of Filipino-Americans are highly educated professionals.

3. Many of our own ventures of foreign companies have been cited for high levels of productivity and quality and in a couple of cases our joint venture partners have looked at the possibility of using Filipino managers for their regional expansions.

4. Our country is very rapidly becoming a hub for the international call business center as Filipino women among different nationalities have been rated the highest for their pleasant voice and disposition and their understandable English.

5. Perhaps most revealing of all, the quality of our workforce has been proven by 7 million Filipinos working overseas today. From professionals to skilled to semi-skilled workers, praise has been heaped by employers and host countries on their superior skills and adaptability to all kinds of tasks and work situation.

6. In the shipping industry, we are the prime supplier of seafarers. Today, Filipinos account for 20% of the total crew requirements worldwide.

In the 2002 World Competitiveness Report, the Philippines was rated low on criteria such as governance, infrastructure, government integrity, bureaucracy, and industrial productivity, but we ranked at the top in the following criteria out of 49 countries surveyed:

1. availability of skilled labor - first

2. availability of senior managers - third

3. availability of qualified IT employees - fourth

4. average working hours per year - fifth

5. flexibility & adaptability of labor force - sixth

For 2003, 59 economies were surveyed and we were no. 21 in government efficiency, no. 19 in economic performance, no. 26 in infrastructure and no. 23 in business efficiency. Though the Philippines slipped down from 18th place in 2002 to 22nd place in 2003, what is significant is the high ratings that we maintained in skilled labor, labor costs, remuneration in services, availability of finance skills, and information technology skills.

The point is clear, as one of the country's leading industrialists says: "The Philippines is a nation blessed in the so-called people skills that are much prized in the world today. There is no question that the Filipinos—our people, our human capital—are our main source of competitive advantage. So we are wise to nurture our human resources as the principal component of our competitive strategy in the world today."

If we have to differentiate ourselves in the market and find a sustainable source of "competitive advantage," the key is our people. Even Robert Reich, the renowned economist and former Labor secretary of the Clinton Administration, has underscored the surpassing importance of people as a resource in this way:

> "As every advanced economy becomes global, a nation's most important competitive asset becomes the skills and cumulative learning of its workforce... Globalization, almost by definition, makes this true. Every factor of production other than workforce skills can be duplicated anywhere in the world... capital,

technology, raw materials, information – all, except for one thing, the most critical part, the one element that is unique about a nation: its workforce."

HOW ARE THEY TREATED BACK HOME?

The Philippine system of institutionalized and highly organized overseas employment is the first of its kind in the world and serves as a model for any labor-sending country. Under the system, Filipinos are allowed to leave to work in countries with friendly bilateral relations with the Philippines, many of which are signatories to international labor and other United Nations Conventions and instruments. They leave only when they have approved employment contracts, verified by Philippine Overseas Labor Officers in various embassies and consulates abroad, with specific employers and well-defined terms and conditions of employment approved by the POEA, which include wage and compensation packages, free transportation and accommodation, overtime pay, holiday pay, rest day, among others. They are issued Overseas Employment Certificates (OECs) that will prove that they are legally processed and authorized to exit as temporary or contract workers. They are covered by insurance that entitles them to death, disability benefits, medicare benefits, repatriation, loan assistance and educational assistance for family members and on-site welfare and legal assistance packages.

The POEA, which issues licenses to private recruitment agencies numbering over 1,300, exercises disciplinary authority over them in cases of violations of recruitment rules and regulations by suspending or canceling their licenses based on the gravity of their offenses. On a yearly basis, the POEA dockets an average of 3,000 recruitment violation cases, 75% of which involve excessive collection of placement fee (authorized fee is only an equivalent of one month salary). These violations are normally combined with two other offenses of misrepresentation (65.68%) and premature collection and non-issuance of receipts (57.61%). Findings of liability based on the merit of the case combined with those dismissed due to settlement of claims between the parties, show an almost similar rate of 73%. Out of these cases, P52.1 million has been ordered refunded excluding the amount of settlement between the parties.

Payment of fines by erring agencies that went to the Bureau of Treasury in 2001 total to P12.33 million compared to P2.98 million in 2000, an increase of 209.80%. For 2002, fines increased to P13,115,104.80. For 2003, an additional P6.878 million were collected from erring agencies.

POEA also protects legitimate OFWs from illegal recruiters by ordering the closure of establishments found to be engaged in criminal activities. We use surveillance and entrapment to gather evidence against them and provide legal assistance in filing cases against them in courts. From 1996, where only one case of closure was reported, two in 1997, two in 1998, five in 1999 and ten in 2000, the figure dramatically jumped to 28 cases of closure in 2001 or 180% increase from 2000 to 2001. For 2002 and 2003, additional 29 cases for each year were recorded.

If we are to base the extent to which the system is able to protect OFWs/OCWs against abuse and exploitation on the number of complainants involved in these illegal recruitment cases which is 4,943 workers, it can be said that it is quite insignificant compared with the average yearly deployment of 700,000 to 800,000 workers. Most of the victims are factory workers, domestic helpers, caretakers and operators including seafarers. Most common countries of destination are Taiwan, Hong Kong, Kingdom of Saudi Arabia, and Brunei. Negligible as the number may be, exploitation, oppression and injustice are not acceptable especially if the victims are the needy and the poor who are forced to leave their families and loved ones for a better life.

What Has The Government To Say About Them?

Without sacrificing the protection and welfare of its citizens wherever they are, the Philippine government has opted for a more pragmatic view on overseas employment.

- Migration is a global phenomenon. Workers from rich and poor countries alike do migrate. Labor migration should be seen in the light of emerging views on globalization.

- Labor-scarce economies will always exert a pull in migration from labor-surplus economies. Not only the producers, but even labor will tend to move from one country to another in a borderless world. Labor may ultimately be perceived as an internationally shared human resource.

- So long as there are imbalances in world economic and social circumstance, people will always migrate for better opportunities, higher wages or realization of personal aspiration.

- Whether the government will encourage or discourage overseas employment, Filipinos will migrate on the basis of their personal choice. It is the responsibility of the government to empower and enable a Filipino worker to make an enlightened choice, and

- He must have access to and/or be provided with vital information that can make him decide wisely, whether to remain in the country or work abroad.

CONCLUSION

The OFW phenomenon is almost a century old and has far exceeded Biblical proportions. The diaspora and exodus will continue in the global world that we all live in today. Our government policies and programs have already taken into account the new realities in labor migration. Leaders of our industry have seen the new business environment brought about by globalization and they, together with leaders of rich countries like America, are one in saying that the "people are the key" to any nation's competitive advantage. In our case, OFWs along with exports, foreign investments have all become the lifeblood of our economy. The contributions of the OFWs are considerable. From 1990-2002, the dollar remittance amounted to US$58.5 billion or an average of US$4.5 billion every year. It excludes remittance through informal channels like couriers, friends and relatives, payroll deductions and door-to-door scheme, estimated to be double the remittance through the banking system. In 2003, the remittance was US$7.2 billion. On the average, it represents 20.6% of the country's export earnings and 6.2% of the Gross National Product.

Mr. Fernando Zobel de Ayala, Co-Vice Chairman of the Ayala Corporation, is indeed correct in saying that the Philippines is blessed in the so-called "people skills" that are highly prized in the world. The private sectors are ready to invest heavily in upgrading the skills of their people. To be globally competitive, they all know that people as "unique" assets must be continually nurtured and enhanced. Our global competitiveness on the quality of our workers was rated top and our market niches for our workers are secured.

If the OFW phenomenon and its economic and political benefits are clear in the mind of people in the world, what about its spiritual dimension? Who is catching God's vision on it? Who is hearing God's call in this diaspora? Has the church already positioned itself strategically in this flow of Filipinos the world over? Even with just the 3 million OFWs alone scattered in over 180 countries, the task of networking is enormous. We also need to ask the question, "Who do we network with?"

These are but few of the questions and reflections that crossed my mind and the time to look for the right answers is now.

Part II

BIBLICAL THEOLOGY

PART II

━━ᴖᴖ⌁ᴖᴖ━━

INTRODUCTION

Having set forth the facts and figures of the Filipino "diaspora" highlighted with the attention that the Philippine government devotes to oversee such contemporary realities in Part I, we now move into the biblico-theological segment of this volume.

Here in Part II, the guiding question is: What does God have to say and what is he doing about the Filipino "diaspora?"

Dr. Narry F. Santos presented his research findings in two steps: He began with a survey on how the term "diaspora" is used in the Bible and during biblical times, then followed by a description of how Jewish "diaspora" (including Jewish Christian "diaspora") is related to Christian missions. His conclusion is that human suffering, persecution and "diaspora" are all God's providential ways in accomplishing Christian missions.

Based in part on Santos' findings and conclusions and integrating other related data, Dr. Luis Pantoja attempted to formulate a theological perspective on the Filipino "diaspora." After an exercise of theological reflection, in summary format; he provided five theses on the Filipino "diaspora" and concluded with fifteen theological propositions.

SURVEY OF THE DIASPORA OCCURRENCES IN THE BIBLE AND OF THEIR CONTEXTS IN CHRISTIAN MISSIONS

Narry F. Santos

INTRODUCTION

The term "diaspora" (διασπορα) refers to the Jewish dispersion (i.e., to the scattering of Jews outside Palestine). It is also the technical name for all the nations outside of Palestine where Jewish people had come to live (Moo 2000: 50).

The Jewish dispersion began in the deportations by the Assyrians (722 BC) and Babylon (597 BC), and later spread throughout the Roman Empire to Egypt, Asia, Minor, Greece, and Italy. Thus, "diaspora" generally refers to Jews living outside of Palestine (Brown 1967: 55).

However, the applicability of the use of diaspora has been widened to any religious or racial minority living within the territory of another religious or political society. In this chapter, I will use the term diaspora as a reference to the Jewish dispersion throughout the known world during the biblical period.

The purpose of this chapter is twofold. First, I seek to survey how diaspora is used in the Bible and during biblical times. Second, I wish to describe how Jewish "diaspora" (including Jewish Christian diaspora) is related to Christian missions.

USE OF DIASPORA IN THE BIBLE AND BIBLICAL TIMES

The term "diaspora" is found in the New Testament, the LXX (or Septuagint), related Old Testament words, and extra-biblical literature during the biblical period. I will briefly discuss the occurrences of diaspora in these different sources.

Diaspora in the New Testament

The verbal substantive, "diaspora" (διασπορα), commonly translated as "scattered," occurs only thrice in the New Testament. The three occurrences are:

1. "The Jews said to one another, 'Where does this man intend to go that we cannot find him? Will he go where our people live scattered among the Greeks, and teach the Greeks?'" (John 7:35 NIV);
2. "James, a servant of God and of the Lord Jesus Christ, to the twelve tribes scattered among the nations: Greetings" (James 1:1 NIV); and
3. "Peter, an apostle of Jesus Christ, to God's elect, strangers in the world, scattered throughout Pontus, Galatia, Cappadocia, Asia and Bithynia" (1 Peter 1:1 NIV).

In John 7:35, the Jews in Palestine raised the questions, "Where does this man intend to go that we cannot find him? Will he go where our people live 'scattered' among the Greeks, and teach the Greeks?" Their questions revealed a lack of comprehension of Jesus' comment, "You will look for me, but you will not find me; and where I am, you cannot come" (John 7:34).

Through these questions by the Jews, I see their use of "diaspora" (scattered), as a reference to the Jewish minority in the midst of other religions, in this case the Greek-speaking environment (Sänger 1990: 311). The "Greeks" (Ελληνας) are a general reference to Gentiles[1], whom Jews would normally call, Greeks (cf. Col. 3:11).

In James 1:1, James greeted "the twelve tribes scattered among the nations" in his salutation. The mention of the "twelve tribes" can either refer to the literal twelve tribes of the nation of Israel or to the figurative "twelve tribes," as a reference to the true people of God (thus, broadening the Jewish roots to include the church of James' day).

Though the figurative sense of Christians (both Jews and Gentiles) may be the possible reference of "the twelve tribes scattered among the nations," it seems better to take the scholarly consensus[2] that the expression refers to the Jewish Christians, who were scattered across the Roman empire. The following references to Jewish institutions and practices contribute to the conclusion of a Jewish audience:

1. the believers that James addressed met in a "synagogue" (James 2:2);

2. the believers shared the assumption that monotheism is a foundational belief (James 2:19);

3. the people believed that the law is central to God's dealings with his people (James 1:21, 24-25; 2:8-13; 4:11-12); and

4. the people understood the Old Testament imagery of the marriage relationship to indicate the nature of the relationship between God and his people (James 4:4).

In 1 Peter 1:1, Peter described his audience as "God's elect, strangers in the world, 'scattered' throughout Pontus, Galatia, Cappadocia, Asia and Bithynia." Like the use of James, the "Petrine diaspora" refers to the scattered communities outside Palestine.

Particularly, Peter listed the Jewish Christians who lived in the Gentile regions of "Pontus, Galatia, Cappadocia, Asia and Bithynia." These localities referred to the northwest quadrant of Asia Minor bordering the Black Sea (Davids 1990: 7), an area that Luke reported Paul was not allowed to evangelize.[3] In addition to a Jewish Christian audience, Peter addressed the Gentile Christians (1 Peter 1:14, 18; 2:9-10, 25; 3:6; 4:3-4). He even applied to them categories that directly related to Jews.[4]

Thus, Peter's use of diaspora can include the "communities of people living outside their native land, which is not Jerusalem or Palestine but the heavenly city" (Davids 1990: 46). These scattered communities were to view their lives on earth as temporary (thus, as aliens, sojourners, pilgrims, foreigners, who belonged to heaven).

Diaspeiró in the New Testament

So far, we have seen the three occurrences of the word diaspora (διασπορα as found in John 7:35, James 1:1, and 1 Peter 1:1). I will now discuss the verb form of diaspora, which is, diaspeiró (διασπειρω). This verb appears in only three instances in the New Testament. These three instances occur in the following verses (all found in the Book of Acts):

1. "On that day a great persecution broke out against the church at Jeru-salem, and all except the apostles were 'scattered' throughout Judea and Samaria" (Acts 8:1b NIV);

2. "Those who had been 'scattered' preached the word wherever they went" (Acts 8:4 NIV); and

3. "Now those who had been 'scattered' by the persecution in connection with Stephen travelled as far as Phoenicia, Cyprus and Antioch, telling the message only to Jews" (Acts 11:19 NIV).

In all these three instances in the Book of Acts, diaspeiró relates to the scat-tering of the Christians of Hellenistic Jewish origin, Greek-speaking Jewish Christians from the diaspora, in areas where there was a non-Jewish majority (Acts 11:19), but also in the area around Jerusalem and toward Samaria (Acts 8:1). The unique contribution of these verses in the use of diaspeiró is that those who were scattered served essential factors in the expansion of early Christianity or to missions (Acts 8:4-8, 40; 11:19-21).

Diaspora in the LXX (Septuagint)

In the Greek translation (i.e., LXX or Septuagint, including the Apoc-rypha) of the Hebrew Old Testament, the technical term "diaspora" is found in 12 passages. These 12 passages are Deuteronomy 28:25; 30:4; Nehemiah 1:9; Psalm 146:2; Isaiah 49:6; Jeremiah 13:14; 15:7; 34:17; Daniel 12:2; Judith 5:19; 2 Maccabees 1:27; and Psalm of Solomon 8:34. They generally refer to the "dispersion of the Jews among the Gentiles" or "the Jews as thus scat-tered" (Schmidt 1962: 99).

The noun "diaspora" is used in the LXX of the exile of the scattered people of God among the Gentiles (Deut. 28:25; 30:4; Psa. 146:2; Isa. 49:6;

Jer. 15:7; 34:17; 2 Macc. 1:27; Jdt. 5:19). Moreover, "diaspora" can refer to both the dispersion and the totality of the dispersed (Isa. 49:6; Psa. 146:2; 2 Macc. 1:27; Psa. Sol. 8:34).

Related Words in the Old Testament for Diaspora

There is no fixed or technical Hebrew equivalent for the Greek word, diaspora. In Deuteronomy 30:4, the Hebrew root is *ndt*, which in the niphil means, "expelled, driven out." The nearest Hebrew term, which may correspond to diaspora is *golah*, or *galot*, or the emphatic *galota* (from the Aramaic root, *galo*).

These three words can mean the process of "leading away," "deportation," or "exile." They can also mean the state of those "led away," "deported," or "exiled." (Schmidt 1962: 99). They have become technical terms for exile or banishment after the destruction of Jerusalem and the loss of the Palestinian homeland. However, in the LXX, they are always rendered with words other than diaspora.[5]

Diaspora in Extra-Biblical Literature

Aside from biblical literature, there is a sufficient amount of extra-biblical sources that pictured the period of the Jewish diaspora.[6] These sources seem to support two main reasons for the Jewish diaspora:

1. **forced deportation** – this source of Jewish dispersion was triggered by conquests of the Assyrian,[7] Babylonian,[8] and Roman (specifically, Pompey)[9] empires. These harsh realities of the conquests would have brought severe wounds to the pride of the chosen people of God. They reminded the Jews of the outworking of God's severe judgment through scattering; thus, emphasizing pain and curse. In addition, the Jews would have been ridiculed and derided (cf. Psa. 79:4, 10) by the enemies of God, because of the Jewish exile; and

2. **voluntary migration** – this source of Jewish dispersion from Palestine to the diaspora, arising from diverse motives, was highly significant.

It was significant, because such migration involved no curse or shame, but a sense of optimism and restoration of dignity and pride. With the voluntary migration came the benefit that the Jews could not be exterminated in a single stroke. However, the destruction of Jerusalem in 70 A.D. and the final ridding of Palestinian Judaism in Hadrian's war[10] did much to disturb this pride of the diaspora.[11]

During the diaspora, there were probably few major cities or regions that were without a community of resident Jews.[12] The origins of the Jewish communities in Babylonia came from the exile, when many Jews decided to remain in Babylonia (despite the permission of Cyrus for the Jews to return to their land; 2 Chron. 36:22-23; Ezra 1:1-4).

There are also evidences of Jewish settlements or communities in Nehardea, Nisibis (Josephus *Ant.* 18.9.1 §§311-312), Seleucia (Josephus *Ant.* 18.9.8-9 §§372-379), Antioch (Josephus *Ant.* 12.3.1 §119),[13] Lydia and Phrygia in Asia Minor (Josephus *Ant.* 12.3.4 §§147-153),[14] kingdom of Bosporus,[15] Egypt,[16] Teuchira, Apollonia, Ptolemais, and Latin-speaking North Africa (Trebilco 2000: 284), Macedonia, Greece, Thessaly, Boetia, Aetolia, Attica, Argos, Corinth, most of the Peloponnese and the islands of Euboea and Crete (Philo *Leg. Gai.* 281-282), and Rome.[17]

By the end of the 1st-century B.C., Philo could claim that "Jews dwelling in Alexandria and Egypt from the Libyan slope to the borders of Aethiopia do not fall short of a million" and "that no single country can contain the Jews because of their multitude" (Philo *Flacc.* 43, 45). Though Philo's figures are not reliable, there is no doubt that the Jewish population did grow fast (Collins 2000: 5).

Evidence seems to point to the direction that the total Jewish population of the diaspora considerably exceeded the Jewish population in Palestine (Tcherikover 1970: 292-295), and that diaspora Jews constituted a group of significant size. Scholars often suggest that five to six million Jews were living in the diaspora during the first century, but such figures can only be speculative.

What is the economic situation of the diaspora Jews? While the general impression from the papyri "is that of a hard-working people earning its living by tenacious labor," there were many who prospered, and no branch of economic life was closed to them (Tcherikover and Fuks 1957-1964: 19; Applebaum 1976: 701-727).

Specifically, Jews of the diaspora were soldiers, land-owning farmers, agricultural laborers, shepherds, artisans, manual workers, traders, merchants, bankers, government officials, and slaves (Trebilco 2000: 286). In some Roman writers, Jewish poverty was a byword (Juvenal *Sat.* 3.14-16; 6.542-547). However, there were also some very wealthy Jews. Thus, diaspora Jews were found in almost all socio-economic strata of that period.

So far, I have surveyed in this first major section the use of the word or concept of diaspora, as seen in the New Testament, in the LXX, in related Old Testament words, and in extra-biblical literature during the biblical period. In the next and last major section, I will describe how Jewish diaspora (including Jewish Christian diaspora) was related to Christian missions.

RELATIONSHIP BETWEEN DIASPORA AND MISSIONS

I will seek to relate diaspora and missions through the contextual check of the diaspora passages for indicative elements in missions. Such contextual check shows God's sovereignty in the Jewish diaspora. In fact, God's sovereignty establishes the framework for the missionary expansion of Christianity.

To establish the relationship between the concept of diaspora and Christian missions, I will check the presence of the concept of missions in the three diaspora passages in Acts and the three diaspora passages in the New Testament.

Checking Out Diaspeiró Passages For Missions

Let's first go to the three occurrences of the word, diaspeiró, in Acts (i.e., 8:1b, 4; 11:19). I will inspect the context of these diaspeiró passages, checking out the presence of Christian missions-related factors.

The earlier context of Acts 8:1b and 8:4 dealt with persecution and martyrdom. In Acts 7:54-60, the stoning of Stephen happened. Right after Stephen's martyrdom, Luke immediately narrated the breaking out of a "great persecution" in Acts 8:1a. Saul carried out this persecution, by trying to destroy the Jerusalem church. He went from house to house, heartlessly and systematically dragging off men and women and putting them into prison (Acts 8:3).

Aside from persecution, the later context revealed the emphasis on missions. The Hellenized Jewish Christians,[18] who were scattered in the diaspora, "preached the word wherever they went." Particularly, Philip (a Grecian Jew, who was chosen as a deacon in Acts 6:5) preached about Christ in Samaria (Acts 8:5). As a result of his preaching and miraculous signs, people listened. Many were healed and were rejoicing (Acts 8:6-7). Many people also believed Philip's message and were baptized (Acts 8:12).

Thus, we can see that persecution (along with martyrdom) became the trigger of the diaspora of Hellenized Jewish Christians. These Christians used their diaspora outside of Jerusalem to be the setting for their missionary efforts. In other words, it was their context of persecution that enabled them to fulfill Jesus' commission that they be witnesses "in all Judea and Samaria" (Acts 1:8).

In its wider context, the persecution of Acts 8:1 and the subsequent missions efforts in Acts 8:4 resulted in the formation of "the church throughout Judea, Galilee and Samaria," which was strengthened, encouraged, and which grew in numbers and lived in the fear of the Lord (Acts 9:31). Thus, the inception of such separate communities can be traced to the persecution during the Jewish Christian diaspora.

What I find fascinating in Philip's missionary effort in Samaria was his boldness to proclaim the message of Christ within a hostile setting. As a Hellenized Christian Jew (who was hated for his being a Christian), Philip moved away from the hostile persecution of the diaspora, and moved toward another hostile environment in Samaria (where Jews were hated by Samaritans).

Historically, the Jews and the Samaritans had a great schism and enmity between each other.[19] Yet, despite historical and cultural hostility, Philip boldly undertook his missionary efforts and saw a great Samaritan harvest of souls.

Let's now check out the diaspeiró context of Acts 11:19 for missionary elements. The preceding context talked about the apostles' hearing the news that the Gentiles were receiving the word of God (Acts 11:1). Peter explained before the Hebraic Jewish Christians how God opened the door to the Gentiles (specifically to the Roman centurion God-fearer, Cornelius, and his household) in Acts 11:2-18. Peter's explanation was received well, to the point that the people praised and said, "So then, God has granted even the Gentiles repentance unto life" (Acts 11:18).

This opening of the missionary doors for the Gentiles was exemplified in Acts 11:19-21. Those who were scattered by the persecution related to Stephen's martyrdom went to the northern portions of "Phoenecia, Cyprus, and Antioch" (Acts 11:19a). Though the missionary efforts already expanded to the point of leaving Palestine, the recipients of their outreach efforts were Jews only (Acts 11:19b).

But the missions extension went further when some "men from Cyprus and Cyrene" (Acts 11:20a) went to Antioch and "began to speak to Greeks also, telling them the good news about the Lord Jesus" (Acts 11:20b). The Greeks (Ἑλληνιστας), as used by the Jews, generally referred to the Gentiles. Amazingly, the Greeks responded in great numbers and "believed and turned to the Lord" (Acts 11:20c), as the Lord's hand was on the missionaries.

Thus, in this strategic passage on the diaspora, we see the further fulfillment of Christ's commission (Acts 1:8), that his people be witnesses to the "ends of the earth" (εσχατου της γης). From the missionary effort to Jews in Jerusalem to Jews in Samaria, the outreach opened widely to the Gentiles, who belonged to the ends of the earth.

Checking Out Diaspora Passages For Missions

We have just explored the missions efforts related to the diaspeiró passages in Acts 8:1b, 4 and 11:19. At this point, let's turn to the three instances of the word, diaspora, in the New Testament (i.e., John 7:35, James 1:1, and 1 Peter 1:1).

We begin with John 7:35. Though admittedly, there is no immediate context of missions in John 7:35 (on the contrary, the context is that of hatred, hostility, misunderstanding and unbelief by the religious leaders toward Jesus; cf. 7:32, 41b-44), the scope of the diaspora is far and wide (i.e., among the Greeks and Gentiles).

Similarly, the scope of missions is far and wide – reaching the nations throughout the world. In the Great Commission, the extent of going and making disciples is to "all nations" (παντα τα εθνη). As we have seen in the previous section, the Jewish diaspora reached many nations. There were only a few major cities or regions that were without a community of resident Jews. Thus, both the diaspora and missions are far-reaching and global in scope.

In addition, the context of hostility and hatred in John 7:35 is similar to the context of suffering and persecution in Acts 8:1. From this similarity, we glean that missions work is usually triggered by hostility, hatred, suffering, and persecution. God's global work greatly expands within the context of pain and persecution.

In James 1:1, the NIV translates the word diaspora as "scattered among the nations" – focusing on the dispersion of the "twelve tribes" "among the nations." In 1 Peter 1:1, the enumeration of the locations in the diaspora (i.e., Pontus; Galatia; Cappadocia; Asia; and Bithynia) shows the far-reaching spread of the Jewish dispersion. This also forms part of the far-reaching spread of missions.

Thus, we have seen in our inspection of the diaspeiró and diaspora passages in the New Testament how God used suffering, persecution, and dispersion as the context for expanding his kingdom and enabling his people to fulfill their commission to become witnesses to all the nations and to the remotest part of the earth. He used the diaspora to expand the missionary work to the Jews, Samaritans, and Gentiles.

CONCLUSION

I have surveyed in this chapter the use of the word or concept of diaspora as seen in the New Testament, in the LXX, in related Old Testament words, and in extra-biblical literature during the biblical period. In addition, I have described how Jewish diaspora (including Jewish Christian diaspora) is related to Christian missions. The relation is evident in God's providential hand in the spread of missions through His chosen tools of suffering, persecution, and diaspora.

ENDNOTES

[1] Though Ἕλληνας may refer to Greek-speaking Jews, like those of the dispersion, who reside in Jerusalem in territorially organized synagogues (e.g. John 12:20; Acts 6:1; 9:29; 11:20), or to non-Greeks (e.g., Mark 7:26), or to Greeks in whose territory the Jews live, the term, Ἕλληναζ, is better taken as Greeks or Gentiles, in general.

[2] Dibelius simply specifies the addressees as the diaspora Jewish Christian church and thus not Palestinian (Dibelius 1976: 47). Other scholars even ventured to name the provenance of the letter. Moffat located the work in Egypt, due to its alleged wisdom affinities (Moffatt 1928). Reicke ad Laws saw similarities of the epistle to Hermas and alleged Roman flavor that they argued for a Roman provenance (Reicke 1964: 6 and Laws 1980: 22-26). Ropes placed James in Caesarea of Palestine-Syria (Ropes 1916: 49; cf. Davids 1982: 28-34).

[3] In Acts 16:6-10, Luke narrated that Paul established churches in the southern area of Galatia. Of course, later, Paul did so in the western province of Asia.

[4] For example, Peter described the Gentile Christians (i.e., who were "once not a people" and now are "the people of God" [2:10a]) as "a chosen people, a royal priesthood, a holy nation, a people belonging to God" (which are descriptions earlier given about Israel).

[5] The Greek words, αιχμαλωσια, αποικια, αποικισμος, μετοικεσια, and παροικια, are associated with these three Hebrew words.

[6] A sampling of these extra-biblical sources are as follows: Artapanus; Aristobulus, Demetrius; *Joseph and Aseneth*; Josephus; *Epistle of Aristeas*; Philo; Pseudo-Philo; *Pseudo-Phocylides*; some of the *Sibylline Oracles; Testament of Abraham* and Wisdom of Solomon. Other sources include some papyri and inscriptions, six excavated *diaspora* synagogues, and texts from non-Jewish authors who wrote their perceptions on Jews and Judaism.

[7] After the death of Solomon (931 BC), the kingdom was divided into two, Israel consisting of the northern tribes with important shrines at Dan and Bethel and the capital subsequently set at Samaria. Judah consisted of the southern tribes of Judah and Benjamin, with Jerusalem as the capital. The northern kingdom of Israel came to an end in the 8th century BC, when Samaria fell to the Assyrians in 722. The Assyrians took large numbers of the population captive and replaced them by immigrants. Cf. 2 Kings 15-17.

[8] In the 6th century BC, the southern kingdom of Judah fell to the invading Babylonians, who then dominated the Middle East. Jerusalem fell in 597 and was

deported in 581 BC Large deportations of the population followed. Following the fall of Babylon to Cyrus of Persia (539-530 BC), Jews were encouraged to return from exile (though a significant number stayed). However, the monarchy was not restored. Cf. 2 Kings 23-25 (cf. 2 Chronicles 36).

[9] Pompey took hundreds of Jews to Rome as prisoners of war (Trebilco 2000: 282).

[10] Emperor Hadrian re-founded Jerusalem in 135 AD, as a Roman colony of Aelia Capitolina (Bruce 1988: 162).

[11] Schmidt comments, "Prior to 70 AD the wounds of earlier expatriations could be healed the more easily because in spite of everything Jerusalem still remained as the holy city and therefore as the focal point not merely of the Holy Land but of the whole *diaspora*. After 70 AD, however, the *diaspora* became, as it were, completely homeless" (Schmidt 1962: 101).

[12] Instances that support the statement that probably few major cities or regions were without a community of resident Jews are as follows: Philo *Leg. Gai* 214, 281-83; *Flacc.* 45-46; *Vit. Mos.* 2.232; Josephus *Ant.* 14.7.2 §115; *J.W.* 7.3.3 §43; 1 Macc. 15:23-24; *Sib. Or.* 3:271-272; Acts 2:9-11.

[13] The Jewish community in Antioch, which was the largest in Syria, probably began in the third century BC.

[14] Between 2210-205 BC, Antiochus III transferred 2,000 Jewish families from Mesopotamia and Babylonia to Lydia and Phrygia as military settlers. This provides unambiguous evidence of Jewish communities in Asia Minor.

[15] Jews lived in at least three towns in the kingdom of Bosporus. A Jewish inscription from Gorgippia dated 41 AD, refers to the manumission of a female slave in a synagogue (Levinskaya 1996: 227-246). The author spends a whole appendix on the inscriptions from the Bosporan kingdom.

[16] The Jewish communities in Egypt were the largest. At the time of the Babylonian conquest, some Jews fled to Egypt (Jer. 43:6-7; 44:1; 46:14). Aramaic papyri of the 5th century BC give evidence of a Jewish military colony at Elephantine, a colony that included a Jewish temple.

[17] A significant number of Jews lived in Rome. Josephus recorded that Pompey brought a number of Jews to Rome as prisoners of war in 63 BC (Josephus *Ant.* 14.4.4-5 §§70-71, 79). He also wrote that 8,000 Roman Jews supported an embassy from Judea (Josephus *Ant.* 17.11.1 §300).

[18] From this time onward, the Jerusalem church appeared to have been a predominantly "Hebrew" body (Bruce 1988: 162). Of course, after the destruction of Jerusalem in 70 AD and Emperor Hadrian's re-founding of Jerusalem in 135

AD as a Roman colony of Aelia Capitolina, the Jerusalem church was a completely Gentile-Christian community – having no continuity with the 1st-century Jewish-Christian church in Jerusalem.

[19] Judah was isolated from the other tribes of Israel in the settlement period (cf. Deut. 33:7). Then a cleavage erupted with the disruption of the Hebrew monarchy after Solomon's death (c. 930 BC). The schism widened when the Samaritans refused to share in the rebuilding of the Jerusalem temple and erected their own temple in Gerizim (Josephus *Ant.* 11.310, 322-324, 346). The hostility continued with the destruction of the Gerizim temple by the Hasmonean ruler, John Hyrcanus, when he conquered Samaria and added it to his kingdom (Josephus *Ant.* 13.256). Though the Roman conquest of Palestine in 63 BC liberated the Samaritans, the unfriendly relations continued between the Jews and Samaritans.

REFERENCES

Primary References

Josephus *Ant.* 11.310, 322-324, 346; 12.3.1 §119; 12.3.4 §§147-153; 13.256; 14.4.4-5 §§70-71, 79; 14.7.2 §115; 17.11.1 §300; 18.9.1 §§311-312; 18.9.8-9 §§372-379; J.W. 7.3.3 §43.

Philo *Leg. Gai* 214, 281-83; Flacc. 43, 45-46; Vit. Mos. 2.232.

Secondary References

Applebaum, S. (1976). "The Social and Economic Status of Jews in the Diaspora," in *The Jewish People in the First Century*, S. Safrai and M. Stern, eds. CRINT 1.2. Assen: Van Gorcum; Philadelphia: Fortress.

Brown, Colin. (Ed.). (1967). *New International Dictionary of New Testament Theology.* Vol. 1. Grand Rapids: Zondervan.

Bruce, F. F. *The Book of Acts.* (1988). Grand Rapids, MI: Eerdmans.

Collins, John J. (2000). *Between Athens and Jerusalem: Jewish Identity in the Hellenistic Diaspora.* Grand Rapids, MI: Eerdmans.

Davids, Peter. (1982). *Epistle on James.* Grand Rapids, MI: Eerdmans.

_____. (1990). *The First Epistle of Peter.* Grand Rapids: Eerdmans.

Dibelius, M. (1976). *A Commentary on the Epistle of James.* Philadelphia: Fortress.

Laws, S. (1980). *A Commentary on the Epistle of James.* New York: Harper and Row.

Levinskaya, Irina. (1996). *The Book of Acts in its First Century Setting: Diaspora Setting.* Grand Rapids, MI: Eerdmans.

Moffatt, J. (1928). *The General Epistles of James, Peter and Jude.* London: Hodder and Stoughton.

Moo, Douglas J. (2000). *The Letter of James.* Grand Rapids, MI: Eerdmans.

Reicke, B. (1964). *The Epistles of James, Peter and Jude.* Garden City: Doubleday.

Ropes, J. H. (1916). *A Critical and Exegetical Commentary of the Epistle of St. James.* Edinburgh: T & T Clark.

Sänger, D. (1990). "διασπορα, διασπειρω" in Horst Balz and Gerhard Scheider (eds.). *Exegetical Dictionary of the New Testament.* Grand Rapids, MI: Eerdmans. 1: 311-312.

Schmidt, Karl Ludwig. (1962). "διασπορα" in *Theological Dictionary of the New Testament,* Gerhard Kittel, ed., Grand Rapids, MI: Eerdmans. 2: 98-104.

Tcherikover, V. (1970). *Hellenistic Civilization and the Jews.* New York: Atheneum.

Tcherikover, V. and Fuks, A. (Eds). (1957-1964). *Corpus Papyrorum Judaicarum. Vol. 1.* Cambridge, MA: Harvard University Press.

Trebilco. (2000). "Diaspora Judaism," in *Dictionary of New Testament Background,* Craig A. Evans and Stanley E. Porter, eds., Downers Grove, IL: InterVarsity. 1: 280-296.

FORMULATING A THEOLOGY OF THE FILIPINO DIASPORA

Luis L. Pantoja, Jr.

⸻⸱⸻

S imply stated, theology is the articulation of what God says or does about any idea or experience that concerns humankind. Throughout history and from a multiplicity of sources, theologians have been formulating cognitive statements and proposing them for factual verification and experiential analysis by others.

If, in the effort to preserve orthodoxy, theology simply rehearses what others have said in the past, it becomes tediously repetitious and pedantic. But theology becomes susceptible to heresy and heterodoxy if it breaks away from an historical continuum and proves to be only novel and contemporary. Because our assigned specific subject itself is novel, very little is written about it that could be repeated. By the same token, since there are no models with which to compare, what we say may be dangerously free albeit contemporary. As a precautionary measure, therefore, this effort towards a theological perspective on our chosen subject is unapologetically tethered to the Bible as its primary source and authority. The Bible is God's initiative of self-disclosure to people in the past involving supernatural actions and verbal messages through chosen spokespersons culminating in the person and work of Jesus Christ and written down by human instruments under the superintendence of the Holy Spirit.[1] To be authentic and reliable, any word from God today about any subject of human concern can only come either directly or at least analogously from the Word of God.

Given this presupposition, our effort to propose a theological framework rejects the primary perspectives of radical liberalism and postmodern revisionism without totally ignoring the insights that their approaches may contribute. For instance, since the exile is "a watershed in discussions relating to the Old Testament" (Grabbe 1998:11), current opinions vary regarding the reliability of the biblical records about it. "Are we dealing with a historical event or an example of virtual reality? Did real people from Judah go to Babylon into exile, only later to return and refound their temple and nation? Or are we dealing with a theological and literary concept which well served the needs of oppressed Jews, religious leaders, preachers, storytellers, theologians and writers, but was created by them from whole cloth—or at least from some rather large off-cuts?" (Ibid.).[2] For our purposes, we affirm the historical reliability of the biblical record. Considering the realities of the present that find analogous correspondence with people's experiences of God in the past, we shall attempt to formulate a theological perspective on the subject of this consultation.

Our concern for the moment is the scattering of people—a significant number of people, specifically the Filipino diaspora. For the purposes of this consultation, we borrow the term diaspora—technically used of Jews who for one reason or another lived or lives outside of Palestine. Because only the Jews received a special election and a "promised land" from God, and because being driven away from it had the notion of a curse and due punishment, and furthermore, because there is the promise and hope of an eschatological return to the land, then only with those specifications can diaspora truly apply. Due to some obvious discontinuities, borrowing and using the term for the Filipino context can only be analogical at best. Furthermore, we shall use the term in this chapter and in the volume without the quotation marks or italicization and, unless the context of some presentations dictates otherwise, we shall utilize it in our discussion as a non-technical and generic English word.

One must also acknowledge the objections raised by Orthodox theologian Fr. Thomas Hopko of using diaspora today in terms of forced dispersions from historical national homelands. Citing him in concurrence is Vigen Guroian (1990:1), who speaks particularly about the Armenians who have a lot of experiential commonalities with the Jewish diaspora. "Diaspora is employed by Armenians in such a way as to set forth a deceiving contrast between a so-called normal Armenian religious existence in a pre-Armenocide Turkey, or in present-day Soviet Armenia or in the Middle East with an entirely abnormal and peripheral religious life of Armenians in America. The deception in such thinking is that there simply is no longer an Armenian religious culture which is normal in the traditional sense." For Hopko and presumably for Guroian, "the only acceptable theological use of the term diaspora is to have it refer to the salvific mission of the church in its temporal pilgrimage as a sign of the promised Kingdom of God." (Guroian 1990:1).

Guroian rightly postulates that "if the Armenian Church communities dispersed here in North America continue to think of themselves as primarily diaspora, the Armenian Church will become increasingly incapable of behaving as church and be increasingly irrelevant for people seeking biblical religious meaning for their lives" (1990:4). This is a good cautionary dictum to all dispersed Christians including the Filipinos and their churches wherever they may currently reside.

While the previous arguments are indeed very insightful, this chapter will subscribe to both diaspora concepts highlighted by Hopko and Guroian and perhaps lean towards the missiological and ecclesiological nuances as they apply to Filipinos. The apostle Paul who proudly identifies himself as being of the seed of Abraham (2 Cor. 2:22) and who is willing to die for his own people (Rom. 9:3), also became one with the people with whom he lived and sought to evangelize so that he became known as the "apostle to the Gentiles." Like Paul, the Filipino diaspora does not need to abandon their original cultural identity or cut their ties to the motherland. They simply need to be awakened to and challenged with the religio-missiological implications of their scattering and settling among the nations.

Task Definition

From the FIN (Filipino International Network) Korea consultation organizers led by Dr. Sadiri Joy Tira, I received the assignment of providing a theological framework or perspective on the Filipino diaspora. Perhaps it is necessary to clarify that our goal is to articulate what God has to say about the phenomenon and experiences of Filipinos scattered in the uttermost parts of the modern world. In this sense, they are the objects of the theology.

Diasporic theology could also mean those theological affirmations issuing from the experiences of the scattered people which they have expressed and written themselves. Thus, the Filipino diaspora are the subjects, the theologians of the process. We opt for the former sense.

Our objective is to talk about God's perspective regarding the Filipino scattering among the nations. To do so, one must appeal first to the Bible and find out what God has to say about the subject. Furthermore, we must depend on the accounts of God's actions towards specific people groups in the Bible and also move beyond God's dealings with the Jews. Then in recognition of God's present activity in human history, we draw upon the contemporary global data and insights particularly about the Filipino context that shall augment and complement the biblical material. From such, we should be able to formulate a theological construct for the Filipino diaspora.

Obviously statistics and demographics are not the focus of this presentation and yet they are indispensable toward the formulation of a theology. By necessity, therefore, the reader is directed to the preceding section on historical demography. One must begin by highlighting some contemporary and global realities.

SOME CONTEMPORARY REALITIES

Brain Gain

In the March 8, 2004 issue of *Newsweek*, the cover story is captioned "Brain Gain" and subtitled: "Countries Losing Their Best And Brightest To The West Is A Good Thing. Really."

"In the age of globalization and easy travel, talent that flies away no longer disappears. Nations that once lamented losing their best and brightest are now figuring out ways to lure them home, or to exploit their talents and money while overseas" (p. 3).

"Russian scientists do lab work in the U.K., while New Zealand's engineers raise bridges in Canada. Cuban doctors treat patients in South Africa, and South Africans teach English schoolchildren. The smartest Chinese and Indians go where they please; fully a third of all scientists and engineers from developing countries are currently serving in the United States, Japan and Europe.

"Traditionally, such footloose talent has been seen as a liability – so many beautiful minds flushed down the brain drain. But that concept is changing. Now many experts speak not of a drain but of brain gain."(p.32)

Brain Drain

But brain drain is a genuine problem in some nations of the world. In the same Newsweek issue, Babak Dehghanpisheh writes about "A One-Way Ticket," that is, that people leave their home countries without the intention of ever returning.

"Not every country benefits when workers go abroad in search of jobs. Each year approximately 200,000 Iranians, many of them highly educated, leave the country for the United States, Canada, Europe and Australia. The International Monetary Fund ranks Iran as having the highest rate of brain drain in the world. The reasons aren't difficult to pinpoint: unemployment hovers around 20 percent and the inflation rate is roughly 15 percent. Government restrictions on investment severely limit business opportunities. In Tehran, university teachers and students frequently moonlight as cab drivers to make ends meet" (p. 35).

Now we engage in highlighting some of the realities of the Philippine scene and of the Filipino diaspora.

Reality Check For The Philippines

Babe Romualdez issues a call for a "Reality Check" on the Philippine situations particularly regarding the societal stratifications that could help explain the average Filipino's desire to migrate elsewhere.

"The Philippines has now grown to 84 million people – AB, 1 percent or 840,000; C – 9 percent or 7,560,000; D – 55 percent or 46,200,000; and E is 35 percent or 29,400,000. By 2010, this would reach 100 million. The wealth of the AB class seems to have dissipated over the years. The middle class is literally thinning out while the D and E brackets are growing daily...

"The reality is as follows: Unemployment grew by 11.4 percent last year, adding roughly 58,000 to the total list of jobless Filipinos, which is 3.93 million. That's more than the total population of some cities in Metro Manila. Even if it were true that one million jobs were created by government last year, it can only provide livelihood to a very small chunk of the D-E population." (2004:10).

Plight And Flight

For the Philippines, the brain drain is real because the opportunities for professional gains seem so limited. Compared with other third world governments, the Philippines has more agencies e.g., POEA (Philippine Overseas Employment Administration), whose Administrator Rosalinda Dimapilis-Baldoz has contributed to this volume, and OWWA (Overseas Workers Welfare Administration), working with and keeping records on the Filipinos who work overseas. In a way, it is good that we keep track and show concern but the downside of that factor is that the Philippines appears to be more concerned with its people working abroad than it is with providing jobs for its people at home.

Conrado de Quiros argues the case for justified departures of Filipinos. Among the case studies, Dr. Elmer Jacinto stands out. Even as he was the top finisher in the most recent medical board examinations, he decided to pursue a nursing career in the hope of making it to the United States. To get the attention of people who should hear his plight, he announced his choice on the occasion of his swearing in as a new physician before the Philippine Medical Association.

Elmer Jacinto grew up in Lamitan, Basilan, reading by kerosene lamp and attending school to the intermittent sound of gunfire. But Jacinto went on not just to finish school but to finish medical school and top the board exams. But after showing he could be one of the best doctors this country has known, he has expressed a desire to work as a nurse in a New York hospital. He has already applied for it and been accepted to it. "While it pains me to do this," he says, "I am looking forward to working abroad and don't want to let the opportunity pass."

"Jacinto encapsulates perfectly the country's fundamental question today. Namely, why should anyone want to stay in it? A doctor from St. Luke's Medical Center told me many of his colleagues – these weren't neophytes, these were doctors who had years behind them – were contemplating leaving the country for Canada and working there as caregivers. I thought then he was exaggerating. I don't know.

"Jacinto moreover exemplifies not just the dilemma of professionals who have to live in a country that is unkind to professionals but of the poor in this country who have languished from horrendous neglect by the national government and of folk in Muslim Mindanao in particular who have suffered from horrendous attention by the military. I suggest Jacinto be haled before the presidential candidates could justify why he shouldn't. Anyone who can persuade him to stay – and not by the simple expedient of bribing him, which is how things get done in this country—gets my vote" (de Quiros 2004:14).

With varying degrees of precision and conviction, many hold to a common set of observations about the plight and flight of Filipinos today. As earlier stated, the more precise statistics are available to the reader from the other presentations in this consultation.

1. The Philippines is overpopulated and economically depressed vying currently for the lowest ranking among the Asian economies and rated in the top ten most corrupt nations in the world.

2. Filipinos are proud of their heritage, highly skilled and educated but underemployed and underpaid.

3. There is a prevailing cynicism and skepticism about the future of the country especially in the light of the political prostitution unashamedly displayed by the traditional politicians in the recently concluded electoral campaign.

4. Whenever an opportunity opens for work abroad, Filipinos opt to leave and, given the chance, they prefer to migrate as families.

5. In most cases, they could only leave as contract workers and be numbered among those with OFW (Overseas Filipino Worker) status. Former Secretary of Education and presidential candidate Sen. Raul Roco insists "OFW" should be replaced by "Overseas Filipinos" as a more inclusive designation.

6. OFWs send foreign currency and contribute substantially to sustain the economy so that some observers conclude that the government encourages working abroad instead of providing jobs locally.

7. To keep their loyalty and the benefits to the country, OFWs are accorded special services by the Philippine government including absentee voting privileges.

8. By a law enacted recently, a Filipino expatriate may regain his Filipino status and is allowed to maintain and function under dual citizenship.

9. A few of the expatriates return to the Philippines to retire or to invest but they also insure their rights to foreign citizenship as a political and economic "parachute."

10. Despite all of the above, there remains a healthy sense of cultural and national pride and a positive consciousness of the Filipinos' role in the global economy.

National Cultural Pride

Filipinos can take heart in the victory of nineteen-year-old Patricia Evangelista, a Mass Communications sophomore of University of the Philippines. According to Brian Hanharan of the British Broadcasting Corporation (BBC), chairman of the 2004 International Public Speaking competition of the English Speaking Union (ESU) in London, Patricia was the unanimous choice over 59 other student contestants from 37 countries.[3]

Here are some excerpts from "Blond and Blue Eyes," the speech that won her the award: "When I was little, I wanted what many Filipino children all over the country wanted. I wanted to be blond, blue-eyed, and white. I thought—if I just wished hard enough and was good enough, I'd wake up on Christmas morning with snow outside my window and freckles across my nose! More than four centuries under western domination does that to you. . . Today, about eight million Filipinos are scattered around the world. There are those who disapprove of Filipinos who chose to leave. I used to. Desertion, I called it. . .

"My country is a land that has perpetually fought for the freedom to be itself. Our heroes offered their lives in the struggle against the Spanish, the Japanese, and the Americans. To pack up and deny that identity is tanta-mount to spitting on that sacrifice. Or is it? I don't think so, not anymore. True, there is no denying this phenomenon, aided by the fact that what was once the other side of the world is now a twelve-hour plane ride away. But this is a borderless world, where no individual can claim to be purely from where he is now. My mother is of Chinese descent, my father is a quarter Spanish, and I call myself a pure Filipino – a hybrid of sorts resulting from a combination of cultures. I come from a Third World country, one that is still trying mightily to get back on its feet after many years of dictatorship. But we shall make it, given more time. Especially now, when we have thousands of eager young minds who graduate from college every year. They have skills. They need jobs. We cannot absorb them all.

"A borderless world presents a bigger opportunity, yet one that is not so much abandonment but an extension of identity . . . We are the 40,000 skilled nurses who support the UK's National Health Service. We are the quarter-of-a-million seafarers manning most of the world's commercial ships. We are your software engineers in Ireland, your construction workers in the Middle East, your doctors and caregivers in North America, and your musical artists in London's West End.

"Nationalism isn't bound by time or place. Leaving sometimes isn't a matter of choice. It's coming back that is. The Hobbits of the shire travelled all over Middle Earth, but they chose to come home, richer in every sense of the word. We call people like these *balikbayans* – those who followed their dream, yet choose to return and share their mature talents and good fortune. A borderless world doesn't preclude the idea of a home. I'm a Filipino, and I'll always be one . . . It's about giving back to the country that shaped me. And that's going to be more important to me than seeing snow outside my windows on a bright Christmas." (Pedrosa 2004:11)

Global Contribution

In the film "Un Dia Sin Mexicanos" (A Day without Mexicans), Californians wake up to discover that a third of their population, all Mexicans, has disappeared. The state's activities grinded to a halt and conditions of emergency prevailed. Using it as his springboard, commentator Michael Tan speculates on what the world will be like without the Filipinos.

On a worldwide scale, royal courts and average households get into disarray because they are dependent on Filipino housekeepers, nannies and caregivers. Hospitals and nursing homes operations have to be curtailed because the physicians, nurses and health care professionals are gone. Internet websites and local area networks halt down, service establishments close shop because shipments are delayed when the Filipino seamen disappeared. Flight schedules are disrupted because airport security posts have no personnel, bank operations cease because the tellers disappeared. The world was quieter and there was much less laughter coming from Filipinos and of those they served.

"I know...I'm exaggerating the contributions of Filipinos to the world..." using a bit of hyperbole to shake people up. As their blurb for the film goes: 'How do you make the invisible visible? Make them invisible.' Tan concludes that he writes not so much for the less appreciative nationals for whom the Filipinos work. He actually writes for Filipinos who "are pretty good at putting ourselves down, at making ourselves invisible." (Tan 2004:15).

INSIGHTS INTO THE BIBLICAL DIASPORA

In Dr. Narry F. Santos' presentation immediately preceding this one, we were introduced to the occurrences of the word diaspora in the Bible and of their significance in the mission of the church. As intended, Santos was mainly descriptive and lexical in his chapter. Given his data, we are served best by the reminder about "the tension between historical description and normative meaning by assigning to the biblical theologian the task of describing what the Bible meant, not what it means or how it can have meaning. However, this objectivity of historical description is too often found to be a mirror of the observer's hidden pre-understanding, and the adequacy of historical description is contingent on one generation's discoveries and postulates. Also, the yearning and expectation of believers and would-be believers will not let biblical theology rest with the descriptive task alone." (Series Foreword by Brueggemann and Donahue in Klein 1979: x). We shall take heed even as we attempt to formulate a theology in light of the biblical history with which the Filipino diaspora can find some analogous experience.

Israel In Exile

Ralph Klein presents an excellent summary and readable account of the biblical material on Israel in exile (1979:1-8). "When the Babylonian armies conquered Judah in the early sixth century B.C., they unleashed a host of physical and socio-economic problems. Already in 597 Nebuchadnezzar exiled from Judah King Jehoiachin, members of the royal family, nobles, landowners, military leaders, elders, craftsmen, priests, and prophets. While these men numbered only ten thousand men or less (2 Kings 24:14, 16; Jer. 52:28), they came from the leadership class and their loss represented a severe blow to the Southern Kingdom. Exile meant death, deportation, destruction and devastation. Israel was a defeated nation that had lost its independence, its land, its monarchy, and its temple" (Ibid.).

Between the fall of the Northern Kingdom (722 BC)[4] and the Southern Kingdom (586 BC), a voluntary mass migration of the Jews was allowed under Nebuchadnezzar. Many went to Egypt and settled there around 650 BC while others settled in Syria. When Alexander the Great founded Alexandria, there were more than one million Jewish residents there (Barclay 1958:43f). One should recall that a certain Apollos, that mighty orator-preacher who was very effective in Jewish conversions, was a native of Alexandria (Acts 18:24).

A third compulsory dispersion of the Jews came about when Pompey conquered Jerusalem in 63 BC and he took many of the Jews to Rome as slaves. In 19 AD, the whole Jewish community was banished from Rome for unjust reasons but many of them made it back to city in due time. Then in 70 AD, Jerusalem and the temple were destroyed by the Roman general Titus which understandably led to more dispersion that prevails to this day. (Ibid.).

Israel's exile as a nation is unique because of the attendant factors that are prominently theological. Not only did they lose the land promised to the patriarchs, they also lost their temple—the tangible symbol of their election and of God's special presence among the people. Given that, the sacrificial system and priesthood also ceased to function. Furthermore, had not God promised an eternal kingdom to David (2 Sam. 7)? Is God trustworthy with his promise then? "In short, almost all of the old symbol systems had been rendered useless. Almost all of the old institutions no longer functioned. What kind of future was possible for a people who traced its unique election to a God who had just lost a war to other deities? What kind of future was possible for a people who had so alienated their God that categorical rejection was his necessary response?" (Klein 1979:3-5)

Because of all the unique features of Israel's experience of exile, we go back to the initial disclaimer that the Filipino and other national diaspora experiences do not have considerable commonality with Israel. Neither can we nor any other nation claim Israel's special election in accordance with the eternal purposes of God. Therefore, when we speak of any contemporary diaspora, we must find a theological basis for such from biblical sources other than those of Israel's exile experience and the Jewish diaspora. This particularizing thesis finds emphasis in Fr. John Meyendorff's *Catholicity and the Church* (cf. Guroian 1990:2). We must grant, however, that the first century Jewish Christians of the diaspora do have commonalities with which we as the church can identify. Furthermore, if only as an additional and particular theological perspective, i.e., evangelical premillennialism, we still affirm a unique future for Israel in the divine eschatological scheme (Rom. 11:1-12, 25-29).

Diaspora or Voluntary Migration

Based on what we have said so far regarding the uniqueness of Israel's exile experience, we must use other biblico-theological concepts in order to frame a theological construct on the Filipino diaspora. For one reason or another, Filipinos migrate voluntarily and rarely involuntarily. Over the years and up to the present, there resulted a considerable Filipino global presence in socioeconomic and religious terms that has caught the attention of missiologists and eventually catalyzed the Filipino International Network. Uprooted from the cultural and family traditions, many migrant individuals become exposed to the gospel and experience the new birth in their newfound homelands or work locales. Local churches got started and developed indigenously in domains where religious freedom prevails but significantly also in many antagonistic and restricted access nations. Filipino pastors leave Manila as "tentmakers," that is, to take on employment elsewhere without necessarily depriving themselves of the opportunities to exercise their ministry gifts and calling in their newfound abodes.

A Theology Of The Filipino Diaspora

So what does God have to say about Filipino migrations and how can we best articulate God's statements for the Filipino diaspora? What doctrinal motifs contribute substantially towards formulating a particular diasporic theology? In reply, we highlight five possible motifs that provide a theological perspective for the Filipino diaspora:

1. GOD: His creative power, sovereign plan for history and providential actions in human affairs.

2. HUMANITY: The natural human design, the mandate to populate the earth and exercise dominion, the fall and the concomitant social dysfunctions.

3. JESUS CHRIST: Redeemer and Savior of all mankind.

4. THE CHURCH: God's new creation of people across cultural and national boundaries and its universal nature and global expansion.

5. THE END TIMES: The multitudes in heaven and the eternal New Heaven and Earth where God dwells with his people.

God

God the Creator

After producing a cosmos (orderly universe) out of chaos (Gen. 1:2) in five days, God created man as the crowning glory, beneficiary and steward of all of God's creation. Although God is the ultimate owner of all things as Creator, this created earth is God's provision not for one specific group of people or nation but to mankind in general as an entitlement. National boundaries and immigration laws are artificial human designs because in the beginning God had intended humankind to populate the earth at will and develop it to suit human needs and purposes. Only in his sovereign choice of the nation Israel in order to accomplish God's redemptive purpose did he specify a people and assign a particular location as their Promised Land (Gen. 12-15). The rest of the earth is freely available to all mankind to conquer, to develop and to own. In general, theological statements on creation affirm the preceding but the nuances of migration and immigration become especially relevant in the context of a theology for the diaspora. Such context is seldom mentioned, if at all, in theology books.

God's Sovereignty

We must affirm that God has an all-inclusive master plan for history based on his steadfast love and infinite wisdom. It is intended to accomplish his purposes and ultimately to glorify his name having been established before the world began but executed in space-time history. It is inclusive of men's free actions and all other available means, at the same time holding man responsible and accountable for his actions yet guaranteeing that everything leads toward the fulfillment of his master plan (see Romans 11 and Ephesians 1:3-14). Whether recognized or not, the sovereignty of God plays a substantial role in the pursuits of mankind, including migration, in order to meet human needs.

God's Providence

Another given in this attempt to formulate a theology is the fact of God's providence. "God is continually involved with all created things in such a way that he (1) keeps them existing and maintaining the properties with which he created them; (2) cooperates with created things in every action, directing their distinctive properties to cause them to act as they do; and (3) directs them to fulfill his purposes" (Grudem 1994: 315f). There is the unseen hand

and inscrutable plan of God at work behind all that takes place in the universe including the conquests among nations, the disenfranchisements of peoples and the consequent migrations voluntary or otherwise.

Man

Human Nature and Design

Combine a mind and a will with two feet and you will have a mobile person in pursuit of what one wants wherever one might find it. Humankind is designed for mobility and conquest. Maybe it is assumed in the theologians' minds but this facet of God's design for man is often a missing ingredient in statements on the doctrine of man. But to account for human migrations as a fact of existence, we must affirm that mobility is endemic to human nature. People reside in or move from one place to another because God made them with such instincts. Thus, the Filipino and other diasporas.

Dominion Mandate

Having finished the physical creation as the provision of resources and the domain for man, God gave Adam and Eve the mandate to multiply and populate the earth. No boundaries were set other than basic human mobility. Man was also given the dominion mandate which implies responsible stewardship, conquest and settlement of the whole earth and indeed even the universe (Gen. 1-2). Subsequent to the flood, Noah and his family were given the same mandate and some additional provisions (Gen. 9). Migrations and settlements are engendered in the dominion mandate.

Unity of Humanity

In a roundabout way, Paul Jewett comments on human unity being made ambiguous by God's command to fill the earth. "'Dispersion'—the spread of the race over the planet—is also ambiguous, resulting on the one hand from the divine command to fill the earth (Gen. 1:28; 9:1) and on the other from the curse of Gen. 11:7, whereby the confusion of tongues destroys human unity....

While we have spoken above about the fundamental unity of humankind...a unity reinforced by the universalism of the gospel...and one which we see as God's final as well as initial purpose—the emergence of nationalism and the desire to preserve racial and cultural distinctives, the fundamentalists' fear of one world and resistance to ecumenism, and distrust of the United Nations all show how firmly we cling to differences. These pressures for continued separations persist even as cultural interpenetration on a spherical planet... and intermarriage work more quietly in the opposite direction." (Jewett and Shuster 1996: 452). The unity of the human race makes possible the ethnic cohabitation and interpenetration of cultures that comes about through human migrations.

Sin and Social Dysfunctions

The first instance of involuntary migration was the result of the fall when Adam and Eve were driven out of their home and denied return access by God himself. Subsequent to the fall, social dysfunctions and values distortions became the rule and mankind had to cope with and compensate for the consequences of separation from God. Although tarnished by the fall and further affected by the murder of his brother, Cain moved about, built a city, named it after his own son and settled down. Civilization developed from the instincts of a fallen creature (Gen. 4), no less than a murderer but one under God's protective and sovereign hand.

Following the flood, God instructed Noah and his sons to be fruitful and re-populate the earth. As the human settlements grew, man decided to build a city at Babel so that they will not be "scattered" (11:4). God entered the scene and confused their language and thus "the Lord scattered" them (11:8). This divine initiative of scattering people had a mild punitive intent. Consequently, cultures developed and civilizations flourished even as they also competed to establish one's superiority over the others, thus the racial and ethnic disparities prevailing in societies today. (Sowell 2003). Cultural jealousy and ethnic superiority claims make migration and acculturation more difficult but not insurmountable as proven by the progressive lives of the Filipino diaspora in their chosen and adopted homelands. In fact, by virtue of the Filipino cultural marginality, adaptation and acculturation are positive qualities for diaspora survival.

Jesus Christ

God-Man

As a theological model of a purposeful change of habitation, none can surpass the import and impact of the incarnation of the Lord Jesus Christ. Being the unique God-Man, however, he was not forced out of his abode in heaven and Jesus was not victimized during his earthly sojourn. He was in total personal control of his destiny except in his voluntary submission to the will of the Father. So there are obvious discontinuities between diasporic peoples experiences compared with that of Jesus Christ. To be unique or "only begotten" means that no other human being can duplicate Jesus' life experiences. His total life and suffering were predestined for mankind's redemption (Acts 2:22-24). Even his physical death was not a matter of involuntary violation of his right to life as it was that he laid down his life for his sheep. But he was a model of voluntary humility (Philippians 2:5-11), and of being rejected even by his own culture and people and yet he was able to accomplish his expressed purpose (John 1:11).

Commission

Mission consciousness may be the best value that immigrants may learn from the example of Jesus Christ. No other person came from heaven to live on earth. All that our human limitations can afford to us in migration terms is moving from one country or culture to another and only in eternity will we be able to dwell in God's abode. Jesus never even crossed any ocean to leave his earthly nation for another earthly domain. And yet ironically the most memorable words from his lips as he returned to heaven were "Go and make disciples of all nations." In other words, Jesus commanded his followers to fulfill the church's mission by crossing national and cultural borders which he himself never did. Of course it may be argued rightly that Jesus did the cross-cultural mission through the Holy Spirit's indwelling presence and empowerment of believers. Only in that way does he truly fulfill his promise "I am with you always, to the very end of the age" (Matthew 28:20).

The Church

If a theology of the diaspora is to find any solid and substantial biblical basis and development, it will rest primarily on ecclesiology as its foundational teaching. What we have asserted as God's original creative design that motivates mankind to become adventurous wanderers and explorers finds a counterpart with the new creation of people whose mobility instincts are infused with and used for spiritual and missiological ends. What is commonly called the Great Commission in Matthew 28:18-20 received some geographical modifiers in Acts 1:8. After the Holy Spirit empowers the disciples, simultaneous witness will take place in Jerusalem, in Judea, Samaria and into the uttermost parts of the earth.

Nature

Etymologically, the word "church" as a designation of people "called out" is immediately depictive of displacement. Thus some interpreters give more force to the preposition "out" or its separatist nuance instead of the verb "called" or its mission implication. Because God's call is the catalyst to the formation of the church, the outcome is a body that transcends ethnic, cultural and national boundaries, thus, we affirm the universal church. But technically, the universal church is nothing more than the sum total of local churches worldwide, whether in Ephesus or Epanima, in Sardis or Sardinia, or elsewhere. It also includes churches of all eras as in the first-century or twenty-first century Philadelphia being reckoned as one body.

Pilgrims On A Mission

In his prayer for the church Jesus emphasized the fact that his followers will have to remain in the world although they have become strangers to it, thus, they are in the world but not of the world. But being sent into the world, they are to be pilgrims dispersed and moving about on a mission.

"I will remain in the world no longer, but they are still in the world, and I am coming to you. Holy Father, protect them by the power of your name—the name you gave me—so that they may be one as we are one... I have given them your word and the world has hated them, for they are not of the world any more than I am of the world. My prayer is not that you take them out of the world but that you protect them from the evil one. They are not of the world, even as I am not of it. Sanctify them by the truth; your word is truth. As you sent me into the world, I have sent them into the world... My prayer is not for them alone. I pray also for those who will believe in me through their message, that all of them may be one, Father, just as you are in me and I am in you. May they also be in us so that the world may believe that you have sent me" (John 17:11-21).

Unlike God's call to Israel, the church as an institution is not fixed to a certain ethnic group or nation. Its dispersion is intentional. Again, Guroian and Hopko's postulate is worth restating: "the only acceptable theological use of the term diaspora is to have it refer to the salvific mission of the church in its temporal pilgrimage as a sign of the promised Kingdom of God" (Guroian 1990:1). Although the church had its beginning in Jerusalem, it was not intended to be identified permanently with that city or with Israel as a nation. The gravitational power center shifts and the perspectives of the greater number of adherents prevail.

Global Expansion

Using modern space adventures imagery, Prof. Andrew Walls of Edinburgh, cites what an outer space visitor to earth would have observed about Christianity over the last twenty centuries (Walls 1996:3ff). About 37 AD, the original Jerusalem Christians were all Jews meeting in the Temple where only Jews could enter. They worshipped on the Sabbath, circumcised their male children, offered animal sacrifices and followed certain rituals in addition to reading the Torah. In the process of time, as Luke recorded it, "a great persecution broke out against the church at Jerusalem, and all except the apostles were scattered throughout Judea and Samaria" (Acts 8:1).

Three hundred years later the visitor comes to the Council of Nicea (325 AD) where those gathered came from all over the Mediterranean world and hardly one of them is Jewish; indeed they are hostile to the Jews...Using the Greek translation of the Jewish canon and another set of sacred writings, they speak of Jesus as Lord and Son of God. In their debate the issue was whether Jesus was *homoousios* with the Father or only *homoiousios* with Him. Precise significance for precise terms was the concern of their metaphysics and theology. Some three centuries later still, the visitor finds himself in Ireland where monks are gathered on a rocky coastline, several standing on ice-cold water up to their necks, reciting the Psalms. What they read are the same holy books that the Greek fathers used and pronounced the same formulas hammered out in Nicea in 325 AD. Easter is their most important festival and their quest for holiness is heroic.

For his fourth visit, the professor from outer space comes to London in the 1840s and finds in Exeter Hall an excited assembly promoting Christian missions to Africa. They began by reading an English language translation of the same book that the early Christians used. They accept the Nicene Creed but refused the ascetic practices of the Irish monks. These Christians are involved in all the processes of life and society. Then in 1980, he visits Lagos, Nigeria to witness a white-robed group dancing and chanting in the streets on their way to their church. They call themselves Cherubim and Seraphim and they invite people to see visions and experience the healing power of God in their services. They use the same book that the Exeter group had, accept the Nicene Creed but are not as precise about the Son and the Holy Spirit and they fast like the Irish but only on fixed occasions.

So what would our visitor have observed? First, that there is a historical connection among the five groups. Christians from Jerusalem preached to the Greeks who, in turn established the vast Eastern Mediterranean complex he observed in 325 AD. Celtic Christianity found its roots from the Greeks but by 600 AD, the balance shifted westward and Ireland became the power center. In the 1840s Great Britain was most notably associated with Christian missionary expansion. By 1980, the balance has shifted again and this time, southwards to Africa. This is Walls' main thesis (Walls 1996:6) and the phenomenon of global Christianity finds further substantiation from Philip Jenkins' new Christendom (Jenkins 2002).

Besides the historical connection, there is also the essential "continuity of thought about the final significance of Jesus, continuity of a certain consciousness of history, continuity in the use of the Scriptures, of bread and wine, of water. These continuities are cloaked with such heavy veils belonging to their environment that Christians of different times and places must often be unrecognizable to others, or indeed even to themselves, as manifestations of a single phenomenon" (1996:7).

In addition Walls' and Jenkins' observation that the gravitational center of Christianity has shifted from the north and west to the southern and eastern hemispheres, population trends also show that the Asians, Latin Americans and the Africans are the predominant numbers in the global migration patterns. Such realities present the case for diaspora missions in terms of evangelistic outreach and mission mobilization more poignantly. Since by personal choice and by employment pursuits, Filipinos are already scattered in various places and the Filipino church has grown significantly at home and abroad, we can afford not only to supply the mission personnel but also to support the missionary efforts.

The End Times

Future Kingdom Now

Regardless of theological and hermeneutical particulars held by theologians, there is a common perspective that ecclesiology and eschatology are mutually affirming doctrinal tenets. For that reason, some simply hold that when Jesus Christ comes again, the church ends and eternity sets in.[5] The future eternal kingdom, the age to come has already irrupted into the present era. As subjects of God's eternal kingdom, Christians are present in this world in a salvific mission to convince people of the fleeting nature of the kingdoms of this world so that nations and peoples will opt to become part of the kingdom of God.

Unlike Jesus, Christians were not sent from heaven to earth. Instead we are earthlings who have become citizens of the heavenly realm yet remaining on earth as pilgrims on a mission. Jesus anticipated our being where he is so we are heaven-bound. "Father, I want those you have given me to be with me where I am, and to see my glory, the glory you have given me because you loved me before the creation of the world" (John 17:24).

Furthermore, speaking specifically to the early Jewish Christians, the writer to the Hebrews cites those heroes of the faith who, quite significantly, have dispelled the notion of an end of their dispersion by a return to their land. "All these people were still living by faith when they died. They did not receive the things promised; they only saw them and welcomed them from a distance. And they admitted that they were aliens and strangers on earth. People who say such things show that they are looking for a country of their own. If they had been thinking of the country they had left, they would have had the opportunity to return. Instead, they were longing for a better country—a heavenly one. Therefore God is not ashamed to be called their God, for he has prepared a city for them" (Hebrews 11:13-16).

Multitudes in Heaven

Ultimately, all scattering of all God's people of all time ends in a future gathering that the apostle John describes. "After this I looked and there before me was a great multitude that no one could count, from every nation, tribe, people and language, standing before the throne and in front of the Lamb. They were wearing white robes and were holding palm branches in their hands. And they cried out in a loud voice: 'Salvation belongs to our God, who sits on the throne, and to the Lamb'" (Revelation 7:9-10). Then later yet, John sees the new heaven and earth and the new Jerusalem where the new creation dwells with God in the new eternal order. "Then I saw a new heaven and a new earth... and I saw the Holy City, the new Jerusalem, coming down out of heaven from God... And I heard a loud voice from the throne saying, 'Now the dwelling of God is with men, and he will live with them. They will be his people, and God himself will be with them and be their God.'" (Revelation 21:1-3).

SUMMARY THESES ON THE FILIPINO DIASPORA

Considering the preceding materials, here is one person's attempt to explain the Filipino scattering among the nations from a biblical perspective.

1. Filipinos are scattered abroad as an affirmation of the divine mandate for dominion. Filipinos harness the options available to mankind in general and in their own ingenious ways and means, they attempt to

make a contribution to modern human civilization. Many countries today have achieved high levels of development through the efforts of Filipinos.

2. Filipinos are scattered abroad because they have basic human needs they intend to meet and personal goals they intend to achieve. Even if conditions in the Philippines happen to be favorable, it is likely that the sense of adventure and the inherent right to be free to pursue their goals will prompt Filipinos instinctively, as they do other nationalities too, to move elsewhere. Somehow with their cultural, linguistic and historical background they are more adept and resilient at coping with change and thus Filipinos are more suited for crossing cultural and geographical boundaries.

3. Filipinos are scattered due to God's long-suffering that allows some inept if not wicked national government leaders to remain in office so that prosperity is long delayed or denied to the country and its citizens so that in turn, its people have become dissatisfied and they leave this "damaged culture" and nation for better places. The Philippines, having plunged deeply into moral depravity, social injustice and idolatry now appears to be plundered mercilessly by powerful nations through globalization in a way similar to what the hordes of Assyria and Babylon did to Israel of old.

4. For whatever other reasons, God scatters the Filipinos and by his providential hand utilizes their displacement to accomplish some good for the country and for God's own kingdom. Through the experiences of cultural uprooting and migration, many Filipinos have been called into God's family. Furthermore, Filipino Christians become conscious that they have been sent into God's harvest through the economic displacement processes many Filipino overseas workers have experienced.

5. Filipinos scattered abroad must take heart. What they may have envisioned as personal pursuits and professional engagement that may have resulted in some displacement and frustration may now take on the additional notion of God's purpose. Christians in particular must see the primacy of mission so that the diaspora goal is not reduced to cultural

preservation in a foreign land but a gospel witness that blooms where one is planted. They must identify with the Jewish Christians—the genuine diaspora—who set aside their desire to return to their own land because they looked forward to the city God has prepared for them.

Whether forced to migrate or voluntarily doing so, displacement has its benefits. Consider these other theological and spiritual benefits people derive from being displaced from the comforts of familiar surroundings. Dr. David Wong challenges the reader to consider what transpires when we leave the familiar and the routine (Wong 2000:121ff).

1. By nature we seek the comfort zone. Routine simplifies life and its many tasks. We settle as creatures of habit into a regular schedule. A component of the comfort zone is familiarity.

2. Inside the comfort zone, we feel secure. As Abraham Maslow affirms in the hierarchy of human needs, the need for safety and security are basic.

3. Inside the comfort zone, we become complacent. Familiar sounds and words reassure, but they also lull us to stupor. Within the comfort zone, we easily become smug, self-satisfied and self-righteous. Those who opposed Jesus were secure in their age-old traditions and regulated their lives with numerous rules. Boundaries that once provided meaning and security had become walls of a prison.

4. From time to time, life takes us outside the comfort zone. We go through transitions and move from one place to another. In a global village, our working life spans many lands on different continents. We adjust to strange cultures, accents, currencies, cuisines, and climates. Technology demands that we adjust.

5. Outside the comfort zone, we are more open to change. Unless we are dislodged from our comfort zone, we become victimized by "paradigm paralysis."

6. Outside the comfort zone, we find the opportunity for growth.

7. God takes us beyond our comfort zone to get our attention.

8. God takes us beyond our comfort zone to help us grow.

Indeed, Filipinos who have left the Philippines and have migrated and settled elsewhere in this modern world have arrived at a wider and deeper sense of God's purpose and calling. As attested to by the vignettes of their personal experiences or the other write-ups on selected case studies in a separate section of this volume, God has shown his hand at work behind the movements of peoples worldwide.

Concluding Theological Propositions

Having processed some available data from the contemporary realities about the Filipino diaspora, and having derived some principles from the instances of human migrations in the Bible, it may now be possible to formulate a theology of the Filipino diaspora with these fifteen propositions.

1. God created the whole earth for man's habitation, development and dominion and holds mankind accountable as responsible stewards.

2. By God's creative design, humankind is mobile and free, thus making voluntary dispersion or migration endemic to human nature.

3. Since humankind belongs to one family, peoples can mutually coexist and co-inhabit the same locale, thus making migration, cultural adaptation and cultural interpenetration possible.

4. Although some civilizations past and present conquer and subdue others, all of them, by design and common needs, thrive on intermingled and cross-fertilized cultural norms and values.

5. By conquest, some nations become subservient to others when territorial boundaries are invaded and their inhabitants are scattered, ergo, the involuntary diaspora as experienced by the Jewish nation and other ethnic groups as well.

6. Although generally voluntary, Filipino migrations are catalyzed, in part, by deprivation in some areas of need but perhaps mostly due to economic hardship. Hardly is it caused by foreign conquests as in the case of the Jews and Armenians.

7. What applies to the original creation design also carries over into the church—the new creation so that human and Filipino mobility and adaptation take on a new missional value.

8. Unlike the Jewish nation with its historic and specific geographical identity, the Christian church is universal in nature and may not be limited to a locality or claimed exclusively by any people group. Because the church is a pilgrim community, she cannot be disenfranchised although she must settle where God sees fit to plant her.

9. General revelation ensures certain commonalities among world religions because God has not left Himself without a witness. Therefore migrant peoples as well as receptor groups can have commonalities that serve as fodder to communicating the gospel.[6]

10. Jesus Christ's great commission is to disciple all nations and it can be accomplished in various ways and means but the church's mission will always include varying degrees of Christian migration voluntary or otherwise.

11. God's promised presence—the indwelling Holy Spirit who empowers for personal life and witness, promised to migrate along with human witnesses.

12. Cultural uprootedness has served as a positive factor that God uses to move people away from their natural family bonds and to free them so that they become open to the gospel call and allegiance to God and subsequently incorporate them into His supernatural family.

13. Providentially, the Filipino global presence today is one of God's more effective tools in penetrating doors "closed" or restricted to general mission efforts. However, mission consciousness is not yet generally ingrained among the Filipino diaspora. They have to be awakened and the mission consciousness has to be cultivated and nurtured.

14. By due necessity, but more likely by God's sovereignty, Filipino underground churches have been established and have proliferated in "restricted access" countries but due to the lack of fellowship and cross-fertilization of biblical and theological insights, errors abound especially among lay preachers and congregations. Thus, such reality legitimizes the call for strategic means of instruction and correctives to meet this need.

15. Ultimately, all scattering of all God's people of all time—Filipinos, Jews and non-Jews alike—ends in a future gathering where "a great multitude that no one could count, from every nation, tribe, people and language" stands before the Lamb and dwells in the new Jerusalem where "God himself will be with them" in the new eternal order (Revelation 7:9; 21:1-3).

ENDNOTES

[1] Cf. J. I. Packer's high view of the Scriptures as indispensable to the formulation of theology in his introduction to the theological craft in Woodbridge and McComiskey (1991: 18ff.). Packer answers the question: "How may we best state and apply the complete Christian faith, topic by topic and as a whole, in the light of the current interests, doubts, assumptions, perplexities, questions, protests, and challenges? Answers to that question, and to all the specific questions into which it breaks down, are built up as the Scriptures are searched and exegeted, as the problems of insiders and the wonderings of outsiders are listened to, as the church's past approaches to the problem areas as reviewed and assessed by biblical teaching, and as that teaching is allowed to interrogate us in its terms about our thinking, believing, and behaving" (Packer 1991: 23-24).

[2] Grabbe specifically cites C. C. Torrey as the original doubter of the historical reliability of the exile concept in Ezra. Furthermore, the title of Robert P. Carroll's treatise "Exile! What Exile?" in the same volume is enough to suggest his similar posture on the historicity of the exile (Carroll 1998: 62-79).

[3] Another recent trophy of Filipino achievement is Dr. Josette Biyo, winner among the 4000 candidates from around the world for the 2002 Intel "Excellence in Teaching Award" in an international competition held at Louisville, Kentucky from May 10-17. Dr. Biyo is a public school teacher from Iloilo. The Massachusetts Institute of Technology Lincoln Laboratory in Boston named a minor planet in her honor.

[4] Later this dispersed group from the Northern Kingdom came to be known as the "ten lost tribes" who, it is believed, will somehow return to the land but only in the end times. The Assyrian invading forces occupied the North and intermarried with the Jews who were left behind. Thus came about the hated Samaritans. (Barclay 1958: 43ff).

[5] Dispensational and its modified counterpart historic premillennialism present a much more detailed scheme of the end times when compared to amillennialism or postmillennialism. The latter is specifically more assertive and optimistic regarding the church's potential to influence the world so as to bring about the conditions depictive of a biblical "millennium" albeit a non-literal one thousand years but figurative of a long period of time (Clouse 1977).

[6] Admittedly, some sectarian and fundamentalist religio-cultural perspectives do not espouse or cater to commonality or compatibility. American immigrant Ravi Zacharias cites this in relation to America. "In a pluralistic society there will always be a struggle to find shared values. But if those shared values are made secondary to

a radically different set of values that, at heart, undermine our national freedoms, America will become purely a means to an end that could be in violation of its own reason for being. (It is interesting to note how difficult Islamic countries make it for those of other faiths living among them, but how demanding Islam can be of the American culture to provide it unlimited freedom.)...Culture is dangerous when it is used to hijack the basic ethos of a nation. If that ethos is not respected, the very strengths that made the country attractive to the immigrant in the first placed are abused" (Zacharias 2002:103-104).

REFERENCES

Barclay, William. (1958). *The Letters of James and Peter. Daily Study Bible*. Philadelphia: Westminster Press.

Carroll, Robert P. (1998). Exile! What Exile? Deportation and the Discourses of Diaspora. *Leading Captivity Captive*. Edited by Lester L. Grabbe. Sheffield: Sheffield Academic Press.

Carrier, Herve. (1989). *Gospel Message and Human Cultures from Leo XIII to John Paul II*. Translated by John Drury. Pittsburgh: Duquesne Univ. Press.

Carson, D. A. and Woodbridge, John D. (Eds.). (1993). *God and Culture. Essays in Honor of Carl F.H. Henry*. Grand Rapids: Wm. B. Eerdmans.

Clouse, Robert G. (Ed.). (1977). *The Meaning of the Millennium: Four Views*. Downers Grove: InterVarsity Press.

Coote, Robert and Stott, John R.W. (Eds.). (1980). *Down to Earth: Studies in Christianity and Culture*. Grand Rapids: W.B. Eerdmans Publishing Co.

Cruz, Gemma Tulud. (2004, March). Beyond the Borders Beyond the Margins. *World Mission Magazine*. Internet: http://www.worldmission.ph. Accessed July 7, 2004.

Dehghanpisheh, Babak. (2004, March). A One-Way Ticket. *Newsweek*. March 8, 2004: 35.

De Quiros, Conrado. (2004). There's the Rub. *Philippine Daily Inquirer*. March 8, 2004.

Eck, Diana L. (2001). *A New Religious America: How a "Christian Country" Has Become the World's Most Religiously Diverse Nation*. San Francisco: Harper.

Escobar, Samuel. (2003, January). Migration: Avenue and Challenge to Mission. *Missiology. An International Review* XXXI:1:17-28.

Evangelista, Sonny. (2004, March). Hidden Agenda? *World Mission Magazine*. Internet: http://www.worldmission.ph. Accessed July 7, 2004.

Grudem, Wayne. (1994). *Systematic Theology. An Introduction to Biblical Doctrine*, Grand Rapids: Zondervan Publishing House.

Guroian, Vigen. (1990). Toward a Diaspora Theology. *Window Quarterly* I:4. Internet: http://www.sain.org/WINDOW/Diaspor2.txt. Accessed July 7, 2004

Jenkins, Philip. (2002). *The Next Christendom: The Coming of Global Christianity*. New York: Oxford University Press.

Jewett, Paul K. with Marguerite Shuster. (1996). *Who We Are: Our Dignity as Human. A Neo-Evangelical Theology*. Grand Rapids: Wm. B. Eerdmans.

Klein, Ralph W. (1979). *Israel in Exile. A Theological Interpretation.* Philadelphia: Fortress Press.

Miller, John J. (2004). *Migration Patterns. Reasononline.* Internet: http://reason.com/9605/Dept.Bk.MillerSOWELL.shtml. Accessed July 7, 2004.

Moreland, J.P. and Ciocchi, David M. (Eds.). (1993). *Christian Perspectives on Being Human.* Grand Rapids: Baker Books, 1993.

Niebuhr, H. Richard. (1951). *Christ and Culture.* New York: Harper and Brothers.

Newbigin, Lesslie. (1986). *Foolishness to the Greeks. The Gospel and Western Culture.* Grand Rapids: Wm. B. Eerdmans.

Newsweek Editorial. (2004, March). Brain Gain. *Newsweek.* March 8, 2004:3-32.

Packer, J. I. (1991). Is Systematic Theology a Mirage? An Introductory Discussion. *Doing Theology in Today's World. Essays in Honor of Kenneth S. Kantzer.* John D. Woodbridge and Thomas Edward McComiskey. (Eds.). Grand Rapids: Zondervan Publishing House.

Pantoja, Luis. (1981). "An Evangelical Critique of Contextualization Theology." Unpublished Th.D. Dissertation. Dallas Theological Seminary.

Pedrosa, Carmen N. (2004). From a Distance. *The Philippine Star.* May 23, 2004.

Romualdez, Babe. (2004). Reality Check. *Philippine Star.* March 7, 2004.

Sanneh, Lamin. (2003). *Whose Religion Is Christianity? The Gospel Beyond the West.* Grand Rapids: Wm. B. Eerdmans.

Smith-Christopher, Daniel L. (2002). *A Biblical Theology of Exile.* Minneapolis: Fortress Press.

Sowell, Thomas. (2002). *Migrations and Cultures: A World View.* New York: Basic Books.

Tan, Michael L. (2004, June). World Without Pinoys. *Philippine Daily Inquirer.* June 16, 2004:15.

Taylor, William D. (Ed.). (2000). *Global Missiology for the 21st Century. The Iguassu Dialogue.* Grand Rapids: Baker Academic.

Walls, Andrew F. (1996). *The Missionary Movement in Christian History.* New York: Orbis Books.

Wan, Enoch. (2003, January). Mission Among the Chinese Diaspora: A Case Study of Mission and Migration. *Missiology. An International Review* XXXI:1: 35-43.

Woodbridge, John D. and McComiskey, Thomas Edward. (Eds.). (1991). *Doing Theology in Today's World. Essays in Honor of Kenneth S. Kantzer.* Grand Rapids: Zondervan Publishing House.

Wong, David W. F. (2001). *Journeys Beyond the Comfort Zone.* Singapore: BAC Printers.

Zacharias, Ravi. (2002). *Light in the Shadow of Jihad.* Sisters, Oregon: Multnomah Publishers.

Part III

MISSIOLOGICAL
METHODOLOGY

PART III

〜〜•〜〜

INTRODUCTION

I n this section, the subject of diaspora in general is studied missiologically with Filipino diaspora as the focus of attention. The phenomenon
of diaspora in human history is by no means a recent development;
tragic from a human viewpoint (such as the millennial-old Jewish diaspora)
but providential missiologically. This section begins with the chapter on "The
Phenomenon of Diaspora: Missiological Implications for Christian Missions"
which is a missiological attempt to describe the phenomenon of diaspora and
delineate its missiological implications.

One of the many characteristics of Filipino culture is "collectivism" especially family solidarity. *Irene,* a Filipino abroad often struggle with family separation and suffer sojourner's homesickness; yet providentially bearing witness to
God's glory and being part of the story of Kingdom expansion are all featured
in "Part IV – Global Strategy" and "Part V – Personal Stories."

"Mission" is the Great Commission of making disciples of all nations
and "missions" is the ways and means of accomplishing "mission." Missiology is the practice and study of both "mission" (biblically, theologically) and
"missions" (strategically and practically). Among missiologists, there is an ongoing debate on matters such as: the necessity to differentiate "evangelism"
to be local and "missions" to be foreign; the conceptualization and practice
of "missions" to be determined geographically, linguistically, culturally and
ethnically, etc.

The chapter by Dr. Tereso C. Casiño is a sincere search for answer to the following questions:

- Are ministries among Filipino countrymen legitimate missionary work?

- If a Filipino pastor goes overseas and conducts ministries among Filipino communities, would he or she be considered a "legitimate" missionary?

5

THE PHENOMENON OF DIASPORA: MISSIOLOGICAL IMPLICATIONS FOR CHRISTIAN MISSIONS

Enoch Wan

INTRODUCTION

D iaspora in a large scale is a recent phenomenon of several decades; yet with strong socio-cultural impact on many countries and people groups.

It is important to provide definition of some key-terms and state the assumptions of this chapter at the outset. Etymologically, (explained in the INTRODUCTION of this book), **diaspora** (from Greek διασπορα) means scattering and the term is used in this chapter in reference to "the phenomenon of large-scale movement of people from their homeland to elsewhere geographically over a period of time (i.e. not mere transient)." The term **migration** is used to describe the movement of people from one location to another with no reference to home country; whereas **emigration** is leaving one's own country for another, while **immigration** is just moving to another country.

It is understood that "mission" is the "Great Commission of making disciples" by carrying out the "missions" (ways and means of accomplishing the "mission") including proclamation of the Gospel, persuasion for conversion, practicing the Great Commandment (of loving God and one's neighbor in holistic ministry), producing disciples and self-multiplying congregations, etc.

The purpose of this chapter is to describe the phenomenon of diaspora and delineate its missiological implications. Important as they may be, discussion and analysis of various factors and multiple forms of diaspora are beyond the scope of this chapter.

SOME OBSERVATIONS

The phenomenon of diaspora occurs in contemporary society as international migration. Some of the factors to accelerate this trend of diaspora are: "the rapid processes of economic, demographic, social, political, cultural and environmental change, which rise from decolonization, modernization and uneven development." (Castles & Miller 1998:139)

Of relevance to this study is "the migration model" which, in the words of the Peruvian missiologist Samuel Escobar, is:

> "The *migration model* has also functioned through the centuries. Migrants from poor countries who move in search of economic survival carry the Christian message and missionary initiative with them. Moravians from Curazao moved to Holland; Jamaican Baptists emigrated to England; Filipino Christian women go to Muslim countries; Haitian believers went to Canada; and Latin American Evangelicals are going to Japan, Australia, and the United States." (Escobar 2000:34)

Large scale diaspora is one of the characteristics of contemporary society. The hundreds of churches of the World Council of Churches (WCC), spread over one hundred countries, have made concerted efforts responding to the phenomenon of diaspora through various WCC branches, such as "Actions by Churches Together" (for emergency needs of refugees and displaced peoples), "Ecumenical Advocacy Alliance" (on justice issues, racism, indigenous peoples rights, women's programs...) and *Uprooted People* (a quarterly newsletter) (Stromberg 2003:45).

Diaspora – A Growing Trend

The magnitude of diaspora is impressive for "members of between 1% and 2% of the contemporary world population has migrated or is migrating" (Jongeneel 2003:29; Jacques 1991)

"By the early 1990s there were about 17 million internally displaced people, 30 million 'regular' migrants, and another 30 million migrants with an 'irregular' status. The combined total of 97 million people represents a doubling of the global migrant population in the space of five years" (Hanciles 2003:146). Of the various continents, sub-Saharan Africa has the bulk (estimated 35 million regional migrants), "followed by Asia and the Middle East. Additionally, most migrants—including the bulk of the world's 17 million officially registered refugees and asylum seekers—stay in their region of origin." (Hanciles 2003:146). For instance, Europe is estimated to have approximately 18 million legal migrants and, additionally, around 2.6 million undocumented migrants. (Jongeneel 2003:29)

Various Forms And Factors Of Multiple Diasporas

Diasporas occur among many countries and continents including Chinese, Jewish, South Asian, Hispanic, Caribbean, etc. for many factors such as economic betterment, social instability, political conflict, conquer or oppression, natural catastrophes, etc. They may take various forms such as orderly/voluntary factors (e.g. migration, emigration, immigration, etc.) or chaotic/involuntary factors (e.g. refugee, prisoners of international or tribal wars, ethnic cleansing, children-at-risk, etc.).

Emergence of Islam and Christianity into Truly Global Religions Historically

During the period of the seventh to twelfth centuries, Islam's expansion was based on migration of the Muslim, covering the area:

> "from Iberia and Morocco in the west to sub-Saharan Africa in the south and as far east as Persia, northern India, and later, Indonesia...as the most successful heir to the Roman and Persian empires, so that the period from roughly 750 to 1750 is conventionally regarded in world history as the Islamic Age." (Hanciles 2003:146)

Similar pattern could be found in the process of expansion of Christianity in the sixteenth and seventeenth centuries and specifically with "50 - 60 million Europeans emigrated overseas' from 1815 to 1915. (Hanciles 2003:146)

South To North Migration Movement

Of the many factors to account for the South to North migration move-ment, political instability and desperate poverty of the many countries in the Southern hemisphere are the most significant ones. S.M. Naseem in recent online write-up entitled "Diaspora and Development" made the following observation: "One of the more benign and virtuous aspects of globalization in the past three decades or so has been the increase in the migration of people from the poorer, labor-surplus economies of the South to the richer, labor-scarce economies migration within the South itself." (Naseem 2004)

Hanciles is critical of the attempt to explain South-to-North migration movement in economic terms to be "simplistic;" especially in the African context. He offered to add to the factor of "contextual pathologies" of the southern continents, "charismatic or neo-Pentecostal Christian movements." (Hanciles 2003:150) He factually made an excellent case by contrasting the vibrant immigrant churches (from non-Western origins) in Western Europe and the USA with the secularized and declining Christian churches. (Hanciles 2003:150-151)

It is interesting to observe that in contrast to the migration movement from South to North, there is the shift of missionary force passing "from North to South at a time when the South is increasingly poor." (Escobar 2000: 33-34)

The Opportunity and Challenge of Diaspora To Christian Community – Unity In The Context of Diversity

The phenomenon of diaspora provides both the opportunity and chal-lenge of preserving demonstrative Christian unity in the context of diver-sity. In his case study on diaspora in Europe, Jongeneel had observed that "The life and activities of the congregations and the churches in Europe are nowadays more pluriform and complex than in previous centuries...due to the language used, worship style practiced, multi-ethnic mix...is both positive and problematic..." (Jongneel 2003:31).

Islamization

Some referred to the phenomenon of recent explosive number of Muslims immigrating to Europe in the last few decades as "Islamization" (Jongeneel 2003:31). This development provides both golden opportunities and major challenges to the Christian church for evangelism.

A Case Study Of Challenges And Opportunities In Spain

Samuel Escobar in his 2002 ASM presidential address highlighted the massive immigrant population: "Official figures show that there are 220,000 Moroccans, 83,000 Ecuadorians, 40,000 Columbians, 35,000 Chinese, 28,000 Peruvians, 13,000 Pakistani and a similar number of Filipinos..." which posted a threefold challenge to the Christian church in Spain:

"First is *the challenge to Christian compassion and sensitivity...* The second challenge is *the need for the churches to take a prophetic stance in the face of society's unjust treatment of immigrants...* The third challenge is the fact that *migration is an avenue for the evangelistic dimension of mission...*" (original emphasis, Escobar 2003:19)

MISSIOLOGICAL IMPLICATIONS OF THE PHENOMENON OF DIASPORA

Theology of Christian Missions

Nowadays, people from various parts of the world who traditionally had been separated geographically and culturally are being thrown together in close proximity due to the phenomenon of diaspora. Henceforth there is an urgent search for and emergence of a theology of Christian missions in terms of multi-culturalism and ethnicity, inter-racial relationship and Christian hospitality.

For example, WCC recently sponsored two meetings on the matters of cultural diversity and Christian unity: "International Network Forum on Multicultural Ministry," November 1999 held in Australia and May 2002 in Thailand. (Stromberg 2003:46)

The participants at these gatherings formulated "a Trinitarian theology of the kingdom of God" to account for "the social realities" and in support of "multicultural ministry" of WCC in the following official statement:

"In God's grace, the love which enables the unity of the different persons of the Trinity also enables us to live in the differences of our cultural and individual particularity...The Holy Spirit brings Christ's reconciliation to the human community in such a way that we are not reduced to a single type but enhanced in the richness of our diversity." (Stromberg 2003:46)

Theoretical Formulation

The phenomena of diaspora occur in different contexts and circumstances; are varied in size, shape, dynamics and impacts; thus, are incredibly complex and unpredictable. However, efforts of theoretical formulation have resulted in multiple numbers of theories such as historical-structural, migration systems, network-complexity, social capital, neo-classical economic, etc. (Castles and Miller 1998:19-29; Massey 1999:34-52; Pessar 1999:53-70).

New Way Of Conceptualizing Non-spatially

Traditionally, the terms used to enable researchers to conceptualize spatially are "local" and "global." However, the phenomenon of diaspora provides a new intermediate state between "local" and "global." The phenomenon of large scale and intensified diaspora requires the formulation of a new paradigm that is "borderless" and of "deterritorialization" in nature. "Most important, global migration movements link the fate of distant communities in a manner that transcends national boundaries and significantly weakens culture-place or identity-place correlation." (Hanciles 2003:148)

A recent posting in the internet by Georgiou provides an apt explanation of this new paradigm of **deterritorialization** – the scope and scale of the task is transnational:

"...diasporic as a defining characteristic of certain minorities
allows us to understand the specificity of the experience of
certain groups which at some stage in their history migrated

and have as a reference a distant Homeland. Because of the direct or the symbolic and historical experience of migration and of deterritorialization, diasporic minorities have some distinct characteristics vis-a-vis other ethnic minorities (such as the indigenous and linguistic ethnic minorities)." (Georgiou 2001)

Hanciles proposed the term "transnational migration" or "transmigration" to label the phenomenon of diaspora with the following description,

"This new paradigm suggests that even though migrants invest socially, economically, and politically in their new society, they may continue to participate in the daily life of the society from which they emigrated but which they did not abandon.' Transmigrants are often bilingual, can lead dual lives, move easily between cultures, frequently maintain homes in two countries, and are incorporated as social actors in both." (Hanciles 2003:147)

A New Way Of Conceptualizing Culturally

In a multi-cultural and multi-ethnic society like USA, there are homogeneous groups that are culturally distinctive from other groups. For example, American-Koreans and American-Japanese are culturally distinctive from one another though they come from homogeneous countries of Korea and Japan. Hawaii and Brazil are the two countries that could be illustrative of cultural and ethnic mix that would frustrate any attempt to identify culturally distinctive groups. The phenomenon of diaspora accelerates the process of mixing resulted in the necessity of a new paradigm of ambiguous ethnic identity or cultural "hybridity," as an alternative to traditional concept of "homogeneity." This on-going process of merging, mixing and emerging in Europe is described by Georgiou:

"Diaspora is not a panacea and should not be considered as the only useful concept to address the experience of certain minorities. The value of diaspora does not erase the importance of concepts such as ethnicity and migration. Rather, diaspora has become an additional concept. It is a useful concept that helps us understand the complexities of multicultural Europe." (Georgiou 2001)

A New Scenario That Requires An Interdisciplinary Approach

Due to the complexity of the phenomenon of diaspora, researchers and care-givers are to combine the use of demographic approach, statistical data, community development, social sciences, etc. Parallel to urban missions (Shipp 1990), Christian response to the phenomenon of diaspora has to be interdisciplinary utilizing theories and methodologies of sociology, anthropology, demography, statistics, etc.

It may be a surprise to evangelical Christians that in the 1990's, the Catholic church in the US had issued an official document comprehensively dealt with the matters of migration and mission. "One Family Under God" (Sept. 1995, revised 1998) was an official document issued by the National Council of Catholic Bishops of the United States covering biblical foundation, sociological analyses and practical guidelines.

Methodological Implications

A New Paradigm

The phenomenon of diaspora requires a new missiological paradigm to cope with the opportunities and challenges emerging from such a development. The several dimensions to this new missiological paradigm are described below:

'Multi-directional' Approach To Christian Missions

The traditional missiological distinction between "foreign missions" and local missions is to be replaced by a "multi-directional" approach to Christian missions as the following book title indicates, The New Global Mission: *The Gospel from Everywhere to Everyone* (Escobar, & Stott 2003). The description of "Paragraph 9 of the Lausanne Covenant" succinctly summarizes it well:

> "Missionaries should flow ever more freely from and to all
> six continents in a spirit of humble service."

Jehu Hanciles advocated the replacement of traditional "European-style linear structures" with the "emerging non-Western" pattern, typical of the phenomenon of diaspora:

"...parallel presences in different circles and at different levels, each seeking to penetrate within and beyond its circle. Contemporary migration is a 'network-driven phenomenon, with newcomers naturally attracted to the places where they have contacts and the buildup of contacts facilitating later moves to the key immigrant centers.' ...the emerging non-Western movement is cellular, travels along pre-existing social relations, rests on charismatic leadership, communicates in songs and signals, and understands the human person in his or her relationship to community." (Hanciles 2003: 150)

"Mission At Our Doorstep"

David L. Ripley (1994) convincingly gave a wake up call to Christians in the USA that due to the wave of large influx of immigrants that began in the 1980s, "mission at our doorstep" is a reality not to be ignored. Samuel Escobar made a similar point for the case in the USA (Escobar 2000:29) as did David D'Amico's article, "Evangelization Across Cultures in the United States: What to Do When the World Come to Us" (D'Amico 2001). Ebaugh and Chafetz's book *Religion and the New Immigrants: Continuities and Adaptations in Immigrant Congregations* provided helpful data on the influx of immigrants and the flourishing of the immigrant congregations in the USA.

It is inexcusable for Christians in the US to not engage in cross-cultural evangelization for it can be done at home in ethnic enclaves (D'Amico) domestically (Long 1996). Jan Jongeneel in his case study on Europe entitled "The Mission of Migrant Churches in Europe proposed three terms to deal specifically with the phenomenon of diaspora as follows:

"(1) *Internal mission (Mission in Non-Western Circles)*... The non-Western Christian migrants are part of their own ethnic, national, and linguistic communities... (2) *Reverse Mission*... Many non-Western migrants do not confine their witness to their own circles. They are convinced of their call to preach the full gospel to secular Europeans as well... (3) *Common Mission*... Mission can also be done by members of established congregations and churches in cooperation with members of migrant congregations and churches – the so called 'common mission'... has referred to 'the vision of a common missionary vocation,'..." (Jongeneel 2003:32)

"Multi-dimensional" Perspective And Holistic Missions

The traditional distinction and dichotomist view of "saving soul" vis-à-vis "practicing charity" should give way to a **holistic** understanding of the Christian faith (i.e. Great Commission and Great Commandment combined) and man's condition (spiritual lostness and human plight): the multi-dimensional understanding of Christian mission and humanitarian responsibility to displaced people in diaspora. The new trend of evangelical missions readily being involved in "holistic" understanding and practice is partially caused and challenged by the phenomenon of diaspora. (Escobar 2000:32-33). This shift towards a multi-dimensional perspective is called "a changed understanding" by Hanciles with elements such as the emphasis on "incarnational" ministry, the adaptation of Johannine model of the Great Commission (John 17:18 and 20:21), and the call of missions as "service". (Hanciles 2003:149-159)

"From the perspective of mission, particularly in the Evangelical world, we have lately observed the mushrooming of holistic mission projects, in which a social component becomes indispensable." (Escobar 2000:32)

In a seminal article entitled "Biblical Issues in Mission and Migration," Professor Christine D. Pohl of Asbury Theological Seminary brought to the forth several missiological implications of Christian responsibility to resident aliens in the context of mission and migration:

"(1) The biblical responsibility to resident aliens suggests that a concern for the physical, social, and spiritual well-being of migrants and refugees should not be peripheral to Christian life, mission, and witness; instead, it should be central. In setting priorities... (2) The biblical accounts suggest the importance of carefully and creatively thinking about how to hold together emphases on alien status and hospitality... (3) In a world of ethnic tensions and vast socioeconomic differences and injustices, acts of hospitality are what Philip Hallie calls 'litter moves against destructiveness'... Hospitality is an important expression of recognition and respect for those who are despised or overlooked by the larger society." (Pohl 2003:9-10)

Lawrence Temfwe issued a similar call for Christians in his article, "Aliens in Our Own Country" (2004) and so did others (Creswell 2003; Guthrie 1998; Moreau 2000).

New Approach – 'Diaspora Management,' Networking And Partnership

"Diaspora management" is governmental utilization of resources provided by former citizens in terms of human (e.g. expertise) and financial (e.g. investment and remittance) resources for "motherland." A case in point is the government of India:

> "One nation exploring 'diaspora management' is India, whose government and the Federation of Indian Chambers of commerce and Industry recently invited 2000 extremely successful 'non-resident' Indians from 63 countries to New Delhi, to determine how the resources and achievements of Indians abroad might be used to uplift India... that Chinese non-residents have invested about $60 billion in China while that number for India is only $1 billion from non-resident Indians... The opportunities that 'diaspora management' has to offer are endless..." (http://trendwatching.com/trends/2003/03diasporamanagement.html)

The Vietnamese government has extended similar friendly gesture to descendents of diaspora Vietnamese abroad. (http://news.bbc.co.uk/2/hi/business/2538455.stm)

Since 1976, Chinese Christians all over the world have maximized the "diaspora management" model to promote world-wide movement for evangelism among the diaspora Chinese by forming the "Chinese Coordination Centre of World Evangelism" ("CCCOWE") in 1976. This movement began with seventy Chinese church leaders, who came together at the International

Congress on World Evangelism in Lausanne, to commence the movement that began with the 1st Chinese Congress on World Evangelization convened in Hong Kong in August 1976. Today, there are Board of Directors from each of the 50-plus worldwide CCCOWE District Committees to coordinate global evangelistic efforts among diaspora Chinese. (For details - http://www.cccowe.org/). The formation and operation of FIN will do well to learn from the model of "diaspora management" and the precedent of CCCOWE.

The traditional Western-based, denominational or national model of Christian mission is to adapt to the new landscape, emerging from the phenomenon of diaspora, to network and partner with the vibrant Christian congregations among diaspora community in many lands.

The new approach would include networking and partnership with local Christian efforts and diaspora Christian community, as proposed by Joshua Tsutada in "Global Cooperation and Networking" (Tsutada 2000). The following quotation sums up the need of partnership in the contemporary context of internal migration or large scale diaspora:

> "Precisely at the point in which the influence of Christianity declines in the West, which turns into a hard mission field because its culture resists the gospel, the new global order has brought the so-called Third World into the heart of North America, Europe, and Japan. Within that environ-ment, Christians from old and new churches are called to new partnerships." (Escobar 2000:29)

Swiss missiologist W. Buhlmann (1986) went as far as stating that "the Third Church" will be the driving force of global mission during the Third Millennium, after identifying the first thousand years of church history to be dominated by the Eastern Church (the eastern half of the Roman Empire) and the second thousand years being led by the Western Church of Europe and USA in growth and expansion.

The global mission movement requires the cooperation and partnership of traditional missionary forces from the West with local ethnic Christians. A case in point is well illustrated by Laura Heikes' study on Hispanic American Christians (in relation to migrant workers in the US) and Latino throughout

South America (in relation to non-Christians in South American countries) due to the following advantages they have: familiar knowledge and psychological connectedness to the diaspora population from personal experience and shared cultural affinity. (Heikes 2003:69-85)

Jongeneel's study on the European situation came to a similar conclusion as quoted below:

> "Migrant Christians and their congregations and churches can help establish Christianity in Europe to renew its mission and evangelism. The changing contexts in Europe, the process of globalization, and other contemporary changes – these challenge all Christians as their established and migrant congregations and churches cooperate together to do mission and evangelism commonly: for the sake of God's glory and humanity's salvation." (Jongeneel 2002:33)

For the new millennium, Escobar proposed "the cooperative model, churches from rich nations add their material resources to the human resources of the churches in poor nations in order to work in a third area." (original emphasis, Escobar 2000:34)

> "...Some missionary presence and activity has been significant, though it seldom gets to the records of formal institutional mission agencies as well as faith missions who are trying to set up connections that will allow them to serve within the frame of this migration movement." (Escobar 2000:34)

Marcel Durst's MA thesis had an interesting title: "Mission through Migration: *Mission Initiatives of Latin American Migrants in Switzerland*." (Durst 2002: xiii) with several insightful points:

> "...some recommendations are made which could help develop partnership in these mission efforts, but could also pose a challenge to Swiss churches: to recognize migration as a potential for unplanned mission, to facilitate sending and receiving missionaries in true partnership, and to network of existing Latin groups and their mission efforts."

New Awareness – Wisdom Required

There must be a new awareness that Christian emigration to the West is part of the trend of diaspora yet the well-meaning efforts to assist suffering Christians in emigration may result in the weakening–even destroying–of the local Christian church. Armenian Christians in Iran is an apt illustration. In 1976, there were 169,000 Christians (0.5% of the population of 33.7 million). Since a "procedure set up in Austria to help Christians to leave Iran and obtain a US visa... refugee status..." was in place, by 1996–twenty years later–there were only 78,000 ethnic Christians left behind (0.1% of the 60.1 million population) (see "Human Rights without Frontiers," Feb 16, 2001 - http://www.strategicnetwork.org/index.php?). Therefore, Christians must act with wisdom when facilitating emigration of Christians to the West in some critical situations.

Altered Ecclesiology in 'Christian Countries'

The adapted form of worship and organizational structure by vibrant & growing ethnic congregations may even impact the Christian community in the host country:

> "The migrant congregations and churches are not just an appendix to the established congregations and churches in Europe. They have their own identity, take their own initiatives, and show leadership: their enthusiasm and experiential knowledge of the non-Christian religions and ideologies pave new ways in missions and evangelism." (Jongeneel 2002:32)

The altered ecclesiology in the hosting "Christian countries" has been discussed by quite a few researchers such as D'Amico (2001), Durst (2002), Escobar (2000) and Hanciles (2003).

• Positive Factor: Demographic Diaspora Facilitates Christian Expansion

The thesis of Jehu J. Hanciles' paper, *Migration and Mission: Some Implications for the Twenty-first-Century Church* is that "recent migration movements, as a critical dimension of contemporary global transformations, have the potential to significantly affect the geographic and demographic contours of the world's major religions and provide a vital outlet for proselytism and missionary expansion." (Hanciles' 2003:146)

After reviewing the development of the Christian church historically and the process of Christian expansion analytically, Hanciles came to a conclusion that "Christianity is a migratory religion, and migration movements have been a functional element in its expansion." (Hanciles 2003:149)

• Positive Factors: Reachable And Receptive

According to Roger Greenway of Calvin Theological Seminary, a leading missiologist in the study of urban mission, considered the migratory phenomenon of diaspora (explosive demographic shift to the city included) is a divine provision of making those who traditionally had been unreachable and resistant to become reachable by and receptive to the gospel. (Greenway 1999:554-555)

Laura Heikes cited the precedent of Moroccan Muslim in Spain in search of works to be reachable by the gospel (Heikes 2003:69-85). Such stories can easily be multiplied by the thousands of similar incidents as part of global mission strategy.

Displaced people are most receptive to the gospel when in transition and undergoing psycho-social adjustment from traumatic experience, separation & suffering (Wan 2003). Among the diaspora, ethnic church often has turned into a community center for mutual aid, social activities, substitute-family, etc. Diaspora Muslim, such as Kurds, Afghans, Somalis, etc. are some examples in Justin Long's study (1996) on their accessibility and receptivity.

• Negative Factor – Statistically Challenging

The phenomenon of diaspora had a negative factor to missiological research due to the statistical challenge of ascertaining accurate figures of various groups. The reasons include: high mobility, the tendency towards cultural/ethnic hybridity, confused identity (due to cultural assimilation, genetic amalgamation of inter-racial marriage, psycho-dynamic marginality of the "self" or divided loyalty), etc.

CONCLUSION

The purpose of this chapter is to describe the phenomenon of diaspora and delineate its missiological implications. Several observations of the phenomenon of diaspora have been made: i.e. massive diaspora is a growing trend internationally and intercontinentally, forms and factors of multiple diaspora, etc.

Several missiological implications have been identified including: search for and emergence of "theology of Christian missions" in terms of multi-culturalism and ethnicity, interracial relationship and Christian hospitality; "theoretical formulation" (e.g. new ways of conceptualizing non-spatially and culturally, etc.); methodological implications (e.g. multi-directional approach of "world missions," missions at our doorstep, holistic missions, etc.)

REFERENCES

Alex Araujo (2000) "Globalization and World Evangelism" In *Global Missiology for the 21st Century*, Taylor, William D., ed., Grand Rapids, Michigan: Baker Book House, 57-70.

Cohen, Robin (1997) *Global* Diasporas: *An Introduction.* London: UCL Press.

D'Amico, David F. (2001) "Evangelization Across Cultures in the United States: What to Do When the World Come to Us." (D'Amico.org - 2001). http://www.damicony.org/warticles/art010.htm

Mickleburgh, Andrew (April 2004) *Bibliography of the South Asian Diaspora and East Africa: An Annotated Bibliography. http://coombs.anu.edu.au/Biblio/biblio_sasiadiaspora.html* (April 2004)

Braziel, Jana Evans & Mannur, Anita (2003) *Theorizing Diaspora: A Reader.* London: Blackwell Publishing.

Buhlmann, W. (1986) *The Church of the Future: A Model for the Year 2001.* Maryknoll, NY: Orbis Books.

Castles, Stephen and Miller, Mark J. (1998) *The Age of Migration: International Population Movements in the Modern World.* New York: Guilford Press. 1998.

Cohen, Robin (1997) *Global Diasporas: An Introduction.* London: UCL Press edited by Stephen R. Warner and Judith G. Wittner

Creewell, Mike (April 08, 2003) "God Cares for Refugees, So His people Must Minister to Them, Worker Says." SBC International Missions Board.

Durst, Marcel (May 2, 2002) "Mission through Migration: Mission Initiatives of Latin American Migrants in Switzerland." Unpublished MA thesis, Columbia International University, German Branch, Korntal.

Ebaugh, Helen R. and Chafetz, Janet S (2000) *Religion and the New Immigrants: Continuities and Adaptations in Immigrant Congregations.* New York: AltaMira Press.

Escobar, Samuel, and Stott, John (eds.)(2003) *The New Global Mission: The Gospel from Everywhere to Everyone* (Christian Doctrine in Global Perspective) 25-46

Escobar, Samuel (2000) "The Global Scenario at the Turn of the Century," In *Global Missiology for the 21st Century*, Taylor, William D., ed., Grand Rapids, Michigan: Baker Book House, 25-46. *Gatherings in Diaspora: Religious Communities and the New Immigration.*

Georgiou, Myria (December 4, 2001) "Thinking Diaspora: Why Diaspora is a Key Concept for Understanding Multicultural Europe," On-Line / *More Colour in the Media: The Multicultural Skyscraper Newsletter*, Vol. 1 No. 4. Tuesday.

Greenway, Roger. "The Challenge of the Cities." In *Perspectives on the World Christian Movement*," 3rd edition. Ralph Winter and Steven Hawthorne, eds. P. 553-558. Pasadena, CA: William Carey Library.

Guthrie, Stan (Jan. 01, 1998). "Global Report: Children at Risk: The Biggest Litter Mission Field in the World?" Evangelical Mission Quarterly, vol. 34:1, pp. 88-94.

Hanciles, Jehu J. (2003). "Migration and Mission: Some Implications for the Twenty-first-Century Church" *International Bulletin of Missionary Research*, Vol.27, no. 4: 146-153.

Heikes, Laura (January 2003). "Una Perspectiva Diferente: Latin Americans and the Global Mission Movement," *Missiology*. Vol. XXXI, No. 1k: 69-85)

Hirschman, Charles et al. (eds.) (1999). *The Handbook of International Migration: The American Experience.* New York: Russell Sage Foundation.

Jacques, Andre (1991). "Migration." *In Dictionary of the Ecumenical Movements.* N. Lossky et al., eds. Geneva/Grand Rapids, MI: WCC/Eerdmans:679-681.

Jana Evans Braziel and Anita Mannur (2003). *Theorizing* Diaspora: *A Reader.* Blackwell Publishing.

Juan, E. San, Jr. (January 11, 2004). "Critical Reflections on the Filipino Diaspora and the Crisis in the Philippines" http://quezon.buffaloimc.org/news/2004/01/67. php Sunday at 0317 PM

Long, Justin (1996). "Megatrend No. 3: Movement of Third-World Peoples." *Monday Morning Reality Check,* Oct. 11.

Massey, Douglas "Why does Immigration Occur? A Theoretical Synthesis," In *The Handbook of International Migration: The American Experience.* Charles Hirschman et al. (eds.) New York: Russell Sage Foundation. 1999:34-52.

Moreau, A. Scott (2000). "Refugee Mission Work" in *Evangelical Dictionary of World Missions.* Grand Rapids, MI: Baker:816.

National Conference of Catholic Bishops (1998). "One Family Under God." Washington, D.C. Office of Publishing and Promotion Services.

Naseem, S.M. "Diaspora and Development" (http://www.dawn.com/2004/01/19/ ebr2.htm.)

Pessar, Patricia R.(1999) "The Role of Gender, Households, and Social Networks in the Migration Process: A Review and Reappraisal," In *The Handbook of International Migration: The American Experience.* Charles Hirschman et al. (eds.) New York: Russell Sage Foundation. 34-52.

Pohl, Christine D. (2003) "Biblical Issues in Mission and Migration," *Missiology*. Vol. XXXI, No. 1k January:35-43.

Ripley, David L. (1994). "Reaching the World at Our Doorstep," *Evangelical Missiology Quarterly,* Vol. 30, No. 2. Also available at the following link: http://bgc.gospelcom. net/emis/1994/reaching.html

Stromberg, Jean S. (January 2003). "Responding to the Challenge of Migration: Churches within the Fellowship of the World Council of Churches (WCC)," *Missiology: An International Review,* Vol. XXXI, No. 1, 45-50.

Shipp, Glover. (April 01, 1990). "Research: A key to successful urban evangelism" In *Journal of Applied Missiology*.

Taylor, William David, and Zacharias, Ravi (eds.) (January 2000). *Global Missiology for the 21st Century: Reflections from the Iguassu Dialogue*. Grand Rapids, MI: Baker Book House.

Temfwe, Lawrence (Mar 22, 2004). "Aliens in Our Own Country" Jubilee Center, . (http://www.strategicnetwork.org/index.php?loc=kb&id=13960&mode=v&)

Tsutada, Joshua (Dec 19, 2000) "Global Cooperation and Networking." Korean World Missions Association.

"Vietnam reaps diaspora windfall." http://news.bbc.co.uk/2/hi/business/2538455.stm

Wan, Enoch (January 2003). "Mission among the Chinese Diaspora: A Case Study of Migration and Mission." Missiology. Vol. XXXI, No. 1:35-43.

6

IS DIASPORA MISSIONS VALID? DISCIPLE-MAKING AMONG FILIPINO KABABAYANS

Tereso C. Casiño

INTRODUCTION

World civilizations developed and expanded by crisscrossing religious, cultural, socio-economic, and political boundaries. For hundreds of years adherents of the Jewish-Christian tradition travelled far and wide, transferred families and homes, moved businesses back and forth, and settled and resettled in lands other than their own. Migration, whether national, regional, or intercontinental, has been one of Christianity's powerful strategies for missionary work. John Howard Yoder observes that for centuries the good news has been brought to new parts of the world "primarily by migration of financially independent Christians" (Hedlund 1982:79). Paul and the church of the second century established this as a pattern. Despite all these, however, questions remain over the legitimacy of doing missionary work among people who share the *same* ethno-cultural, religious, and socio-political backgrounds.

This chapter explores the following concerns: Are ministries among Filipino *kababayans* (countrymen) legitimate missionary work? If a Filipino pastor goes overseas and conducts ministries among Filipino communities, would he or she be considered a "legitimate" missionary? The plan of this essay is to identify key "reservations" regarding the legitimacy of Filipino diaspora ministries. It will then attempt to establish the legitimacy of missions among

Filipino diaspora on the basis of the nature and task of the Great Commission. This chapter will specifically argue that the missionary task is *inclusive* rather than *exclusive*, *strategic* rather than *primarily ethnic*, and *soteriological* rather than *sociological*.

RESERVATIONS REGARDING THE LEGITIMACY OF DIASPORA MISSIONS

Not all Christians are ready to recognize ministries among Filipino *kababayans* abroad as a legitimate missionary work. The Scripture makes no distinction in principle between missionary activity among the Jews and among the Gentiles (Bavinck 1960:69-70). But there are still reservations with regard to doing missions among people from the same ethno-linguistic backgrounds. To some, Filipino diaspora ministry is not a legitimate missionary work because it is not a church-planting activity among indigenous ethno-linguistic groups. Others insist that missions is primarily cross-cultural, so diaspora missions, being conducted among one's *kababayans*, merits no biblical legitimacy. The rest simply doubt the validity of diaspora missions since it does not fall under the category of the *highest priority*. Each of these arguments merits an explanation.

The Indigenous Argument: Missions is Primarily Planting Churches Among Indigenous People Groups

The denomination's Global Missions Board was just set up and the officers were elected that day. The chairman called for a meeting—the first for GMB—and I was invited to sit in as a representative from the seminary. As a guest, I opted to listen to the discussions. The newly elected missions executives were excited about the prospect of recruiting and sending Filipino missionaries overseas. They discussed about budget, support, and fundraising but left little amount of time to discuss on policies and procedures. The discussion bogged down on budget! So, I raised my hand and said, "I know of a vast missionary need that CAN be fulfilled without requiring the Convention to raise a huge budget." Heads turned and eyebrows were raised. "As you know," I pressed on, "our Convention has over a hundred Filipino pastors living overseas. They are evangelizing Filipinos in Hong Kong, Singapore, Middle East, Europe, Taiwan, Korea, USA, to mention but a few. Why does the GMB not certify them as *missionaries* among diaspora communities? The Convention may prepare a directory of all these overseas pastors, certify them as ministers of the gospel, and then organize and mobilize them for missionary services and support. All we need to do is to commission them at the local church level first, then the Convention level next." "That's not missions," interrupted the newly elected GMB president. "Missions," he confidently declared," is primarily among indigenous groups." "What do you mean *primarily indigenous?*" I inquired politely. "It is the planting of churches among indigenous people in Indonesia, Nepal, Bhutan, or India," he replied. I did not press on to avoid extended discussions and be branded antagonistic.

The Convention's GMB did manage to send a missionary family to a Hindu-dominated country a few months after that inaugural meeting. *Sadly enough, because of pressure from a few local leaders, the missionary family returned to the Philippines while the announcement about their departure was still circulating among local churches in the Convention!* A few months after the incident, the missions executive resigned from his local church position and the GMB and flew to a neighboring Asian country to serve as a "missionary" among Filipinos!

The "indigenous argument" appears attractive since it views missions primarily from a sociological perspective. Certainly making disciples that results in planting indigenous churches is part of the objective of the Great Commission. The Bible, however, is silent about the status of those who work among their kababayans, *and, so dismissing their ministry as less missionary is theologically unnecessary.*

The Cross-cultural Argument: Missions is Primarily Reaching Out To People From Different Nations

Questioning the legitimacy of diaspora ministries never came across my mind until a conversation I had with an American missionary in 1989. Early on I realized that even among "veteran" missionaries on the field, there is a high degree of reluctance to consider diaspora missions among fellow countrymen as biblically valid and thereby theologically legitimate. The denomination was sending a Filipino family to Canada to *do missionary work*. The American missionary bluntly rejected the idea because the family would be working with their Filipino *kababayans.* In her missionary logic, a Filipino pastor ministering to Filipinos in Canada should not be called a missionary nor his ministry activities be considered missionary in nature. "The Great Commission covers all nations," I quipped. "Does it not include Filipinos?" "Yes," she replied, "but missionary work is only legitimate when it is conducted cross-culturally, not inter-culturally!"

Citizenship, of course, appears to be the main issue here. The above logic states that a Filipino can be a missionary only when he or she conducts ministry functions among Canadians, Americans, Europeans, or anyone holding a non-Filipino passport. This sounds interesting except that this socio-political perspective does not seem to tally with reality on the field as the following similar incidents show:

> "Are you a Filipino?" I asked. "Yes, with an Austrian passport!" was her reply. I was glad to hear a curt reply at the International Baptist Church in Vienna. Six months prior to that, my wife and I had a meeting with a woman in Paris. "I'm from Cebu," she announced candidly, "but married to a French. So I'm now holding a French passport." "Oh, great!" I muttered with a sheepish smile. At Frankfurt airport, Cecille and I were standing in a long cue waiting for our turn, when suddenly a woman from behind asked for our passports. We politely showed our travel documents. The woman's countenance changed as she declared in Tagalog, *Filipino din ako, pero German passport ang hawak ko* ("I'm a Filipino, too, but holding a German passport!").[1]

The Highest Priority Argument: Missions Is Primarily Among E-3 Cultures

In the '70s missions scholars and practitioners debated on the so-called "degrees" of missions based on Acts 1:8. The most vocal among them was Ralph Winter, who created quite a stir at the 1974 International Congress on World Evangelization in Lausanne, Switzerland.[2] Winter classifies evangelism into E-1, E-2, E-3.[3] He sees "cultural" rather than "geographical" distance in this classification, thereby putting Jerusalem and Judea under E-1 category, labeling it as "near neighbor evangelism." E-1 evangelism requires disciples to cross the "boundary" that separates their Christian community from that of the "world immediately outside" although they share the same culture and language.[4] E-2 evangelism refers to the *Samaritan sphere* whereby disciples have to cross a "second frontier" after crossing, of course, the frontier that gaps the church and the world. This frontier may come in varied forms. It may include spiritual, philosophical, ideological categories, which both Christians and non-Christians share because of their place of residence. This also involves "crossing a frontier constituted by significant (but not monumental) differences of language and culture."[5] Despite the necessity and importance of E-1 and E-2 spheres, Winter argues that E-3 evangelism is the highest priority. He writes, "The people needing to be reached in this third sphere live, work, talk, and think in languages and cultural patterns utterly different from those native to the evangelist."[6]

The heavy stress, however, on E-3 evangelism does not depreciate the significance of E-1 and E-2 degrees of evangelism. In Winter's missiological framework, E-3 evangelism is the highest priority in modern missions, but E-1 and E-2 spheres set the motion for E-3.[7] "The master pattern of the expansion of the Christian movement is first," Winter argues, "for special E-2 and E-3 efforts to cross cultural barriers into new communities and to establish strong ongoing, vigorously evangelizing denominations, and then for the national church to carry the work forward on the really high-powered E-1 level."[8]

Missiological Priority Or Missiological Strategy?

Winter's notion of E-3 evangelism as the highest priority is worth taking a second look. The Lord Jesus Christ visualizes global missions with Jerusalem as the temporal *beginning* point. Acts 1:8 unfolds the universal scope of this concern for world missions. The message of repentance for the forgiveness of sins available only in Jesus Christ should be made known to all nations, to all people groups around the world.[9] This universal missions, however, as Luke 24:47 states, should begin in Jerusalem. Contrary to Winter's "highest priority" rendering of the missionary text, Jesus' priority here is "the nations" (collective), a priority that could not be categorized by way of degree of importance. The reference to geographical locations like Jerusalem, Judea, Samaria, and the uttermost part of the world alludes to a device that highlights the significance of universal missions from a *soteriological perspective*. Winter seems to be correct in pointing out that "cultural distance" is what bringers of the good news need to overcome, although the notion of "geographical distance" also needs to be highlighted. However, it is the "theological distance" (i.e., people's need of salvation in Jesus Christ alone, people who are mentioned by their geopolitical and cultural distinctions) that the soteriological dimension of mission becomes distinct.

Viewed soteriologically, Acts 1:8, first and foremost, alludes to an effective *missiological strategy* rather than a *missiological priority*. The text appears to offer a basic concentric missional strategic layout rather than highlighting a world missions priority in terms of degrees. Simply put, Acts 1:8 rules out *ethnic preference* over *soteriological strategy*. The *King James Version* renders the text more forcefully: "But ye shall receive power, after that the Holy Ghost is come upon you: and ye shall be witnesses unto me **both** in Jerusalem, and in all Judea, and in Samaria, and unto the uttermost part of the earth." There is a strong exegetical support in the use of the *en te*, i.e., "both" which the King James Version rightly maintains. *En* is a preposition in a dative case, while *te* is a conjunction and in coordinating form. Modern versions like the *New International Version* and the *New Revised Standard Version* omit *en te* in Acts 1:8. *En te* stresses *equal concern* rather than *highest priority* for universal missions, irrespective of their religious and political orientation, culture, and locations, with Jerusalem as the beginning geographical point. Again the whole tenor of Acts 1:8 is not *missions priority* but *equal concern for* and *equal responsibility to* "the nations."[10] This means that the Great Commission is decidedly *strategic* rather than primarily *ethnic*. The need for Christ's saving grace remains the sole determinant in discipling persons, whoever they may be, wherever they are, and whatever citizenship they hold.

THE BIBLICAL BASIS OF DIASPORA MISSIONS

Reservations regarding Filipino diaspora missions result from the over-emphasis on the ethnic or cultural-anthropological dimension of the missionary task. Reluctance in acknowledging diaspora ministry as a legitimate missionary work lies in the notion that it is *within* one's cultural context. Any attempt to make disciples *outside* one's cultural framework or context is considered legitimate! Of course, most of the reservations come from *contemporary* rather than *biblical* understanding of missions.[11] This calls for a serious review of the nature, intent, and task of the Great Commission. It is tempting to use logic in responding to these arguments. However, because diaspora ministries belong rightly to the Great Commission, it is important to let biblical data speak. In the following pages, I will argue that diaspora missions is valid on the basis of the nature and task of Jesus' Central Commission. I will then conclude by illustrating this with the missionary experiences of Paul and the continuing diaspora nature of the universal church.

The Soteriological Intent Of The Great Commission

Key missionary texts stress that God's love is universal (inclusive) and shows no preference for ethnic origin or nationality.[12] The love of God is global in scope and effect (extensive) and can transform individual lives (intensive) regardless of people's religious, cultural, political, economic, social, and historical backgrounds. The Great Commission bears the following components: the **Person** (Jesus Christ), the **Power** (Holy Spirit), the **purpose** (make disciples), the **people** (all the nations), the **process** or **procedure** (going, baptizing, teaching) (Casiño 2001:167). On this basis, the core intent of the Great Commission is *decidedly soteriological,* nothing less nothing more.[13] *Mission,* then, refers to the total plan, process, and work of God for the salvation of people through all ages. All implementation and forms of this plan done by the covenant people of God and through the universal church are called *missions.*[14]

The Task Of The Great Commission: Make Disciples Of All The Nations

The Great Commission promises an expansive vision of universal missions, covering the *panta ta ethne* (all the nations).[15] The main verb in Matthew 28:19-20 is *matheteusate* (literally, "make disciples").[16] Three participial clauses modify this central verb, namely, going ("when you go"), baptizing, and teaching.[17] *Matheteusate* indicates "summary action, something to be undertaken at once," thus, an action that is "either transient or instantaneous" and needs no "dilly-dallying" (Banks 1991:75). Unfortunately many still misread this text by placing a heavy emphasis on "going" rather than "disciple making." As de Ridder laments, "What is tragic about this wrong emphasis so frequently attributed to the command of Christ is that the entire demand is isolated from the whole witness of the Bible, and the '*going* into all the world' becomes the fulfillment of what Christ demands. Obviously, not everyone can go into all the world, but each can start from where he is" (De Ridder 1979:184).

The Identity of All The Nations

> "Therefore go and make disciples of all nations, baptizing them in the name of The Father and of the Son and of the Holy Spirit, and teaching them to obey everything I have commanded you. And surely I am with you always, to the very end of the age." (Matthew 28:19-20 NIV).

The identity of *panta ta ethne* puzzles biblical scholars, theologians, missionaries and missions strategists as to how it applies to the missionary task.[18] History is replete with records of how a simple error in deciphering the identity of *panta ta ethne* could result in the hampering of missionary efforts.[19] Protestant mission is a good case in point. Shortly after the geographical expansion of Reformation, many Protestants showed lack of enthusiasm for missions because of a defective theological view regarding the timing of the fulfillment of the church missionary task in relation to *panta ta ethne*.[20] Martin Luther, in particular, interpreted the Great Commission as that given to the first century apostles and fulfilled by them, so the church did not have to pursue it.[21] Evidently this obscured the true missionary nature of the church and put much of the Protestant mission, especially within the Lutheran circles, on the sideline in the ensuing years.[22] In fact the first attempt by a Lutheran to do missionary work was only about 1664, when Baron Justinian von Weltz "issued a clarion call to the church to assume missionary responsibilities" (Kane 1982:76).

Traditional Reading Of Panta Ta Ethne

For years mission scholars have debated on whether "the nations" could be identified as the Jews only, the Gentiles only, or both Jews and Gentiles as object of the Great Commission.[23] Those who read *ta ethne* as the *Jews or Israel only* find support in Jesus' specific instruction in Matthew 10.[24] Accordingly "nations" here should be identified as Israel because of the interplay of *goyim-ta ethne* words in Jesus' instruction about mission.[25] Another "traditional reading" identifies the *Gentiles only* as "the nations."[26] Here, Gentiles become the only object of the missionary activity of God because they are not part of the covenant which God made with Israel.[27] Thus, as "excluded people," they are to be reached alone with the message of God's love and forgiveness.

When Jesus' universal message and vision for mission is taken into consideration, *panta ta ethne* unfolds an inclusive identity.[28] Here "the nations" include both *Jews and Gentiles* as the object of the missionary activity of the church. In such case, the Jews are now among many nations.[29] An inclusive understanding of "the nations" emphasizes the centrality of Jesus Christ and the significance of his substitutionary death at Calvary and his resurrection on the third day.[30] This means that to be Jewish does not mean "privileged position" before God as Jews, along with their Gentile counterparts, need Jesus Christ for salvation. As R. C. H. Lenski pointedly writes, "What diversity exists among the nations of the earth: race, color, location, climate, traits, achievements: yet they are all included in this command, for all are sinners, all have souls, all need and are capable of salvation through the grace of God."[31]

Contemporary Reading of Panta Ta Ethne

The recent surge of evangelical missions all over the world introduces new insights into the phrase, "the nations." The emergence of the Church Growth Movement, as it is known today, under the leadership of Donald McGavran and Peter Wagner, brings so much attention to a contemporary "sociological reading" of *panta ta ethne*. Out of this basic sociological reading comes an expanded reading of "people groups" that bears implications for the legitimacy of missions among Filipino diaspora communities.

• **People Groups**

Some missiologists and scholars identify "the nations" as "people groups" or "all peoples."[32] This stress on ethnic category or people groups follows a sociological reading informed by McGavran's experience in the social settings of India and Vincent J. Donovan's work among the Masai ethno-linguistic group in Kenya. Of course, the main weakness of this category lies in its failure to fully depict the pluralistic categories of the social strata of the modern society as shown in the missiological reading of *panta ta ethne*. In this categorization, *panta ta ethne* refers to "families of mankind," i.e., tongues, tribes, castes, lineages of men, or "peoples of earth" (McGavran 1980:22, 56). Roger E. Hedlund concurs, "The concept is embedded in our Lord's Commission to the Church as rendered by Matthew. The mission of evangelization has proceeded on this basis from the First Century onward."[33]

• **Dispersed Nations**

Another sociological reading of *panta ta ethne* as "people groups" alludes to the "dispersed nations," i.e., the migrants or peoples from various lands scattered all over the world. People under this category are transient, moving constantly from one place to another. These diaspora groups may include students, people in business, tourists, military personnel, professional and non-professional workers, diplomats, envoys, among others.[34] Their relocation relates to personal circumstances, aspirations, or choice of career and employment. Diaspora people under this category choose not to give up their original citizenship. This category speaks of millions of family members waiting in their respective countries for a loved one—a husband, a wife —a mother, a sister or a brother to come home. Although their social and psychological displacement is not lifelong, it is enough for them to become vulnerable to psychological, mental, and at times, spiritual disorientation. Some of them may have a hard time reintegrating themselves to the society they once left.[35] The rest of them, of course, have to struggle with either "culture shock," "culture uprooting," or "culture reentry shock."[36] The impact upon host nations is great, and at times, disturbing. Local churches in host nations need to have a strong biblical theology of missions so that they could formulate mission policies and design mission activities relevant to the needs of the migrants or "dispersed nations."

• **Gathered Nations**

"Gathered nations" refer to people groups that permanently reside in countries other than their own (i.e., the immigrants). These people become legal immigrants and are assimilated into the culture of the country they choose to give political allegiance to. This category may include the political refugees and exiles, scientists and professionals who opt to settle down and practice their profession in another country; husbands or wives of inter-cultural marriages, children of first-degree immigrants, among others. But unlike the transient migrants, the immigrants choose to be permanently uprooted socially, politically, and at times, religiously.[37]

• **Closed Nations**

"Closed nations" refer to people groups, which, by virtue of their locations and religious system, become openly hostile to the good news of Jesus Christ. This includes Islamic countries and a few Hindu or Buddhist-oriented societies where Christianity faces a lot of difficulties.[38] People in the category of "hostile nations" may also include those who are residing in communist countries where the missionary and interpretive tasks of the church are hampered by political or religious ideologies (Kane 1986:179-181).

In retrospect, given the expansive and inclusive vision of Jesus regarding contextual mission and evangelization, the phrase *panta ta ethne* calls for an integrated reading—sociologically, theologically, missiologically.[39] A narrow reading of the phrase violates the original missionary intent that the Lord of the Great Commission has for all peoples in the world, regardless of their race and ideologies, and consequently, hinders the contextual character of divine truth.[40]

• **Strategic Missions: A Sketch of Paul's Diaspora Missions**

Paul is a diaspora missionary *par excellence*. His *missionary theology* develops out of a specific calling (missionary identity: "apostolic consciousness"), vocation (missionary task), and motivation (missionary lifestyle). His mission is "mission in certain strategic centers" (*Zentrumsmission*).[41] Paul thinks and *missionizes* in a highly strategic fashion, which accounts for his regional rather than *ethnic* approach to disciple making. He chooses key strategic places "that have a representative character."[42] Paul's missionary work covers interfaith (intercultural), intrafaith (intracultural), and multi-faith (multicultural) ministries. The stress on *faith* rather than culture brings the missionary task back to its soteriological base, which dominates the missionary texts.

Interfaith Missions: Missions Among Same Ethno-Linguistic Cultures

Much of Paul's *interfaith missions* take place during his "first missionary journey" (Acts 13:1-15:35). Here Paul reaches out primarily to his fellow Jews, whose language he fluently speaks and religious customs he himself practices. In this *interfaith missions*, Paul crosses no language and cultural barriers. He understands the significance of proclaiming the good news to those who share his Jewish faith. His missions among the Jewish diaspora communities are *intentional* rather than *incidental*. To him, the good news of salvation should be preached to the Jews who share his traditional faith.[43] In reaching out to the scattered Jews across the Roman Empire, Paul sets a model, for succeeding diaspora missionaries. As a diaspora preacher, Paul knows the most strategic place for gospel proclamation, i.e., the synagogue—the Jewish "religious comfort zone."[44]

Intrafaith Missions: Missions Among Shared But Mixed Cultures

Paul's diaspora missionary work covers the mixed blood, e.g., the half Jews and half Greeks, or pure Jews holding both Jewish and Roman citizenships. As a Jew holding two citizenships, Paul understands his strategic missionary status. Not much is written on this *intrafaith missions*, probably because most of the activities here take place during Paul's "second missionary journey" (Acts 15:36-18:22), which lasted three years. It is no coincidence, then, that Paul "recruits" Timothy—a half-Jew and a half-Greek—to join his small band of itinerant preachers to conduct diaspora ministries in strategic places of the Roman Empire.[45] Timothy's presence reinforces Paul's commitment to reach out to people whose culture he partly shares and whose language he himself speaks.

Multifaith Missions: Missions Among Diverse Cultures

At the rejection of his message, Paul turns to the Gentiles, a shift in missions strategy but not necessarily in priority. This multi-faith diaspora missions covers most of the second and third diaspora missionary journeys (Acts 15:36-21:17). Paul covers the Eastern Mediterranean region and crosses totally different worldviews, philosophies, languages, and cultural manners and customs. In his trailblazing diaspora missionary work, Paul proclaims the good news in places where Christ's love is not known, thus, enduring hostilities and persecutions from both Jews and Gentiles.[46]

• The Diaspora Nature of the Universal Church

Diaspora ministries find their greatest support in the diaspora nature of the universal church. The New Testament church developed, expanded, and spread out in diaspora conditions and environments (Matt. 26:31, 32; Acts 8:1, 4; 9:31). The ensuing centuries through which the ministries of the church unfolded in all dimensions involved intercultural, intracultural, and multicultural missions. In all these undertakings, the objective was the same, that is, to make disciples of all nations. Richard de Ridder concludes:

The Christian Church still lives in diaspora. But it is a diaspora with a purpose....

The whole diaspora of the church can only be understood in terms of its apostolic mission—a going forth from its central authority under commission, and to return when at the end of the age the mission of the Great Apostle is completed. The Church's diaspora is being sent out by Christ. The gathered ones go out to gather yet others. The significance and purpose of the Christian diaspora is to be found in its mission dimension.[47]

CONCLUSION

Diaspora missions among Filipino *kababayans* has a strong case. As long as Filipino missionaries are faithful in fulfilling the central task of making disciples of Filipinos and other nationalities across the world, their efforts contribute to the fulfillment of the Great Commission. Contrary to a contemporary notion that missions is primarily cross-cultural or simply indigenous, the missionary texts makes no distinction in disciple-making among Jews and non-Jews. The Great Commission is decidedly *soteriological* in that "all the nations" need to have personal access to the good news of salvation in Christ.

ENDNOTES

1   These stories echo around the world where Filipinos work, immigrate, and change citizenship after fulfilling legal requirements. Questions remain on whether or not a diaspora Filipino can be considered a legitimate missionary once he or she changes citizenship in another country. If, for instance, a Filipino minister who works among the Filipino communities in America becomes an American citizen, would he or she be called an "American missionary" to the Filipinos? Debates on this issue continue even among missiologists today, and there are no easy answers as far as citizenship is concerned.

2   Insights in this section are drawn primarily from Tereso C. Casiño, "The Text in Context: An Evangelical Approach to the Foundations of Contextualization in the Asian Setting" (Ph.D. diss., ACTS/Asia United Theological University, Seoul, 1996), 79-83, unless otherwise stated.

3   For a fuller treatment, see Ralph D. Winter, "The Highest Priority: Cross-Cultural Evangelism," in Let the Earth Hear His Voice, ed. J. D. Douglas (Minneapolis, MN: World Wide Publications, 1974), 213-241.

4   Winter explains, "Whoever we are, wherever we live in the world, we all have some near neighbors to whom we can witness without learning any foreign language or taking into account any special cultural differences" (Ibid., 218).

5   Ibid., 218.

6   Ibid.

7   Cf. William Dyrness, Let the Earth Rejoice (Pasadena, CA: Fuller Seminary Press, 1983), 148.

8   Winter, "The Highest Priority," 220. "We are thus forced to believe," claims Winter, "that until every tribe and tongue has a strong, powerfully evangelizing church in it, and thus an E-1 witness within it, E-2 and E-3 efforts coming from outside are still essential and highly urgent" (Ibid.).

9   David Filbeck argues that "the Great Commission is based on the ability of people in other cultures and speaking different languages to also 'do theology'" (Yes, God of the Gentiles, Too [Wheaton, IL: Billy Graham Center, Wheaton College, 1994], 195).

10   Ferdinand Hahn, in his insightful analysis of the Great Commission in Matthew, finds a striking balance between the importance of missions to the Jews and Gentiles. Unlike Winter, Han sees mission to Israel as the priority. "This mission," however, notes Hahn, "is only carried out rightly if at the same time the universal commission is observed by working among all nations" (Mission in the New Testament, trans. Frank Clarke [London: SCM Press, Ltd., 1965], 110-11).

[11] Fur further discussion on this debate, see Andreas J. Kostenberger, "The Place of Mission in the New Testament Theology: An Attempt to Determine the Significance of Mission within the Scope of the New Testament's Message as a Whole," available from http://www.ajkostenberger.com/pdf/NT%20Theology%20and%20Mission.PDF;Internet; accessed August 13, 2003.

[12] John 20:21; Mark 16:15-16; Matthew 28:19-20; Luke 24:46-47; Acts 1:8.

[13] J. Sam Simmons puts it succinctly, "Salvation is not just at the heart of mission; salvation is the heart of mission" ("The Missionary Motivation of God's Salvation," in Missiology: An Introduction to the Foundations, History, Strategies of World Missions, ed. John Mark Terry, Ebbie Smith, and Justice Anderson [Nashville, TN: Broadman and Holman Publishers, 1998], 129).

[14] Tereso C. Casiño, "God Has No Favorites! Critical Components of Apostle Peter's Missiological Paradigm," Torch Trinity Journal 6, no. 1 (November 2003): 165. "Mission," notes George W. Peters, refers to the "total biblical assignment of the church of Jesus Christ... Missions is the "sending forth of authorized persons beyond the borders of the New Testament church and her immediate gospel influence to proclaim the gospel of Jesus Christ in gospel-destitute areas, to win converts from other faiths or non-faiths to Jesus Christ, and to establish functioning, multiplying local congregations who will bear the fruit of Christianity in that community and to that country" (A Biblical Theology of Missions [Chicago, IL: Moody Press, 1972],11].

[15] The designation, "Central Commission," appears more accurate in rendering the whole tenor of the missionary text compared to the traditional use of the phrase, "Great Commission." See Richard R. de Ridder, Discipling the Nations (Grand Rapids, MI: Baker Book House, 1979), 184.

[16] This form has a limited entry in the New Testament as noted in the following passages: Matthew 13:52; 27:57; 28:19; Acts 14:21.

[17] de Ridder, 184. The verb matheteusate is in an imperative, aorist, active, second person, plural form which provides the force of other verbs mentioned in verses 19 and 20. In verse 19, the verb poreuthentes (literally: "when you go") is a participle (but in an imperative sense) in aorist, passive deponent, nominative, masculine, second person, plural form. The verb baptizontes (literally: "baptizing") is a participle (in imperative sense) in a present, active, nominative, masculine, second person, and plural form. In verse 20, the verb didaskontes is a participle (imperative sense) and is a present, active, nominative, masculine, second person, plural form, while the verb terein is in an infinitive, present, active form.

[18] The adjective panta is accusative, neuter, plural, which, if attached to the noun ethne (accusative neuter plural), would stress "universal inclusivity," covering the peoples of diverse nationalities or cultures.

[19] See Kenneth Scott Latourette, A History of Christianity (New York: Harper

and Row, Publishers, 1953), 703-100; J. Herbert Kane, 73-75; Johannes Verkuyl, Contemporary Missiology: An Introduction, trans. Dale Cooper (Grand Rapids, MI: William B. Eerdmans Publishing Company, 1978), 18-25; Ho-Jin Jun, "Reformation and Mission: A Brief Survey of the Missiological Understanding of the Reformers," ACTS Theological Journal 5 (June 1994): 160-178.

[20] Gustav Warneck promotes this view, but not without a challenge from a few contemporary missions scholars. For further discussion, see David Bosch, Transforming Mission (Maryknoll, NY: Orbis Books, 1991), 244-248.

[21] Martin Luther, Luther's Works, vol. 12, ed. J. N. Lenker (Minneapolis, MN: Lutherans in All Lands Co., 1907), 25-26, 183-84, 214-16.

[22] As early as 1555, however, an early attempt was made to do what John C. Thiessen calls as "missionary colonization," namely, the Calvin-Coligny Expedition to Brazil. Thiessen explains, "It was to be a place of refuge for persecuted Protestants and at the same time serve as a center from which to reach the Indians" (A Survey of World Missions [Chicago, IL: Inter-Varsity Press, 1955], 18).

[23] For varying positions see, Joachim Jeremias, Jesus' Promise to the Nations (Naperville, Il: Alec R. Allenson, 1958), 19, 39; James O. Buswell III, A Systematic Theology of the Christian Religion, vol. 2 (Grand Rapids, MI: Zondervan Publishing House, 1962), 419-420; Johannes Blauw, The Missionary Nature of the Church (New York: McGraw-Hill, 1962), 85; John Murray, The Epistle to the Romans, vol. 1, reprint ed. (Grand Rapids, MI: William B. Eerdmans Publishing Company, 1971); Donald Senior and Carroll Stuhlmueller, The Biblical Foundations of Mission (Maryknoll, NY: Orbis Books, 1983), 252.

[24] For a fuller discussion on the relationship between Matthew chapters 10 and 28, see Hahn, 127-128; Roger Hedlund, Mission to Man in the Bible (Madras, India: Evangelical Literature Service, 1985), 196-206.

[25] Joachim Gnilka, "Der Missionsauftrag des Herrn nach Matthaus 28 und Apostelgeschichte I," Bibel und Leben (1968): 1-9, cited by Verkuyl, Contemporary Missiology, 106.

[26] See D. Hare and D. Harrington, "Make Disciples of All the Gentiles (Matt. 28:19)," Catholic Biblical Quarterly 37 (1975): 359-369. Cf. Delos Miles, Introduction to Evangelism (Nashville, TN: Broadman Press, 1983), 128.

[27] L. A. Hoedaker, however, thinks otherwise: "The appearance of the church does not stamp the way of Israel as an obsolete or dead-end road" ("The People of God and the Ends of the Earth," in Missiology: An Ecumenical Introduction, ed. F. J. Verstraelen [Grand Rapids, MI: William B. Eerdmans Publishing Company, 1995], 168).

[28] de Ridder observes that *panta ta ethne* "when used in the sense of the Gentiles, is often used with no sense of plurality of the nations; that is, it is used non-sociologically. It designates, then, all the individuals who do not belong to the chosen people. The

significance of this designation is that the community of the Gentiles (together with the Jews) has taken over the place of Israel as the locus of the redemptive work of God" (188).

[29] See John P. Meir, "Nations or Gentiles in Matthew 28:19?" Catholic Biblical Quarterly 39, no. 1 (January 1977): 95-102. Georg F. Vicedom defines *ethne* as "men and nations outside of God's congregation or outside of the dominant culture" (The Mission of God, trans. Gilbert A. Thiele and Dennis Hilgendorf [Saint Louis, MO: Concordia Publishing House, 1965], 102). Karl Barth sees this from an eschatological perspective, that is, a "new eschatological community," gathered among the Jews and Gentiles. He dismisses the idea of *ta ethne* as "made disciples," charging that such "interpretation once infested missionary thinking and was connected with the painful fantasies of the German Christians." Barth concludes that this interpretation is "worthless" ("An Exegetical Study of Matthew 28:16-20," in The Theology of the Christian Mission, ed. G. H. Anderson [New York: Abingdon Press, 1961], 64). For an insightful summary and assessment of Barth's understanding of mission, see Waldron Scott, Karl Barth's Theology of Mission (Downers Grove, Illinois: InterVarsity Press, 1978). See also Filbeck, 193-196.

[30] Senior and Stuhlmueller argue that Jesus stresses on an inclusive view of God's people and relativizes the "identity" of the "elect people" (152-158). They note, "Although the term *ethnos* ("nation") is used almost exclusively of Gentiles in the Gospel and in biblical literature in general, it is unlikely that Matthew excludes the Jews altogether. Israel is an entity no longer the place of mission: now the boundaries have fallen back and `all nations' have access to the gospel of the kingdom. In Matthew's theology no single group has any privileged status as God's people" (The Biblical Foundations for Missions, 252).

[31] R. C. H. Lenski, The Interpretation of St. Matthew's Gospel, vol. 3 (Minneapolis, MN: Augsburg Publishing House, 1964), 173. Senior and Stuhlmueller concur, "Now both Jew and Gentile come as ethnois before the gospel to be judged on the basis of their response to God's gracious offer of life" (252).

[32] Vincent J. Donovan, a Catholic missiologist, notes that "*ethne* would refer more to ethnic, cultural groups, the natural building blocks of the human race" (Christianity Rediscovered [Maryknoll, NY: Orbis Books, 1978], 29-30). Not everyone, of course, is happy about this reading of *panta ta ethne*. Vinay Samuel and Chris Sugden, for instance, dismiss the idea of "people group" claiming it as an invention of "multinational agencies" that seek to bypass the national church" ("Mission Agencies as Multinationals," International Bulletin of Missionary Research 7, no. 6 [October 1983]: 152).

[33] Hedlund, Mission to Man, 202. "All nations," claims Dyrness, "may not mean every individual, but people from among all nations" (Let the Earth Rejoice, 149).

[34] In Korea alone, there is an estimated 500,000 foreigners who temporarily reside in the country for various reasons. The factory workers, numbering more than

200,000, comprise almost half of these transients. These transients also need the good news of salvation in Christ. They, too, are identified in the *panta ta ethne* of the Great Commission.

[35] Some of the major problems that transient residents face when they return to their own culture are as follows: (1) conflict—they cannot simply reintegrate and have a hard time picking up where they left off; (2) disconfirmation—people's expectations of them sometimes fail as the expatriates show different habits and cultural behavior; (3) renegotiation—expatriates try to modify acquired behavior. For further discussion, see Art Freedman, "A Strategy for Managing 'Cultural' Transitions: Re-Entry from Training," in Cross-Cultural Re-Entry: A Book of Readings, ed. Clyde N. Austin (Abilene, TX: Abilene Christian University, 1986), 19-27. See also in the same volume, Nancy Koehler, "Re-Entry Shock," 89-94; Robert R. Faulkner and Douglas B. McGraw, "Uneasy Homecoming: Strategies in the Re-entry Transition of Vietnam Veterans," 103-118.

[36] Overseas foreigners who return to their countries face many challenges because they have to leave an expatriate social and cultural lifestyle, deal with new educational environments, handle cash flow or disposable income, employment shock, and manage problems of housing and property acquisition at home country.

[37] The plight of immigrants is sometimes very disturbing. Sidney L. Werkman observes, "A major geographic change necessitates an adaptation to new culture and language, new friends, new neighborhoods and schools, as well as novel social and recreational activities" ("Coming Home," in Cross-Cultural Re-Entry: A Book of Readings, ed. Clyde N. Austin [Abilene, TX: Abilene Christian University, 1986], 9). Across the Asian region, next to the Chinese in population are Indians who number more than 20 million (1995 estimate) outside their country and could be found in almost all countries in various parts of the world. The Indian migration patterns include (1) "indentured" labor or "coolie" labor; (2) "passage" or "free passenger," (3) brain drain to industrialized countries, and (4) contract labor emigration to the Gulf region (S. Vasantharaj Albert, A Portrait of India-III [Madras, India: Church Growth Association of India, 1995], 41).

[38] For statistics intended primarily for mission strategy of these "closed nations," see Patrick Johnstone, Operation World (Grand Rapids, MI: Zondervan Publishing House, 1993), 15-31.

[39] Pierce Beaver admits that "geographical ends of the earth have disappeared in a time of jet travel and a worldwide Church, but there are social, cultural, ideological, and spiritual 'far-ends' of human society in profusion" ("The Apostolate of the Church," in The Theology of the Christian Mission, ed. Gerald H. Anderson [New York: Abingdon Press, 1961), 264).

[40] Seok-Hwan Kim, a Korean missiologist and missionary to the Philippines, insightfully notes, "There is no freedom for any Christian to exclude some nations when Jesus said, 'all nations.' Disciples do not go only to those who welcome them

and praise them. The nations who do not know Jesus may not welcome his disciples, but Jesus' disciples need to go to them also" (Disciple's Bible Study- Stage 3 [Seoul: Disciples Publication, 1994], 11).

[41] Bosch, Transforming Mission, 130. These strategic centers include Philippi for Macedonia, Thessalonica for Macedonia and Achaia, Corinth for Achaia, Ephesus for Asia, and Rome for the whole empire.

[42] Ibid. Bosch observes, "In each of these [cities] he lays the foundations for a Christian community, clearly in the hope that, from these strategic centers, the gospel will be carried into the surrounding countryside and towns" (Ibid.).

[43] After their commissioning in the church at Antioch (Acts 13:1-5), Paul and Silas went down to Seleucia and Cyprus. Upon arriving in Salamis, the two proclaimed God's Word in synagogues. Reaching out to the diaspora Jews appears urgent in Paul's first diaspora missionary journey.

[44] Soon-Tae Kwon highlights this strategic approach to diaspora missions by labeling Paul's first missionary journey with the subtitle, "From Jews to Gentiles through the Synagogue" ("An Analysis of Contemporary Models of Missions Among the Selected Baptist Churches in Seoul, Korea in the Light of Paul's Models of Missions," Th.D. diss., Asia Baptist Graduate Theological Seminary, Philippines, 2000), 22-28.

[45] In observing Jewish custom, Paul circumcises Timothy because of the Jews living in the area (Acts 16: 3).

[46] The debate on whether there is a single or unitary church or two "competing missions," that of Peter and James in Jerusalem and Paul in Antioch, continues. While Paul's historical contribution to first century Christian missions could not be ignored, it will be "historically misleading" to highlight his singular prominence at the expense of Peter and others. After all, it was Peter, not Paul, who pioneered cross-cultural missions. For further discussion, see Casiño, "God Has No Favorites," 163-183; Michael Goulder, St. Paul versus St. Peter: A Tale of Two Missions (Louisville, KY: Westminster John Knox Press, 1995).

[47] de Ridder, 217. Hoedemaker stresses that "the church not only has its start geographically and historically in Israel but is also rooted materially in the question and promise of the covenant" (168).

REFERENCES

Albert, S. Vasantharaj (1995). *A Portrait of India-III*. Madras, India: Church Growth Association of India.

Austin, Clyde N. ed. (1986). *Cross-Cultural Re-entry: A Book of Readings*. Abilene, TX: Abilene Christian University.

Banks, William (1991). *In Search of the Great Commission: What Did Jesus Really Say?* Chicago, IL; Moody Press.

Barth, Karl (1961). "An Exegetical Study of Matthew 28:16-20." In *The Theology of the Christian Mission*, ed. G. H. Anderson. 55-71. New York: Abingdon Press.

Bavinck, J. H. (1960). *An Introduction to the Science of Missions*. Translated by David Hugh Freeman. Grand Rapids, MI: Baker Book House.

Beaver, Pierce (1961). "The Apostolate of the Church." In *The Theology of the Christian Mission*, ed. Gerald H. Anderson, 258-268. New York: Abingdon Press.

Blauw, Johannes (1962). *The Missionary Nature of the Church*. New York: McGraw-Hill.

Bosch, David (1991). *Transforming Mission*. Maryknoll, NY: Orbis Books.

Buswell III, James O. (1962). *A Systematic Theology of the Christian Religion*. Vol. 2. Grand Rapids, MI: Zondervan Publishing House.

Casiño, Tereso C. (November 2003). "God Has No Favorites! Critical Components of Apostle Peter's Missiological Paradigm." *Torch Trinity Journal* 6, no. 1: 163-183.

_____. (November 2001). "A Worldview Approach to Designing Missions Strategies Among Asian Cultures." *Torch Trinity Journal* 4, no. 1: 167.

_____. (1996). "The Text in Context: An Evangelical Approach to the Foundations of Contextualization in the Asian Setting." Ph.D. diss., ACTS/Asia United Theological University, Seoul.

De Ridder, Richard R. (1979). *Discipling the Nations*. Grand Rapids, MI: Baker Book House.

Donovan, Vincent J. (1978). *Christianity Rediscovered*. Maryknoll, NY: Orbis Books.

Dyrness, William. *Let the Earth Rejoice*. Pasadena, CA: Fuller Seminary Press, 1983.

Filbeck, David. (1994). *Yes, God of the Gentiles, Too.* Wheaton, IL: Billy Graham Center, Wheaton College.

Freedman, Art. (1986) "A Strategy for Managing 'Cultural' Transitions: Re-Entry from Training." In *Cross-Cultural Re-Entry: A Book of Readings*, ed. Clyde N. Austin. 19-27. Abilene, TX: Abilene Christian University.

Gnilka, Joachim. (1968). *"Der Missionsauftrag des Herrn nach Matthaus 28 und Apostelgeschicte I."* Bibel und Leben: I-9.

Goulder, Michael. (1995). *St. Paul versus St. Peter: A Tale of Two Missions.* Louisville, KY: Westminster John Knox Press.

Hahn, Ferdinand. (1965). *Mission in the New Testament.* Translated by Frank Clarke. London: SCM Press, Ltd.

Hare, D. and D. Harrington. (1975). "Make Disciples of All the Gentiles (Matt. 28:19)." *Catholic Biblical Quarterly* 37: 359-369.

Hedlund, Roger E. (1982). *Building the Church.* Madras, India: Evangelical Literature Society.

_____. (1985). *Mission to Man in the Bible.* Madras, India: Evangelical Literature Service.

Hoedaker, L. A. (1995). "The People of God and the Ends of the Earth." In *Missiology: An Ecumenical Introduction,* ed. F. J. Verstraelen, 157-171. Grand Rapids, MI: William B. Eerdmans Publishing Company.

Jeremias, Joachim. (1958). *Jesus' Promise to the Nations.* Naperville, Il: Alec R. Allenson.

Johnstone, Patrick. (2001). *Operation World.* Grand Rapids, MI: Zondervan Publishing House.

Jun, Ho-Jin. (June 1994). "Reformation and Mission: A Brief Survey of the Missiological Understanding of the Reformers." *ACTS Theological Journal* 5: 160-178.

Kane, Herbert. (1982). *A Concise History of the Christian World Mission: A Panoramic View of Missions from Pentecost to the Present.* Grand Rapids, MI: Baker Book House.

_____. (1986). *Understanding Christian Missions.* Grand Rapids, MI: Baker Book House.

Kim, Seok-Hwan. (1994). *Disciple's Bible Study-Stage 3.* Seoul: Disciples Publication.

Kostenberger, Andreas J. (August 13, 2003). "The Place of Mission in the New Testament Theology: An Attempt to Determine the Significance of Mission within the Scope of the New Testament's Message as a Whole," available from http://www.ajkostenberger.com/pdf/NT%20Theology%20and%20Mission.PDF;Internet.

Kwon, Soon-Tae. (2000). "An Analysis of Contemporary Models of Missions Among the Selected Baptist Churches in Seoul, Korea in the Light of Paul's Models of Missions." Th.D. diss., Asia Baptist Graduate Theological Seminary, Philippines.

Latourette, Kenneth Scott. (1953). *A History of Christianity.* New York: Harper and Row, Publishers.

Lenski, R. C. H. (1964). *The Interpretation of St. Matthew's Gospel.* Vol. 3. Minneapolis, MN: Augsburg Publishing House.

Luther, Martin (1907). *Luther's Works.* Vol. 12. Edited by J. N. Lenker. Minneapolis, MN: Lutherans in All Lands Co.

McGavran, Donald A. (1980). *Understanding Church Growth.* Revised Edition. Grand Rapids, MI: William B. Eerdmans Publishing Company.

Meir, John P. (January 1977). "Nations or Gentiles in Matthew 28:19?" *Catholic Biblical Quarterly* 39, no. 1: 95-102.

Miles, Delos (1983). *Introduction to Evangelism.* Nashville, TN: Broadman Press.

Murray, John (1971). *The Epistle to the Romans.* Vol. 1. Reprint Edition. Grand Rapids, MI: William B. Eerdmans Publishing Company.

Peters, George W. (1972). *A Biblical Theology of Missions.* Chicago, IL: Moody Press.

Samuel, Vinay and Chris Sugden (October 1983). "Mission Agencies as Multinationals." *International Bulletin of Missionary Research* 7, no. 6: 152.

Scott, Waldron (1978). *Karl Barth's Theology of Mission.* Downers Grove, IL: InterVarsity Press.

Senior, Donald and Carroll Stuhlmueller (1983). *The Biblical Foundations of Mission.* Maryknoll, NY: Orbis Books.

Simmons, J Sam (1998). "The Missionary Motivation of God's Salvation." In *Missiology: An Introduction to the Foundations, History, Strategies of World Missions,* ed. John Mark Terry, Ebbie Smith, and Justice Anderson. 129-147. Nashville, TN: Broadman and Holman Publishers.

Thiessen, John C. (1955). *A Survey of World Missions.* Chicago, IL: Inter-Varsity Press.

Verkuyl, Johannes (1978). *Contemporary Missiology: An Introduction.* Translated by Dale Cooper. Grand Rapids, MI: William B. Eerdmans Publishing Company.

Vicedom, George F. V. (1965). *The Mission of God.* Translated by Gilbert A. Thiele and Dennis Hilgendorf. Saint Louis, MO: Concordia Publishing House.

Winter, Ralph D. (1974). "The Highest Priority: Cross-Cultural Evangelism." In *Let the Earth Hear His Voice,* ed. J. D. Douglas, 213-241. Minneapolis, MN: World Wide Publications.

Part IV

GLOBAL STRATEGY

PART IV

—⚒—

INTRODUCTION

Missiology is composed of three interdependent disciplines, that is: theology, the social sciences (history, sociology, and anthropology), and strategy. Having discussed the historical demography of the Filipino diaspora, Biblical theology, and missiological methodology in the preceding chapters, we now come to the natural outworking of these subjects. What can we do with the statistics and the analyses presented?

Strategy is vital to the execution of a task. We ask, "How can we effectively mobilize the Christians in the Filipino diaspora to help fulfill the Great Commission? Are there effective tools and resources available to utilize for the effective preaching of the Gospel and the discipling of Christ's followers? Are there existing strategic models to be emulated? Because the task of world evangelization is so great, how can we better partner and pool our resources for greater impact?

At the recent FIN-sponsored consultation, missions strategists and practitioners were invited to brainstorm and to craft strategic global mobilization, equipping and resourcing of Filipinos Christians in the diaspora. Dr. Sadiri Joy Tira, International Coordinator of the Filipino International Network; Dr. Henry Tan, President and CEO of GlobalLEAD Inc.; Dr. Brian Fargher of Campus Crusade for Christ; and Mr. Bob Lopez National Director of Philippine Missions Association, presented models of mobilization and equipping tools for discipleship and evangelism. Rev. Charlie H. Mance, Sr. Pastor of the River of Life Alliance Church in Calgary,

Alberta, Canada presented a case study on the Filipino-Canadian missions thrust, while Rev. Rodrigo Felomino, a Filipino missionary to Hong Kong presented on cooperative evangelistic strategy in Hong Kong. Ms. Venus Hannah Galvez shared how Filipinos in Japan are reaching the locals; the leaders of KSPS in Singapore and Dr. Ronald Adhikari in Taiwan also shared their thoughts and experiences regarding Filipino ministries in their host countries. These models and strategies are transferable to individuals and organizations engaged in evangelism and discipleship.

FILIPINO INTERNATIONAL NETWORK: A STRATEGIC MODEL FOR FILIPINO DIASPORA GLOCAL® MISSIONS

Sadiri Joy B. Tira

—◆—

INTRODUCTION

This chapter presents a missiological strategy for reaching the world for Christ through the mobilization of the Filipino Christians in diaspora.[1] It will focus on the Filipino International Network as a model of missiological strategy presented to the Filipino diaspora.

When mapping out a missions strategy, the basic question is: How will we begin? The answer is: we must begin by seeking and discovering God's plan. Missions strategists must discern God's agenda and recognize what He is doing to accomplish His plan. Our mission is, in fact, God's mission as missions originates from His heart. This is *"Missio Dei"* (Vicedom 1965: 4-11). As missions strategists, we must understand that "we begin... where missions begins—with God" (Webster 1965: 1), and so our strategies must be found in His "blueprint" and what He is already doing in the world. We must then align ourselves with His plan and direction.

The scattering or dispersion of nations, and their gathering, is a major biblical theme (see Genesis 11, Revelation 7, 22). The case of the Filipino diaspora (i.e. dispersion), though the dispersion is primarily economical, is being used by God to gather other nations to worship Him.

The Filipino International Network (hereafter referred to as FIN) is a *kairos* movement, referring to a divinely appointed window of opportunity. This is because God raised the movement to respond to unprecedented opportunities to reach the nations through the Filipinos in diaspora. In God's providence and sovereignty, Filipinos have been widely dispersed for a divine purpose. It is a tremendous opportunity for Filipinos to engage and participate in the fulfilment of the Great Commission and the achievement of the ultimate goal of missions. The ultimate goal of missions is not church planting, the building of hospitals, nor literature distribution; rather it is the gathering and worshipping of the nations around the Triune God's throne as described in Revelations 7, and the healing of the nations from the pain resulting from their sins, as illustrated in Revelations 22.

The FIN vision took shape as men and women of God around the globe started to take notice of the mass dispersion of Filipinos, in what I refer to as Limited Access Regions (LAR)[2], and as they started to recognize a divinely-planned "strategy" already in place. These visionary individuals later formed a strategic partnership in the form of FIN to help fulfill the goal of missions. They embraced the Matthean Great Commission (Matthew 28:18-20), and acted on the Lukan mandate which I call "glocal® missions." Glocal® missions means "thinking and acting locally and globally simultaneously."[3]

A BRIEF HISTORY OF FIN

Coffee Connections

Ground-breaking movements often start out as ideas passed back and forth between like-minded individuals. Sometimes over a cup of coffee or a cup of tea. Often times the unstructured ideas collect and take root in the "mind and heart" to form a singular vision. In the case of FIN, the initial "brainstorming" took place in a tiny restaurant over breakfast, coffee, bacon and eggs.

An Edmonton businessman (let's call him John) and I had casually met on several occasions previous to one catalytic meeting. I had then expressed that we needed the Jesus Film videocassettes for the First Filipino Alliance

Church's upcoming New Immigrants and New Citizens Sunday. Enthusiastic to participate in reaching out to the new immigrants, John agreed to provide us with the Jesus Film videocassettes.

This initial meeting was soon followed by a series of meetings during which we interacted over early morning breakfast or cups of coffee, and discussed the acceleration of the fulfillment of the Great Commission. At one point in our conversation I wondered out loud about Socrates. And asked John: "What did they say about Socrates and his wisdom again?" To which John responded "Didn't Socrates acquire wisdom not because he knew the answers, but because he asks the right questions at the right time.

Not to outsmart Socrates, my friend and I had many questions. In one of these meetings, we talked about the millions of Filipino nationals living and working outside their homeland as a result of the growing poverty and political instability in the Philippines. We had both heard of the rise of the Filipino "Overseas Contract Workers" (hereafter referred to as Overseas Filipino Workers, or OFWs) – Filipino expatriates working under contract in countries outside the Philippines such as Hong Kong, Singapore, Japan, Saudi Arabia and the Gulf States, and in many other countries; there are also thousands of Filipino sailors or seamen. Both of us wondered how many Christians there were out of the millions of Filipinos living and working in the "10/40 Window."[4]

We also wondered how many OFWs were leaving their homeland everyday. To answer our question, we researched the OFW presence across the globe and found, for example, over a million Filipino OFWs in Saudi Arabia alone! We also heard that there were over 400,000 in Hong Kong, 50,000 in Singapore, 40,000 in North Africa, and 25,000 in Israel. There are also Filipinos in South Asia. There are thousands of Filipinos in the Islamic, Buddhist, Jewish, Hindu, and Western worlds. With the coming turn over of the British Colony to Peoples Republic of China (in 1997) we wondered (in 1993) what would happen to the Filipinos in Hong Kong. How many Filipinos would remain to work in Hong Kong under the Chinese rule?

The presence of the OFWs in the 10/40 Window gave us the idea to motivate, equip and mobilize Filipinos in the Middle East, North Africa, Far East and North East Asia. We continued to meet for interaction and prayer meetings over breakfast at the Edmonton Inn. Then in 1994, a whole new door of opportunity was opened for the vision that had taken root in our hearts and minds.

Simultaneously the Lord had been working in the hearts of a handful of men, (e.g., He was also moving in the hearts of several Campus Crusade for Christ (CCC) leaders in USA, Europe, and the Philippines. The late Dr. Bill Bright, founder and former President of CCC International himself, endorsed this vision when he met with us in Edmonton in May 1996.

During the first five years of the 1990's God's Spirit was also stirring hearts of the Filipino Believers in Europe (with the formation of the European Filipino Christian Workers Network), in Japan (Filipino Japanese Network), in Singapore and Hong Kong. In these countries Filipino church leaders formed their respective ministerial associations. Over the years I have had the privilege of interfacing with these diaspora leaders at their conferences. Evidently, God was moving among the Filipino diaspora.

A Gathering of Like Minds

A handful of CCC leaders and I met from April 11-14, 1994 in Amman, Jordan. One day, these men were traveling in a bus from Amman to the ancient city of Petra (Jordan). On their way to Petra, they huddled at the back seat of the tourist bus for casual conversation but with a specific agenda. The topic of discussion was the "possible outreach and mobilization strategies" and "discipleship models" for Filipino ministries in LAR of the world. During the Amman consultation, the group reached a consensus that there [was] an urgent need of ministering (evangelism, discipleship resourcing and lay leadership training) to the OFWs. They also agreed that Filipinos and other ethnic groups (Koreans, South Asians and Africans) have a great potential to impact regions with limited access to the Gospel recognizing that God [had] providentially placed these people... in these regions for a specific reason in His plan of saving the nations. Hence, the mobilizing strategy should not be limited to OFWs only.

Further research in the following months and trips to *pind da pinoys,*[5] would further show us what God was doing in various regions of the world;

our vision expanded when we saw the potential ministry presence that the Filipinos had all over the world.

At the same time, God was moving the President's Cabinet of the Christian and Missionary Alliance (C&MA) in Canada with the vision I had shared with them after doing more research on the Filipinos in the 10/40 Window. The leadership of the C&MA Canada at that time was ready to launch into non-traditional C&MA missions strategy. Around the same time God was placing in the hearts of FFAC members a strong desire to become more actively involved in global missions. During their Extended Night of Prayers, held monthly, members would pray that God would raise up workers from their midst and that God would open new doors for them to play a strategic role in the fulfillment of the Great Commission. Between January and April 1995, the leadership of FFAC prayed and waited for God's direction. A passage from the second chapter of the book of Habakkuk captivated their hearts. We read in Habakkuk 2:1-3 (NIV):

> [1] I will stand at my watch and station myself on the ramparts; I will look to see what he will say to me, and what answer I am to give to this complaint. [2] Then the LORD replied: "Write down the revelation and make it plain on tablets so that a herald [2] may run with it. [3] For the revelation awaits an appointed time; it speaks of the end and will not prove false. Though it linger, wait for it; it will certainly come and will not delay.

They pondered the vision that God had given them, and like Habakkuk they wrote down the vision, submitted it to those who would play a strategic role in its fulfillment, and waited for the appointed time in which the vision would be realized.

Cyprus Baby

In the process of waiting, and "running" with the vision, a consultation was organized to take place in Larnaca, Cyprus, from May 3-6, 1995. Dr. Brian Fargher, a CCC staff member based in Edmonton, coined an apt title for this consultation, naming it the "First Filipino International Networking

Consultation '95." This term would be neutral denominationally, encouraging a strategic synergy of various like-minded organizations and local churches, and connoted religious neutrality, appropriate for the religious communication sensitivity required in LAR. At the consultation, the connections that started over coffee would give birth to a relational (that is a relationship-run) movement that would multiply and mature over time. The term "Filipino International Network" became the name given to the "movement" that emerged from this '95 Consultation. It soon reached far beyond Larnaca, spreading across the 10/40 Window and the western world, particularly North America.

Thirty-one delegates from Europe, various Limited Access Nations (LAN), the Philippines, and North America gathered at the Henipa Hotel, a site that would be used again in the future. Evangelical leaders with a strategic ministry involving Filipino expatriates, and several missions consultants, were invited, as well as visionary OFWs whom I had met on my research travels.

The goals of the consultation were to (a) remind participants of the mandate to fulfill the Great Commission; (b) to encourage and motivate Christian OFWs in the 10/40 Window; (c) to remind the participants of the priority of evangelism and discipleship; (d) to share the vision of the Filipino diaspora's role in global missions; (e) to gather strategic information from the participants; (f) to share available resources with the participants.

As the delegates interacted and sought God's face together, they identified several critical issues that needed to be addressed to make "Operation Trojan Horse"[6] an effective reality. These vital issues were: the need for prayer mobilization; the need for a communication tool such as a prayer bulletin or newsletter to link the network; leadership conferences for church leaders in strategic limited access regions; the need to minister and strengthen Filipino expatriate families[7] through Family Conferences; the recruitment of teachers and trainers to conduct evangelistic and discipleship training in the 10/40 Window; and the need to expand the network into other countries where there is a high number of Filipino OFWs.

The three-day consultation culminated in the signing and adoption of the "Larnaca Covenant." The Larnaca Covenant affirmed (a) "the Lordship of

Jesus Christ in His Church and over the nations" (b) "the Great Commission as a mandate to all believers for the 10/40 window and the world" (c) "the sovereignty of God in placing Filipino believers in the 10/40 window and the world." The delegates committed to "pray for one another," "to share resources for greater effectiveness in reaching the 10/40 window and the world," and "to recruit, train and mobilize Filipino believers as tentmakers and career ministers to the 10/40 window and the world" while "continuing dialogue and strategy meetings." The signing of the "Larnaca Covenant" signified the official birth of FIN and became its guiding document.

Before leaving Henipa Hotel two important decisions were made by the participants: (1) Rev. Sadiri Joy Tira was given the mandate to implement the newly signed "covenant" (2) A new partnership was forged during the concluding communion service when Dr. Valmike Apuzen an evangelical leader from the Philippines reminded the delegates of the missiological implications of the Last Supper. I vividly recall Dr. Apuzen's exhortation: "We can not partake in communion without embracing the Great Commission of our Lord Jesus. Paul understood this when he wrote: "For as often as you eat this bread and drink this cup, you proclaim the Lord's death till He comes" (I Corinthians 11:26)." Apuzen's remark became the commissioning words for everyone as they returned to where God had "planted them." As a result of the Larnaca Consultation a new movement was born.

'Glocal'® Collaborations

Soon after the consultation in Cyprus, a new partnership of "glocal®" proportions was set in place with four initial partners. In FIN's case it refers to the like-minded people in Edmonton who forged a partnership having global implications. The consultative partnership was set into place to oversee and provide accountability to the newly-hatched FIN initiative. The major partners of the FIN partnership were: First Filipino Alliance Church, Klemke Foundation, the C&MA in Canada, and CCC in Canada. These partners represented a local church, a Christian foundation, an evangelical denomination and a para-church organization.

These collaborative organizations provided FIN with initial funding and logistics for the network. A simple Memorandum of Agreement (MOA) was signed to seal their respective commitments to the movement. As the vision of FIN was introduced to other local congregations, mission agencies, and like-minded individuals, the network of "partners" grew, and eventually regional committees were established in several limited access regions, Far East Asia, and North America. Partners would cast the vision to other Christians committed to "glocal® missions" in places where Filipino Christians were located as FIN extended its partnerships across the globe.

First Filipino Alliance Church (FFAC) is a prime example of glocal® partnership, as it ministers locally, nationally, and as it extends its ministry around the globe by partnering with FIN. FFAC formed the prayer base for FIN's ministries, embracing FIN as an extension of their own ministry, and praying fervently for FIN just as a mother prays for her child. Frequently throughout the year, the congregation releases their Senior Pastor to represent them, ministering to Filipinos all over the world. They also provide FIN with international headquarters in Edmonton. In recent years, FFAC would commission some of its members to partner with FIN internationally as Christian workers. Certainly, a local congregation that releases its resources, including many of their members, and their pastor, for a global ministry is "thinking and acting locally and globally simultaneously."

Growing and Going

The FIN movement would be fueled by four key components, that is: trusting relationships between partners; networking of individuals and organizations committed to the Great Commission and FIN's vision of seeing Filipinos actively participating in this task; communication making like-minded people aware of God's work in and through the Filipino diaspora Christians; and the gathering of workers who would strategically influence others to take part in the task at hand. Consultations would play a significant role in keeping the movement growing and going.

Five more significant consultations would be held after the historical consultation in Cyprus. From September 19-20, 1996, Filipino evangelical leaders from several denominations and para-church organizations met in

Puerto Azul, Philippines with representatives from the FIN partnership and Philippine government officials, for a "Ministry and Missions Consultation" regarding "The Church and the Filipino Overseas Contract Workers." Having been made aware of the needs and missions potential of the millions of Filipino OFWs or OCWs, the delegates would present and sign the "Puerto Azul Declaration," committing to partner in "extend[ing] beyond the Filipino OCWs to include all Filipinos, whether in the Philippines or abroad, and to make disciples among all nations." The delegates of the Puerto Azul Consultation would "officially endorse FIN as a networking movement that [would] facilitate the delivery of related ministries and services" to the Filipino diaspora. This consultation held in the Philippines would result in a spreading awareness among Filipino Evangelical leaders of the necessity to strategically train and prepare Filipino OFWs for their service in other lands, and would further connect Filipino Christians for a joint effort in fulfilling the Great Commission. For the first time, FIN was represented at the Second National Tentmaking Conference sponsored by the Philippine Mission Association in Tagaytay, Philippines in December 1996. Furthermore, the consultation would bring the participants to the realization that the Philippine Overseas Employment Administration (POEA) could play a significantly strategic role in deploying Filipino "tentmakers." The POEA was indirectly becoming "the largest sending agency" of Filipino "tentmakers." The consultation participants would start praying for a greater Christian influence in POEA so that a greater mobilization of the "tentmaking" force could be achieved.

The Puerto Azul Consultation in 1996 would be followed by the "Filipino North American Prayer Advance '97" held in Midland, Texas. There, Filipino Christian leaders from across North America gathered with FIN consultants and partners to pray and fast "for revival among the millions of Filipinos dispersed worldwide." Affirming The Larnaca Covenant and The Puerto Azul Declaration, the delegates at Midland would endorse FIN "as a catalyst movement that [would] facilitate concerted prayer networks among the Filipino diaspora." The participants committed themselves "to pray for one another; to mobilize [their] respective congregations and contacts for extraordinary prayer and to seek God's face; to initiate, encourage, and influence other Filipino North American believers to participate actively in future regional and national Prayer Advances" and "to help the Filipino Christian diaspora to go beyond cultural lines and seek ways to love, serve and share the Gospel to the people of their host country and to other internationals residing in their midst." The Midland Prayer Advance would challenge Filipino North American pastors and congregations to participate in global missions, through prayer, and active involvement in motivating and mobilizing the Filipino Christian diaspora.

In 1998 three more consultations were sponsored by FIN for regional Filipino leaders in Far East Asia held in Singapore; Middle East and North Africa in Manama, Bahrain; and the historical International diaspora Leaders Consultation in Camp Nakamun, Alberta (Canada). These consultations broaden the FIN network not only among Filipinos in the diaspora but also with other ethno-cultural diaspora networks (e.g. South Asians, Chinese, Vietnamese, Black, Persians, Japanese, Spanish-Latinos, Koreans, etc.).

Seven years after the FIN birth in Cyprus, a network of 54 participants from five continents including LAR, and 11 key countries including the USA, Canada, Israel, Korea, Hong Kong and Germany, converged in Singapore to celebrate God's work through His Filipino children, and to pray and plan for FIN's next steps. The keynote speaker, Dr. Thomas Wang, founding general secretary of the Chinese Congress on World Evangelization (CCOWE) and chairman of the time-specific AD2000 Movement, reminded the participants of God's sovereignty in placing them where they were at that given time. He urged them to be active participants in the fulfillment of the Great Commission, and he expressed his dream of one day seeing a second (after the Chinese with CCOWE) worldwide diaspora group deliberately and strategically organize for world missions; the Filipinos and FIN being an answer to prayer.

The consultation would culminate in the calling and organizing of a "FIN Global Committee" that would aid in the future initiatives and planning of FIN. Before leaving, the consultation would also reword its mission statement, from the original:

FIN "is committed to motivating, equipping, and mobilizing Christian

Overseas Filipino Workers (OFWs) around the world to help accomplish the Great Commission" to the revised: FIN *is a catalytic movement of Christians committed to motivate and mobilize Filipinos globally to partner for worldwide mission."*

MINISTRY CHANNELS

FIN has five primary channels of ministry. These are: Prayer Advance, New Life Training Curriculum, Family Life Ministry, Jesus Film distribution, and the organizing of regional and international strategic consultations.

Prayer Advance

FIN founders hold that at the heart of missions strategy is seeking God's heartbeat and work in the world. Prayer, therefore is crucial, and actually the "backbone" of missions strategy. To build a network of prayer, Prayer Advances[8] (a new spin on the traditional term "Prayer Retreat" to suggest a forward action and results) are conducted in cities worldwide with a significant Filipino population, particularly in the 10/40 window. At Prayer Advance, participants bring brief reports from their area of the globe to lift up their "area" together. In an article published in the Alliance Life Magazine (no date), Dr. Brian Fargher, one of the visionary men who was instrumental in launching FIN describes the very first Prayer Advance held in Edmonton in 1996 as a "role model," explaining that Prayer Advance was "implicitly based on Jesus' words in Matthew 9:36-38: His compassion, the opportunities and the exhortation to pray for harvesters." Prayer Advance continues to be organized by FIN's regional committees in each region on an ongoing basis throughout the year.

New Life Training Curriculum

FIN plans and sponsors an ongoing number of strategically conducted discipleship-training seminars throughout the year and around the globe, using CCC's five-level New Life Training Curriculum in regions where access to discipleship training is needed by the Filipino tentmakers. NLTC is a curriculum that trains disciples of Jesus to become "multiplying disciples" continuing on the cycle of evangelism and discipleship. NLTC has been organized in Japan, Canada, and mostly in Limited Access Regions where it is difficult to access training. Over a thousand "trainees" have been trained on how to effectively become "multiplying disciples" and their numbers have increased tremendously in recent years.

Family Life Conference

Further, in response to the high rate of broken marriages and families in OFW communities, FIN's Family Life Ministry conducts conferences (also using CCC material) in cities where there is a large OFW presence to aid in strengthening marriages. Family Life conferences are designed to help people build godly homes by teaching God's blueprint for marriage and family. This is done by providing practical, biblical resources on marriage. It encourages couples, in FIN's case, particularly OFWs and mixed-marriage (when one spouse is Filipino and the other of a different culture) to keep their marriage vows, build up their family relationships, and teach their children about the meaning, purpose and responsibilities of marriage.

Jesus Film

FIN has also been involved in providing Filipino congregations and individuals with the Jesus Film for evangelistic purposes. The Jesus Film is the life story of Jesus Christ based on the Gospel of Luke. The Jesus Film is available in over 700 languages, and FIN aids in distributing these to OFWs for the Filipino community and oftentimes for their hosts. During the past seven years, close to 50,000 Jesus Film in video and DVD formats were distributed through the FIN networks.

Strategic Consultations

Finally, FIN organizes and sponsors both regional and international "strategic consultations." (This consultation in Seoul, South Korea is an example of these strategic consultations). These consultations provide the

Filipino leaders who participate with a special time to brainstorm for more creative ways to mobilize the Filipino diaspora, to network with each other and to build trans-denominational connections for the advancement of the Gospel. Participants are encouraged to expand the vision of God's work through the Filipino diaspora.

CONCLUSION

Evidently, FIN is a *Kairos* strategic movement to help fulfil the Great Commission and the achievement of the ultimate goal of ever-present Christian missions. The unseen but ever-present architect of FIN is none other than the Holy Spirit who is the administrator of Christian missions.

As a strategy for "glocal® missions," FIN is one of the most cost-effective missions strategies. It is a proven partnership model between local churches, denominations, Christian organization, para-church groups, and missions enthusiasts.

FIN is a story of strategic connections between the Filipino diaspora congregations and their counterparts in the homeland – the Philippines. FIN is also a story of visionary men and women committed to the cause of Jesus Christ. It is a story of modern-day children of Isachar. Moreover, it is a story of people who took courage because of their faith in God (c.f. Hebrew 11).

Finally, FIN is a story of the Filipino diaspora impacting other nations for the glory of God. Let me close this chapter with these first-hand observations:

- In Bahrain OFWs connected with FIN helped launch a Sri Lankan congregation. Also in Qatar OFWs connected with FIN are reaching out to their fellow expatriate workers from Nepal. I had the privilege of meeting and ministering to these Brethren. In Northern UAE a group of Chinese from mainland China came to Christ and were baptised and for several years have worshipped God with Filipinos. Who can orchestrate the gathering of foreign workers in a third country?

- In Hong Kong FIN distributed the Jesus Film in video cassettes to Filipino Care Givers (FCG). One of the recipients showed it to the

Chinese children under her care. The children saw in the film how Jesus calmed the storm. In turn they asked their maid to pray and ask Jesus to stop the rain so that they will be able to go to school. The maid prayed and the rain "stopped"! Amazed of what happened, the children invited Jesus to come into their lives as the maid led them to prayer. Consequently, the children showed the film to their parents who later became followers of Jesus themselves. In almost every high rise building in Hong Kong there are many OFWs who are Christ servants.

• In Japan, FIN sponsored an NLTC among OFW ladies married to Japanese men. Some of these women brought their husband during the training sessions and in turn heard the Good News. They accepted the message and surrendered their lives to Jesus Christ. Several of them were baptized by FIN trainers before the end of the training sessions. It must be reported that some of these men were notorious gangsters — members of Japanese mafia! Some of the greatest miracles that are happening today are hardened lives changed by the gentle Holy Spirit. Indeed, miracles happen today! Who are best to penetrate the Japanese society with the gospel of Christ but Filipina wives married to Japanese men?

It has been observed that anti-western sentiment has increased significantly in many regions of the world in the recent years following 9/11, or the September 11, 2001 bombing of the World Trade Centre in New York City (USA). In the face of spreading fear of violence and growing alienation between people, the Church must be the primary model of how the gospel gathers all people together. The Church must take on the role of "peacemaker." In a world transformed by migration, often due to violence and strife, Filipino Christians have been prepared by God to broker reconciliation and peace among alienated individuals and groups. The Filipinos, in their loving and humble spirit, have won the hearts of many. They have become bearers of the Good News and their message has been accepted by many of their peers, employers, and hosts. They have in fact become peacemakers and gatherers.

FIN is an unprecedented movement among the Filipino diaspora. It is a movement that emerged from a divinely-inspired vision to make disciples of the thousands of Filipinos scattered across the globe. This vision, given to people committed to the fulfilment of the Great Commission, is being used to challenge a new generation of men and women to become multiplying disciples, gatherers and peacemakers to the nations. Let us pray that more will be inspired and embrace FIN's mission and vision. May the dispersion of the Filipino nation result to the gathering of many.

ENDNOTES

[1] Diaspora is the scattering or dispersion of a specific people group due to "religious or political persecution or to seek economic opportunities and political freedom" (Pierson cited in Moreau, 2000, 275).

[2] Limited Access Nation/s (LAN) is a Christian & Missionary Alliance (C&MA) term for the more commonly used term, Creative Access Nations (CAN). CAN is "a country which limits or forbids the entry of Christian missionaries and for which alternative legal means of entry are required to enable Christians to live for Christ" (Johnstone and Mandryk, 2001, 755). LAN and CAN are synonymous. Limited Access Region (LAR) is a cluster of LAN or CAN specifically located in the 10/40 Window, (e.g. Islamic world, Jewish world, Hindu world, and Buddhist world).

[3] I understand the Great Commission according to Matthew in Matthew 28:18-20 and Christ's commissioning his disciples to be his witnesses in Acts 1:8 as "glocal® missions." This is making disciples of all nations in our increasingly "globalized" and "borderless" world; this may include preaching and teaching, training, church planting, compassionate-ministries, and other strategies to make disciples of Jesus Christ. The making of disciples must be conducted in all places at the same time for all people. Hence, the Matthean-Lukan missions agenda is "glocal® missions." An example of a New Testament church practicing "glocal® missions" is the church in Antioch as described in Acts 11:19-30 and Acts 13:1-3. The Antioch congregation was reaching out to the local people, but they were also extending their ministry beyond their geographical region by commissioning missionaries Barnabas and Saul. This is a biblical model of what I call "glocal® congregation" doing "glocal® missions" that is "thinking and acting locally and globally simultaneously."

[4] 10/40 Window — Louis Bush, former Executive Director of A.D. 2000 & Beyond, coined the term "10/40 Window" referring to the "window" extending from ten degrees north to forty degrees north of the equator. This region extending from West Africa to East Asia is home to the majority of the world's unreached people groups, including the Muslims, Hindus, and Buddhists.

[5] "pind da pinoys" — is a play on the Filipino accent which would often pronounce the sound for the letter 'f' as 'p,' so "find" as "pind," and 'th' as 'd,' hence "the" as "da." Pinoys is slang for "Filipinos."

[6] Operation Trojan Horse was the initial project embraced by the C&MA Canada to help launch FIN. It was coined by Wally Albrecht, former Vice-President for Global Ministries.

[7] Most OFWs are geographically separated from their loved ones who are left behind in their homeland. Effective Kingdom workers need to have healthy marriages and relationships.

[8] During the pre-planning of the first Prayer Advance in Edmonton in April 1996, Dr. TV Thomas (Director of Centre for Evangelism and World Missions in Regina, Saskatchewan, Canada) suggested to me not to use Prayer Retreat, Prayer Summit, or Prayer and Fasting, but Prayer Advance. The late Rev. John Bearg, national prayer coordinator for CCC Canada, endorsed this event. The main features of Prayer Advances are the gathering of participants around the Lord's table for the "breaking of bread," followed by prayer for unity among Filipinos in the community before intercessory prayer is offered for the host countries and other needs of Filipinos in diaspora. Most Prayer Advances, if not all, result in greater networking and cooperative evangelism among Filipinos. In many occasions, Filipino pastors and congregations reconcile and forgive each other after being divided and deeply wounded. Prayer Advances in LAR, for example, have been used by God to bring revival among Filipino congregations.

REFERENCES

Fargher, Brian L. (n.d.). "Prayer Advance '96." *Alliance Life* (no date) 24.

FIN News. (2002-2003). Quarterly Publication of the Filipino International Network. Volumes IV & V.

Johnstone, P. & Mandryk, J. (2001). *Operation world*. Carlisle, Cumbria, Canada: Paternoster Lifestyle.

Moreau, A. Scott, ed. (2000). *Evangelical Dictionary of World Missions*. Grand Rapids, MI: Baker Book House Company.

Tira, Sadiri Emmanuel. (2002). "Global Missions and Local Congregation: A Case Study of the First Filipino Alliance Church in Edmonton, Alberta, Canada." D. Min. dissertation. Jackson, Mississippi: Reformed Theological Seminary.

Vicedom, George. (1965). *The Mission of God*. St. Louis, MO: Concordia Publishing House.

Webster, Douglas. (1965). *Unchanging Mission* – Biblical and Contemporary. Philadelphia, PA: Fortress.

APPENDIX 1

FILIPINO INTERNATIONAL NETWORK
GUIDING DOCUMENTS

Larnaca Covenant

We, the participants of the Filipino International Networking Consultation '95, representing various Filipino believing communities in the Middle East, Gulf States, North Africa, North America, and the Philippines affirm:

- the Lordship of Jesus Christ in His church and over the nations,
- the Great Commission as a mandate to all believers in the 10/40 window and the world,
- the sovereignty of God in placing Filipino believers in the 10/40 window and the world.

Therefore, we commit:
- to pray for one another,
- to share our resources (information, personnel, infrastructures, materials, finances, strategies) for greater effectiveness in reaching the 10/40 window and the world,
- to recruit, train, and mobilize Filipino believers as tentmakers and career ministers for the 10/40 window and the world,
- to continuing dialogue and strategy meetings.

We, the participants of FIN Consultation '95 covenant ourselves to this declaration on this day, May 6, 1995.

The Puerto Azul Declaration

Believing that the Triune God has revealed Himself and His will in the inerrant Bible consisting of sixty-six canonical books, and has commissioned us as members of His church to make disciples of all nations by preaching the good news of salvation solely by grace through faith in Jesus Christ until He returns bodily to usher in the eternal order,

And having met for a Ministry and Missions Consultation regarding "The Church and the Filipino Overseas Contract Workers (OCWs)" on September 19 and 20, 1996 at Puerto Azul, Cavite, Philippines,

And having been made aware of the needs as well as the missions potential of the Filipino OCWs.

We hereby commit ourselves to partnership intended to enhance the ministry effectiveness of agencies and individuals to assist in the efficient deliver of services to OCWs.

Furthermore, we agree:

* to widen our focus and extend beyond the Filipino OCWs to include all Filipinos whether in the Philippines or abroad, and to make disciples among all countries; and
* to establish the standards of biblical and theological evangelicalism and to maintain a high level of professionalism in the delivery of such services;

In recognition therefore of the need for a coordinated international effort, we officially endorse the Filipino International Network as a networking movement that will facilitate the delivery of related ministries and services.

Midland Affirmation

We, the participants of the historic Filipino North American Prayer Advance '97 in Midland, Texas recognize the urgent call for Filipino Christian leaders in North America and around the world to gather for prayer and fasting for revival amongst the millions of Filipinos who are scattered all over the world.

We affirm the Larnaca Covenant and the Puerto Azul Declaration endorsing the Filipino International Network as a catalyst movement that will facilitate concerted prayer networks among the global Filipino Diaspora.

Therefore we commit ourselves to the following:

* to pray for one another.

- to mobilize our respective congregations and contacts for extraordinary prayer and seeking God's face.
- to initiate, encourage, and influence other Filipino North American believers to participate actively in future regional and national Prayer Advances.
- to help the Filipino Christian Diaspora to go beyond cultural lines and seek ways to love, serve, and share the Gospel to the people of their host country and to other international residing in their midst.

We, the participants of the Filipino-North American Prayer Advance '97 make this statement of affirmation on this day, November 16, 1997.

APPENDIX II

FIN Sodality Partnership Diagram

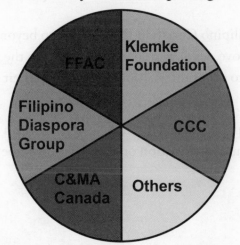

- The **Christian and Missionary Alliance (C&MA) Canada** provide funding for FIN's administration expenses.

- **FFAC** releases their Senior Pastor to serve as FIN's international coordinator; releases some of their members to conduct NLTC trainings, provide office space, and communication equipment.

- The **Klemke Foundation** provide funding for evangelistic and discipleship trainings (NLTC and Jesus Film); sponsor strategic FIN consultations.

- **Campus Crusade for Christ (CCC)** provides evangelistic tools and discipleship materials; release personnel to conduct NTC training; release International School of Theology/Asia (ISOT) staff.

- **Filipino Diaspora Groups** provide local hospitality to FIN training teams and local coordination for FIN sponsored events.

- **Others:**

  - Dr. Benzon Professional Corporation provide funding for strategic consultation.

  - Kryptor Management Consulting provides professional assistance (financial accounting and audit).

  - Individual sponsors for FIN projects (e.g. Prayer Advance, Family Life Conference).

8

THE NECESSITY OF TRAINING THE FILIPINO DIASPORA

Henry H. Tan

INTRODUCTION

The dispersion of the Filipino people across the world is a documented fact. The question that poses a challenge is, "What is God's purpose for the Filipino diaspora?" Why are they dispersed the way they are? Surely, it must be beyond the obvious reasons of making a living. Looking at what happened with the Jews in the first century, it is clear that through the dispersion of the Jews due to persecution, the gospel was brought to other pasts of the world.

> "On the day a great persecution broke out against the church at Jerusalem, and all except the apostles were scattered throughout Judea and Samaria." Acts 8:1b (NIV)

> "Those who had been scattered preached the word wherever they went. Philip went down to a city in Samaria and proclaimed the Christ there." Acts 8:4-5 (NIV)

The Filipinos are placed in a similar situation. Suffering from economic 'persecution,' millions have braved the challenges working for a living in foreign countries. Searching for a better life, the Filipino has ventured forth to all parts of the world – ranging from the Antarctica in the north to Australia down under and from Japan in the East to the United States in the West. Large numbers of them are in the Middle East. In fact, there are significant groups of Filipinos in countries where the nationals are non-Christians.

Looking at the grand scheme of things, one could say that God has super-naturally chosen the Filipinos to be His ambassadors throughout the world. The Filipino diaspora reveal the following realities that they:

- have met the Lord since arriving at their destination;

- have led other Filipinos in their host countries to the Lord;

- have started churches amongst the Filipinos;

- have even led a few locals to the Lord;

- are excited about discovering their purpose for being in another country; and

- have caught the vision of seeing movements of spiritual multiplication take place in their (temporary for most) adopted land.

Somehow the Lord has especially blessed the Filipino. Filipinos are generally friendly, flexible, adaptable, gifted with music and the ability to learn languages quickly. Everywhere Filipinos go they quickly learn the local language (usually just by watching local TV programs). The very make-up of the Filipino people lends to their becoming effective 'fishers of men.' The strengths and gifts of the Filipino people lay mostly in the interpersonal arena – relationships – the very area that our Lord emphasizes through the Great Commandment.

> Jesus replied: "'Love the Lord your God with all your heart
> and with all you soul and with all your mind.' This is the first
> and greatest commandment. And the second is like it: 'Love
> your neighbor as yourself.' All the Law and the Prophets
> hang on these two commandments." Matt.22:37-40 (NIV)

In the light of how the Lord has uniquely created the Filipino to be most adept at relating with people, it would seem that we would be remiss if we overlook the training of the Filipinos for the task that the Lord may have for them as they are being dispersed worldwide. They need to be trained because they are already "on- site" for the work of the Lord in all these places across the globe.

Everyday there are hundreds, if not thousands of Filipinos who are leaving the country looking for employment. Perhaps we should seize the opportunity to equip those who desire to be trained prior to their departure from the Philippines. It is imperative that we do so if we are to be good stewards of the people He has already raised for HIS work. By identifying the places with communities of Filipinos, FIN has an additional responsibility of stewardship. How we assist our Filipino brothers and sisters to live their lives for Him is critical. The challenge is for us to bring a smile to God's face by living our lives to the fullest for Him such that people would be attracted to the God who lives inside our hearts.

A large number of those leaving the Philippines go to Limited Access Nations. These are countries that may not allow missionaries to come to their country. But today we have millions of Filipinos in Limited Access Nations who need the Lord. And for those diaspora Filipinos who already know the Lord, they will also need the fellowship of other Christians.

With the significant number of diaspora Filipino Christians in Limited Access Nations, perhaps God is opening up an avenue to allow Christians to get into such countries for His purposes. If we do not train those going to these countries, would we be held accountable for those living there?

EQUIPPING AND TRAINING CHRISTIANS BEFORE THEY LEAVE THE PHILIPPINES

It has to start back in the Philippines. *Church-based training.* If churches would embrace the Filipino diaspora phenomenon as part of their missions effort, they can provide Orientation Leadership Seminars to adequately prepare potential leaders for their role in obeying the Great Commission in their host country. It would be such a tremendous opportunity for the local churches in the Philippines to sponsor these evangelical Christian OFWs first by providing them with the necessary leadership skills. The local Philippine church in a critical way becomes the authentic prayer partners and leadership sponsors for the outgoing OFWs in their new role as non-traditional "missionaries" to their "kababayans" in the host country.

FIN could motivate the vision, provide training, and encouragement to the churches to consider this vital but often neglected missions strategy. The preparation for those going would include topics on: living overseas; understanding the local culture and way of life; studying the Word; evangelism and discipleship; leading small groups; spiritual multiplication; personal development plan; and others. It would be invaluable for each person to experience the joy of leading people to the Lord and following them up while preparing to leave. Learning while doing the ministry at home is critical to success in a foreign land. More than doing, however, is the fact that each person must be growing in their 'being' – their walk with God. Somehow, each Christian must be reminded anew that Christianity is about developing his or her relationship with Christ. This is what Christianity is all about. When they minister overseas, what they are helping new believers to focus on is really their walk with God—developing their relationships with Jesus Christ—and learning to multiply spiritually.

> Jesus called them together and said, "You know that those who are regarded as rulers of the Gentiles lord it over them, and their high officials exercise authority over them. Not so with you. Instead, whoever wants to become great among you must be your servant, and whoever wants to be first must be slave of all. For even the Son of Man did not come to be served, but to serve, and to give his life as a ransom of many." Mark 10:42-45 (NIV)

It is through serving and adopting the attitude that was in Christ Jesus that we will be able to earn the right to be heard so that eventually everyone will bow down before Jesus acknowledging Him as Lord.

> "Your attitude should be the same as that of Christ Jesus: Who, being in very nature God, did not consider equality with God something to be grasped, but made himself nothing, taking the very nature of a servant, being made in human likeness. And being found in appearance as a man, he humbled himself and became obedient to death – even death on a cross! Therefore God exalted him to the highest place and gave him the name that is above every name, that

at the name of Jesus every knee should bow, in heaven and on earth and under the earth, and every tongue confess that Jesus Christ is Lord, to the glory of God the Father." Philippians 2:5-11 (NIV)

EQUIPPING AND TRAINING FILIPINO CHRISTIANS IN THE NEW COUNTRY

Traveling throughout these countries where there are significant numbers of Filipinos, one will certainly find different kinds of churches. Most of the churches are led by laymen who, by virtue of their limited knowledge (which is much more than the new Christians), have been appointed as pastors. Most, if not, all have no formal Bible training. The first recipients of training would have to be the pastoral leaders. They would need training in handling the Word of God, conflict resolution, shepherding their flock, preaching, turning a passage into a message, leading small groups, church organization and, most of all, a tender heart for God and all that God loves.

FIN could offer the pastoral leaders modular courses where they don't have to leave their ministries in order for them to be better equipped and trained. Programs need to be developed where over a period of two and a half years (three modular courses per year), participants would be more adequately prepared for their responsibilities as pastoral leaders.

Another key area of concern is that of seeing *church planting movements* take root in each of the countries where there are Filipinos. Pastoral leaders must catch the vision of seeing multiplication of churches whereby new converts can be nurtured and loved. Church planting training must take place if FIN is serious about reaching the locals for Christ.

The second group of people who needs training would be the lay people in Church. To be involved in mobilizing Filipinos by first reaching them with the gospel, the lay people must be trained in 'making conversations count,' transitioning from current events/situations to the gospel presentation. They must learn to master at least one tool for evangelism, follow-up and discipleship. Once there is mastery of a tool, they would have the foundation to be flexible in their presentations.

Leading small groups is a skill that can be acquired through training. Since having large groups may prove to be dangerous in some countries it is imperative that 'churches' be small so as to escape detection by the authorities. Thus in small groups the leaders can skillfully facilitate the adult learning process.

One essential truth for all believers is that of knowing why they exist. Purposefulness in life is absolutely necessary for believers to live lives that are meaningful. So often, even believers live as if they have no purpose. How tragic it would be for believers to wake up one day to discover that they have basically squandered their lives by simply existing and not really living the life that God intended for them. FIN exists partly to help bring purposefulness to lives through Jesus Christ. Training in this area would be most beneficial to Filipinos all throughout the world.

Basic Bible study skills where they can learn from the Word is a must. How can we grow if we do not have a steady diet of God's word to apply in our lives? For all this to happen there needs to be trained disciplers who can continue the transforming process life to life. What an exciting day it would be to see disciplers equipped to disciple people who would in turn disciple others.

> "And the things you have heard me say in the presence of
> many witnesses entrust to reliable men who will also be
> qualified to teach others." 2 Timothy 2:2 (NIV)

Another area that is important would be that of learning to discern needs of the local people and to creatively serve them by helping meet their needs. Every time you help meet someone's needs it would be perceived that you care for and love them. It is interesting to see in Nehemiah 9 that they were taught first before their physical needs were met.

> "You made known to them your holy Sabbath and gave them
> commands, decrees and laws through you servant Moses. In
> their hunger you gave them bread from heaven and in their
> thirst you brought them water from the rock; you told them

to go in and take possession of the land you had sworn with uplifted hand to give them." Nehemiah 9:14-15 (NIV)

Both are important. Feeding them with truth and physical food go hand in hand. We must not lose sight of their spiritual need even as we deal with their material needs. Too many organizations in seeking to provide both have been seen to only provide for their material needs. This is not adequate. We need to help people see the sufficiency of Christ in their lives. To excel in this area, training must be provided to help our leaders become adept at discerning needs and to creatively help meet them.

The truth of the matter is that God has 'sent' Filipinos into the world for His purpose. He has done His part. We must now do ours—making sure that the Filipinos are trained to carry out His Commandment and Commission. Let us look with anticipation to all that He has in store for the Filipino people as we trust Him to see the whole world transformed in Him.

THE PRACTICAL AND INSTRUCTIONAL COMPONENTS OF OUTREACH

Brian Fargher

INTRODUCTION

One of God's first commands to Adam and Eve was to go forth and multiply. Look at this command through the lens of 2 Tim 4:4 and it reminds us that God is very interested in multiplication, not just addition.

Tom is a vibrant Christian worker, talented and energetic. When he arrived he asked me, "What advice do you have for me?" I almost begged him, "Don't leave an empty desk when you move on. Coach lots of people to do ministry even better than you do it." Tom's a great speaker so he grabbed all the speaking opportunities. He's a great lecturer so he gave workshops on leadership. When he moved on he didn't leave an empty desk – he sold it! In five years he hadn't coached a single person. Soon the waves subsided and life went on as though Tom had never been there.

Those of who are having fun in ministry usually have no trouble with the addition but we often struggle with the multiplication. We get so taken up with what we are doing, simply because we enjoy it so much, that we spent little or no time multiplying ourselves. If you question this try a little experiment. Keep track of the numbers of hours in a week that you do ministry, and the number of hours that you invest in coaching others to do ministry.

Many of us excuse ourselves by saying, "That's what schools and seminaries are for. If people want training they can go there." For huge numbers of Christian workers Bible School or seminar is not an option. If each of us adopted Frank Lauback's literacy teaching adage, "each one teach one," we'd made a fantastic contribution to the number of trained workers. Field training, or 'on-the-job' training has a large number of obvious advantages, and very few disadvantages. The most obvious is that it can major on the practical.

But any training module must have an objective. For practical purposes let's say that the objective of the training we're considering is "preach and pull in 'fish.'" Extrapolated, that means verbalizing the Good News of Jesus' death and resurrection and encouraging the listeners to say Yes to Jesus' offer of a renewed relationship with the Creator. If that were an easy assignment there would be a lot more people doing it. What makes it difficult is that to achieve the objective, the worker has to go out and find listeners.

In order to do this, a person needs at least four things: vision, convictions, commitment and skills. Note that 'information' is not one of the most important things. The more information the minister has, the greater the breadth and depth there will be to the ministry, but I've been privileged to work with many people who possessed a limited amount of information, but a supernatural amount of vision, conviction and commitment, and then the Holy Spirit supplied, as he promised to do, the gifts they needed for ministry.

In order to major on the *practical,* let's begin with the one practical component of Great Commission ministry. There are a wide variety of resources people can use but in the 21st century, the *Jesus* film continues to be among the best.

JESUS FILM

The two biggest advantages of the *Jesus* film are its availability and its versatility. Wherever you are in the world you can very quickly obtain a copy in just about any language you want. Once you have the DVD or some other format in your hand you can use it in a wide variety of ways. Perhaps the most important thing to remember is: the Jesus film is just a resource. I like the saying, "God uses people, and people use resources."

It is irrelevant for us to question whether God can use the film without the intervention of people: of course he can. Our concern is to maximize the potential of the film. That means that we want as many people as possible to say Yes to Jesus' invitation, whether the promise we zero in on be the one in Matthew 11:28, John 4:24, or any other one. Whenever I make use of this resource I want as many people as possible to respond. So what can I do to make that possible?

But first, let's just note in passing some of the ways we can use it:

1. We can slip it into a package and give it away without the person who received it knowing what he/she has received. That's a bit like the primitive 'burn and scatter' method of sowing grain: you set fire to some bush or grass, wait until the ashes have cooled and it looks like it's going to rain, and you thrown some grain into the ground. Sure; some of it will sprout, but it's an inefficient way to farm. If a blind giveaway is the only way, then it's a good way.

2. Asking a person if they want a copy. This has at least two variations. You may never meet the person who accepts a copy; e.g. groups of people distribute the Jesus film on the streets of Sydney on any of about 90 languages. They do not expect to meet any of the recipients again. I have offered the Jesus film to hundreds of householders with the stipulation: May I return in a week and get your opinion of the film? This method has advantages and disadvantages.

3. Inviting them to view a showing. Millions of people have seen the Jesus film in theaters and in outdoor showings. Some of the comments I will make about the next option apply to this one. Perhaps the major disadvantage of large showing, is the difficulty of having any on-going contact with those who indicate making a response. For me personally, whenever I am able to choose one of the four, I would choose the next one. For me it has lots of advantages and not a lot of disadvantages.

4. Requesting a family to host a showing. If this is done well, it is one of the best evangelistic presentations I can imagine. It contains the best of all methods. What are some of the advantages?

   • The most important one is that the whole family is together on their turf.

- The viewers are hosting the showing and can invite their friends.

- Interaction is much more likely when the viewers feel comfortable.

A Malaysian couple began coming to our church. They wanted to know who Jesus was. I got to know the man just enough to feel free to ask him: "Have you and your family ever watched a film called Jesus?" They had never seen it. So I said to him: "It gives a great overall picture of who Jesus is and why he came into the world. The film is based on the Bible. It is two hours long and the ideal way to watch it is half at a time. What would you think of having in your home on two successive Sunday afternoons?" He agreed. On two successive Sunday afternoons, he hosted a showing of the Jesus film. Even though I was still learning how to do this, the showing was a huge success.

Since then I have learned from others and from personal experience a lot of things about such showings. The following are four important things I need to be prepared to put in place in order to make the showing as successful as possible:

1. I need to be very clear about the fact that this film is interactive, and not just informational.

2. I need to tell people why this film is important to me.

3. I need to tell the viewers that I'm going to ask for a response.

4. I need to give them a form to fill in at the conclusion of the showing.

New Life Training Curriculum (NLTC)

NLTC is a set of training materials put together by Campus Crusade for Christ International and used around the world for training staff and volunteers both on the campuses and in the community.

The instructional component of training is absolutely essential. Without it, a sustainable and successful ministry is impossible. When such ministries are built only on practical strategies, they are difficult to sustain because they don't have a foundation to support them over the long haul.

Convictions and concern are equally essential. One without the other will produce a dysfunctional ministry. Without concern people are usually not interested in connecting with Outsiders. But concern without convictions rarely results in ministry. The instructional component of training is directed towards developing convictions. This takes time. Convictions cannot be developed in a crash course.

When convictions and concern are developed together they add up to commitment. This is the one and only thing that will make Outreach an ongoing success. This means that the primary purpose of training materials is to establish principles which will build convictions; it is not the instructional contents of the materials themselves. Some of the key principles or core values that are required for the instructional process are noted below.

Only Practitioners Teach

In some ways this was a hard decision for us to make. But because role modeling is more important than content or mode of delivery, it was and continues to be, a necessary decision. Unless people are personally involved on a regular and structured basis in Outreach, they are in no position to encourage others to get involved.

This decision also functions as an effective filter to prevent people who have lost interest in Outreach from continuing as facilitators. From beginning to end, the message must come through loud and clear that practice is more important than theory. In Outreach the experts are not those who have theological degrees or public speaking skills, but those who connect with people in whose lives God is working, share as much as possible of the Good News with them and expect God to continue his work in their lives. These connecting and sharing skills are things that any committed person can acquire.

Everyone Does All Of It

There is no one who specializes in any one part of Outreach and training. If we have a special interest in Bible studies, we naturally gravitate to them and want to skip Outreach. The specialization can go the other way as well:

people get so taken up with Outreach Visitation that they don't want to provide the basic instruction that new believers need.

All four parts of the Great Invitation are treated as equally important: the going, the preaching, the integrating into the Believers' fellowship and the training to reproduce.

Instruction Is Work-Related

The purpose of everything we do is to connect with people who need to hear the Good News. All of the instruction is directed towards that goal. Outreach belongs in a different category from personal witnessing. The former is a structured ministry while the latter is a biblical lifestyle. The former includes the latter, but the latter does not include the former. Instruction times resemble training an apprentice rather than classroom or Bible study. Hopefully participants are constantly asking: How will this help me in Outreach ministry?

No instruction is given just to provide information. Unless the teaching material is work-related, it is irrelevant. This assists the facilitators in making material relevant and practical. Everyone involved can immediately apply what they are learning because they can see for themselves how the facilitators are applying it.

Team Teaching

The primary purpose of team teaching is to train facilitators. Team teaching has many other advantages, but the greatest contribution it makes is in preparing new facilitators. As a mature facilitator works with a new person, it is relatively easy to give instruction. After the session, it is also convenient to assess the session together and talk about what went well and areas needing improvement.

One of the major benefits of team teaching is that it produces a pool of skilled people to make presentations. It also provides opportunities for everyone who so desires to be involved in this aspect of the ministry.

Skeletal Outlines

Skeletal outlines are the bare bones of the message or seminar, the rough outline that the facilitator will assist the trainees to flesh out. These outlines have their strengths and weaknesses, but in my experience the strengths outweigh the weaknesses. In many ways it is safer for facilitators to work from a complete text or a fill-in-the-blanks model, but the disadvantages are greater than the advantages.

The two major weaknesses of skeletal outlines are:

- The facilitator comes unprepared and chatters, tells stories and jokes, or launches into sermons to fill in the time.

- The trainees may leave the session with large blank spaces in their training manuals. This is a very frustrating experience for them.

Weaknesses are easy to overcome by training facilitators properly. Attempting to avoid these risks by allowing facilitators to read from an instructor's manual is counterproductive.

But the following are some of the strengths of using skeletal outlines:

- The facilitator is able to contextualize material for the group and setting. If the facilitator uses a text book or a fill-in-the-blanks approach, it is very difficult if not impossible to contextualize the material.

- The facilitator is able to have much more personal input into the training session. He or she is not as tied to the notes.

- Because there is more participation the chances of the training session becoming a monologue are considerably reduced.

- It gives the facilitator a flexibility that no other approach provides.

Assignments

The most important learning is what the trainee does on his or her own. This is why we have found assignments to be a vitally important part of the training. Each training unit has twenty study questions which participants are encouraged to answer in their own time. Each trainee is assigned a mentor who offers assistance to the trainee so that he or she is able to complete the assignments.

Assignments also provide an effective evaluation of how well the facilitator did in presenting the material. If the trainees are unable to do the assignments or get many answers wrong, it indicates that the facilitator did not do a good job.

Assignments also serve as a filtering mechanism. Those who are willing to put time and effort into doing assignments are highly committed and will be in the process for the long haul. People who 'don't have time' for assignments won't seem to be able to find time for Outreach either. In most cases their problem is not time but commitment.

Content

In the training materials we have chosen to use, there are 40 instructional units. We often spread these forty units over eight months (September to April). There are a number of reasons for this:

- It gives trainees time to participate in the training and move into practical ministry.

- It gives trainees time to do their assignments and thus assimilate the material. Those whose commitment is low to begin with have lots of time to think through the whole process and grow spiritually over a period of eight months.

- It provides a period of time for trainees to adjust their ministry responsibilities so that they can plan for greater involvement in local-church Outreach ministry.

Timetable

Almost any time frame, other than crash courses, can be used for the instruction. It has been our experience that a training weekend, i.e. two and a half hours on Friday evening and four hours on Saturday morning each month for eight months, works well.

Importance of Basic Level

Over the years one of the most important lessons we have learned is that the Basic level of the training process is the most important component. It is easy to think that Basic is just one of four levels and if people miss a bit here and there in Basic they will pick it up as they go along. Such turns out not to be the case.

Basic level is like boot camp. It separates the 'men' from the 'boys.' It has an important filtering function. People who can't make it through the requirements of Basic, especially the practical, are not going to apply themselves as they move along.

Summary of Contents

The training process is more important than the brand name of the materials. But the materials we have been using have proved to be very user-friendly and effective. They are worth taking a serious look at by anyone considering training people in Outreach. The training materials we use are New Life Training Curriculum referred to as NLTC.

NLTC is a series of forty training units developed by Campus Crusade for Christ, and used internationally in many different languages, for training people in Outreach ministry.[1] In most countries NLTC is the backbone of training given to people interested in joining Campus Crusade for Christ staff. Usually those who join CCC staff go through all four levels of NLTC twice: once before they join and again during new staff training.

Because of its heavy emphasis on practical requirements, NLTC is a unique training process: Two thirds of training time should be given to practical work and one third to instruction. Without the emphasis on practical application there is nothing unique about the materials.

In the context in which we are using NLTC our main objective is to train spiritual leaders in Outreach and disciple-making for local-church ministry. People are being trained to be bi-vocational staff of the local church rather than of Campus Crusade for Christ. For people who are more interested in personal development ('discipleship') or church-life ministry, NLTC may not be the best training materials. NLTC is strongly oriented to Outreach, based on the outreach concept of target area saturation evangelism. In fact, without target area saturation evangelism, NLTC is deprived of its unique market niche and becomes just another training program in evangelism or witnessing. In such cases, because it is being misused, it may be less effective than other materials on the market that are prepared especially for personal evangelism and witnessing.

Implementation of the practical component will vary from location to location, but structured and consistent target area saturation evangelism must be part of the process. In our case, trainees are strongly encouraged to be involved in structured outreach from a local church one evening a week, 6:30 - 8:30. The evening will vary depending upon the location.

The NLTC material (Basic, Intermediate, Advanced and Leadership) has three themes:[2]

- Spiritual formation (development). The emphasis here is on the promotion of interior spirituality. The individual's personal devotion and commitment is of top priority. It cannot be overemphasized that who we are is more important than what we do. All four levels of the training material come back to this theme repeatedly.

- Skill development, especially contacting and communicating skills. How to meet people and pass on to them what God has for them are the two main skills in which every Outreach Minister needs to excel.

- Strategy formulation and implementation. Many people have spiritual depth and communication skills, but are never able to translate them into action. This is because they have never been taught how to formulate and implement a strategy that is effective in the area in which they live and minister. If a person is interested only in sharing the Good News within his or her network of contacts, training about formulating and implementing strategy is not necessary. But for people who are committed to reaching everyone everywhere, learning how to formulate and implement strategy is vital.

These three areas of instruction need to be the major interest of everyone involved in Outreach. There is no limit to their breadth and depth. In much instructional material, the trainees can move through the material and put it on the shelf. Not so with this material. It has to stay with Outreach Ministers the rest of their lives. They will be reviewing and restating it as they teach it to others.

The combination of spiritual formation, skill development and strategy formulation and implementation is unique and highly effective. The three parts of the training create attitude, skills and knowledge. No participant is ever given the impression that he or she has acquired all there is of the three. Effective ministers will be working on improving attitudes, skills and knowledge the rest of their lives.

The instructional part of the training is divided into four parts: Basic, Intermediate, Advanced and Leadership. Each part has ten units. As long as time is given for assimilation and assignments, the training may be done in a wide variety of ways. In our case we do it once a month on a Friday evening and Saturday morning during which we cover five units. The training centre incurs a number of operating costs as it operates so trainees need to pay for that.

Overview of Contents of NLTC Basic Level

The following is a brief description of the contents of Basic NLTC, illustrating how the ten teaching units are tied together, and how each one contributes to the overall objective of the training. For the sake of convenience the material is divided into two parts called *Messages and Seminars*; the first message is designated BM#1 and so on. When we present the material we usually alternate messages and seminars; that is the reason why the messages and seminars are alternated in the brief descriptions given below. In most cases seminars are somewhat more practical in nature than the messages.

The overall objective is to train spiritual leaders in Outreach and disciple-making for local-church ministry. Right from the beginning it is important for all participants to understand that this is ministry training, not a course in personal evangelism or witnessing.

How to Experience God's Love and Forgiveness (BM#1) is foundational for all spiritual leaders. It is important for every participant to be experiencing a dynamic relationship with God. Only then are they able to be effective spiritual leaders. God's love and forgiveness is one of many topics to which the training returns again and again.

How to Present 'Knowing God Personally'[3] (BS#1) is one of the first skills that an Outreach Minister needs to develop. Printed material is one of the resources God has given and everyone needs to know how to use it effectively. In this presentation, trainees are encouraged to understand the principles underlying the material.

The person who is experiencing God's love and forgiveness wants to know *How to be filled with the Holy Spirit* (BM#2). In this context 'filled' means directed and empowered; the emphasis is on the lifestyle of the person going into ministry. When spiritual leaders are directed and empowered by the Holy Spirit, their lives and ministries will resonate a supernatural quality.

Every piece of printed material has some unique feature so we want to be able to use our resources as effectively as possible. *How to Present 'Knowing God Personally' part II* (BS#2) provides training on the key questions and responses that are part of a Gospel Presentation. Trainees will learn to ask the key questions comfortably and naturally, as well as to give appropriate answers.

The directing and empowering of the Holy Spirit is something that the Believer can experience all the time. *How to Walk in the Spirit* (BM#3) is about the Spirit-filled lifestyle. The ministry of the Holy Spirit must be experienced and demonstrated in the personal life of the worker. Everyone involved in Visitation Outreach needs to be able to say, without any mental reservations, "I am being directed and empowered by the Holy Spirit."

We not only want people to make a decision to follow Christ, i.e. to be a disciple, but we want them to grow. *How to Present 'Knowing God Personally' part III*

(BS#3) gives us some ideas of how we can do this. This unit introduces the skill of follow-up.

"Witnessing is wearisome," some would say. That's because they don't understand *How to Witness in the Spirit* (BM#4). When used incorrectly, or by an untrained person, the use of a printed booklet may seem mechanical. But when Believers understand that witnessing is part of the Spirit-filled Life, then they want to witness. When Believers understand that sharing the Good News is part of the Spirit-filled life they gain a new freedom and boldness.

We want to understand and experience the Spirit-filled Life, and we want to be able to explain this supernatural lifestyle to others. *How to Present the Spirit-Filled Life part I* (BS#4) enables the trainees to explain to others how they too can be directed and empowered by the Holy Spirit.

People then need to see that what has been presented so far is all part of a grander scheme. *How to Help Fulfill the Great Commission* (BM#5) encourages each person to lift up their eyes and see a world that needs to hear the Good News.

The Great Commission is something that everyone can be involved in right away; Jesus told his disciples to begin in Jerusalem. *Developing a Personal Ministry Strategy* (BS#5) sows some seeds that will not germinate for some considerable time. It encourages the participants to formulate a strategy that will help them begin in their Jerusalem and reach out to the world (Acts 1:8).

The two key words to keep in mind in the instructional component of training are: principles and convictions. Principles are applicable in every situation and enable those in training to take the material and apply it in whatever ministry position they find themselves. Convictions empower people to keep going through the tough times; they enable them to accept outreach as a ministry rather than an optional activity to be pursued occasionally.

CONCLUSION

The instructional component of the training process is the glue that binds everything together. Without this glue the practical component (the initial bubbling enthusiasm) dissipates and disappears.

Unless the practical component is treated as a non-negotiable essential, the Outreach potential of the instructional material becomes plans, promises and predictions: nothing gets done.

The instructional component is an absolute necessity, but the practical component is even more important.

ENDNOTES

[1] Information on the NLTC materials, Basic, Intermediate, Advanced and Leadership are available from: Campus Crusade for Christ. http://www.crusade. org. Phone (604) 514-2000. Box 300 Stn A, Vancouver, BC, V6C 2X3

[2] These three themes express in different language the three concepts of any and all effective education: attitude (spiritual formation), skills (abilities) and knowledge (strategy formulation and implementation).

[3] Would You Like to Know God Personally? is an update of The Four Spiritual Laws. In conversation it is abbreviated to KGP. It is available in bulk from Campus Crusade for Christ; see contact addresses in note 1 above.

THE PHILIPPINE MISSIONS ASSOCIATION (PMA) TENTMAKING AGENDA: RAISING AN ARMY OF OUTSTANDING FILIPINO WITNESSES

Robert Ferdinand K. Lopez

INTRODUCTION

T entmaking missions mobilization is one of the flagship ministries of the Philippine Missions Association (PMA). Through the Philippine Council of Evangelical Churches (PCEC), the PMA is mandated with the task of mobilizing the Filipino Church to active and effective involvement in cross-cultural missions. The goal of the PCEC and PMA is to have 200,000 missionaries by 2010 which it aims to achieve through its Tentmaking Missions first in Asia and all over the world.

BACKGROUND

PMA came into existence in 1983, at about the same time the rate of deployment of Filipinos abroad as contract workers started to grow by leaps and bounds. This continuing trend led to the popular acronym OCWs to refer to the Filipino overseas contract workers abroad. At that time, the term used in mission circles for "Tentmaking" was bi-vocational missions. It was regarded as inferior to traditional missions. For many, missions meant sending donor-supported missionaries whose specific mandate was to share the Good News of salvation to the "heathen." However, the fact that more than 80%

of the world's population live in countries that do not issue missionary visas, altered the sole use of traditional global missions strategy. The global reality that Christian churches could no longer send traditional missionaries to reach a majority of the world's population, gave the notion of tentmaking a more serious consideration and practical approach for global Missions.

This reality has helped mission executives and church leaders realize the strategic value of Tentmaking as a platform for access to these countries. As a result, new western organizations such as Tentmakers International Exchange and Global Opportunities evolved, with a focus on encouraging primarily the Western church to adopt Tentmaking as part of the missions program of churches and denominations. New books on Tentmaking found their way into Christian bookstores and mission libraries.

TENTMAKING IN THE WESTERN CHURCH

Tentmaking works on the premise that the 'tentmaker missionary" gains entry into a country by securing a work visa within his/her area of occupational or professional expertise. These work contracts, however, are often in third world and developing countries, which are able only to offer low compensation packages and sub-standard working conditions, unlike that of the West.

For many Western tentmakers, especially those who are married and have families, additional funds will have to be raised to cover living expenses in the mission field. In some instances, these professionals will work for a number of years in their own countries in order to work and live in the mission field for a couple of years without having to be dependent on the income they generate as tentmakers. When their funds are spent, they return home and sometimes repeat the process.

Though their sacrifices are commendable, this practice also raises questions from the local nationals. It is difficult for them to understand why a Westerner would want to work in their country under such substandard conditions. Hence, this leads to the nationals suspicious of the Westerners' motives for coming to work in their country.

THE SCATTERING OF FILIPINOS

As opposed to the Western situation, many Filipino Christians are forced to seek employment abroad because job opportunities are either scarce or not attractive in the Philippines. Oftentimes, the income offered Filipinos abroad would be far more substantial than what they would be making back home. However, their income is not sufficient for family status under their work visas.

Most Filipinos continue to accept these overseas contracts and with resilience, endure the long separation from their families. Today, almost a tenth of the Philippine population work abroad either as immigrants or OCWs. This staggering figure translates to nearly 8 million Filipinos.

Divinely Dispersed

The steady deterioration of the Philippine economy has led to an increasing number of Filipinos seeking greener pastures. Among them are evangelical Christians. In the same manner that the believers in Jerusalem dispersed to Judea and Samaria to escape the persecution that broke out against the Church (Acts 8:1), Filipino Christians have been fleeing the economic oppression in the Philippines. Many of the countries where these believers find work are considered "graveyards" of missions. Some of these do not even have an indigenous church movement.

It is estimated that hundreds of thousands of Filipino believers have been positioned by God in some of the most spiritually needy places in the world where traditional missionaries have been barred from entering. It is believed that a majority of them come together regularly as a Filipino church, fellowship or bible study group in the host country. Some of them are actively engaged in witnessing. We thank God that thousands of Filipino believers today have come to know the Lord while serving as OFWs through the witness of their Filipino Christian co-workers. Sadly, their intentional witnessing efforts are with Filipinos.

Two Developments

It has been noted that most of the Filipino diaspora churches are independent churches and do not necessarily have denominational affiliations. This has led to two developments.

First, some of these diaspora churches began "reverse-church planting" when members of their congregations started Bible studies upon returning home. These Bible study groups sometimes grow to small fellowships and, rather than be affiliated with local churches in their area, become daughter churches of the diaspora church. Later on, the "mother church" status is transferred from the OFWs church to their largest congregation in the Philippines when their key church leader goes home "for good" to provide leadership to the growing number of congregations. The OFWs church then becomes considered as their missions church. Some small but prominent denominations in the Philippines such as Day by Day Christian Fellowship and the Lord Reigns Ministries are examples of this.

The second development is that some OFWs who have served in a pastoral capacity abroad find themselves "dislocated" from ministry upon their return to the Philippines if their OFWs church does not have an organized congregation in their hometown. Oftentimes, their lack of theological training or non-recognition of their ministry record abroad by some local church leaders in their hometown have led to their being "sidelined" or being "under-utilized" in the local church.

It is with this as a backdrop that PMA has began formulating a program that will empower Filipino churches both in the Philippines and abroad to become launching pads of the gospel to the *Unreached* and *Unevangelized*.

MOBILIZING THE FILIPINO CHURCH

The word "missions" is often misunderstood among Filipino church leaders as doing church planting in another province or in some remote part of the country. This is probably due to the usage of the word by American and European missionaries more than half a century ago. Missions is indeed doing church planting in the Philippines since it was a cross-cultural for them. Also, the common mindset of missionaries then was missions had to be directed to the economically weaker, remote or "backward" communities. It is for this reason that most of the early work of missionaries was done in the hinter-lands among tribal peoples. This is true not only in the Philippines but in other parts of Asia, Africa and South America. Often, this work consisted of providing material assistance along with the preaching of the gospel. This has become for many Filipino church leaders, particularly in the rural areas, the definition or model of engagement in missions.

With this definition, missions has been perceived as difficult and unnec-essary since it represents a drain in the human and material resources of the often financially-strapped local church. A regular pastor's income, though often augmented by the kind-hearted support of relatives, is barely enough to cover for one's family's basic needs. There is unspoken fear that if their church begins to financially support missions work, there will be even less given to the pastor or lesser funds available for other church programs.

Furthermore, in recent years the Church has been stirred up by books and seminars on church growth through membership addition. The idea of sending out and supporting their best-trained church workers to become missionaries has become all the more less appealing and is sometimes viewed as counter-productive to their programs.

Mobilizing the Leaders

PMA, as a network of mission agencies and missions-oriented churches, has declared its goal to help raise up 200,000 Outstanding Filipino Witnesses (OFWs) by the year 2010. This entails the massive mobilization of churches inside and outside the Philippines. We are currently focusing our mobiliza-tion efforts on the leadership of denominations, local churches and ministe-rial fellowships since they are the prime movers and influencers. They also are the ones who may block or discourage their church members from engaging in Tentmaking missions if they feel it threatens their church programs.

The Tentmaking strategy is being presented to these leaders as the most viable platform for Filipino churches to fully engage in the Great Commis-sion. PMA, through its Tentmaking mobilization network, is reaching out to pastors through leadership seminars and consultations to plant vision and help address the misconceptions stated earlier. They are encouraged to mobilize their own churches and help prepare their members who are planning to work abroad to be witnesses for the global marketplace. PCEC, under the able leadership of Bishop Efraim Tendero, is helping clear the way for PMA to meet with the leadership of denominations and prominent local churches to present the Tentmaking Agenda.

One premium for the church to send out tentmakers is in the area of finances. Unlike supporting career missionaries, commissioning and caring for their own tentmakers will not be a burden on the church's coffers since the latter are gainfully employed. It is highly probable that the church's income, on the contrary, will increase because of the larger tithes and offerings coming from the tentmakers and their families.

Vision casting has not been limited to churches in the Philippines. Filipino pastors and lay workers serving as OFWs in Asia and the Middle East have also been challenged to use their occupations as platforms for cross-cultural ministry. Diaspora churches in Hong Kong, Japan, Malaysia and in the Arabian Peninsula have been exhorted to bring their witness beyond the Filipino community in their host country and reach out to locals and other non-Filipino expatriate workers. The advantage of mobilizing the diaspora churches is that they are already established in the mission field. Every member of the church has the potential of becoming an effective tentmaker-missionary if motivated and properly trained.

PMA has also began sounding a trumpet call among Christian businessmen to consider setting up businesses that will facilitate the deployment of Filipino believers as OFWs. This can happen by setting up or operating overseas manpower recruitment agencies and sourcing for job orders in countries that need to be impacted with the Christian message. Another option will be to become investors in other countries and hire qualified Filipino Christians.

Natural Evangelists

Almost all of the OFW brethren are not considered tentmakers because their reason for going abroad is primarily financial. Most of them did not see their relocation to be an expansion of witnessing opportunities. Therefore, they did not seek to be equipped for their new arena of ministry and have left without any training in cross-cultural witnessing and discipleship.

By the grace of God, Filipinos are friendly and hospitable and these traits cause others to be attracted to us. This is very evident when Filipinos are gathered in community such as in a church service or a bible study. It may be for this reason that Filipinos are said to be natural evangelists. We try to make our guests as welcome and as comfortable as possible. Because of this, non-Filipinos would openly express their appreciation of our friendship and genuine care.

It is not, therefore, surprising to find non-Filipinos in our diaspora churches. On the many different occasions I have been in a diaspora church service, I have noticed the presence of other Asians, Africans and even Caucasians. Like Filipinos, they are expatriate workers. Admittedly, most of them have been believers prior to their attendance in these Christian services. They come out of a need for spiritual nurturing and fellowship. But there are those who have come to know the Lord Jesus Christ through Filipinos. Some just walked into a church service out of curiosity. Others came because they were invited by a Filipino co-worker or neighbor. Still others came because their Filipino spouse is a believer. Once in a while, you will find non-Filipinos among those who respond to an altar call.

But not everyone returns and becomes a committed member of the congregation. As so often is the case, church visitors do not get followed-up. Attendance of new believers is inconsistent. Many of them never get to be discipled. Truly, the fruits of purposeful witness often do not last long. This brings us to the second element of the PMA tentmaker mobilization program.

Equipping an Army

Short and practical Tentmaking training programs have been developed by various Philippine-based missions training organizations to provide practical missions education for the local church, the pastor and the prospective tentmaker. These programs are in modular format to allow flexibility of time for both trainers and trainees. Tentmaker seminars conducted by PMA in partnership with other missions training agencies for denominations and ministerial fellowships are often tailored to fit the type of audience and the time constraints of the participants. In such cases, follow-up seminars are scheduled to cover the other important topics that have not been taken.

The Tentmaking curriculum is designed to help the candidate tentmaker to handle the peculiarities of living, working and ministering as an OFW. The objective of the training program is to help tentmakers nurture Christ-like character, develop ministry and church planting skills, sensitively witness to members of specific religious blocks, cope with cross-cultural and work-related stress and manage finances properly.

In educating the local church, PMA conducts a seminar that provides guidelines in how to set up an "OFW Desk" in their church to effectively process and prepare their prospective tentmaker for overseas deployment and ministry. It also gives pointers on how to provide care and affirmation of the OFWs family members who will have to stay behind.

These training programs are gradually being exported to diaspora churches. A network of missions trainers are being challenged to make themselves available for short-term trips to different parts of the world to help equip the expatriate Filipino Christians. The task is to train OFW pastors and their leaders to be trainers themselves and make the training modules reproducible and transferable in order to equip as many as possible in the shortest time and at the least expense. Those who get trained in the Philippines prior to their deployment as OFWs will be able to train others when they get integrated into a diaspora church.

PMA also encourages local churches to develop a strong discipleship and church planting program. It is recognized that it is the responsibility of the local church to provide a strong biblical and theological foundation for their members. Theological courses and ministry skills-enhancement programs are constantly being promoted to pastors to help them raise up strong and passionate disciples. Discipleship at home is key to making disciple-makers of the nations.

BUILDING A GLOBAL DATABASE

Lofty as it may appear, the goal of raising 200,000 tentmaker missionaries is doable. Statistics from the Philippine Overseas Employment Administration and demographic estimates extrapolated from year 2000 census figures all point to this to be well within the realm of possibility. But in order to track the progress of achieving this goal, a global database of Filipino Christian ministries and tentmakers must be set up and professionally managed. It is imperative that we take stock of what has been and is being done by Filipino churches all over the world in terms of cross-cultural witnessing. There is also a need to have a database of Christian professionals and highly-skilled workers who are considering to serve as tentmaker-missionaries. Oftentimes, there is difficulty matching job openings with the occupationally qualified individuals since no database of Christians professionals exist.

PMA has began networking with Christian research groups, denominations, churches and mission agencies, as well as Filipino church networks outside the Philippines such as the Filipino International Network (FIN) to help create the database. There is an impression that almost all local churches in the country would have a member or a relative of a member who has gone overseas either as an OFW or an immigrant. The FIN will play a central role in helping facilitate the global information exchange network to become a reality. The database itself will become the property of the global Filipino church although it is managed by PMA. Regular reports will be made to the PCEC, FIN, denominations and other partners in the project.

The Challenges Faced

With over 51,000 local congregations in the country according to the DAWN survey conducted last 2000, this research will be a Herculean task. It will be nothing less than a census. The resources required will be stratospheric. However, the gathering of information will be a partnership effort and will be an ongoing work with no fixed deadline. This will be done simultaneously with the mobilization of churches and denominations. As earlier mentioned, the endorsement of PCEC is going a long way in getting denominations and churches to participate in this database management project.

Furthermore, due to the fluidity of OFWs, keeping the database updated will be even more challenging. Careful management of data will be crucial for the information to be credible.

There are three options for OFWs when their employment contract has run its course, which in most cases are either two or three years. The first is contract renewal, if their services are still desired by their former employer. Professionals like engineers, nurses, accountants, and programmers, more often than not, get their contracts renewed repeatedly. However, it is but natural for some to seek better income opportunities with other employers. This may sometimes entail returning to the Philippines for a while or landing a job in another country. The last option is to re-integrate into Philippine society in the least difficult way. This is often the least desired choice that OFWs are forced to take when either job alternatives elude them or the pressure of family concerns bring them back home. This condition of multiple scenarios presents the greater challenge in managing the database. It will take a major commitment on the part of all parties providing information to keep this global database current. A secure system of global communication will be set up with PMA serving as the hub for exchange of information as well as regular updates received.

Given the confidential nature of the information stored, this database will not be connected to the internet and neither will it be accessible through local area networks to prevent computer hackers from sabotaging it.

Strategic Global Linkage

Keeping accurate records is not only meant to keep track of our progress in achieving the goal of empowering 200,000 Filipino believers to be Outstanding Filipino Witnesses. More significantly, it will help link the Filipino churches around the world with motherland churches and denominations. It will help address the lack of recognition and affirmation of pastors and lay leaders of OFWs churches among their peers in the Philippines. Hopefully, it will also alleviate the concern of some OFWs churches that they are only being valued because of their financial resources.

But what I consider the most important advantages of this linkage are in the areas of member care, accountability and strategy.

The Filipino diaspora churches serve the families of OFWs by providing a place for spiritual nourishment, care and affirmation by their loved ones.

These brethren gather out of a common need for fellowship and encourage-ment that is further aggravated by their separation from their families and friends. They undergo bigger struggles with lust and covetousness because of the dangerous mix of loneliness and strong purchasing power. It is in this arena that we recognize the incalculable value of the Filipino diaspora churches as they, by the grace of God, help keep the believer stay on course.

But then, as I had mentioned in the earlier part of this chapter, no rela-tionships exist between our churches and those in the diaspora. We suspect that almost all motherland local churches subconsciously think that their responsibility of oversight and care for their members cease or cannot be done practically once the latter leave the country. It is rare that OFW brethren are formally recognized and commissioned as tentmakers by their local church. Most of the time, no effort is made on part of the leadership of the local church to arrange for their OFW members to be received by another Chris-tian organization or diaspora church in the country where they will be living and working for the next couple of years. These are wasted opportunities since churches on both sides stand to benefit by connecting with one another. Member care and accountability concerns of the OFWs' mother church are immediately addressed when the diaspora church formally acknowledges her responsibility of pastoral oversight of the OFWs. The receiving church gets an additional worker that they did not have to disciple and train. Both churches can share on the tithes and offerings of the tentmaker-OFWs over whom they are jointly responsible spiritually.

Strategic Battlefield Placement

These diaspora churches are also the frontliners in the spiritual battlefield. As in the natural realm, the overall effectiveness of the frontline combat units is determined by their connectedness to their mother units. By communi-cating essential information about their condition and situation, the enemy's troop strength and position, plus other vital information to the mother unit, the frontline units can provide guidance so that the right personnel, equip-ment and supplies may be deployed in a manner that will have the greatest chance of victory.

In the same vein, when diaspora churches are linked to motherland churches, there will be more effective ministry in the frontiers. When motherland churches send their tentmaker-OFWs to their diaspora counterparts, they get to participate in the kingdom work of the latter. They are the reinforcements that are always needed in the field. They may help in the evangelization and discipleship of our countrymen. Better still, they may influence the diaspora church to become seriously involved in cross-cultural outreach.

When a partnership between motherland and diaspora churches is established globally, this may be the most formidable force ever assembled against the strongholds of darkness all over the world.

OUR DECLARATION

PMA declares its dependence on the Holy Spirit for guidance and empowerment. We are not daunted by the dimensions of implementation because we put our trust in God's ability. We seek only that our Heavenly Father and our Lord Jesus Christ be glorified in the outworking of these plans. It is very clear to us that success is the product of God's sovereignty and grace. It is such a privilege to partake, with the rest of the Universal Body of Christ, in preparing the world for the grandest homecoming of all time – the RETURN OF THE KING OF KINGS!

EVANGELISM STRATEGIES IN THE DRAGON ARENA

Rodrigo C. Felomino, Jr.

INTRODUCTION

I n 1978, the first Filipino Protestant Church was planted in Hong Kong. It is estimated that there are now more than 100 Filipino churches – this includes the Roman Catholics and other non-Protestant churches. When the Church growth movement started in 1955, the focus was centered on specific and limited countries. In the middle '60s until the late '70s, church growth experts began to assess and evaluate growth of churches in many countries but not much study has been done on churches planted by Filipinos for the Filipinos in other countries including Hong Kong.

Hong Kong is now often referred to as "Asia's world City". With all the modern sophistication of the 21st Century, Hong Kong is enriched by the colorful traditions of its ancient Chinese Culture and the conglomerate presence of its Western and European and Asian neighbors. As a financial hub of Asia and the world, Hong Kong is considered as one of those developing city that had entered the World's top 10 economies – proving its economic strengths.

Combined with the network of financial offices and headquarter and its proximity to the "largest" prospect of clients – the Mainland China, business is not just booming but also expanding. Considering the favorable working conditions in Hong Kong and its high wages and liberal visa policy, it has attracted nationals from some 170 countries who can visit visa free for periods varying from seven days to six months. It was reported that in the year

2000, passenger arrivals and departures totaled 144 million. Hong Kong is considered to have one of the lowest unemployment problems in Asia. With most of the people working, demand for domestic helps becomes a necessity – an opportunity that allowed Filipinos, Indonesians, Thais and other Asian neighbors to come as domestic helpers. The present status of Hong Kong is shaped by its location and culture. It has a good record in terms of business opportunities and investments. The Hong Kong 2002 Information Services Department of Hong Kong SAR Government gives a summary as to why Hong Kong is a city of opportunity:

In view of such great global market and business opportunities, work and money defines the lifestyle of many Hong Kong people. For many husbands and wives who are working someone has to take care of the children and or old parents (common in many Chinese homes). This is where many of the foreign domestic helpers come in. According to Hong Kong laws, Foreign Domestic Helpers (FDH) "may be admitted subject to the conditions that they have relevant experience, that their employers are bona fide Hong Kong residents who are prepared to offer reasonable terms of employment including suitable accommodation and wages not lower than a minimum level set by the government, and that the employers are willing to provide for the maintenance of the helpers in Hong Kong as well as to meet the costs of repatriation of the helpers to their country of origin".

With the increase of more available jobs and strong economic growth, demand for foreign domestic helpers has increased over the past two decades. By the end of 2002, there were 237,104 of such helpers in Hong Kong, an increase of 0.78% compared with the number of 235,274 in 2001. A good percentage of the foreign workers are from the Philippines. As of last report by the Philippine Consulate, there are more than 143,000 registered Filipino domestic helpers accredited by the Philippine Overseas Employment Administration (POEA), working in Hong Kong.

RELIGIOUS FREEDOM IN HONG KONG

Under the "One Country, Two Systems," religious freedom is one of the fundamental rights enjoyed by Hong Kong residents; the Basic Law and some relevant legislation protect it. Thus, the exercise of one's faith is freely expressed in Hong Kong. As early as 1841, the presence of a Protestant community was already recorded. In the latest report, it has been estimated that there are more than 500,000 Christians in Hong Kong. About 51% of which are Protestants and 49% are Catholics. The evangelistic work of churches and missionaries resulted to the establishment of independent churches since the 1970s – this includes Protestants and Roman Catholics.

Here's a recent report on the Protestant Christians living in Hong Kong:

> "About 300,000 Protestant Christians live in Hong Kong. The Protestant Church is made up of over 1,300 congregations in more than 50 denominations with many independent churches. The Baptists form the largest denomination, followed by the Lutherans. Other major denominations are Adventist, Anglican, Christian and Missionary Alliance, Church of Christ in China (representing the Presbyterian and Congregational traditions), Methodist, Pentecostal and Salvation Army. With their emphasis on youth work, many congregations have a high proportion of young people."

It is in the context of this religious freedom that many denominations and local churches found a rich ground for church planting. It is also due to this religious freedom that no "persecutions" have been experienced by the Filipino churches as compared to those in their counterpart in the Creative Access Nations (CAN).

FILIPINOS IN HONG KONG

Although there is no clear record as to when the first Filipinos came to Hong Kong as domestic helpers, it was in the late 1960s that a good number of women were able to find job as "amahs". In the middle of 1970, the number of domestic helpers grew steadily that it also became the decade where many denominations in the Philippine started sending missionary workers to Hong Kong. The exact number could not be accurately established because of the many undocumented or even false documents used by some of these workers. In Hong Kong, a few cases of overstaying workers have been reported. From as high as 200,000(estimate) in 1995 to 1996, Filipino domestic helpers are now down to just more than 126,500 (The Sun report, March 2004). Despite the decrease in numbers, the Filipinos are still considered the largest expatriate community in Hong Kong. Their presence is so strong that during holidays and Sundays, "Central belongs to them." In fact, because of the great number, two blocks of the road in Central are closed to traffic, and someone even commented, "When the Filipinos are out on Sundays or Holidays, the 'rich and the powerful' get out of Central because it belongs to the Filipinos."

Hong Kong has one of the best protective mechanisms for foreign workers, yet there are still many cases of abuses being reported. Unlike European and North American countries, most Asian countries do not grant residency status or citizenship to most of their foreign workers. The government of Hong Kong does not allow domestic helpers to work outside that which is stipulated in their contract. Contract period is good for two years and unless the employer signs for the extension of the contract, no domestic helper is allowed to find another employer until the two year contract has been completed. Termination of contracts is allowed under the law with certain conditions. Domestic helpers need to go home first to their country of origin until a new working visa is granted by the Hong Kong government. The last few years have been difficult in Hong Kong due to the economic downturn — less job opportunities, businesses folding up, slumping costs of properties and a strong competition from Mainland China.

Yet, in the midst of these difficulties and uncertainties, the Filipinos are as pliant as ever — thriving and growing stronger in their resolved to move on in establishing God's kingdom by putting up churches and fellowship groups in Hong Kong.

RESULT OF THE SURVEY CONDUCTED AMONG THE FILIPINO PROTESTANT CHURCHES

a. Number of churches: 60 (a few other smaller churches/groups have yet to be identified and classified)

b. Number of Services: 145-150 services (this includes weekday Fellowship groups)

c. Number of Adherents: 25,000 plus or minus

d. Status of Filipino Churches :

1. Chinese Church Sponsorship: 15 churches

2. International Church Sponsorship: 10 churches

3. Philippine Mission Affiliated: 20 churches

4. Independent (not in the above categories): 15 churches

FILIPINO CHURCHES IN HONG KONG

The growth of the Filipino churches in Hong Kong may be considered exceptional and phenomenal. It seems that the same entrepreneurial attitude of the local people of Hong Kong is also evident among the Filipinos who are also doing ministry works and planting churches. Although there is an appearance of "division," among denominations, it cannot be denied that the presence of these churches is an indication of good harvest. The responsiveness and openness of the Filipinos in Hong Kong and the effectiveness of various denominations in doing evangelism contributed to the establishment and growth of churches.

The majority of the Filipino churches were established by various denominations from the Philippines following up their own people in Hong Kong. This is true in most of the mainline denominations. Many of the Independent churches come from the Charismatic and Pentecostal traditions. And since many are hardly bound by organizational "red tapes" they are able to establish their fellowships faster than mainline churches.

There are two officially organized Ministerial Fellowships in Hong Kong: The Filipino Ministerial Fellowship and the Association of Filipino Ministers. A group of Filipino Baptist churches also has a strong ministry among the Filipinos living in Hong Kong. The Filipino Ministerial Fellowship as an organization provides an avenue for these fellowships to be united.

Based on statistics, there will probably be more than 60 Protestant churches in Hong Kong, although most of the newly established churches were just in the last 10 years; and Filipino churches have an estimated membership of at least 25,000.

UNIQUE CHALLENGES AND OPPORTUNITIES

• The Hong Kong government law allows one day off each week for domestic helpers, providing them time for rest, reconnecting with loved ones and friends, and the freedom to exercise their religious beliefs. This gives opportunity for most churches to reach out and conduct evangelistic events and hold worship services for their members. But it is also in this context that other forces compete for the attention of many of the Filipino domestic helpers, (i.e., civic and hometown organizational meetings, sports, business and part-time jobs, etc. – although not allowed by HK labor laws).

• Most of the Filipino churches are self-supporting but need to find a place for their worship and fellowship. Due to the high cost of rents, many of these churches have difficulty supporting full-time workers. At least one fourth of these churches are led by "tentmakers" (domestic helpers or professionals who are leaders of their congregations). Most of the Filipino churches rent flats for their meetings. It sometimes serves as a place of refuge for terminated OFWs.

• Members of Filipino churches are mostly women. It is not unusual to see churches with no male members – except may be the pastor. Leadership is then placed under the care of the women including eldership (even for denominations who normally, do not appoint women elders in the Philippines).

• By law, a domestic helper is allowed to work outside the provision stipulated in the contract. It has been observed that in most of the Filipino churches, more than half of the people are professionals or college graduates. Many are from the teaching profession. Because of this many Chinese employers are interested in hiring Filipino domestic helpers since they can also be "tutors" of their children.

• Five years ago, there were about 175,000 to 180,000 Filipinos in Hong Kong. This year, however, it has gone down to just around 130,000. This may be attributed to the influx of Indonesian and Thai helpers who are willing to receive lower monthly wages than what is required by law. The Indonesians, for example, doubled their number the last five years.

• Hong Kong has one of the best transportation and communication systems in Asia and maybe in the world. It is quicker to move from place to place either by trains, buses, and ferries. Telephones are so accessible that one will never be lost in the "jungle city" of Hong Kong. This aids the churches in ministering to their members even to the far-flung areas of Hong Kong.

• Local Chinese churches initiatives may also have contributed to the growth of the Filipino churches. A few of these Chinese churches have sponsored and supported work among the Filipinos by providing them free space for their fellowship; a few have even provided monthly support for Filipino church workers. The same is true with some international churches who have invited Filipino pastors from the Philippines to come to Hong Kong so they can minister to their fellowmen abroad.

• Filipino pastors from the Philippines can come to Hong Kong even without local sponsors. An automatic free 14-day visa status is granted to anyone who comes to Hong Kong. A few of these churches have started their ministry in Hong Kong using this strategy. One can also apply for a three-month visa allowing longer time for ministry and establishing of fellowship groups. Another possible option is to come and work as a "tentmaker." We have a few churches that fall under this category.

• Because of the strategic location of Hong Kong, Christian ministry opportunities abound. Bible scholars and experienced ministry practitioners from North America and Europe have regularly stopped in Hong Kong and conducted various seminars and conferences without any restrictions from the government. This has also benefited Filipino pastors and churches. For example, in December 2003, Dr. Enoch Wan graciously accepted the invitation of the Filipino Ministerial Fellowship to conduct a seminar in Hong Kong on the topic: "Understanding the Chinese People from a Pastoral, Anthropological and Personal Experience." This was our first attempt to help Filipino workers understand the Chinese people better. The seminar was attended by 34 pastors and church leaders. The other goal was for Filipino pastors to understand the mindset of Chinese in Hong Kong so they can help their members understand their employers. In previous years, through FIN initiatives, we have invited speakers and lecturers from the Philippines to conduct seminars for leaders in the area of leadership and counseling.

Specific And Effective Strategies

The Filipino churches are creative and resourceful in their evangelism strategies.

Hope in Crisis Ministry

In Hong Kong there is no such thing as "security of tenure" among domestic helpers. They can be terminated any time. Some of them find it hard to adjust for different reasons, and so breaking of contracts is a regular occurrence. In most cases, many of them have no place to go hence a need for shelter. This is where termination centers come in. Most Filipino churches have flats (homes of their workers) but many times serve as "shelters" for terminated OFWs.

A good number of churches have seen the potential impact of this to minister and a good number have rented flats exclusively to use as "Home of Refuge." Churches like Alliance Churches ("the Filipino Center"), Evangelical Community Church (the "Oasis"), Free Believers in Christ ("Haven of Rest"), Methodist English Speaking Congregation (Bethune House) and a few other groups seized that oportunity and have rented flats for that pupose. These "houses of refuge" became a place where many Filipinos come to know the Lord. They provide food for the body and refreshment for the soul. In fact, many churches that operate using this strategy have reported an increase in their membership.

Many Filipino domestic helpers involved in labor cases get support from pastors and church ministers who accompany them in court hearings and provide them with moral, emotional and spiritual support.

Filipino workers' greatest struggle is not just the fear of losing their job or being terminated; many of them have left family, husband, children and parents and this has created a lot of emotional and psychological problems. This is where the support of our churches and the ministry of our pastors come in.

Airport Reception Ministry

It is estimated that around 70 to 100 Filipinos arrive in Hong Kong International Airport in any given day, many of them for the first time.

While some are excited, others are apprehensive and scared because of reported bad experiences of other domestic helpers. They do not know anyone and would be meeting either their agent or their employers for the first time. This is where a good ministry begins. The strategy of the pastor is to meet them at the airport and hand them a "calling card" (although once the employment agency finds this out, they confiscate the card) and phone cards (to call) home. This allows them to call back home and inform their families that they have arrived safely in Hong Kong.

A clear system is yet to be formulated about this particular strategy. Some pastors have combined their resources and came up with just one card, that include their names, the names of their churches and telephone numbers. This combined effort is being tested.

Use of the Airwaves

In a survey done by a local radio station, results revealed that 54% of Filipinos in Hong Kong listen to a commercial Filipino radio station (1040 A.M. Band). This inspired a number of pastors to join forces in sponsoring Christian programs to reach out through radio. In May this year, four Filipino churches have combined their resources and began broadcasting to cater to a good number of Filipino listeners. One program is even broadcast in the Ilocano dialect since a good number of Filipinos in Hong Kong speak the language.

CHURCH PLANTING PROGRAM IN HONG KONG

The following strategies have been employed by Filipinos who have planted churches in Hong Kong:

• Denominations from the Philippines follow-up their members who are working in Hong Kong. A good number of denominations and local churches have done this.

• "Short-term missions." Local churches and denominations send their pastors on short-term missions trips until a viable congregation is organized, after which a permanent worker is sent to pastor the group.

• "Divine Appointments." There have been pastors who went on their own and tried to see whether the Lord has open doors for them. A few churches have been organized as a result of this.

• International congregations with Filipino members inviting Filipino pastors to become part of the ministry. Most of the international congregations have Filipino fellowships with corresponding Filipino workers.

• Local Chinese churches initiating and supporting the work. One good example is Fairview Park Alliance Church. As the story goes, a storm hit Hong Kong and a number of Filipinos were caught in the rain and could not find a place to hide. The Chinese ministers invited them inside the church for shelter. Later, they started sharing the gospel to them, and soon a Filipino fellowship was born.

CHURCH PLANTING IN REVERSE

One of the most exciting things about what God among doing in the Filipino churches in Hong Kong is that He turned it into a 360-degree mission—"missions in reverse." The former "mission field" is now becoming a strong supporter of church planting in the Philippines. Almost all the big Filipino churches in Hong Kong are doing church planting in the Philippines. They do this by providing monthly support for their chosen church planters, either attached to their denomination or directly under their supervision. The Alliance Filipino Fellowship is now supporting six church planters in the Philippines. They do not only provide monthly support but also assist in the purchase of a piece of land and the construction of the building. According to policy, church planting can only be started in places where at least five of the present or former members of the Fellowship in Hong Kong are residents of the area. (See Appendix).

FILIPINO CHRISTIAN CHURCHES AT THE "DOORSTEP"

While the majority of the Filipino churches are independent; a good number of churches are either attached to an international church or under the umbrella of a Chinese church. At least 14 churches are considered to be directly under the Chinese ministries. This includes support of the worker, place of venue and supervision by a Chinese coordinator. Most Filipino churches have not done intentional effort to reach out to the Chinese or even to other nationalities. One Filipino church that stands out is "His Sanctuary Services." They have catered to both Indonesians at one time and now to the Sri Lankans. In fact, they have a regular attendance of at least 65 people during their Sunday services.

The biggest prospect though is Mainland China. So far, only a few churches have done intentional ministry in China. The IXTHUS have sent some of their workers to China to reach the Chinese by teaching English in schools. The Alliance denomination has a couple and three single ladies working as tent-makers in China.

Filipino churches are also in the doorstep of other Asian countries. A few churches have now reached out to Macau: Free Believers, Grace of Jesus Fellowship, Jesus is Lord Church, His Sanctuary, and Revival Christian Church. They are primarily reaching out to the Filipinos but are hopeful that they can have ministries to the people of Macau as well. In Taiwan, the following have planted churches: Free Believers and Jesus is Lord. The Alliance Group in Hong Kong is now making an initial step to reach out to Taiwan, Korea and Japan.

CONCLUSION

The potential of 25,000 Filipino Christians have not been fully tapped. For one, the "each to his own" attitude still prevails. It is a little difficult to have a concerted effort in a larger scale. In fact, the FMF is primarily just the association of pastors and workers but not of churches. It seems that pastors are amenable to come together but doubly hard for churches to come together.

What can be done to tap the potential of such a large group of believers for worldwide outreach? The answer is obvious – unity and concerted effort; but how to implement them is still a question that remains unanswered. The

Filipino Ministerial Fellowship in their February meeting had approved to extend an invitation to the FIN leadership to host a global conference in Hong Kong. This would create a larger effect—a united ownership that "we are bigger and greater than we think." There is much that we can do if we join hands in partnership and work together; not divided by denominations or human limitations but as a united body of Christ.

APPENDIX

Kowloon Tong International Congregation
Alliance Filipino Fellowship
Church Planters Support

In obedience to the Lord's command to "make disciples of all people groups," the AFF has committed itself to work with CAMACOP in her church-planting program in the Philippines. The AFF will provide monthly salary support to CAMACOP – approved church planter for a period of seven years according to the following schedule:

Year 1 to Year 3: 6,000 pesos per month (approximately HK$870.00/mo.)
Year 4 to Year 5: 4,500 pesos per month
Year 6: 3,000 pesos per month
Year 7: 1,500 pesos per month

Some Guidelines for the Church Planting Projects:

1. It must be approved by the CAMACOP as a viable project after surveys have been made.

2. The CAMACOP must be willing to provide church planters for the place.

3. The CAMACOP must be willing to give counterpart support in addition to what the AFF will provide (this may come in the form of house rentals, transportation expenses and ministry expenses of the church planter).

4. The church will be encouraged to submit a quarterly ministry report to the CAMACOP and the AFF.

5. Additional requests of support for special needs by the AFF-supported church planters will be treated on a case-to-case basis; (i.e., chairs, hymnals, musical instruments, evangelistic crusades, etc.), but the amount would not exceed P5,000 per church, per year. This will be approved when funds are available.

6. AFF-supported church planters who will have big projects like buying of church property or construction of building will be considered depending on the availability of funds. Such projects must be approved by the CAMACOP.

7. Request for assistance from other church planting areas outside the AFF-supported church planters will only be considered if endorsed by the CAMACOP and that aid will only be considered if funds are available. One time assistance of not more than HK$1,000 per church will be granted. Only three churches can avail of this assistance per year.

A CASE STUDY: MOBILIZING "CANADIAN-PINOYS"

Charlie H. Mance

—————

INTRODUCTION

To say that Canada is a nation of immigrants would be an understatement. According to Statistics Canada, the country has absorbed 13.4 million immigrants over the last 100 years with the highest intake taking place in the nineties. (http://www12.statcan.ca/english/census01/products/analytic/companion/etoimm/canada.cfm) (accessed on March 2, 2004)). Over the span of 20 years—from 1970 to 1990—2.7 million immigrants entered the country (Ibid). The immigration rate accelerated further from 1991 to 2000 when 2.2 million immigrants arrived. In 2003 alone, close to a quarter of a million immigrants were accepted (http://www.parl.gc.ca/information/library/PRBpubs/bp190-e.htm#aourpopulationtxt (accessed on March 2, 2004)).

As the number of childbirth per Canadian female continues to drop, immigration will become more crucial to the country, whose fertility rate fell to a record low of 1.49 in 2000 (http://www.statcan.ca/Daily/English/020926/d020926c (accessed on March 2, 2004)). With the current fertility rate, deaths are predicted to exceed births in 20 to 25 years so that at that point immigration would account for all population growth (http://www.statcan.ca/Daily/English/020703/d020703a.htm (accessed on March 2, 2004)).

With immigrants from around the world settling in Canada, the missions field has moved right into the backyards of Canadians, literally in many instances. It is encouraging that Canadian churches and denominations are finally realizing that these newcomers, increasingly Asian and non-Christian, represent the most accessible mission field given the receptivity of newcomers to the gospel (McGavran 1970:248-249). Brian Seim notes that because immigrants are often lonely and unsure of themselves in the Canadian context, they "are wide open to overtures of Christian love" (Seim n.d. 9).

Newcomers to Canada present a double-sided opportunity. Not only do they constitute a local audience for the gospel but also a global force for the gospel. In other words, believers in the immigrant groups can be mobilized for missions especially to their own people. In a paper arguing for the mobilization of the diaspora ethnic groups, T.V. Thomas says:

> "It is often easier to motivate Christians and churches to address the reaching of their own ethnic people. Though no group should ever be encouraged to employ that as their sole focus for evangelism, it is perfectly natural to see ethnic Christians being recruited for ministry to their own people." (Thomas 1998:3).

Believers in the diaspora groups eventually bring the gospel beyond their ethno-cultural boundaries. This is reminiscent of the Jews in Jerusalem who were dispersed by persecution, and in the process proclaimed the gospel to other people groups (Acts 8).

So the $64,000 question is how do we mobilize an ethnic group in diaspora for the Great Commission? This paper seeks to answer that question. The first part of this paper presents the immigration scene in Canada and how Canadian "Pinoys"[1] fit into the larger ethno-cultural milieu of the country.

The second part explores the Alliance model for mobilizing Filipino-Canadians at the national level through the Conference of Filipino Alliance Ministries (CFAM). The third part explores how one of CFAM churches, the First Filipino Alliance Church in Edmonton, carried the step further by mobilizing Filipinos at the global level.

The Canadian Immigration Landscape

Last summer, my wife Judy's sister came to visit Canada and wherever she and her family went, they were struck by how green the scenery was. Then last winter, my sister in-law and her family returned for the holidays. This time the monotony of whiteness of the "snowscape" left a different yet vivid impression. To them, Canada was either all green or all white.

Canada as the Second Most Multi-racial and Multi-cultural Country

Canada's physical landscape may appear to have two tones for most of the year, but its demographic landscape is one of the world's most "colorful." Out of a 2001 total population of 31,021,300, 5.4 million people were born outside Canada (http://www12.statcan.ca/english/census01/products/ analytic/ companion/etoimm/canada.cfm#proportion_foreign_born_highest (accessed on March 2, 2004)). This comes out to 18.4 percent of the population, the highest proportion in 70 years (Ibid.). More than 200 different ethnic origins were reported in the 2001 census question on ethnic ancestry [http://www12. statcan.ca/english/census01/products/analytic/companion/etoimm/canada. cfm#Top (accessed on March 2, 2004)].

With 18.4 percent of its population declaring themselves as first-generation immigrants, Canada today is the world's second most multi-racial and multi-cultural country. Only Australia tops the list with 21.9 percent of its 2001 population born outside the country [http://www12.statcan.ca/english/ census01/products/analytic/companion/etoimm/canada.cfm (accessed on March 2, 2004)]. In comparison, only 11.1 percent of the U.S. population was classified foreign-born in 2000 (Ibid.).

The influx of immigrants is most palpable in the major urban centers of the British Columbia, Ontario, and Quebec, which together absorb 9 out of every 10 new Canadians (http://www12.statcan.ca/english/census01/products/analytic/ companion/etoimm/canada.cfm (accessed on March 2, 2004)). Toronto is possibly the world's most ethno-culturally diverse metropolis in the world with 4 out of 10 of its residents reporting in 2001 to be foreign-born (Figure 1) [http://www12.statcan.ca/english/census01/products/analytic/companion/etoimm/subprovs.cfm (accessed on March 2, 2004)].

Immigrants Increasingly Asian and Less European

One notable development in the immigration scene was that during the first 60 years of the last century, European countries such as the United Kingdom, Italy, Germany and the Netherlands were the primary sources of immigrants to Canada (http://www12.statcan.ca/english/census01/products/analytic/companion/etoimm/canada.cfm#immigrants_increasingly_asia). In addition to Europe, the United States was also a traditional source of immigrants to Canada (accessed on March 2, 2004). The balance, however, has gradually shifted towards Asia starting in the mid-1970s with the influx of the Indochinese "boat people." Today 7 out of the top 8 source nations are in the Asian continent [http://www12.statcan.ca/english/census01/products/analytic/companion/etoimm/canada.cfm#immigrants_increasingly_asia (accessed on March 2, 2004)].

The Escalating Filipino Factor

The Filipinos are recent comers to Canada.[2] The recency of their entry into the country is shown by the fact that between 1946 and 1964, only 770 Filipinos were admitted to the country (Laquian 1973:1). But from 1964 onwards, they steadily increased so that the Philippines ranked fifth from 1971 to 1980, and sixth from 1981 to 1990 among the top eight origins of immigrants [http://www12.statcan.ca/english/census01/products/analytic/companion/etoimm/subprovs.cfm (accessed on March 2, 2004)]. The country jumped to the third spot in 1991 to 2000, behind China and India.[3] The Filipino language (Tagalog) is now the fifth most common non-official (not English and not French) language spoken at home [http://www12.statcan.ca/english/census01/products/analytic/companion/etoimm/canada.cfm#immigrants_speak_nonofficial_language_home (accessed on March 3, 2004)].

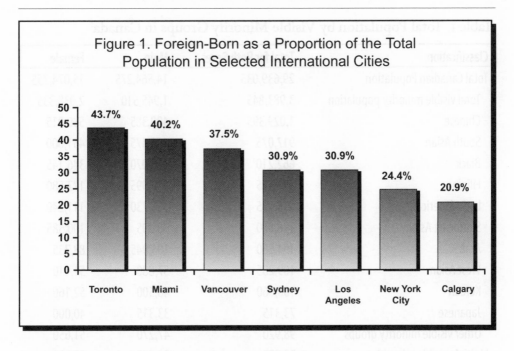

Figure 1. Foreign-Born as a Proportion of the Total Population in Selected International Cities

According to the most recent count, Filipinos now number 327,550 and constitute today's fourth largest visible minority[4] group in Canada (Table 1) [http://www12.statcan.ca/english/census01/products/standard/themes/ RetrieveProductTable.cfm (accessed on March 3, 2004)]. More than half of them (54%) live in Ontario with the rest found mostly in British Columbia, Manitoba, Alberta, and Quebec [http://www.asiapacificresearch.ca/stats/people/ demographics_dataset1_byprov.cfm (accessed on March 3, 2004)].

In addition to the immigrants are the migrant Filipinos, e.g., professionals on work visa, students, live-in caregivers, etc. The Commission on Filipinos Overseas reported that 9,737 individuals in this category arrived in Canada in 2002 (http://www.cfo.ph/statistics/emigrant_country.htm (accessed on March 3, 2004)). Since 1981, Canada has hosted 151,127 Filipino migrants (Ibid.). There are no available data on how many of these eventually stayed on to become immigrants although it has been noted that compared to other visible minorities, Filipinos are mostly likely to become immigrants [http://www.ops.gov.ph/visit2002/backgrounder_can. htm#Filipino%20Immigrant (accessed March 4, 2004)]. All these figures are bound to grow as more Filipinos come to Canada either to work or to settle for good.[5]

Table I. Total Population by Visible Minority Groups in Canada[6]

Classification	Total for Both Sexes	Male	Female
Total Canadian Population	29,639,035	14,564,275	15,074,755
Total visible minority population	3,983,845	1,945,510	2,038,335
Chinese	1,029,395	499,385	530,015
South Asian	917,075	465,475	451,600
Black	662,210	316,070	346,145
Filipino	308,575	130,995	177,580
Latin American	216,975	105,730	111,240
Southeast Asian	198,880	98,295	100,585
Arab	194,680	105,945	88,735
West Asian	109,285	57,880	51,410
Korean	100,660	48,500	52,160
Japanese	73,315	33,315	40,000
Other visible minority groups	98,920	47,270	51,650
Multiple visible minorities	73,875	36,655	37,220
All others	25,655,185	12,618,770	13,036,420

The believers among the 7 million strong migrant Filipinos scattered in many countries represent a tremendous force that could be harnessed for world evangelization. Dalrymple argues that the Filipinos are one of the two ethnic groups from Asia uniquely prepared by God to be in the forefront of missions in the next few decades.[7] The Filipinos' dispersion, largely fueled by economic reasons, coupled with their characteristics as an industrious, hardworking and resilient people, have been a windfall to the Great Commission.

A Canadian government report noted that the Filipinos' "long history of cross-cultural relationships with various eastern and western civilizations have made them inherently multicultural in outlook" and naturally adaptable to the Canadian mosaic (Gartner 1979:6). According to the Asian Center for Missions, Filipinos are an excellent fit to reach the world, particularly Asia, because "appearance-wise they are not a shocking sight to their Asian neighbors – like the striking white Americans. Politically, they carry very little baggage, for they were not imperialistic" (Shubin 1998:40).

The Christian Filipinos dispersed overseas, mostly as OCWs (overseas contract workers), are uniquely and divinely placed to evangelize their own countrymen and to penetrate host countries, many of which are closed to traditional missions strategies (Dalrymple 1996:5). Aside from the OCWs, the immigrant Filipinos in the First World represent another pool of potential missionaries (Shubin 1998:38-40).

Given these possibilities, churches must identify, train, send, and support Pinoys, who can go as professional missionaries or as tentmakers to the nations of the world.

Mobilizing Filipino Canadians At The National Level

The Formation of The Council for Filipino Alliance Ministries

Although the Canadian Christian and Missionary Alliance (CMA) began their work among Filipinos in Canada as early as 1983 with the planting of the First Filipino Alliance Church in Edmonton followed by subsequent church plants in other major cities, it was not until 1990 that these churches banded together to form the Council of Filipino Alliance Ministries (CFAM). CFAM then became the vehicle for the mobilization of Filipinos in Canada.[8]

Three watershed events preceded CFAM's formation. First, in October 1988, Rev. Sadiri Joy Tira, the founding pastor of the First Filipino Alliance Church, convened a meeting in Edmonton of denominational leaders and pastors from each of the four organized Filipino-Canadian Alliance congregations. The meeting focused on the denomination's interest in accelerating the birthing of Filipino Alliance churches in Canadian cities with a sizable Pinoy community.

Second, the pastors of the four organized churches gathered again in January 1990 in Edmonton to plan a joint nationwide evangelistic concert featuring showbusiness-personality-turned-itinerant-evangelist Ray Ann Fuentes from the Philippines. Third, the pastors, together with the new CMA's Vice President for Canadian Ministries, Dr. Stuart Lightbody, met for another round of consultation in Edmonton on October 13, 1990. It was out of these historic meetings that CFAM was born. Rev. Tira, the prime mover behind CFAM's formation, was appointed by the council as its first national coordinator with the subsequent approval of the denomination.

On May 21-23, 1991, CFAM met for the first time as a Council in Saskatoon, Saskatchewan. To reach and mobilize Filipino-Canadians, Rev. Tira presented a ten-year plan, which had six key components: (1) evangelism and birthing of Filipino-Canadian churches; (2) church development; (3) development of pastoral and lay leadership; (4) participation in global missions; (5) networking with Alliance World Fellowship (AWF), Filipino Association of the Christian and Missionary Alliance Churches in America (FACAMA), and Christian and Missionary Alliance Churches in the Philippines (CAMACOP); and (6) internal and external promotion of CFAM through literature.[9]

The plan was adopted by the Council, which also embraced four goals, three of which were vital to the mobilization of Canadian Filipinos: (1) the calling of a biennial national missions conference, (2) planting of Filipino churches in cities with a sizable Filipino community, and (3) training and development of leaders.[10]

Mobilization Through the Biennial Family Missions Conference

The CFAM pastors agreed at their 1991 Saskatoon meeting to hold a "Family Missions Conference" every two years just prior to the week of the CMA's General Assembly[11] with the objectives of (1) promoting awareness of the Canadian Alliance's global missions program, (2) raising support for missions, and (3) recruiting candidates for missions (Tiangson 1997:3-4).

The first Family Missions Conference was held on July 2-4, 1993 at Camp Nakamun in Busby, Alberta with the First Filipino Alliance Church as its host.

> "The conference was envisioned and brought to fruition under the direction of Rev. Joy Tira, pastor of First Filipino Alliance Church in Edmonton and the coordinator of the Council of Filipino Alliance Ministries. The stated purpose of the conference was to encourage Canadian Filipinos to get involved in world evangelization. The objective was met through the

inspiring and motivating addresses by the plenary speakers, the informative workshop sessions and the times of corporate singing. It was obvious that the conference had been a time of divine visitation. What the Spirit had set in motion was enthusiasm, the encouragement and commitment among the Canadian Alliance Pinoys for mission." (Friebel 1993:2).

The first mission conference was followed by the following events:

- The second Family Missions Conference at the Rayner Centre on Lake Diefenbaker, Birsay, Saskatchewan, on June 28-30, 1996. Host church: Filipino Community Church in Saskatoon.[13]

- The third Family Missions Conference in Aylmer, Quebec, on July 3-5, 1998. Host churches: Filipino Alliance Church of Toronto, Ottawa Filipino Community Church, and Mississauga – Hamilton Filipino Ministries.[14]

- The fourth Family Missions Conference in Three Hills, Alberta, on June 30 to July 2, 2000. Host church: River of Life Alliance Church (formerly Calgary Filipino Alliance)

- The fifth Family Missions Conference in Otterburne, Manitoba June 27-29, 2003. Host church: Church of the Living Hope (formerly Winnipeg Filipino Alliance Church).[15]

These conferences share four characteristics. First, the focus on missions that was strongly evident in the first Family Missions Conference was maintained in the later conferences. The plenary-session topics and the workshops in these succeeding conferences, while not all on world missions, ultimately reminded the CFAM constituency of the missionary genes of its denomination. In some of these conferences several missions organizations, Bible colleges, and seminaries set up booths for information and recruitment purposes.

Second, offerings were taken in all these conferences to support various missions causes. For instance, the 2000 Family Missions Conference in Three Hills, Alberta, set the record for the highest offering for missions. Over $4,000 was raised and given to different needs relating to Alliance missions. At the last missions conference in Otterburne, Manitoba, close to $1,000 was raised for the Filipino International Network. That amount, albeit small, went towards helping defray the cost of holding this consultation here in Korea.

Perhaps more important than the money raised at these conferences was the awareness generated among the participants of the need to not just pray for but give to missions as well. This has resulted in long-term support for missions. For instance, from year to year since 2000, the top givers to Alliance missions and to the scholarship for Bible college and seminary students in the Filipino church in Calgary were members of the organizing committee for the 2000 Family Missions Conference in Three Hills, Alberta. There is no doubt that the conference is a factor in raising financial supporters for missions in the CFAM congregations.

Third, these conferences were occasions for challenging people to consider missionary service, either long-term or short-term. No hard data exists as to how many have actually made a decision to be a missionary as a direct result of the challenges given during these conferences. Neither do we know how many of these decisions translated into actual deployment of people in the field.

However, some anecdotal accounts are encouraging. For instance, 25 people were reported to have responded to Dr. T.V. Thomas' altar call for missionary service during the last plenary session at the 1993 conference in Busby, Alberta.[16] Among those who responded were two ladies who were with the Toronto delegation.[17] A few years later they obtained theological education in Toronto and went overseas as Overseas Missionary Fellowship missionaries in the fall of 2003. One is now ministering to Moslem university students in southern Philippines while the other is working with impoverished children in Phnom Penh, Cambodia.

Fourth, the conferences became commissioning events. For instance, the 2000 conference in Three Hills, Alberta, will be remembered as the time when Dr. Hayson Valencia, an Alliance missionary from the First Filipino Alliance Church, was commissioned as a tentmaker to a "limited access nation."[18] At the 2003 missions conference in Otterburne, Manitoba, Tonyvic Tira, also a member of the First Filipino Alliance, was commissioned as a short-term missionary to work with Campus Crusade for Christ in reaching out to the Moslems in southern Spain.

The next Family Missions Conference will be in Vancouver on July 1-3, 2005. The three CFAM churches in British Columbia will jointly host this event which will be unique in that there will be a simultaneous track for second-generation Filipino Canadians. The goal of this parallel conference is to challenge them to take their place in this ongoing mobilization of Canadian Pinoys for world missions.

Mobilization Through the Birthing of Churches

When CFAM was formed in the fall of 1991, there were only four "organized" Filipino-Canadian Alliance churches.[19] The decade-long plan adopted in 1992 called for the planting of ten new churches by the end of 1995, a goal that was not readily met (Tiangson 1997:2). However, by 1997 and 1998, there were 9 and 11 organized churches, respectively.[20]

Today CFAM has 15 organized churches from the Pacific coast to the Atlantic seaboard.[21] In addition to these thriving congregations are Filipino groups, existing within predominantly white Alliance churches, which have the potential to become local churches.[22]

Table 2 shows the combined statistics for the member churches.

Table 2. Combined Statistics for the CFAM Churches[23]

Category	1998	1999	2000	2001	2002	2003
Number of organized churches	11	11	13	14	15	15
Inclusive membership	1,281	1,406	1,547	1,857	1,905	2117
Professions of faith	256	339	449	404	327	302
Baptisms	41	80	59	64	107	79
Sunday attendance	1,004	1,011	1,039	1,394	1,546	1,907
Sunday school attendance	472	537	599	684	802	Not Available
Giving to Alliance overseas missions	$38,281	$42,748	$40,700	$49,742	$53,869	$53,000
Gross income	$838,865	$961,622	$1,081,131	$1,294,954	$1,480,281	$1,800,000

Mobilization Through Recruiting and Developing Leaders

Leadership recruitment and development represent the third avenue for mobilization of Canadian Pinoys in the CFAM model.

From the beginning, CFAM was committed to raising leaders from its own congregations and releasing them for service. Departing from the practice of its American counterpart—the FACAMA, which routinely imported pastors from the Philippines to lead its churches—CFAM went for indigenous development of leaders. Rev. Tira, in the *Plan for the Decade: Reaching and Mobilizing Canadian Pinoys*, contends:

> "We need to develop our own leadership. Hence, we should not encourage immigration of pastors from the Philippines. I believe the most effective workers are those who are already here in Canada. Let us encourage our young people to respond to the call of God. However, we recognize the urgency of starting Filipino ministries in those cities identified [for church planting]. Therefore, we will consider importing church planters from the Philippines. Only workers endorsed by CAMACOP leadership should be allowed for pastoral leadership. *The importation of church planters from CAMACOP should not be understood as a long-term strategy but only for the next few years.* Personnel from CAMACOP should go through the licensing procedures and ministerial orientation of the Canadian C&MA Districts."[24]

Rev. Julius Tiangson, who became the next CFAM National Coordinator in 1997, echoed the same sentiment:

> "Our thrust to plant churches will require experienced or inexperienced personnel. We need to be sensitive to God as personnel approach us from outside the C&MA. *The recruitment from outside ... need to be viewed as a short-term solution to our present lack of available personnel.* Great care and wisdom need to be exercised in the process.[25]

Table 3 summarizes the background of current CFAM pastors. First, half of the current sixteen (16) CFAM pastors came from within its constituency,

Table 3. Background of Pastors Prior to Joining CFAM

Church	Pastor(s)	Background Before Joining CFAM
Filipino Christian Alliance Fellowship (Vancouver, B.C.)	Rev. Ricky Mapa	A former member of the First Filipino Alliance Church. Came to Canada on landed immigrant status. No previous pastoring experience.
Fraser Valley Alliance (Surrey, B.C.) North Vancouver	Pastor Jeff Barrun	A former member of the Filipino Christian Alliance Fellowship. Was a visa (Regent College) student from the Philippines church. Had previous pastoring experience in the Philippines.
Filipino Alliance Church	Pastor Patrick Loo	A former member of the Filipino Christian Alliance Fellowship. Was a visa (Regent College) student from the Philippines before pastoring the Filipino Alliance Church of Toronto and then the North Vancouver Filipino Alliance Church. Had previous pastoring experience.
First Filipino Alliance Church (Edmonton)	Rev. Dr. Sadiri Joy Tira	Was a visa seminary (Canadian Theological Seminary) student from the Philippines before planting the church. No previous pastoring experience but had extensive cross-cultural training through Operation Mobilization.
River of Life Alliance Church (Calgary)	Rev. Charlie Mance	Was former member of the First Filipino Alliance Church. Was a visa student (University of Alberta; Canadian Theological Seminary) from the Philippines. Acquired landed immigrant status. Attended Tyndale seminary. No previous pastoring experience.
River of Life Alliance Church (Calgary)	Rev. Arnold Magtulis	Was a member of the River of Life Alliance Church Was a visa student from the Philippines (Prairie Bible Institute; Prairie Graduate School) before joining the church as second pastor. Had previous pastoring experience.
River of Life Alliance Church (Calgary)	Pastor Serelito Caderma	Was a member of the Filipino Community Church. (Saskatoon). A second-generation Filipino Canadian and a graduate of the Alliance's Canadian Bible College with no previous pastoring experience.
House of Prayer Alliance Ch. (Calgary)	Pastor Francis Herras	Came directly from the Philippines from a Pentecostal denomination. Had previous pastoring experience.
Regina Filipino Alliance Church	Pastor Jack Gonzales	A former member of the First Filipino Alliance Church. Came to Canada on a landed immigrant status. No previous pastoring experience.

Filipino Community Church (Saskatoon)	Rev. Dan Fabella	Came directly from the Philippines from the CAMACOP. Had previous pastoring experience.
Church of the Living Hope (Winnipeg)	Rev. Fred Sebastian	Came to Canada on a landed immigrant status. Was a CAMACOP pastor. Had previous pastoring experience.
Filipino Alliance Church of Toronto	Rev. Dr. Asterio Wee	Came directly from the U.S. from FACAMA. Had previous pastoring experience.
Christ-Centered Alliance Church (Scarborough)	Pastor Ben Mapa	This was formerly an independent charismatic church that affiliated with the Alliance in 2002. Came to Canada on a landed immigrant status. No previous pastoring experience.
Gateway Christian Life Centre - Mississauga	Rev. Julius Tiangson	Was a visa worker (accountant) while planting the church. Became an immigrant and pastored the church. No previous pastoring experience but had some church-planting experience from the Philippines.
Gateway Christian Life Centre - Brampton	Pastor Ed Bolante	A former member of the Gateway Christian Life Centre in Mississauga before planting the church. Came to Canada on a landed immigrant status. Was a lay pastor in the Middle East.
Filipino Community Church (Ottawa)	Pastor Aurelio Vito	Came directly from the Philippines. Was former president of the Navigators in the Philippines. No previous pastoring experience.

i.e., they were former members of CFAM congregations. They were either landed immigrants attending a CFAM church or visa students from the Philippines attending a CFAM church. These were individuals, therefore, already familiar with the Canadian Alliance denomination.

Second, six of the 16 pastors, or 38 percent, represent Canadian Pinoys who were recruited from the laity in the CFAM churches. In contrast to the others who had come with previous pastoral experience in the Philippines, these individuals had no pastoral training. Their gift to lead and pastor became apparent while they were attending CFAM churches. (Eight others had prior pastoral experience from the Philippines before joining CFAM).

Third, 12 out of 16, or three quarters of CFAM pastors, had been in Canada for some time, either as immigrants or visa students, before obtaining theological education and, or pastoring the church. This means that they are already familiar with the Canadian context prior to the start of the ministry.

Only three came directly from the Philippines while another came from the United States.

Fourth, 10 out of 16, or 62 percent, of CFAM pastors come from Alliance background prior to becoming a CFAM pastor. Three came from independent charismatic churches; two, Baptist; and one, Pentecostal.

Sixth, CFAM is starting to see the emergence of second-generation leaders with the hiring of a youth pastor, a Saskatchewan-born Filipino, in July 2003 by the River of Life Alliance Church in Calgary. The Gateway Christian Life Centre in Mississauga is considering calling a second-generation Filipino pastor this year.[26] This is consistent with CFAM's goal to see its young people respond to full-time ministry.

Seventh, 14 out of the 16 (87 percent) CFAM pastors have at least a Bible college education. Eight have seminary degrees from Canada, two have earned their Doctor of Ministry degrees from Canada and two have Doctor of Ministry degrees from the US.

Emerging lay leaders who sense a call to the pastorate or missions were encouraged by CFAM to seek formal theological education as a preparation for ministry. The Centre for Intercultural Studies at the Canadian Theological Seminary was to play a key role in leadership training and development.[27] Churches were also encouraged to support these people in prayer and finances with a few of the churches setting up scholarship funds.

CFAM is committed to releasing its best people for global evangelization. Leading the way is the First Filipino Alliance Church, which has sent three Filipino Canadians to Canadian Bible College (CBC) and ten to Canadian Theological Seminary (CTS). Of these, four have become vocational ministers, (Tira 2002:131-132)[28] three have become career Alliance missionaries,[29] two have completed their missionary apprenticeship and waiting for direction to go overseas,[30] and one is on staff with Campus Crusade for Christ (CCC) in Canada. These figures do not include tentmakers and those who have gone on short-term missions overseas.[31] Given its relatively small size, the First Filipino Alliance has excelled in mobilizing a sizable number of workers.

Other churches have started to follow the lead of the First Filipino Alliance. For example, Calgary's River of Life Alliance Church has stepped up to the plate. It began encouraging people to consider full-time Christian ministry in 1999, the year it set up a scholarship fund. One graduated from seminary in 2000 and has joined the church as its congregational care pastor with plans of eventually serving overseas. Two more completed their Bible college education in 2001 and 2002. One has gone on to do her Master of Divinity at CTS and the other moved to Three Hills, Alberta, where her husband is completing his studies at the Prairie Bible Institute. The couple is also thinking of overseas compassionate ministry. The church has three other CTS students and one Bible college student who are all considering missionary service.[32]

CFAM is slowly achieving its dream of becoming a sending organization that will release the best of its people for church planting and global evangelization (Tiangson 1997:5).

Of the various denominations with work among Filipino-Canadians, the Christian and Missionary Alliance has one of the most comprehensive national strategies and a nationwide network of local churches to mobilize Filipino Canadians.

MOBILIZING FILIPINO CANADIANS AT THE GLOBAL LEVEL

The Significant Role of The First Filipino Alliance Church

The First Filipino Alliance Church and its founding pastor, Rev. Tira, were key players in the Alliance model of a country-wide mobilization of an ethnic group.

First, the church and its pastor were catalytic in the formation of CFAM. The early history of CFAM's mobilization of Filipino Canadians for church planting and global missions is intertwined with that of the church and its pastor. The early church planters who went to Regina, Toronto, and Calgary were lay leaders from the said church while the first batch of Filipino Canadians deployed overseas as Alliance missionaries was entirely from the church.

Second, the church and its pastor took mobilization seriously at the local church level. The church leaders, beginning with its pastor and elders, constantly highlighted missions as a defining characteristic of the church. And it walked the talk by encouraging its members and adherents to participate in missions conferences (Tira 2002:130-131),[33] short-term overseas missions (Ibid.),[34] and medical and dental missions (Ibid.).[35] In addition to the pastor, 14 other individuals have gone overseas under FIN projects to train Filipino and non-Filipino overseas workers (Ibid.). It has also commissioned a professional couple, who have moved to a Middle Eastern country, as tentmakers (Ibid., 132)

Third, the church and its pastor took the mobilization a step further: it launched what has become its, and also CFAM's, de facto global mobilization arm – the Filipino International Network (FIN).

The Emergence of the Filipino International Network

The story behind FIN began in 1993 when First Filipino Alliance Church's leaders prayed earnestly to make a significant contribution to world missions. That year God began to work in the hearts of certain individuals, who would later become the church's partners in launching FIN.

The first of such partners was an Edmonton businessman who had met with Rev. Tira prior to the significant "catalytic" meeting. At this initial meeting Rev. Tira requested for Jesus Film videos, which the First Filipino Alliance intended to give away during its New Immigrants and New Citizens Sunday in October 1993.

This pivotal meeting was followed by subsequent meetings during which the two men talked about how the Great Commission's fulfillment could be hastened. In the course of their many conversations Tira casually mentioned that there were over a million Filipinos leaving the Philippines as OCWs. The businessman was incredulous. For the two, there came a sudden realization that a million Filipinos overseas was a staggering statistic that their interest in global missions could not overlook. Both seriously began to consider how the Christian OCWs in the Middle East and Gulf Region could be motivated, equipped and mobilized through the Jesus Film (Ibid. 119).

Rev. Tira came up with an action plan to distribute the videos in the Middle East, which was presented to the Dr. Ben de Jesus, the Executive Director of the AWF, who in turn encouraged Rev. Tira to present the plan to the CAMACOP leaders (Ibid.).

A whole new vista opened when this businessman invited Rev. Tira to address the April 11-14, 1994 regional meeting in Amman, Jordan of the Campus Crusade for Christ representatives in the Middle East. During that meeting the OCW phenomenon was discussed and a consensus was reached that: (1) there was an urgent need to minister to the Filipino OCWs through evangelism, discipleship, and lay leaders training and (2) the evangelical Christians among the Filipinos and other ethnic groups, e.g., Koreans, working in the region had the great potential to impact their host countries, the vast majority of which were closed to traditional missions (Ibid. 121).

At this meeting Rev. Tira was asked to conduct a demographic study of the area. So from June 26 to July 14, 1994, Rev. Tira and a First Filipino Alliance elder travelled through the region, connected with Filipino church leaders and tentmakers, and were exposed to the great potential for a ministry there (Ibid. 122). Among other things, they discovered that the Filipino believers were among the most aggressive in sharing their faith with some even witnessing to the Arab Moslems.

Upon his return to Canada, Rev. Tira gave a report on the encouraging results of this survey trip to his own denominational leaders, who were supportive of the initiative. The vision of a ministry to the Filipino OCWs in the Middle East and Gulf states was soon dubbed as "Operation Trojan Horse" by Rev. Wally Albrecht, the then Vice President for Personnel and Missions for the CMA in Canada (Ibid. 123).

Then at the invitation of AWF's Executive Director, Dr. Ben de Jesus and Rev. Tira met key Philippine evangelical leaders on January 11-23, 1995. He gave an encouraging report on the results of his survey trip and the Philippine leaders received the findings and recommendations with enthusiasm (Ibid. 122).

On May 3-6, 1995, an important meeting called the "Filipino International Network Consultation '95," was convened in Larnaca, Cyprus.[36] Attended by 31 delegates from Europe, the Middle East, the Gulf states, North Africa, the Philippines, and North Africa, the consultation discussed the need to (1) fulfill the Great Commission; (2) encourage and motivate Christian Filipino OCWs in the 10/40 Window; (3) remind the participants of the priority of evangelism and discipleship; (4) share the vision of the Filipino diaspora's role in global evangelization; (5) gather strategic information from the participants; and (6) share available resources with the participants (Ibid. 123-124).

Two things emerged from this Cyprus meeting: the emergence of FIN as a global movement to mobilize Filipino OCWs and the Larnaca Covenant that affirmed, among other things, "the sovereignty of God in placing Filipino believers in the 10/40 Window and the world" (Ibid. 125-126).

Soon after the Larnaca meeting, Dr. Henry Tan, the National Director of Campus Crusade for Christ in the Philippines, and was one of the participants, made a recommendation to the First Filipino Alliance's board of elders to allow Rev. Tira to serve as FIN's coordinator. This recommendation was accepted by the church and later affirmed by the denomination. The church redefined Rev. Tira's ministry description to allow him to serve as FIN's International Coordinator. Hence, FIN became a ministry of the church. Aside from the church, the other partners were a private foundation based in Edmonton, the CMA in Canada, and CCC in Canada. The partners would provide FIN with an international headquarters in Edmonton and logistics for operation. (Ibid. 126).

As the vision of mobilizing Filipino OCWs was introduced to other churches, organizations, and other mission-minded individuals, the network of FIN partners grew and eventually regional FIN committees were established in the Middle East and Gulf states, Far East Asia, and North America (Ibid. 127-128).

Two more significant events followed. One was the September 19-20, 1996 Puerto Azul Consultation in Cavite, Philippines, where FIN representatives met with Filipino evangelical leaders from several denominations and Christian government officials. The leaders endorsed FIN as a networking movement that would facilitate the mobilization of Filipinos in the diaspora. Then followed the "Filipino North American Prayer Advance '97" in Midland, Texas, where Filipino Christian leaders from the United States and Canada gathered with FIN representatives to pray and fast for revival among Filipinos scattered worldwide (Ibid.).

THE OBJECTIVES AND GOALS OF FIN

The objectives of FIN are to motivate, equip, and mobilize Filipino OCWs around the world to accomplish the Great Commission. It is also committed to train Filipino diaspora pastors and lay leaders to better serve their congregations and mobilize them to reach out cross-culturally (Ibid. 127-128). To accomplish these objectives, FIN has set these goals:

(1) mobilization of a prayer base to blanket FIN with intercession;

(2) training of OCW Christian leaders and lay people through CCC's five-level New Life Training Course and CCC's Family Life Conference;

(3) recruitment of tentmakers; and

(4) calling of regional consultations to keep the vision fresh and workers focused. FIN is also active in providing congregations and individuals with the Jesus Film for evangelistic purposes (Ibid. 128-129).

Lastly, FIN would also play a large role in the placement of Alliance missionaries in Limited Access Nations.

CONCLUSION

The Conference of Filipino Alliance Ministries presents a model for mobilizing Filipino Canadians at the national level through a coherent strategy for church planting and development, recruitment and development of homegrown leaders, and the convening of a biennial national missions conference.

The First Filipino Alliance Church, a CFAM church, carried the mobilization to the global level through its launching of the Filipino International Network whose stated mission is to motivate, equip, and mobilize Filipino overseas contract workers around the world for the fulfillment of the Great Commission.

ENDNOTES

[1] "Pinoys" is the slang for Filipinos.

[2] Other recent immigrants to Canada are the Latin Americans, Arabs, and West Asians.

[3] Ibid. The top 8 source nations were: 1. People's Republic of China; 2. India; 3. Philippines; 4. Special Administrative Region of Hongkong; 5. Sri Lanka; 6. Pakistan; 7. Taiwan; and 8. United States.

[4] http://www.statcan.ca/english/Pgdb/defdemo40e.htm (accessed on March 3, 2004). The Canadian Employment Equity Act defines visible minorities as "persons, other than Aboriginal peoples, who are non-Caucasian in race or non-white in colour." Under this definition, regulations specify the following groups as visible minorities: Chinese, South Asians, Blacks, Arabs, West Asians, Filipinos, Southeast Asians, Latin Americans, Japanese, Koreans and other visible minority groups, such as Pacific Islanders.

[5] The author noted that an increasing number of Filipinos arriving in Canada as immigrants are those that had worked for many years in the Middle East and had no plans of returning to the Philippines.

[6] http://www12.statcan.ca/english/census01/products/standard/themes/RetrieveProductTable.cfm (accessed on March 3, 2004).

[7] The other group is the Koreans. Terry A. Dalrymple, "Strategic Opportunities for the Philippine Church in World Evangelization," Evangelicals Today, March-April 1996, 5.

[8] The name was changed late in 1997 to Conference of Filipino Alliance Ministries. The name change was necessitated by a shift in the nature of CFAM. From an association of pastors of Filipino Alliance churches, it became a "conference" – a formal network of Filipino congregations within the CMA in Canada. See Julius Tiangson, "A Network of Filipino Churches in Canada!" CFAMLink, January 1998, 1.

[9] See Sadiri J. B. Tira, "Plans for the Decade: Reaching and Mobilizing Canadian Pinoys," a paper presented at the Annual Conference of the Council of Filipino Alliance Ministries hosted by the National Office of the Christian and Missionary Alliance in Canada, May 21-23, 1991, Saskatoon, Saskatchewan, Canada, pp. 1-8.

[10] The last goal of producing a church planting manual to guide Filipino pastors did not materialize.

11 At the July 2002 Family Missions Conference in Three Hills, Alberta, CFAM decided to move the holding of the conference in between the biennial CMA General Assembly.

12 Plenary speakers included Benjamin de Jesus, then Executive Director of the Alliance World Fellowship; Dr. T.V. Thomas, the Director of the Centre for Evangelism at the Canadian Bible College and Canadian Theological Seminary; Dr. Arnold Cook, then Vice President for Missions for the CMA in Canada; Rev. Vergil Schmidt, then senior pastor of Grande Prairie Alliance Church; and Rev. Sadiri Joy Tira, the founding National Coordinator of CFAM and pastor of the First Filipino Alliance Church.

13 Plenary speakers were Rev. Joseph Arthur, founder of the Philippine Student Alliance Lay Movement (PSALM); Dr. Arnold Cook, then President of the CMA in Canada; Dr. Valmike Apuzen, the President of the Christian and Missionary Alliance Churches of the Philippines; and Rev. Sadiri Joy Tira, then the National Coordinator for CFAM and senior pastor of First Filipino Alliance Church.

14 The plenary speakers were Rev. David Rambo, former Alliance missionary to the Philippines and later president of CMA in the U.S.; Dr. Stuart Lightbody, Vice-President for Canadian Ministries, Christian and Missionary Alliance in Canada; and Rev. Julius Tiangson, CFAM National Coordinator.

15 Plenary speakers were Dr. Henry Tan, trainer from the International School of Leadership, Campus Crusade for Christ (USA); Jun Vencer, Executive Director for Leadership Development, Dawn Ministries; and Rev. Sadiri Joy Tira, International Coordinator for Filipino International Network (FIN).

16 This is according to the report of the missions and evangelism committee of the host church. The report is photocopied in Sadiri Emmanuel Santiago Tira, "Global Missions and Local Congregation: A Case Study of the First Filipino Alliance Church in Edmonton, Alberta, Canada," D. Min. dissertation, Reformed Theological Seminary, 2002, p. 342.

17 The author had the privilege of praying for them when they responded to the altar call at the end of the last plenary session. These two ladies were pioneers of the Filipino Alliance Church in Toronto.

18 "Limited access nation" refers to a country that bans or restricts the entry of missionaries and pastors.

19 In the Alliance parlance, an "organized" church refers to self-supporting, self-governing, and self-propagating church. These four organized churches in 1990 were the Filipino Christian Alliance Fellowship in Vancouver, the First Filipino Alliance Church in Edmonton, the Filipino Community Church in Saskatoon, and the Winnipeg Filipino Alliance Church.

[20] Multicultural Statistics 1997: Filipino Churches, The Christian and Missionary Alliance in Canada, 30 Carrier Dr, Suite 100, Toronto, Ontario, Canada. Multicultural Statistics 1998: Filipino Churches, The Christian and Missionary Alliance in Canada, 30 Carrier Dr, Suite 100, Toronto, Ontario, Canada

[21] These churches by provinces and their pastors are: (1) British Columbia - Filipino Christian Alliance Fellowship in Vancouver (Rev. Ricky Mapa); North Vancouver Filipino Alliance Church (Pastor Patrick Loo); Fraser Valley Alliance Church in Surrey (Pastor Jeff Barrun); (2) Alberta - First Filipino Alliance Church in Edmonton (Rev. Dr. Sadiri Joy Tira); River of Life Alliance Church in Calgary (Rev. Charlie Mance, Rev. Arnold Magtulis, Pastor Serelito Caderma); House of Prayer Alliance Church (Pastor Francis Herras); (3) Saskatchewan - Filipino Community Church in Saskatoon (Rev. Dan Fabella); Regina Filipino Alliance Church (Pastor Jack Gonzales); (4) Manitoba - Church of the Living Hope in Winnipeg (Rev. Fred Sebastian); (5) Ontario - Filipino Community Church in Ottawa (Pastor Aurelio Vito); Filipino Alliance Church of Toronto (Rev. Dr. Asterio Wee); Christ-Centered Alliance Church (Pastor Ben Mapa); Gateway Christian Life Centre - Mississauga (Rev. Julius Tiangson); and Gateway Christian Life Centre – Brampton (Pastor Ed Bolante); (6) Quebec - Christ Community Church in Montreal (currently in search of a pastor).

[22] A good example of this is the Filipino fellowship within Rexdale Alliance Church in Metro Toronto.

[23] *Multicultural Statistics 1997: Filipino Churches.* The Christian and Missionary Alliance in Canada, 30 Carrier Dr, Suite 100, Toronto, Ontario, Canada. *Multicultural Statistics 1998: Filipino Churches.* The Christian and Missionary Alliance in Canada, 30 Carrier Dr, Suite 100, Toronto, Ontario, Canada. *Multicultural Statistics 1999: Filipino Churches.* The Christian and Missionary Alliance in Canada, 30 Carrier Dr, Suite 100, Toronto, Ontario, Canada. *Multicultural Statistics 2000: Filipino Churches.* The Christian and Missionary Alliance in Canada, 30 Carrier Dr, Suite 100, Toronto, Ontario, Canada. *Multicultural Statistics 2001: Filipino Churches.* The Christian and Missionary Alliance in Canada, 30 Carrier Dr, Suite 100, Toronto, Ontario, Canada. *Multicultural Statistics 2002: Filipino Churches.* The Christian and Missionary Alliance in Canada, 30 Carrier Dr, Suite 100, Toronto, Ontario, Canada.

[24] Sadiri J.B. Tira, "Plans for the Decade: Reaching and Mobilizing Canadian Pinoys," p. 3.

[25] Julius Tiangson, "Directions Beyond 2000," p. 4.

[26] This has been confirmed by the author through a telephone conversation with the Gateway's Rev. Julius Tiangson.

[27] Sadiri J. B. Tira, "Plans for the Decade: Reaching and Mobilizing Canadian Pinoys," p. 5. The Centre for Intercultural Studies is no longer in operation.

[28] Sadiri Emmanuel Santiago Tira, "Global Missions and Local Congregation: A Case Study of the First Filipino Alliance Church in Edmonton, Alberta, Canada," pp. 131-132. These are Rev. Ricky Mapa, senior pastor of Filipino Christian Alliance Fellowship in Vancouver; Rev. Charlie Mance, senior pastor of River of Life Alliance Church in Calgary; Pastor Jack Gonzales, interim pastor of Regina Filipino Alliance Church; Rev. Samson Aragones, pastor for evangelism at Rexdale Alliance Church in Metro Toronto; Rev. Ricardo Habacon, church planter with the Baptist in Richmond, B.C.

[29] Ibid. These missionaries are Rev. Hayson Valencia, limited access nation (LAN); Mr. Raul Santos, LAN; Maria Pablo, LAN.

[30] Ibid. Shawn Kelly and Iris Kelly completed their missionary apprenticeship last December 31, 2003 at the River of Life Alliance Church.

[31] Figures are given later in the paper.

[32] Two of these seminary students originally came from Edmonton's First Filipino Alliance Church.

[33] Sadiri Emmanuel Santiago Tira, "Global Missions and Local Congregation: A Case Study of the First Filipino Alliance Church in Edmonton, Alberta, Canada," pp. 130-131. Over the years, the church has sent five delegates to IVCF's Urbana Missions Conference and two to the Student Missionary Advance Mission Conference in Hamilton, Ontario.

[34] Ibid. A total of 14 from the church have gone to join short-term overseas missions trips with Operation Mobilization and Campus Crusade for Christ.

[35] Ibid. Two members of the church, including a dentist, had gone to join these trips.

[36] Ibid., pp. 123-124.

REFERENCES

Dalrymple, Terry A. (1996). "Strategic Opportunities for the Philippine Church in World Evangelization." *Evangelicals Today*, March-April 1996, 6-7.

FIN Ministry Brochures. Filipino International Network, P.O. Box 54035, 10130 – 79 Street, Edmonton, Alberta, Canada.

Friebel, Kelvin (1993). "Canadian Pinoys Advance!" *Alliance Life*, November 10, 1993, 2, 22.

Gartner, Joseph (1979). "Filipino Canadians," Ottawa: Research Branch of the Library of Parliament, October 10, 1979.

Laquian, E. R. (1973). *A Study of Filipino Immigration to Canada.* Ottawa: United Council of Filipino Associations in Canada, 1973.

McGavran, Donald (1970). *Understanding Church Growth.* Grand Rapids, Michigan: Eerdman Publishing Co., 1970.

Multicultural Statistics 1997: Filipino Churches. The Christian and Missionary Alliance in Canada, 30 Carrier Dr, Suite 100, Toronto, Ontario, Canada.

Multicultural Statistics 1998: Filipino Churches. The Christian and Missionary Alliance in Canada, 30 Carrier Dr, Suite 100, Toronto, Ontario, Canada.

Multicultural Statistics 1999: Filipino Churches. The Christian and Missionary Alliance in Canada, 30 Carrier Dr, Suite 100, Toronto, Ontario, Canada.

Multicultural Statistics 2000: Filipino Churches. The Christian and Missionary Alliance in Canada, 30 Carrier Dr, Suite 100, Toronto, Ontario, Canada.

Multicultural Statistics 2001: Filipino Churches. The Christian and Missionary Alliance in Canada, 30 Carrier Dr, Suite 100, Toronto, Ontario, Canada.

Multicultural Statistics 2002: Filipino Churches. The Christian and Missionary Alliance in Canada, 30 Carrier Dr, Suite 100, Toronto, Ontario, Canada.

Seim, Brian. *Reaching Newcomers to Canada: The Samaria Principle.* Scarborough, Ontario: SIM Canada, n. d.

Shubin, Russel G. (1998). "The Escalating Filipino Force for the Nations." Mission Frontiers U.S. Centre for World Mission, September-December 1998, 40-41.

Thomas, T. V. Mobilizing the Diaspora in Canada for Mission. A paper presented at the International Leadership Conference hosted by Lausanne Canada, March 9-12, 1998, Tyndale College & Seminary, Toronto, Canada.

Tiangson, Julius. (1998). "A Network of Filipino Churches in Canada!" CFAMLink, January 1998, 1-2.

Tiangson, Julius. (1997). "Directions Beyond 2000." A paper presented at the Annual Conference of the Council of Filipino Alliance Ministries hosted by the National Office of the Christian and Missionary Alliance in Canada, May 23-24, 1997, Willowdale, Toronto, Canada,

Tira, Sadiri Emmanuel. (2002). "Global Missions and Local Congregation: A Case Study of the First Filipino Alliance Church in Edmonton, Alberta, Canada." D. Min. dissertation, Reformed Theological Seminary, 2002.

Tira, Sadiri Emmanuel. (1991). "Plans for the Decade: Reaching and Mobilizing Canadian Pinoys." A paper presented at the Annual Conference of the Council of Filipino Alliance Ministries hosted by the National Office of the Christian and Missionary Alliance in Canada, May 21-23, 1991, Saskatoon, Saskatchewan, Canada.

WEBSITES ACCESSED

http://www12.statcan.ca/english/censuso1/products/analytic/companion/etoimm/canada.cfm (accessed on March 2, 2004)

http://www.parl.gc.ca/information/library/PRBpubs/bp190-e.htm#aourpopulationtxt (accessed on March 2, 2004)

http://www.statcan.ca/Daily/English/020926/d020926c.htm (accessed on March 2, 2004)

http://www.statcan.ca/Daily/English/020703/d020703a.htm (accessed on March 2, 2004)

http://www12.statcan.ca/english/censuso1/products/analytic/companion/etoimm/canada.cfm#proportion_foreign_born_highest (accessed on March 2, 2004)

http://www12.statcan.ca/english/censuso1/products/analytic/companion/etoimm/canada.cfm#Top (accessed on March 2, 2004)

http://www12.statcan.ca/english/censuso1/products/analytic/companion/etoimm/canada.cfm (accessed on March 2, 2004)

http://www12.statcan.ca/english/censuso1/products/analytic/companion/etoimm/subprovs.cfm (accessed on March 2, 2004)

http://www12.statcan.ca/english/censuso1/products/analytic/companion/etoimm/canada.cfm#immigrants_increasingly_asia.

http://www12.statcan.ca/english/censuso1/products/analytic/companion/etoimm/imm.cfm (accessed on March 2, 2004)

http://www12.statcan.ca/english/censuso1/products/analytic/companion/etoimm/canada.cfm#immigrants_increasingly_asia (accessed on March 2, 2004)

http://www12.statcan.ca/english/censuso1/products/analytic/companion/etoimm/canada.cfm#immigrants_speak_nonofficial_language_home (accessed on March 3, 2004)

http://www.statcan.ca/english/Pgdb/defdemo40e.htm (accessed on March 3, 2004).

http://www12.statcan.ca/english/census01/products/standard/themes/ RetrieveProductTable.cfm (accessed on March 3, 2004).

http://www.asiapacificresearch.ca/stats/people/demographics_dataset1_byprov.cfm (accessed on March 3, 2004).

http://www12.statcan.ca/english/census01/products/standard/themes/ RetrieveProductTable.cfm (accessed on March 3, 2004).

http://www.cfo.ph/statistics/emigrant_country.htm (accessed on March 3, 2004).

http://www.statcan.ca/english/Pgdb/dofdemo40.htm (accessed on March 3, 2004).

http://www12.statcan.ca/english/census01/products/standard/themes/RetrieveProductTable.cfm (accessed on March 3, 2004).

http://www.impactresearch.ca/stats/people-demographics_data.asp?type=byprovince (accessed on March 3, 2004).

http://www12.statcan.ca/english/census01/products/standard/themes/RetrieveProductTable.cfm (accessed on March 3, 2004).

http://www.cbp.statistics-emigrant-counts.htm (accessed on March 3, 2004).

MINISTRY TO FILIPINO ENTERTAINERS AND JAPINOS

Venus Hannah Galvez

T he recent advances in technology, communications, transportation, and entertainment often overshadow recent social developments in society. While the karaoke, digital video disc, webcams, cell phones, PDAs, laptops, computer games and many electronic gadgets are innovations in entertainment, they only reveal a deeper desire for human interaction. Companionship, live shows and nightclubs thrive as a business—better understood in the economics of demand and supply. Nevertheless, behind this degrading skin business, one witnesses that customer-entertainer connections slowly but surely, open opportunities for international relations. In many cases, the customer-entertainer relation leads to intermarriage. Eventually, the influence of the foreign spouse on the once homogenous clan becomes more visible in the next generation—on the lifestyle and future direction of mixed-race children.

Stories of growing Filipino migration to Japan, as dominated by entertainers, catch the attention of both the local people and other foreigners. The Japanese media coverage on Filipinos' activities describes "unusual" sights and sounds in the community. The Filipinos' rituals and Sunday Service attendance from "back home" are carried over to Japan and intermarriage with the locals do not take away this religiosity. Roman Catholic and International churches are filled with Filipinos. Many churches were planted and transplanted to keep up with their spirituality. Here, the Japanese-Filipino children (Japinos) and the Japanese in-laws are exposed to Filipino Christianity.

Indeed, the Filipinos may have left home, but they have transported with them their beliefs, tradition and culture. This chapter focuses on the Filipino presence in Japan, with emphasis on the sovereignty of God in their migration, and on His grace that has included them in His salvation plan for Japan.

EXODUS FROM THE PHILIPPINES, INFLUX IN JAPAN

Many Filipinos who come to Japan do not return to the Philippines, and those who do return to their homeland, aim to return to Japan with their relatives and friends in tow! Filipino entertainers are currently the largest migrant group in Japan, and their increase in population is indirectly dependent on Japan's economic condition. You can hear Filipino entertainers speak of *companion-dates, branded fashion, assorted gifts, side trips and reasonable tips* as affected by the rise and fall of the "mighty yen."

Furthermore, many second- and third-generation Filipino-Japanese born in the Philippines are also migrating to Japan. Some of them are professionals, but end up working in factories and construction sites. More Filipinos are expected to migrate to Japan because of the common knowledge that the Japanese population is in rapid decline. Former British ambassador to Japan from 1980-1984, Hugh Cortazzi writes,

> "The average annual immigration in recent years of some
> 50,000 would need to go up more than 10-fold to 640,000
> a year to offset the rapid decline in the productive age popu-
> lation. It would require a revolution in Japanese attitudes to
> accept such an increase, and it could not be achieved without
> serious social strains." (Cortazzi 2004).

Filipino women in Japan, former entertainers, are teased about being more productive than the Japanese women, and now it is observed that the Filipino-Japanese children are more visible on school campuses. Many short-term Filipino entertainers are directly and indirectly encouraged to marry Japanese.

Indeed, one would question who would trade the convenience of life and the easy attainment of money in Japan for the poverty "back home." Hence, with the influx of Filipinos in Japan, economists and politicians in the Philippines configure the Filipina-entertainers migration as billions of monetary contribution, while sociologists and religious practitioners view them as agents of change in the society.

Historical records show that the first western foreigners to reach Japanese soil were Portuguese traders and Jesuit missionaries who arrived in Kyushu, Japan in 1542. Most of the Western Japan warlords then welcomed Christianity because trade with overseas nations often included the sale of arms, which were sought-after commodities in those days.

The "closed door policy" which has traditionally marked Japan's view of immigrants, goes back to the Edo Period (1600~1868), when the most famous Shogun in Japan, Tokugawa Ieyasu, eradicated the decentralized feudal system and established the military government (bakufu) in the city of Edo, now known as Tokyo. Although one of Ieyasus' advisors, Will Adams, was an Englishman, Ieyasu perceived European influence such a threat to the newly-found national stability that he decided on a Closed-Door Policy. Ieyasu restricted virtually all cultural and diplomatic relations with the outside world. Those who ventured abroad were executed on their return to prevent any form of 'contamination.'[1]

Lim Hua Sing, professor of Economics at Waseda University, affirms in her article *"Utilizing foreign talents to achieve economic growth"*:

> "The U.N. Population Division warned at the end of 2000 that Japan needs to accept 610,000 immigrants annually in order to maintain the current level of employable population under the period of the extreme low birthrate. Japan appears to be still under the influence of the Closed-Door Policy, which took place in 300 years of the Edo period. Japan is still a homogenous society and closed toward foreigners whose cultural backgrounds are of variety and heterogynous...It would take a long time for Japan as a whole to psychologically be ready to accept massive immigrants." (2003)

The mass migration of Filipinas to Japan and their inclusion in Japanese society is, hence, no less than phenomenal, given Japan's traditional view of foreigners and immigration.

Filipino Entertainment Industry in Japan

The Philippine relations to Japan may go further than the recorded stories on the martyrdom of the first Filipino saint, Lorenzo Ruiz, in Nagasaki in 1637. Interestingly, "while strolling in Hibiya Park, Tokyo in the spring of 1888, the Philippine national hero Jose Rizal listened to an orchestra playing Viennese waltzes. He was pleasantly surprised to learn that some of the musicians were Filipinos" (Ocampo 2003).

The Filipino entertainment industry in Japan would then date back to pre-World War years. The economic boom in Japan in the 20th century resurrected this relation and even paved the road for more entertainers to work for longer periods in the country. It is beyond the common Filipino's imagination how easily money is earned from entertainment in Japan, as singing and dancing are taken as mere pastimes in the Philippines.

Despite the high standard of living, the high technological facilities, the extraordinary transportation, and the high-tech communication system, the Filipino entertainer soon discovers that these conveniences do not meet the emotional or social needs of their customers. Since financial success is the Filipino dream, it is inconceivable to the Filipino entertainers why rich people like the Japanese are still not happy and secure. More inconceivable is the news of the Japanese's high rate of suicide. Again, the Filipinos look up to their customers' wealth but are taken aback by the fact that material abundance cannot satisfy them. The Japanese and the Filipinos are in actuality both seeking true happiness and security in life. The Japanese may take pride in their latest models of cell phones, DVDs, PDAs, laptops and desktops, but behind their economic success and superior communication system lies a deep longing for companionship. This desire for companionship is often manifested in the temporary relief of live entertainment.

The growing entry of Filipinos to Japan reflects a three-dimensional reality: economic survival of the sending party, social problems of the receiving field and spiritual discovery of the involved individuals. The hunger for reality, as ordained by our Sovereign and Gracious God, would help them come to terms with their real spirituality.

Economic Survival of the Entertainers

Philippine diplomatic sources say that Japan has the third largest concentration of overseas Filipino workers after Saudi Arabia and Hong Kong. According to figures provided by the Philippine Overseas Employment Administration, 94 percent of Overseas Filipino Workers (OFWs) in Japan are employed as Overseas Performing Artists (OPA) and 95 percent of them are women who earn as much as US$800 a month. There are approximately 185,000 Filipino entertainers in Japan who send home around US$200 million each year. The Philippine government allows the deployment overseas of Filipino women as young as 18 years old. In order for them to obtain a visa from the Japanese Embassy, they must present an Artist Record Books (ARB).

It is unfortunate that Filipina entertainers in Japan have come to be known as "Japayuki," which was an original concoction made by Japanese media referring to young girls working as prostitutes. Apparently, good performances in Japan are not based on singing or dancing but on how many customers are attracted by the entertainer every night.

From between 10,000 to 15,000 entertainers deployed annually in the early 1980s, the numbers have risen to between 40,000 and 80,000 yearly in the past four years. According to the Philippine Overseas Employment Administration (POEA), there are 240,548 documented Filipinos in Japan as of 2001.

In the 1980s, the Filipino entertainers in Japan were considered professional, multi-talented artists who could sing, dance and speak the local language. Now with the fast and high demand of entertainers, the recruiters and promoters deploy any young Filipina even without high school education or musical talent. The question remains: who would trade a high-paying job in Japan with house and lot, branded clothes and jet-setting lifestyle with just 4-6 hours of work, to round-the-clock housework in Hong Kong, care-giving service in the Middle East, or prison-like factory work in Taiwan? In an interview with OWWA Welfare Officer Josephine Sanchez-Tobia, she divulged:

"It is a perception that working in Japan means big money. Moreover, this is a particular industry where educational attainment is nonessential. We hear tales about a provincial lass, a high school dropout with a good singing voice, someone with good looks and who can dance; they are all encouraged to work as a guest relations officer in clubs or lounges. This becomes a stepping-stone in securing an entertainment visa in Japan and a means to earn dollars fast! Nowadays, having no singing and dancing abilities does not deter deployment to Japan. A recruiter would entice a Filipina informing her that her job is to just sit and pour drinks to customers and get paid in yen, yen that will allow her to buy the latest appliances and accessories while working as Overseas Performing Artist." (Talorete 2004)

Social Problems in Target Area

Although mostly unreported, many Japanese are so lonely that they resort to either suicide or live entertainment by foreigners. In 2001, there were 31,042 suicides reported in Japan. It was the fourth consecutive year that the number topped 30,000 — a per-capita rate more than twice that in the United States (http://www.msnbc.com/modules/expoprts/ct_mail.asp?/news/922190. asp). Their material wealth and socio-cultural setup cannot fill the emptiness of their life. The high demand for entertainers in this wealthy Asian country exposes the loneliness still experienced in the midst of materialistic pursuits.

The high-tech entertainment media is not as attractive as the live performances of the Filipino entertainers. On Mondays, many Japanese men rush to nightclubs after office or factory work for them to ease the tension of the coming week's workload. On Fridays, they go back to "wining and dining" to forget the problems they encountered the whole week.

Analysts blame the social problems in Japan as a "complex mix of factors, including Japan's flagging economy, a breakdown in social values, and the loss of family stability." In 1999, divorce hit a record high. "There has just been too much violent social change," said Biten Yasumoto, a social psychology professor at Sanno University near Tokyo. "This has given birth to a huge number of problems." Figures released by Japan's Health Ministry in 1998, when 32,863 people committed suicide substantiate that the Japanese suicide statistics is high by international standards (Lies 2000). The United States has roughly the same number of suicides a year but its population is twice the size of Japan's.

One Thursday showed 31,385 people killed themselves in 1999. Analysts said cultural differences were important. No religious prohibitions exist against suicide in Japan, and it is sometimes seen as a way of escaping shame or saving loved ones from embarrassment or financial loss."[2]

Spiritual Discovery of the Involved Individuals

A Japan-based civic group called on religious and militant groups to join the campaign against the continued deployment of Filipino entertainers abroad. "Let us all destroy this national disgrace. Stop the trafficking of women. Our national honor is priceless. We must defend it at all cost, at all times." The Philippine Women's League of Japan pass on their views on *Japayuki* by coming up with the following information:

> "Filipinos rank first in the list of foreign drug offenders in Japan. Majority are women working as hostesses in Japanese bars and night-clubs. They work from 5 p.m. to 4 a.m. seven days a week with only one or two days off a month. They are also forced to go on the mandatory *dohan* or dates with customers even during their supposed sleeping hours at daytime. So, to stay awake in their jobs, they resort to stimulant drugs such as *shabu* and bron. Also, according to testimonies given to the police, they take *shabu* in order to stay slim and sexy for they are heavily fined when they gain weight. Another serious repercussion of the deployment of Filipino bar hostesses to Japan is the alarmingly increasing number of broken homes and illegitimate children. To politicians back home, therefore, we ask and beg—STOP THE DETERIORATION OF FILIPINO MORALITY! STOP THE JAPAYUKI NOW!" (http://japan.co.jp/~ystakei/pw11.html).

Filipino groups in Japan circulate and demand responses to the hate e-mail by Art Bell, a US-based radio talk show host, which states, "In Japan, Filipinos are heavily discriminated against. The only Filipinos that can live successfully in Japan are the Filipino prostitutes."

There are unending issues of the expatriates' presence in Japan. Many more controversies revolve in the recruitment and deployment of the Filipino entertainers. The Japanese people may get the entertainment they seek, but both parties use each other for their own temporary relief. The Japanese Immigration crackdown on nightclubs these days is partly due to the promoters' illegal activities—employing more entertainers than stipulated in the business contracts, and for requiring other odd jobs.

Many Filipino entertainers, out of convenience, end up marrying their customers. For many Filipina entertainers it is a premeditated plan that if executed successfully, will grant them a resident visa and would enable them to work without having to give "a cut" to their recruitment agency. On the other hand, the Japanese family ends up having a foreigner in their close-knit homogenous clan, which entails much adjustment on language and culture.

Who could fathom or even question God's sovereign will? A God who allows the migration of Filipino entertainers to an affluent yet lonely Japanese society. How can we measure His grace in choosing to save and use these lowly, uneducated young women to reach out to the closed-knit, homogenous Japanese family?

By virtue of marriage, these Filipino women and men who are former entertainers, are now inside the circles of close-knit Japanese families. Their reach and influence are more intensive and extensive than the reach of traditional missionaries. Given the proper orientation and training in missions, these Filipinas can be effective witnesses of the gospel. It is God's amazing grace that saves the "worst sinners" in this society, molds them into the people He wants them to be, and uses them as instruments for His kingdom-building in Japan.

In the light of God's sovereignty, grace and truth, we simply picture both the Japanese and Filipino people and their circumstances as divinely appointed by God. This is not to justify the demand for entertainment by the Japanese or the supply of the material provision for the Filipinos. For God loves these Filipino entertainers so much that His masterplan for Japan involves saving their customers, Japanese family and friends through them. I have been blessed to see the fruits of this mission and I am committed to pray that God would raise missionaries and spiritual multipliers among the singers, dancers, entertainers, bar girls in nightclubs, and among their

Japanese customers. With our intentional outreach, Filipino entertainers will come to red light districts and all over Japan!

> "But God chose the foolish things of the world to shame the wise; God chose the weak things of the world to shame the strong. He chose the lowly things of this world and the despised things." (I Corinthians 1:27-28 NIV)

TESTIMONIALS OF MODERN-DAY MISSIONARIES IN JAPAN: THE FORMER FILIPINO ENTERTAINERS

Our unchanging, true and eternal God is the same God of the Filipino entertainers. The only God who extended His grace to Abraham who lied, Moses who killed, David who committed adultery, Paul who persecuted the believers, and to Rahab who lived a sinful life. He is our forgiving and merciful God. He is a potter who can mold the Filipino entertainers to be His modern-day missionaries to a closed-door Japanese society.

Below are true-to-life stories of 12 Filipino entertainers with their real names so that you can interview and associate with them if ever you come to Japan. I have personally ministered to them and still keep my communication with some of them. They represent the hundreds of Filipinos who came to know Jesus Christ and who I personally met in Japan in my 12 years of ministry.

Alona is a beautiful and young entertainer who married her Japanese customer and now has two children. Her family lives with her Japanese in-laws. She accepted Jesus as Savior and Lord of her life and is now actively sharing her new-found faith and inviting her friends, relatives and Filipino entertainers to her home Bible studies and to church. Her Filipino store serves as a contact point for Filipinos in Japan. She is instrumental in our evangelistic house blessing ceremonies and reaches out to homosexuals married to Japanese men.

Erie is a former lesbian who came to Japan as a professional singer in a nightclub. God has transformed her into a lady minister at a Japanese church. In 1997, I invited her to attend the Asian Mission Congress in Thailand.

There she was extremely challenged to financially support international outreaches while being directly involved in Japan missions.

Beth, a former *Japayuki* who caused the removal of her Filipino parents' church leadership position when she came to Japan. She was a cult member for 18 years, but is now an active evangelical church member since she came to know Jesus last year. She often invites her Filipino and foreign friends to church and exercises her gift of hospitality. She taught her Filipino-Japanese son to pray and to share testimonies during Sunday worship services. Her Japanese relatives live in the province and are her potential mission targets!

Carol, a former entertainer married to a Japanese man. She is one of the most active Christians in our Tokyo Church. She shares her Christian faith to her Japanese husband and often invites her friends, who are still entertainers, for home Bible studies and church activities. Together with her contacts, we aim to have a local Filipino-Japanese church near her place.

Emmy only finished her elementary studies and became a professional dancer. She came to Japan as an entertainer and met the Lord Jesus Christ. She surrendered her life and committed to work for Him in a Japanese church that introduced her Japanese husband, mother-in-law and daughter to Jesus Christ. With on-the-job outreach training, she worked with our mission in ministering to many Filipinas married to Japanese in Kanagawa Prefecture. Our Filipina contacts are mail-order brides, "*shokai*" (introduced by friends and relatives to marry a Japanese) and her fellow nightclub workers. The husbands of these Filipinas have attended Japanese Christian gatherings and home Bible studies conducted by a Japanese pastor. Their Filipino-Japanese children are now attending a Japanese church Sunday school where their Filipina mothers are praying for them to become future pastors and missionaries.

Espie is a former nightclub entertainer, but now a factory worker. She came to know Christ only last year (2003) and now regularly attends our Sunday worship services. Her Japanese husband may have divorced her but her Christian testimony attracted her daughter to come to church. Her daughter has since learned how to pray and share God's faithfulness in her life. She invites people to church and shares her faith with her workmates.

Jennifer is one of the oldest Filipina entertainers whom I respect for her openness and honesty. With her permission for this interview and report, she admitted to have had married three times already, and is again a divorcee. Her overnight visit to our Filipino Christian Ministry Network (FCMN) Mission Center led her to acknowledge her personal situation and she prayed to accept Jesus as Savior in November 2003. In March this year, we joined a Japanese church near her new apartment in Tokyo; a three-minute walk from her former apartment of eight years. The local church just opened their doors to International Ministry after 45 years of existence. It's a double blessing and joy for us because the old church invited us to this new outreach and they would like our mission group to help them start it; better still, Filipinos are most welcome to join them. It's also the first time for Jennifer to enter a Christian church in Japan after 26 years of living here. Her birthday was two days before our agreed Sunday worship together and she celebrated on Saturday night. Still, she came straight to worship service even with a "hang-over." She was surprised to hear the English sermon because this was her personal Bible reading earlier, "How to be Born Again." She admitted to have understood the Japanese translation better than the direct English preaching. Please pray for her growth and sphere of influence: for 15 years she has belonged to a Japanese bowler's association with 126 members; she has more Japanese contacts than most of her fellow Filipinos. She cherished the memories when she worked with her younger sister in a nightclub where customers where fond of their singing and dancing. Her sister, Jocelyn, came to know Jesus in 1990 and now coordinates the Intercessors for Japan in the Philippines (see Jocelyn's personal written testimony in Appendix).

Judith, at age 13, came to Japan as an entertainer but became a drug-user-pusher and later married her Yakuza boss who gave her capital to start a Filipino restaurant. She received a gospel tract in our weekly evangelism outreach in Metropolitan Tokyo and was later followed up by a Filipino Christian counselor. When she accepted Jesus Christ as her Savior and Lord, changes were evident in her life. She employed jobless Filipino Christians and allowed her restaurant to be a worship place for Filipinos. Many came to know Jesus in this place and the restaurant income supported Filipino missionaries and Christian outreaches. Her mission extended to the Philippines when she purchased land for a church building in her hometown. She also attends Japanese churches and special Christian gatherings to share her testimony and to spiritually feed her two Filipino-Japanese children.

Judy was a Mama-san or leader of about 15 Filipino entertainers. She came to know Jesus through the outreach of Emma, a Filipina housewife in Hokkaido, who was also instrumental in the conversion and baptism of her Japanese husband and children. Our mission group sent Bibles and gospel tracts to Emma who distributed them to Judy and the Filipino entertainers. All of these Filipino women accepted Jesus as Savior and Lord. They became so discontent with their entertainment jobs that they chose to go back home to the Philippines without finishing their contract. Judy soon returned to Japan to marry her Japanese boyfriend. She is now a housewife with two children and is actively attending a Japanese church in Hokkaido.

Mary Grace is a college graduate who ended up as a hostess in Japan. She is considered a four-timer since she travelled as entertainer for four times before she settled as housewife of a Japanese, her customer during her first contract as Overseas Performing Artist. I met her during our Japanese Language School graduation and I invited her to join our Sunday worship service last March. Praise God for His saving grace that she is now a new believer. We found a new factory job for her and now she would like to mend her broken relationship with her family in the Philippines who disowned her when she became an entertainer in Japan.

Shirly is a former model and nightclub worker. She is now managing a construction business. She was instrumental in planting two Filipino-Japanese churches in Saitama and Kanagawa Prefectures. She is married to an Okinawan Japanese who now supports the Filipino ministry by offering their house for worship and outreaches.

Tess came to Japan as a nightclub singer. When she came to know Jesus, she began leading worship in her church. She is now using her talents for the Lord. She underwent Ministry Training (New Life Training Center) with us on evangelism, discipleship and church leadership last year and prayed to become a spiritual multiplier. She now shares her faith to her Japanese husband and workmates in the factory.

Our God is truly amazing! He alone can reach these lowly members of the society and even use them for His Kingdom-building in Japan. In His sufficiency, many of these Filipino entertainers now find genuine satisfaction, peace and security in their lives and this is what they share to the people around them. For what they experience with Christ and for who God is, they testify faithfully!

Our church in Japan is a powerful testimony of what God can do in the lives of Filipino entertainers and expatriates. The members derived the name God's Grace Christian Fellowship because it is a fellowship of sinners saved by the grace of God. The members of our congregation are equipped for Japan evangelization and are mobilized for prayer-intercession through the Intercessors for Japan (IFJ).

By God's grace, I have personally met and ministered to hundreds of Filipino entertainers who accepted Jesus Christ as Savior and Lord of their lives. Many of them now attend home Bible studies and Sunday worship services. They have testified on how they tried to share Christianity with their Japanese Buddhist customers, club owners and managers. They have expressed how their lives have been changed and that they desire to look for a job outside the entertainment industry. I have been connected with many Filipino entertainers through my regular column at *Pinoy & Pinay Magazine* as many of the Filipino entertainers in Japan read inspirational articles with quotations from the Bible. Some of them became my regular callers for prayer and counseling.

RAHAB MINISTRY IN FOREIGN COUNTRIES VIS-À-VIS MINISTRY TO FILIPINO ENTERTAINERS IN JAPAN

The Rahab Ministry of the Samaritan Purse in Thailand and Youth With A Mission outreach in the red-light districts in Holland are considerably well-focused and intentional.

Their organization and support challenges us to strengthen our base as we seek partnership with like-minded mission organizations in order to have more resources (personnel and finance). The ministry to Filipino Entertainers in Japan is long-term through a series of outreaches: *First-timers, Returnees,*

Married to Japanese, and Mother of Filipino-Japanese children. Economics Professor Alvin Ang, Filipino Ph.D candidate at Osaka University, helped us realize that our ministry to the Filipino entertainers in Japan is unique because we are not only bringing them to Christ but also training them to be church-based servant leaders in Japan and beyond! Indeed, our holistic ministry in Japan is not only looking for alternative jobs for the Filipino entertainers but also training them as spiritual multipliers and lay church leaders.

To better understand our ministry in Japan, some simple categories and some brief descriptions of the Filipino entertainers must be discussed.

First-Timers

Filipino entertainers who have their first six-month contract to Japan are called "first-timers." They are known as "talento" or talents. They arrive in groups and stay together in a rented apartment. Their boss (sacho) and leader (Mama-san) do not allow them to go out unless they are with their group members. Reaching out to them is difficult and so we give them gospel tracts instead since we are not permitted to spend more time with them.

Some of them read the magazine where I am a regular columnist and they secretly call me for prayer and counseling. Others call me before they report for work at 6 p.m. and then call again for confession and other prayer requests at around 4 to 6 a.m. I have not personally met most of the callers, but have chatted with them on the phone many times.

Returnees

When asked why the Filipino entertainers come back to Japan, they say that they are especially requested (shimei) by their Japanese customers. They take pride in their singing and dancing skills and how much business they bring in to the nightclubs they work in.

These Filipino entertainers are more open to conversation and seek counseling on intermarriage with the Japanese and their future in Japan. Their jobs require them to go out with their customers (*dohan*). Some come to church.

An entertainer-returnee who came to know Christ in our outreach testifies, "I came to Japan to seek the mighty yen but Jesus the Almighty God found me."

Married to Japanese

Though many of the Japanese who go to nightclubs are divorced, most Filipino entertainers still choose to marry their customers. These entertainers who fall into the trap of marriage are blinded by the "big money" given to them by their Japanese suitors. They often realize later that this "investment" by his or her customer is like a dowry. It is a one-time gift but out of sense of indebtedness, the Filipino entertainer agrees to marry this customer.

Some couples live together before they marry or until they have a child. In many of our experiences in Japan, when a Filipina becomes pregnant, she longs to connect with other Filipinos. This is a good opportunity to reach out to them and root them in God's Word and church ministry.

The Filipino converts start to share their Christian faith to their Japanese husband and in-laws. But the pressure from their families back in the Philippines who expect their continued financial support causes a strain on their faith. Temptation to go back to nightclub work or to go through abortion is very strong. Some compromise their faith by going back to their former way of life while attending our home Bible studies. We let the Spirit of God work in their hearts as we seek to find alternative jobs for them. We have success stories like Espie's and Beth's even though it takes time for them to accept and adjust to lower-paying jobs with longer hours of work and more demanding responsibility.

Mothers to Filipino-Japanese Children

The Filipino entertainers who have Filipino-Japanese children have mixed emotions on having children with two different cultures. It is a big challenge for them to learn the Japanese culture, language and culinary art for the sake of their children. There is a heavy responsibility to attend school functions and to remain sober knowing that they are closely scrutinized by the Japanese mothers and that the other children are indisposed towards them.

Our ministry to this group of Filipinos is more taxing because of the necessary multifaceted way of presenting biblical principles on parenting, roles of family members, church involvement and community association. A number of seminars and workshops on personal and church-life direction are conducted for them. We encourage them by casting on vision for Christian movement in Japan through their Filipino-Japanese children (Japinos). Now like the Filipino mothers, we Filipino full-time missionaries in Japan envision many of the Japinos becoming pastors and missionaries among the Japanese and even around the world!

Church Planting Initiatives

In the past ten years, church planting initiatives have been launched by different denominations and Christian organizations among the Filipino OFWs in Japan. Some of these denominations are the Jesus Is Lord Fellowship (from the Philippines), the Christian & Missionary Alliance, and several Baptists and Pentecostal groups.

The FCMN and God's Grace Christian Fellowship (GGCF) are to be noted for their intentional church planting work among the Filipino entertainers and Japinos.

Many Filipino entertainers have attended our worship services and have joined in the different ministries of GGCF, specifically the home Bible studies which we call *Weekdays Cell Groups*. GGCF worship centers are called *Sanctuary*, which is open to the public 24 hours a day, 7 days a week. Since the Filipinos in Japan work in different shifts and the entertainers go home anytime of the day, the Sanctuary is a welcome solace for them after their jobs.

Ministry Challenges in Japan

Believing that the gospel is for all, we intend to reach all the Filipinos in Japan especially the entertainers. We also aim to train them to reach out to their Japanese family, clan, workmates, friends and spheres of influence.

Since majority of the Filipinos in Japan are women entertainers who eventually marry the Japanese nationals and then have Filipino-Japanese children, we actually give more focus on them. As we see the influx of Filipinos in Japan, we envision them like a Trojan Horse entering closed-knit families and establishing God's Kingdom. The fast-facts below on Japan challenge us to keep on with our prayer-intercession until we witness Japan as the *Land of the Risen Son*.

Population:	125,860,000
Size:	377,847 km²
Density:	333 people/ km²
Capital:	Tokyo
Cities:	672
	With no church: 9
	With only 1 church: 74
Towns/Villages:	2,562
	With no church: 1,734
	With 20,000 population – no church: 75
Churches:	8,900
Members:	543,816
	Member/church: 69
	Member/population: 4.3/1000
Worship attendance:	266,970
	Attendance/church: 34
	Attendance/population: 2.1/1000
Missionaries:	2,362[3]

Prayer Points

Awareness. There needs to be an awareness of the reality of what is going on in the world with regard to prostitution. Pray that more Christians would see and understand the need for prayer and response.

People. Pray for the men, women, and children who are involved or affected by the entanglement of prostitution or sex slavery.

Children. Pray specifically for the children who are being sold into prostitution and are physically, mentally, and emotionally abused.

Current Ministries. Pray for the ministries that are already working to provide help for the men, women, and children involved in prostitution: wisdom, provision, strategy, protection, favor. Some of these ministries are: White Lotus (Cambodia), Rahab Ministries (Thailand), The Cleft (Amsterdam), Linda's House of Hope (Australia), and World Vision.

Laws. Pray for governments worldwide to make righteous decisions with regard to the laws on prostitution and also for wisdom on how to enforce those laws.[4]

ENDNOTES

[1] Japanzone, Your guide to Japan and Japanese Culture, Japan-guide.com

[2] Elaine Lies, Japan Suicide Rate Clings Near Record High, Corporate Watch in Japanese Transnational Resource and Action Center (TRAC), Friday June 30, 2000. http://www.corpwatch-jp.org

[3] Operation Japan, JEMA & OJ Publishing Committee, Edition 2000.

[4] The Sex Industry- Trafficking of Women and Children, Youth With A Mission. http://www.ywamperth.org.au/articles.asp?name=11

REFERENCES

An Outreach to all women of Faith & Hope: Hearts for Christ Ministries. http://www.heartsforchrist.org/womenofword/rahab1.htm

Cortazzi, Hugh (2004). Japan Spotlight (January/February 2004), Japan Times, March 10, 2004.

Holy Bible. New International Version. http://bible.gospelcom.net/cgi-bin/bible?language=english&version=NIV&passage=Ecclesiastes+3%3A9-14&x=15&y=12 *Japans chilling Internet suicide pacts,* MSNBC News Link http://www.msnbc.com/modules/exports/ct_email.asp?/news/922190.asp

Japanzone, your guide to Japan and Japanese Culture, Japan-guide.com http://www.japan-guide.com/e/e2134.html

Laverinto, Jocelyn (2003). *Praying for Spiritual Missiles To Be Launched in Japan,* Inori Shinbun, The official Prayer-Newsletter of the Intercessors for Japan, Anniversary Issue, November 29, 2003.

Lies, Elaine. Japan Suicide Rate Clings Near Record High, Corporate Watch in Japanese Transnational Resource and Action Center (TRAC), Friday June 30, 2000. http://www.corpwatch-jp.org

Ocampo, Ambeth R. (2003). *Filipino and Japanese links,* Philippine Daily Inquirer, Friday Jul. 04, 2003.

Operation Japan, Edition 2000, JEMA & OJ Publishing Committee Pinays in Japan, Philippine Women's League of Japan, http://japan.co.jp/~ystakei/pwl1.html

Sing, Lim Hua. (2003). *"Utilizing foreign talents to achieve economic growth,"* Asia Network, January 24, 2003.

Smith's Bible Dictionary, http://bible.crosswalk.com/Dictionaries/SmithsBibleDictionary/smt.cgi?number=T3572

Talorete, Butch N. (2004). In the eye of the storm, *Philippines Today,* March 10, 2004

YWAM publication. The Sex Industry- *Trafficking of Women and Children,* http://www.ywamperth.org.au/articles.asp?name=11

APPENDIX

Personal Written Testimony of
a Former Entertainer-Turned-Prayer Mobilizer for Japan
by Jocelyn N. Laverinto, IFJ-RP Coordinator

I was broken hearted and depressed before I came to know the Lord Jesus in the year 1990, believing that committing suicide was the only way out of my emotional misery. There was no sense of meaning in my life anymore because my Japanese lover had abandoned me. I had lost the pleasure of eating. I suffered sleepless nights. I isolated myself, locking myself inside my room, alone, wallowing in the pain of rejection and abandonment from a lover who promised me the moon and the stars. I tried to conceal my inner pain because of shame to admit that I was a victim of unrequited love. However, the more I suppressed my heartache, the more I become broken inside. The pain was so severe that it was like pouring vinegar into my wounded and bleeding heart. And I wanted to die!

In my yearning to die, the true Lover of my soul knocked at the door of my heart. A friend of mine told me that the only Person who could take away the pain in my heart was Jesus Christ! Suddenly, I realized that I was the one who had abandoned God. I ran away from His grace and mercy. I had rejected His love and lost my memory on how to get back home. Unknowingly, He sent His emissaries to bring me back to where I truly belong – I belong to the Kingdom of God! I was the prodigal daughter who was found wounded, naked, almost destroyed by Satan, yet my Father in heaven rescued me! He provided me with clothes of righteousness, peace and the joy of the Holy Spirit.

I have tasted the goodness and protection of God because I was brought back into His presence. But what about those people who have lost their way before, just like me? Where are they now? What is their present condition? While asking these questions, I remember the place where I became emotionally wounded and spiritually disabled. The shackle of strongholds of Japan such as idolatry, lawlessness, materialism, death, and deception have captured and prevented me from going back to the Master of my soul, Jesus Christ. This revelation has given me an intense inner desire to kneel down and mobilize more intercessors so that powerful spiritual missiles (Divine power, 2 Corinthians 10:3-5) from the mighty God can be launched to demolish the spiritual strongholds of Japan. Such prayers will also allow missionaries in Japan (ground warriors) to penetrate the inner camp of the enemy (Satan) and retrieve the prisoners of war (the people loved by God, including my sister, Jennifer Yanagi).

God inspired me to be a part of Intercessors for Japan-Philippines (IFJ-RP) in mobilizing churches all over the nation to pray for the evangelization of Japan. He gave me a vision of many churches as they prayed in unity just like a "Burning Bush." This vision came into reality as I travelled to Davao City, Cebu City and Leyte last November 8 to 16, 2003 in mobilizing churches to intercede for Japan.

14

THE KAPATIRAN NG MGA SIMBAHANG PILIPINO SA SINGAPORE (BROTHERHOOD OF FILIPINO CHURCH IN SINGAPORE)

Interview with
Rev. Reynaldo 'Rey' Solano & Ms. Godiva Ysip

I n 2003, over 50,000 Filipinos were counted as working and living in Singapore making it one of the top Asian destinations for OFWs. They work in Singapore as medical workers, IT professionals, household workers, and construction workers. In July 1998, Kapatiran ng mga Simbahang Pilipino sa Singapore (KSPS) was founded to respond to the OFW need for spiritual care and guidance. Since their start in 1998, 22 congregations have become affiliated with KSPS.

Rev. Rey Solano and Ms. Godiva Ysip are two of KSPS' leaders. Here a FIN News Editor interviews them and talks to them about their ministry to the Filipinos in Asia's Lion City.

FN: How many Filipino congregations are there in Singapore? How many organized Filipino churches are there?

RS: To my knowledge, there are more or less 36 Christian Filipino organized congregations to date, existing mostly under the covering of a local church. Of these churches, 22 are members of KSPS headed by a Filipino pastor. Of the remaining 14 churches, one Hawaiian-Japanese lead five, while Singaporeans lead the remaining eight, with Filipino leaders assisting them. Only one church is fully accredited by the government as a religious body operating on its own.

At least three large churches have a significant number of Filipino parishioners but do not have a distinct "organized" Filipino church. They exist as small groups and they meet for social functions. There are also at least five known pseudo-Christian groups that have regular Sunday meetings. Several Roman Catholic churches have organized Filipino groups actively involved in their parishes.

FN: When was KSPS formed and what was it that brought you all together?

GY: In the mid '90s, Rev. Aow Kwong Bu, former pastor of Queenstown Baptist Church (QBC) encouraged the Filipinos in Singapore to unite for the sake of the ministry of the Lord.

RS: KSPS was formed in 1998. We were all brought together by our passion to reach primarily the Filipinos and other expatriate workers. The Filipino pastors recognized a common goal and purpose.

The first meeting of the group took place at QBC. In attendance were Pastors Wilfredo "Dong" Adriano (International Baptist Church), Nida Simeon (QBC), and a representative from Grace Assembly of God. The second meeting was an organizational meeting and was attended by more pastors: Joy Cera and Esther Chelliah (Wesley Methodist Church), Rey Paano (Calvary Charismatic Centre), Jingle Cortes (Brethren Mission Church, now Papuri Christian Fellowship), Elvie Sinel (Word for the World, now Word International), Florence Tay (Paya Lebar Methodist Church), and Esther Ong (Faith Methodist Church).

FN: How often do you meet?

RS: We meet regularly for fellowship and prayer every last Sunday of the month.

FN: You mentioned that KSPS is now organized. What is your association's objectives and what cooperative ministries do you do to reach the Filipinos, other expatriates, and their host nation?

GY: The objectives of KSPS since its inception has always been in the area of cooperative evangelism, fellowship among pastors and leaders, training, prayer, social action, and information dissemination.

RS: Yes, the objective of the group revolves around the common agenda of reaching out to the Filipinos in Singapore with the Gospel of Christ by conducting various activities that caters to this objective. Four major activities are planned annually as a cooperative activity geared for outreach and fellowship:

1) prayer convocation in February

2) evangelistic meeting in June (before or after Independence Day)

3) pastors and their family fellowship in December

4) sports outreach (basketball and volleyball tournaments) – these used to be once-a-year activity. Now with committed volunteers to oversee it, we are holding our 3rd Conference this coming September (2004).

GY: Some of the KSPS past projects had brought the following personalities from the Philippines to minister to our countrymen: Nonoy Zuñiga, Dr. Ely Javier, Ray-An Fuentes, Princess Punzalan, Tirso Cruz III, Coney Reyes, and Evangelist Kumar Abraham and his group of singers called The Wind.

As Rey mentioned, annual prayer gatherings, evangelistic meetings, and sports festivals have been part of KSPS' regular activities. Some churches offer short courses on computer technology as a contact point for non-Christians.

We have also been involved in many community projects such as raising funds for the victims of Mt. Pinatubo and for the victims of the earthquake that hit Baguio City badly in 1990. KSPS has also always been supportive to the Philippine Embassy in Singapore. Our member churches help the Embassy in information dissemination, counseling runaway domestic helpers, gathering people for the Embassy events, and visiting hospitalized Filipinos.

FN: It is encouraging to know about your concerted efforts. What are your respective ministries among Filipinos in Singapore? How do you help the community in practical day-to-day matters?

RS: Primarily, I pastor a church aimed at reaching the Filipinos. This includes personal counseling, visitations, encouragement through preaching and study of God's Word, training for church and small group leaderships.

I also belong to a pool of community leaders actively working together to address some of the needs of the Filipinos in Singapore. We all work hand-in-hand with the Philippine Embassy. For two years, I have been involved with a local non-government organization (NGO) in giving appreciation to OFWs, for example, a citywide search for the "Most Outstanding Employer" and the "Most Outstanding Domestic Helper." For a time, I chaired the United Council of Leaders in Singapore. This group comprises the heads of different Filipino community organizations. Several times, I have been involved in finding solutions to domestic disputes and legal. There were times that I have been called as a material witness in court cases between a domestic helper and her employer.

GY: My ministry among Filipinos in Singapore is to disciple a small group of Filipino domestic helpers who are employees of the Singaporeans attending worship in our church. We meet every Sunday morning using a cell group format. We have our own Filipino worship service, Bible study and prayer meeting. I teach some skills in evangelism, discipleship, and follow-up. I also do a few counseling and conflict resolution between employers and their maids.

FN: How did God prepare you for ministry in Singapore?

RS: I had the privilege of having some Singaporean classmates during college and seminary days in the Philippines. They gave me insight and a feel of what it is to be Singaporean. Through them my personal knowledge of their country, its people, and their culture was expanded. But it was my one-and-a-half month ministry exposure in Penang, Malaysia that gave me a better perspective of the life and culture in the region. My ministry involvement in reaching the small Filipino community in Penang also gave me first-hand experience about the lives of Filipinos in a foreign land. After that, I had two short visits in Singapore where I ministered and had fellowship with pastors and members of the churches in Singapore. It allowed me to interact with various Filipinos working in Singapore.

GY: I was a member of Christ for Greater Manila's (CGM) evangelistic team from 1984-1990; worked for my home church as discipleship coordinator from 1990-1993; and was an Operation Mobilization missionary in

England from 1993-1995. I have been in Singapore since 1996. All these missions exposure has prepared me to minister in Singapore.

FN: You are both very busy with your church ministries. Tell us how you got involved with Filipino International Network (FIN)?

GY: FIN brought together pastors, churches and organizations from different countries whose main goal is to reach out to Christian Filipinos and their host nations.

RS: I got to know FIN through KSPS. In 2002, I chaired the Singapore Planning and Coordinating Committee for the first FIN Global Consultation. I represented KSPS in the recent July 2004 consultation held in Seoul, Korea. I am also serving as member of the FIN Global Committee.

GY: My own first exposure to FIN was when I attended the FIN consultation in Taipei, Taiwan in 1997. I then helped organize the FIN-Far East Asia Regional Consultation in April 1999 and I was further exposed to the growing FIN partnership when we, KSPS, hosted the FIN Global Consultation here in 2002. I was helping KSPS in the preparation of this historic event; working closely with the KSPS chairperson and FIN's International Coordinator.

FN: So, now that you are ministering in Singapore, how do you see yourself contributing to FIN?

GY: In the past I personally coordinated two FIN events held here in Singapore, namely the Far East Asia Regional Consultation in April 1999 and the Global Consultation in 2002. I just graduated from Bible College with a degree of Master of Arts in Education and Intercultural Studies. I may be able to contribute to the ministries of FIN in the areas of missions and evangelism. I was a missionary with Operation Mobilization for two years in the UK before coming to Singapore, so maybe I can contribute as a resource on this. Since my work in church is mainly among the locals, (Singaporeans), I may be able to contribute by teaching Filipinos how to work with the locals.

RS: FIN has a global perspective and has always worked in partnership with other members of the Body of Christ. This networking model has always been the strongest under-girding factor of our association here in Singapore.

KSPS started working together in 1997 with a common goal in reaching the Filipinos being paramount to each individual church's sets of beliefs. FIN expands this idea of networking globally. I see FIN as a global catalyst in mobilizing Filipinos to help reach the world for Jesus Christ.

KSPS can contribute to FIN in many ways. We have many resources in Singapore. We need to combine these resources for cooperative missions work. It is important to cast the vision to all the local churches. There are excellent training opportunities in this country. It is important that we maximize the potentials of these and and share them with the congregations. My dream is for the KSPS to become a strong receiving and sending congregation.

How can I contribute to FIN? First of all, to diligently and faithfully pastor the Filipinos here in Singapore. Second, to encourage other pastors and congregations to embrace FIN's mandate to "motivate, equip, and mobilize Filipinos for missions."

FN: What strategies are the Filipino churches with KSPS using to reach their hosts and other expatriates, and how has FIN helped facilitate this ministry?

RS: Cooperative event outreaches. FIN helped us work together and in the past resourced us with evangelistic tools and discipleship training materials. Above all, FIN has given us the vision to see beyond our geography. As I said earlier, my dream for the KSPS is to become a strong missions base in Far East Asia.

GY: I agree with Brother Rey.

FN: Thank you very much for participating in this interview. KSPS showcases "cooperative model" and unity in the Body of Christ. It is our hope and prayers that other Filipino congregations outside their homeland will follow your model in Singapore. God bless you and your respective congregations.

GY: Thank you for this privilege of taking part in this interview.

RS: I look forward to reading FIN's publication. Thank you.

15

FORMOSA, WITH LOVE
Interview with
Dr. Ronald Adhikari

F rom the outskirts of Taipei, the capital city of Taiwan (Republic of China), one would discover why Taiwan is known as the Ilha Formosa, "the beautiful island." Its beautiful scenery—the mountain peaks reaching the clouds—has been attracting Filipino fishermen for many decades who fished in the Northern China Sea. Now that Taiwan is a modernized industrialized megalopolis, it has been attracting, no longer just Filipino fishermen, but factory workers, IT professionals, construction workers, and domestic helpers. In recent years, thousands of Filipinos have migrated to Taiwan as Overseas Contract Workers.

FIN News has interviewed Dr. Ronald Adhikari, a worker who has been ministering in Taiwan. He is not a Filipino, but he has played a significant role in the FIN movement.

FN: Dr. Adhikari, how is it that you ended up in Taiwan? In retrospect how do you see how God has prepared you for ministry in Taiwan?

RA: Way back in 1968 I was praying for Taiwan and God impressed upon my heart Isaiah 55:5 which I took to be God's promise. It took me 25 years of preparation and I am still learning God's ways.

Initially, the seven years of student ministry in India was an exciting pilgrimage of faith. In Singapore, much of my cherished prejudices and paradigms about the ministry shifted radically. In Korea, the main lesson I learned was about authority structures in other cultures and my submission and trust in God in a changing world. Residing and studying in five Asian countries, the USA and New Zealand, gave me the experience of being a global citizen, learning the languages, and finding means and ways to witness for the Lord.

The ten years of Church planting and seminary teaching in the Philippines was another training ground. And the Lord opened the way for me to enter Taiwan while I was ministering to the Chinese Churches in the USA.

FN: It's a good thing that you spent some time in the Philippines, because here in Taiwan, you minister to many international workers, particularly to Filipinos. What exactly is your ministry among Filipinos in Taiwan?

RA: Well, let me share with you some of the things we are doing:

1. Networking among the Filipino pastors, Chinese Christian leaders interested in missions and keeping in touch with Churches as well as some Christian agencies in the OCW-sending countries.

2. Assisting Filipino fellowships—speaking at meetings or inviting speakers, participating in evangelistic outreach programs, finding funds for special programs, counseling, mentoring.

3. Vision casting among the Chinese churches so that they may see the need to reach out to the foreigners at their doorsteps.

4. Raising prayer warriors for this strategic ministry all over the globe.

FN: Would you happen to know how many Filipino churches there are in Taiwan?

RA: Among the 80,000 Filipino OCWs in Taiwan, approximately 4,000 meet for worship and fellowship on Sundays. (The Roman Catholics may have 7,000.) The three largest groups are JIL, Word for the World and Free Believers Fellowship. JIL alone has established 24 fellowship groups all over the island. In the larger 12 cities of Taiwan, there may be two to four Filipino fellowships. Altogether there may be 80 to 100 meeting places on Sundays. This includes the English services that Filipinos attend.

FN: That's a lot of Filipinos! They must have a lot of potentials for ministry to their hosts as well. Do you know what strategies the churches are doing to reach their hosts?

RA: Yes,

1. Many have tried the direct confrontational gospel presentation, but much of the enthusiasm has subsided because of miscommunication, language barrier, and ignorance of cultural understanding of religion.

2. Praying for the hosts' spiritual enlightenment and silently witnessing by living is a good method; but it is difficult to evaluate its effectiveness in the short duration of employment.

3. Most have found it rewarding to invite the Chinese to the worship services, which are lively and contemporary, and especially appealing to the younger generation. Those learning English find the Filipino fellowships as a very good place to practice their language skills. Several Chinese friends became Christians within a short time. Filipinos married to Chinese nationals do make serious efforts to win their spouses to Christ. The approximate conversion rate among the Taiwanese is one person to every 100 Filipino conversion.

4. One Filipino missionary team, after laboring for several years, has recently planted a Chinese Church in Taichung. They are showing that Filipinos can be used to evangelize Chinese but one must be prepared for the long years of witnessing.

FN: You are now a FIN-partner from Taiwan; how did you get involve with FIN whose headquarters are across the globe in Canada?

RA: When I attended a conference for tentmakers with Global Intent (sponsored by PMA, PCEC etc.) in Tagaytay, I came to know about FIN. I kept Dr. Tira's outline and his paper about FIN and began to make connections with Filipinos and pastors. This resulted in writing a research about OCWs in Taiwan. Then I attended the FIN conference in Singapore along with a jet-set Filipino pastor from Taiwan. I continued to keep in touch with Dr. Tira ever since.

FN: How is God using your background and ministry to prepare you for ministry with FIN?

RA: My original background is from a remote corner of India in the state of Mizoram, which has a Christian population (85%), and an average income of US$350 per year. Yet, the Baptists and Presbyterians alone are able to send out over 2,000 missionaries (Cf. Operation World, Patrick Johnstone). Johnstone describes it this way, "No nation on earth has sent out so many of their people as missionaries." And I had the privilege to be raised in the midst of such an ongoing movement.

When I lived in Singapore and Korea, I became more sensitive about the great missionary movements taking place. It was a conviction that something similar was taking place in the Philippines in spite of the difficulties and problems the country was facing. I believed that the Philippines will be another major missionary-sending nation and that the Filipinos have an important role in global missions.

I took it as a personal confirmation when I heard of the two Filipino pastors who were arrested, tried, condemned and had their head shaved in preparation for execution in a jail in Riyadh, Saudi Arabia, and the reason for their conviction was witnessing for Christ on Arab land. These two pastors eventually returned to the Philippines. To me they were living martyrs! Not only are the Filipinos adaptable and suitable to meet cross-cultural challenges anywhere in the world but also, Filipino believers are willing to face martyrdom.

I am challenged and excited to be where God is moving among His people in a special way, and FIN is an integral part and an important instrument in this dynamic movement.

FN: Where does FIN fit into the Filipino-Taiwanese context? How can FIN facilitate the ministry of the Filipino congregations in Taiwan?

RA: There are several ways FIN could facilitate the ministry of the Filipinos.

1. Designing special training programs such as tentmaking, to prepare them for a life of ministry. In Taiwan, Filipinos need to understand something about Chinese religion.

2. Finding connections to network in other countries and to find openings for employment and ministry for a continuing witness.

3. Encourage the establishing of OCW Churches in the major cities of the Philippines, for their anticipated return home.

4. Ordination of qualified leaders as tentmaking missionaries.

5. Holding conferences and consultations.

6. Pastoral visits especially to those in remote areas.

FN: While you are in Taiwan, how can you contribute to FIN?

RA: By prayer, giving and serving the Filipinos in Taiwan towards a global ministry. To be a catalyst in the formation of Filipino ways of planting churches, doing missions and working out training programs for tentmakers; networking and connecting key Filipinos to FIN in my travels, and partnering with Filipinos to reach other nations particularly to those unreached.

FN: It has been great to partner with you over the years. Now let's talk about the other OCWs from other countries that you mentioned earlier. Is it true that many Filipinos work side by side in "high-tech" factories with other contract workers from countries like Thailand and Vietnam?

RA: Around 8,000 Filipinos work in the same factories and around 4,000 in the high-tech industries along with Thais and Vietnamese. The smaller private factories have a good mixture of workers. The Thais in the high-tech section may be less than 1,000 and the Vietnamese even less.

FN: In some places they live together in the dormitories provided by their Chinese employers. Please describe the relational dynamics of these multinational workers.

RA: Many of the larger dorms designed for 15 persons may have 20 to 30 people sharing the space. The smaller rooms designed for a couple may have five to eight people, each with a bunk bed.

Even in large workplaces the workers try not to mix up but some have to live together. Most employers separate the groups because of past racial tensions which flare up sometimes. The tendency for a foreign worker is to find his own group outside the workplace after working hours.

Working together in the same department under Chinese supervisors creates no problems as long as they keep up with the demands. There is respect and politeness in their relationships and they tolerate one other and work together.

The ladies have a closer bonding among the different nationalities. They all try to learn the basic means of communication which is Mandarin. They are seen to be going out together.

FN: I think that Filipinos are generally easy-going and adaptable so it would be relatively easy for them to make connections, even among other nationalities. You mentioned earlier that the Filipino believers are active in evangelism. Can you give us some examples of how these Filipino believers reach out to the other nationalities?

RA: There are evangelistic activities among the Filipinos and Taiwan's locals. It is becoming a common sight to see old Chinese people in their wheelchairs clapping their hands while singing Christian choruses in a Filipino meeting. It is neither strange to see a Children's Sunday School activity in English for Chinese children in a Filipino service.

There are three Chinese ladies who are studying conversational English in Lotung, Ilan County; they were recommended to visit the Filipino service to practice their English among the Filipinos. They attended the meetings faithfully and they also began to like the fellowship and the lively worship. Someone gave witness to them and they became Christians and were baptized. They are now serving both in the Chinese host church and also among the Filipinos.

Two Thai lady workers were befriended by Filipino ladies in Erhlin, Changhua county. They attended the services and enjoyed the Filipino meetings. They were beginning to understand the gospel when they had to leave Taiwan. It takes a while to see Thais become believers.

At the 8th anniversary of Word for the World, Joyce brought her Chinese husband, whom she had tried to explain the gospel to in English and her broken Chinese during the five months of their married life. The husband was interested but could not fully grasp the meaning. At this anniversary meeting, they were given a special seat where someone could explain the gospel to him. When the preacher gave the invitation to come forward to accept the gospel, he did. We all rejoiced.

In Taichung City, at the Community Church English service, a Chinese gentleman and two Indonesians usually joined the Filipino fellowship. One

Indonesian accepted the Lord and after a year, the Chinese gentleman was baptized. The Filipino fellowship was the main instrument leading to their conversion.

FN: Dr. Adhikari, I have one final question: How can the readers of this book effectively pray for the ongoing ministries of the Filipino believers in Taiwan?

RA: We would like to see at least one Chinese church in every major city involved in reaching out to the foreign workers at their doorstep.

This involvement would include sponsoring a Filipino pastor to minister among the Filipino community and train them to become soul winners and church planters, even as lay workers.

Pray also for pastors who can minister in Thai, Indonesian Bahasa and Vietnamese to evangelize, disciple and train converts for witnessing and church planting.

FN: Dr. Adhikari, again it has been a pleasure to partner with you over the years. May God continue to use you to bless many Filipinos and other nationalities in Taiwan and beyond.

RA: Thank you for this opportunity to share with you how God is moving in our part of the world. I continue to pray for FIN's ministry around the globe.

Part V

PERSONAL STORIES

Part V

PERSONAL STORIES

PART V

—⟨⟨⟨·⟩⟩⟩—

INTRODUCTION

There are hundreds of anecdotal reports about Filipino Christians who are actively participating in missions and whose lives are colorful. In this section several true stories are shared; stories of hardship, suffering, injustices, as well as joy and triumph. Some of the writers did not make it to Seoul, South Korea but they submitted their piece following the Consultation. These select ethnographic reports and personal stories are printed in order to inspire and encourage the followers of Jesus Christ, particularly the Filipino Church in the diaspora. These stories are also shared to solicit prayers for those in the front-line, especially those Filipinos in the diaspora who are suffering and deeply wounded for the sake of the Gospel.

Some of the people whose stories are included here live in places where religious freedom is granted; others, however, of them work in restricted regions, making it necessary to use pseudonyms and fictitious places.

We encourage the reader to celebrate the advance of the Good News and the faithful stewardship of God's servants in all walks of life. We also invite the reader to regularly uphold these men and women and the hundreds they represent in prayer.

ALL TO ALL PEOPLE: SAMPLES OF DIASPORA FILIPINOS MAKING KINGDOM IMPACT

Lorajoy Tira Dimangondayao

INTRODUCTION

In recent decades thousands of Filipinos have travelled across the seas in pursuit of greater fortune. Many have taken jobs as temporary workers in foreign lands, giving support and relief to host nations. Many others have settled in other countries, flourishing in their adoptive communities as immigrants and citizens. As they work in myriad industries and locations, thousands of them are making Kingdom impact outside their homeland as they interact with their new communities abroad.

Approximately 93.19% of Filipinos call themselves "Christian" (Johnstone & Mandryk 2001), and of this majority, a conservative estimate of 7% (Tira 2001) claim to be genuine followers of Jesus Christ. Because of this Christian majority, the Philippines has become known as Asia's first and only Christian nation. The Filipino Christians are so devout that according to Attorney Rosalinda Dimapilis-Baldoz (Administrator of the Philippine Overseas Employment Administration), every Filipino overseas directly or indirectly bears the name of Christ. With Filipinos found in almost every industry, at every level of management, and in every strata of society, Christian Filipinos are positioned to be effective witnesses for Jesus Christ wherever they are situated. Christian Filipinos recognize God's providence in placing them in all corners of the globe to serve people of all sorts. They become like the Apostle Paul who "bec[a]me all things to all [people]...for the sake of the gospel."

I am privileged to have personally met many who are witnesses of the Gospel beyond the borders of their Philippine homeland. For the purpose of this chapter I have conducted interviews with several of them—some in person, others by phone, and the very distant ones via email. In most cases I have used their actual names; however in the case where security is a concern, names have been changed. Pseudonyms are indicated by an asterisk. These people have graciously shared their lives with me, and these are their stories.

To provide a general background by which we can better understand the Christian Filipinos and their impact on their communities, this chapter will first present a general profile of Filipinos who have left the Philippines, including those who have chosen to take residence outside country. This brief description will be followed by real-life stories of several Christian Filipinos, who are representative of the thousands making a far-reaching impact for the Gospel of Jesus Christ. The word "diaspora," coming from the Greek term meaning disperse or to spread about, will be used in this chapter to refer to "the dispersion or spreading of something that was originally localized (as a people or language or culture)" (Wordnet 2003), specifically referring to Filipinos who have moved from their homeland, the Philippines, to live or work in another geographical location.

THE WORLD OF THE FILIPINO MIGRANT

In order to understand the profile of the Filipino migrant, one must look at the world in which Filipinos find themselves. While this section will discuss common destinations of Filipinos, it is not an exhaustive discussion of all destinations for Filipino migrants.

In most cases, the Filipinos leave their homeland for personal advancement (e.g. career, education). The majority of advancement opportunities for Filipinos are found in North East and Far East Asia, the Middle East, North Africa, and the Arabian Peninsula. The Western world (North America, Western Europe, Australasia, New Zealand) is also a frequent destination.

Filipinos are also deployed to work at sea on ocean-going vessels and oil rigs. The diaspora also includes the thousands of students seeking higher education in prestigious universities worldwide.

North East and Far East Asia

Singapore and Hong Kong have become the commercial and banking centers of Asia. Japan, South Korea, and Taiwan, and to some extent Thailand have become technological hubs of the world. Indonesia and Malaysia are fast becoming industrial countries. Brunei also has become a major oil-producing country. Vietnam, in recent decades has become a major textile-producing country in the world. These countries have imported laborers and factory workers, construction workers, scientists, engineers, domestic workers, and women entertainers from the Philippines.

The Middle East, North Africa, and The Arabian Peninsula

The Middle East, North Africa, and the Arabian Peninsula are currently the center of production of the world's indispensable commodity. To accelerate their production, they needed to build airports, roads, commercial centers, seaports and housing for their booming population. There has been an outpouring of Filipino migrant workers to this region. They work in construction, hospitals, commercial centers, airports, schools, and homes. There are thousands of engineers, architects, doctors, dentists, nurses, medical technologists, sales clerks, teachers, drivers, and domestic workers (e.g. nannies, caregivers) deployed to this region.

The Western World

The Western world, which includes North America, Western Europe, Australasia, New Zealand, is the most affluent region of the world. It is the current center of political, military, and economic power. These countries often seek out the most talented and best-trained "cream of the crop" from the Philippines. Western countries hire Filipino nurses, doctors, technocrats, scientists, lawyers, business people, skilled trades people, and at times even military personnel. Many Filipino students also travel to these countries to pursue higher education. In the Western world, the Filipinos contribute to the advancing economy. They serve to strengthen the political, military, and economical grip of the West.

The Philippines also deploys talented Filipinos who contribute to the international arts sector, sharing their skills in drama, singing, mixed media, fashion, and industrial design. Filipino artists can be found in world-class cities around the world such as London and New York. Also deployed by the Philippines are the sea-based workers. The Filipino seafarer is famous, and some say that a Filipino can be found on any and all seafaring ventures.

Making "Home"

While most Filipinos who leave the Philippines are deployed as temporary workers, and who must repatriate to the Philippines after the completion of their contracts, many who leave choose to settle down and "make home" in other countries.

It is interesting to note that in most cases, the West welcomes the foreign-born to take permanent residence and even citizenship in their countries. Many Filipinos who leave for the West for career or education choose to permanently reside for economic reasons and personal advancement. Thus, they become "adopted children" of these nations. This is a stark contrast to the immigration policies of most countries within the other two regions discussed, in which migrants such as Filipino workers are only encouraged to stay for as long as they are needed by the host nation.

In places where their stay is limited, Filipinos who prefer to stay longer frequently find means of extending their visas. Many are able to legally renew their contracts over long periods of time, but many also resort to other means of extending their stay on foreign soil. In some places like Japan and in many Middle East and North African countries where Filipinos are invited to stay only for a limited time, intermarriage between Filipinos and locals are gaining popularity in order for them to extend their stay in the host country.

However, intermarriage is not limited to these countries and it is obvious that not all intermarriages are related to immigration issues. Modern Filipinos, who are themselves a product of mixed races and cultures, are more receptive to intermarriage with non-Filipinos. These marriages between Filipinos and locals produce children of mixed cultures and race. The Filipino blood is infused with these races, and the Filipino culture blended into the local culture. Indeed Filipinos are contributing to the formation of a new kind of "global family"— a mixture of bloods and cultures—and the children of such families play a significant role in the bridging of races and cultures.

In our modern times when workers travel throughout the world for work, students enroll in universities across the globe, and children refer to themselves as "part Filipino, Irish, and Lebanese," many Filipino Christians have taken the opportunity to become "all to all people," playing a special role as "adopted children" and as contributors to host countries. They are indeed in strategic positions for potential Kingdom impact.

ALL TO ALL PEOPLE: THE CHARACTERISTICS OF FILIPINOS

Teodoro A. Agoncillo, a respected Filipino Historian, noted that "the common traits [of the Filipinos] are probably basically Malay and characterize the Filipinos as a people" (accessed 2004). These basic traits have fused with foreign influences to result in some outstanding traits common to the average Filipino. It is these traits that make Filipinos an asset to the countries in which they work and live. Combining this with their Christian heritage makes Filipinos in diaspora natural witnesses of Jesus Christ with great potential for impact wherever they are planted.

The Three 'A's

While it is difficult to pinpoint what exact characteristics make the Filipinos special, particularly those in diaspora, some of these common traits have been particularly valuable in helping them adjust to other cultures, win the respect of other nationals, and express their faith in distant countries. These outstanding traits will be explored using Efraim Tendero's (a Christian Filipino leader) three 'A's—highly adaptable, acceptable, and accessible.

Their adaptability, acceptability, and accessibility can be credited to a multitude of influences. In contrast to the population in many other Asian nations, the Filipino population is racially and culturally heterogeneous. Both blood and culture have been influenced by the Polynesians, Malays, Indonesians, Indians, Chinese, Arabs, Spanish, Americans and Japanese. This diversity of influences is evident in the physical features of the Filipino people and in their cultural and linguistic patterns.

Adaptable

The Filipinos are adaptable because their culture is a multicultural blend of East and West. Their culture, though basically Eastern, reflects the adjustments Filipinos have made through the years to western culture and customs. Evidently, the Filipinos seem to have one foot in the East and one foot in the West.

The Filipinos are not only culturally adaptable, but they are also generally linguistically flexible. It would seem that the Filipinos have fine-tuned their language-acquisition skills through the practice of the 80-plus Philippine dialects. Out of necessity to communicate, an average Filipino speaks three to four dialects, perhaps using all dialects in the course of a day. To add to their knowledge of Philippine dialects, their extended exposure to both the Spanish and American cultures have left them with working knowledge of English and Spanish. Many Filipinos still remember when they were required to take Spanish courses in school, and most Filipinos can converse fluently in American English. Filipinos today are gifted at learning new languages, this being an advantage as they move to distant lands. Indeed, the Filipinos have become natural linguists, chameleon-like in their shift back and forth between dialects and languages.

It is significant to note that the Filipinos have, over the years, experienced all kinds of sufferings such as foreign invasions, regional conflicts and wars, political revolutions, natural calamities and disasters, and epidemics of all kinds. The average Filipino has also suffered at the hands of corrupt government leaders and a corrupt system that favors the wealthy minority. Massive corruption in the Philippines has robbed the average Filipino of basic rights and opportunities to advance economically. Consequently, the Filipinos have become a "broken" but "resilient" people. It is through their hardships and suffering that the Filipinos have learned to endure, make do, accommodate, integrate and easily adapt to any situation and society.

Acceptable

In addition to their being adaptable, the Filipinos are acceptable. As a people, Filipinos have a special ability to connect and put people at ease. This is due to the positive points of the Filipino character, including friendliness, generosity and hospitality, ability to identify with others, and a happy disposition.

Filipinos are generally very friendly, warm, and generous, often giving their very best to family, friends, and guests whether in material or emotional support. In general, Filipinos love to give! This is expressed in the action of hospitality. As Agoncillo puts it, "one patent Filipino trait that immediately commends itself to the foreigner is his hospitality" (accessed 2004). Hospitality is perhaps the most admirable trait of the Filipinos. This penchant for giving is coupled with the Filipinos' deep sense of gratitude, as expressed by the term *"utang na loob,"* roughly translated a "debt of gratitude" which they regard as a life-long obligation to repay a favor and an act of kindness.

They are also known to be a kind-hearted people who are quick to identify with those blessed to call them friends. They will rejoice with friends at times of celebration and mourn with them in times of sorrow. The Filipinos are also known to be sympathetic and their ability to identify often extends to those beyond their circle of friends. In addition, Filipinos highly value loyalty, and are known to be loyal to their family, country, and to their religious and social affiliations (Zaide 1999).

Perhaps the impetus for their hospitality and kindness is their generally "happy" disposition. In an article published in *The Economist* (2001), Felipe de Leon, professor of Filipinology at the University of the Philippines, is quoted, "In every survey ever conducted, whether the comparison is with western or other Asian cultures, Filipinos consider themselves by far the happiest." While this statement may seem exaggerated, it presents a picture of the happy nature of the Filipinos in general. This is a valuable characteristic in this generation when people find themselves displaced, and "scattered" far from home. It has been observed that the Filipinos' friendly and happy outlook help them to easily bridge cultural gaps and make them "acceptable" to their hosts.

Moreover, in our present world situation where violence, terrorism, and ethnic strife are prevalent, the Filipinos who, as a nation, have no history of aggression, have also gained favor as peace-loving people. Their unassuming and humble temperaments make them "acceptable" to a generation that is often wary and hypersensitive to potential threat.

As workers, Filipinos in general have the reputation of being diligent and hardworking. These qualities certainly make them "acceptable" to their host nations, particularly to their employers, coworkers, and peers.

Accessible

Filipinos are also accessible. The Philippine archipelago is located at the intersection of air and sea routes. Hundreds of international sea vessels and aircraft arrive at Philippine points of entry every day, giving Filipinos access to all sorts of travel. Thus the Filipino can easily travel to the east, west, north, and south. Furthermore, the country has diplomatic relations with most nations, giving qualified Filipinos entry with reasonable requirements.

The 'X' Factor: The Filipino Difference

From early church history, Christians have used 'X' as an abbreviation or shorthand for the word 'Christ' as in the example of "Xtian." This comes from 'X' or Chi, being the first letter in the Greek word for Christ. The 'X' Factor used in this section refers to the Filipino difference — the difference being that in addition to being adaptable, acceptable, and accessible, Filipinos are also distinctly known for their Christian majority.

As was initially noted, approximately 93.19% of the Filipino people call themselves Christian (Johnstone & Mandryk 2001), giving them the title of "Asia's only Christian Nation." The Christian factor in their national profile makes Filipinos an oddity in their Asian region and they have a reputation for being very religiously devout. It seems that no matter where they are in the world, religious Filipinos will find fellow worshippers and places to express their faith. As regards the Christian majority, Sonia M. Zaide, a Filipino historian observes:

> "The Philippines can be expected to play a great missionary role in bringing the gospel of Christ to other tribes and nations of Asia. In the past, most other Asians have rejected Christianity because of their suspicions of the Western missionaries and Western imperialistic aims. However, the Filipinos do not have that problem, for we have no history of conquest of other Asian lands and we readily—even enthusiastically—accept Christianity, which forms part and parcel of our cultural heritage from the West. Thus today, Filipinos... can bring Christianity to many Asian lands that would otherwise be closed to the gospel." (1999:24)

While we cannot presume that all Filipinos who confess to being Christians are active and growing followers of Christ, we may estimate that at least seven percent (Tira 2001) of Filipino Christians are making a difference for Christ in the way they live their faith in their personal lives and in their places of work. If Zaide's observations are correct, then we can also safely estimate that approximately seven percent of Filipino Christians are playing the role of "unofficial missionaries" making an impact for the Great Commission in lands that are otherwise closed to the gospel.

Undoubtedly, many of the Filipinos in the diaspora have to some degree assimilated within the local practices and cultures. However, the Filipino traits listed above are still evident in the values and behavior of diaspora Filipinos. They are still generally adaptable, acceptable, accessible and devout in their faith. With their unique combination of common traits, shaped by history and circumstances, Filipinos are clearly well equipped for Kingdom impact.

KINGDOM IMPACT

Filipinos are making a positive impact in their places of work and in the communities that they are a part of. Christian Filipinos, in particular, are making Kingdom impact as they reach all parts of society. Below are true stories of Filipinos who God is using to touch lives and call people to serve the Lord. They are representative of the seven percent who are making a Kingdom impact for the gospel. While their backgrounds and stories vary extensively, common threads link their stories, providing us with inspiration as we serve our host communities. These common threads are that these individuals acknowledge God's providence in placing them where they are; they maximize their God-given resources; they practice Kingdom ethics; and they bloom where they have been planted. It can be said that despite their personal tragedy, economic circumstances, and the political instability in their homeland, these individuals have made the choice to take the opportunity to "become all things to all [people] so that by all possible means [they] might save some." (1 Corinthians 9:22)

Acknowledging God's Providence

We read in the Bible about Joseph and Daniel who worked in Egypt and Babylon, respectively. They were forced by circumstance—Joseph was sold by his brothers, while Daniel was taken away from his home as a captive. They were displaced, living among people of different values and customs. Their displacement, however, was changed by God for His purpose. While their experiences may differ from those of Joseph's and Daniel's, the cases of Linda, Mike, Teddy, and Marietta are examples of God's sovereignty in placing workers in "high places" so that they could make an impact for the Kingdom. Though Linda, Mike, Teddy, and Marietta are far away from their homeland and are living among people of a different language and culture, one can only imagine how many people they may influence and what the result could be for the Kingdom.

Designing for a King – Linda*

Linda is a talented interior designer who was hired as the head designer of a king's palace. Not only is she known as an expert in her field, but she has become known for her thoughtful and gentle disposition which she attributes to her personal relationship with Jesus Christ. Through the years, her employers have come to trust her, value her services, and even respect her faith in Jesus Christ. She has also become a confidante to a handful of royal ladies, and Linda has sensed a growing eagerness to learn more about Jesus.

Teaching at the Top – Mike*

Mike moved to the West with his family as a young man. Early on in his life he decided to devote his life teaching young people how to become better members of their community and good citizens of their countries. He studied and trained on how to assist people in learning. After serving his adoptive country for many years, he responded to an opportunity to be an instructor in a country traditionally closed to the West. Despite his western upbringing, Mike was able to enter that country and maintain a teaching position because of his Filipino background. Though Mike "had it all" in his adopted home country, he chose to work in a foreign land to respond to their need for high quality teaching, and in the hopes of living out his faith in Jesus Christ as a witness to his students and hosts. Since he is very friendly and admirably intelligent, Mike has been able to influence many people in his host country to seek "the truth" about Jesus Christ.

Friends in High Places – Teddy*

The Gulf States' economy boomed ever since it became a major oil-producing region. This caused the city states to rapidly expand infrastructures such as hospitals, schools, shopping centers, and airports. Like many Filipinos who have been hired since the late 1970s, Teddy works for a major airline company owned by one of the Gulf States. He is known to be a dependable and well-respected employee, and his unassuming, approachable, and jolly disposition win him the friendship of his coworkers and superiors alike. Though he is an unassuming and simple man, he counts many high-ranking officials in his city as friends. While it is rare for average Filipino workers to make friends with members of the affluent class in their host countries, Teddy has won the trust of many locals and he is often a guest in the homes of his high-ranking friends, which are normally non-accessible to other expatriates. God has strategically placed good-natured Teddy in a position to impact lives through his friendship and personal testimony.

*Introducing the One Who Calms Storms — Marietta**

Thousands of Filipinas are employed in Hong Kong as domestic helpers. Many are nannies who care for the children of working Chinese parents. Thousands of these nannies are sharing their faith with their employers, impacting whole families with the gospel of Jesus Christ. Just before the turnover of Hong Kong to China in 1997, the Filipino International Network (FIN), saw the need to equip these strategically-positioned nannies with evangelistic and discipleship training. Training was organized along with the distribution of Jesus Films in English, Tagalog, and Cantonese. The films were intended to be used by Filipino workers in reaching their *kababayans* (countrymen), their employers, and hosts. A number of nannies attended. One of them was Marietta, a nanny working for an affluent Chinese family. One stormy morning soon after the completion of her training, Marietta was granted a special opportunity to use her newly acquired skills and her Cantonese copy of the Jesus Film when her charges were dismayed about having to miss school. Marietta showed them the scene of Jesus calming the storm and asked them if they too would like to ask Jesus to calm their storm. By afternoon the storm had cleared and the children were able to go to school with their new knowledge of Jesus, the one who calms storms. This led to a unique opportunity for Marietta to tell the children's parents about Jesus Christ. Marietta's employers are now active members of a local Hong Kong congregation. Marietta and other Christian nannies like her are in a unique position to care for families and to make an impact on the families they serve.

God is using these men and women as His witnesses in the lives of their employers. Their stories are examples of the impact Christian workers are making in some of the world's most influential homes as they recognize God's providence in placing them where they are.

Maximizing God-given Resources

The early believers where exhorted by the Apostle Paul to "serve God with their spiritual gifts" including the gifts of prophecy, exhortation, and giving (Romans 12). Malu, Lulu, Robert, Judith, Terry, Celso and their gifted team, and Rebecca are great examples of Filipinos following the Biblical exhortation. In the cases of Malu, Lulu, Robert and Judith, Filipino-Canadians are sacrificing their own time and financial resources to train people to share their faith, often spending their vacation time to travel overseas to Filipino International Network-sponsored training seminars. In the case of Terry and Celso and the OFWs they work closely with, Filipino expatriates are using their skills and abilities to advance the kingdom in the region where God has placed them. Rebecca, on the other hand, is a Filipino-Canadian who is supporting missionaries and missions initiatives with her own funds. Kingdom advancement requires the giving of time, funds, and personnel.

Teachers Without Borders — Malu, Lulu, Rob, and Judith

There are Filipinos in the diaspora who sacrifice their own time and resources to participate in Kingdom work. Such is the case of these four individuals who are regularly scheduled to train people in foreign countries throughout the year. Malu, Lulu, Rob, and Judith all have day jobs that keep them busy. Malu is a researcher, Lulu is a busy pastor's wife, Robert is a business manager and his wife Judith is a full-time housewife who devotes the bulk of her time to raising their three young children. As busy as they are, these four find the time to travel for Filipino International Network at least three times a year to teach Filipinos how to share their faith in Jesus Christ. They often use their vacation days and pay for their ministry trips. Through their travels to conduct training seminars, they have ministered to many Filipinos, encouraging them to use all their gifts and talents for God's glory. They have trained hundreds of Filipino believers in many cities across the globe to share their faith and become multiplying disciples. Filipino believers in many cities across the globe have been touched by their examples. These four people are making an impact as teachers without borders.

Using Their Gifts — Terry, Celso, and Team

Fifteen years ago, Terry left the Philippines to be the Executive Secretary of a multinational accounting company, managing "the life" of the Chief Executive Officer. Terry is highly organized and has a knack for turning plans into reality. She now serves as a leader in FIN and has been a key player in organizing Filipino International Network initiatives, particularly in her region. She is an encouragement to other believers who, like her, have been away from the Philippines for extended periods on account of overseas work. Terry is making an impact using her gifts and skills to organize Filipino International Network initiatives (e.g. evangelistic and discipleship training, Family Life Conferences, distribution of Jesus Films in her region).

In the early 1980s, Celso moved to a rapidly-growing country to work as an engineer. Celso is a dependable worker, and is accepted by his peers. He has made a commitment to devote his time and resources to assist in advancing the Great Commission. Celso is currently serving as a regional coordinator with FIN. He oversees initiatives and actively encourages other Filipino Christians to become actively involved in missions. Celso is a good leader and is being used to impact the people around him for Christ.

Terry and Celso work with a talented team of OFWs in their region who are using their gifts and abilities to advance the Great Commission in their part of the world. Luz and Jess, Jerry, Marlene, Malu and Randy, Butch, Jun, Erik, Ronie, Freddie, Vil, and Hennie, are some of the members of this team of workers who are associated with FIN, and who, like Terry and Celso, are providing leadership in motivating and mobilizing Filipino Christians for global missions in their region.

Supporting the Cause — Rebecca

It is very encouraging to meet people who recognize the urgency of global missions and who will give of their resources to assist in advancing the Kingdom. Rebecca is one such person. Rebecca left the Philippines for the Middle East in the late 1980s. For several years she worked there as a dentist before migrating to Canada in the early 1990s. In Canada she continued practicing her profession, and is now one of the most sought-after dental professionals in her city. After being encouraged at her local church to participate in missions in whatever way she could, Rebecca decided to become a financial supporter of the FIN. She now sponsors FIN initiatives such as strategic consultations and some training initiatives. Rebecca seeks ways to reach out locally and globally. Aside from her involvement with FIN, Rebecca leads her staff from her two clinics in weekly Bible studies (many of her staff are not yet followers of Jesus Christ), and actively involves herself in her local church by supporting the local ministries. Though she is a very busy woman, Rebecca makes it a point to participate in at least one short-term dental missions outreach. This year she returned to the jungles of Brazil for the second time to assist in a dental mission to low-income Brazilians. Rebecca may not be a full-time missionary, but she certainly is actively involved in making an impact wherever God places her, and through whatever opportunities are presented to her.

These men and women are using their God-given resources to make an impact for the Kingdom. Though they are busy and have responsibilities to their families and in their workplace, they maximize what God has given them—whether time or financial resources—to participate in sharing the Gospel. It is important for diaspora Christians to realize that their resources are God-given, and that these resources are multiplied for God's glory when returned to Him.

Blooming Where They (Diaspora Christians) are Planted

In the Book of Jeremiah, the Jewish captives living in Babylon are admonished to build houses and dwell in them, and to seek the peace of the city where they have been taken (Jeremiah 29:5-7). Just like the Jews who flourished in the cities where God had taken them, Mercedes, Ed and Nila are "blooming" and are contributing to the growth of their new homes away from their homeland, the Philippines. Diaspora Filipinos must bloom where they are planted so that they can connect with the locals in the communities where they settle.

Connecting the Dispersed – Mercedes

The United States of America has become known as a "melting pot" — a place where people from all over the world immigrate to to start anew and to find a new home. It is here that Mercedes, a veteran journalist and member of the Philippine intelligentsia, has settled and found new beginnings. The former senior editor of the Philippines News Agency and chief of the Foreign Information Division of the Bureau of National and Foreign Information (BNFI) of the Department of Public Information of the Philippines, and diplomat to

Eastern Europe, now calls the eastern United States "home" along with her Romanian husband and children. Mercedes makes an impact through her writing and her ability to network immigrant people. She continues to write for *Business World* of Manila, and various other communications, including *Charisma*, a Christian magazine based in the United States. In an interview, Mercedes states: "God has placed me in an area where there is a need for writing up, documenting and publishing the community life of Filipinos in America. Communications is a community need for survival, visibility and unity." Indeed her writing connects the "scattered" Filipinos with their home-land. Mercedes not only connects people through her writing, but she also actively participates in the life of her community, serving community organi-zations as a volunteer publicity person. Aside from this, Mercedes maximizes her skill at connecting by sending out letters of encouragement to pastors, their spouses, church women, and senior citizens. She further helps Filipino seniors by organizing trips to go to government senior centers for fellowship and meal programs, health check-ups, visits to the community bread house for their supply of free bread, and visits to the immigration and naturaliza-tion offices and to the libraries. Mercedes makes it a priority to pray for young people and the schools in her neighborhood, and hosts dinners for members in the community. Her cross-cultural marriage and family are an encourage-ment to both European and Asian friends. By connecting fellow immigrants and expatriates through writing and community work, Mercedes is making an impact both locally and globally.

Turning Musicians Into Worshippers — Ed and Nila

Filipinos are world-famous for their musical skill and entertainment skills, and music is often a connecting factor for Filipinos who love to play instruments together, sing, and dance. In Chicago, Illinois, a husband-and-wife team are being used by God to turn musicians into worshippers. Both coming from successful music-related careers in the Philippines, Ed and Nila moved to Chicago, Illinois with their young family to join the ministry team of a local church that ministers to a cross-cultural congregation. Nila, who is trained in music pedagogy and who served as music director of a large urban church in the Philippines, is serving as the music and worship director at their church in suburban Chicago. She plans the music for the church's gatherings (e.g. Sunday services, weekly gatherings, and special cantatas and choral events), and encourages and trains members of the congregation to use their voices and their musical instruments to "make a joyful noise to the Lord." Ed, an accomplished concert pianist and orchestral director in the Philippines, is the official pianists at their church. During the week, he directs several choirs in the area and trains musicians working with various cultural associations.

Ed and Nila reach out to their community, both within the multicultural neighborhood where their house is located, and beyond–to the community of immigrant Filipinos living in the Chicago area. At Christmas, they have made it a tradition to invite neighbors who are not yet followers of Jesus Christ for caroling around the piano and to share with them the reason they celebrate Christmas. They regularly host dinners at their home with the purpose of sharing their faith, and in recent months they have started discipling their contacts who have come to know Jesus Christ through their testimony. In addition to their regular church involvement and community outreach, Ed and Nila regularly invite traveling Christian workers to their home for fellowship and a time to renew their strength for more travel, treating them with that well-known Filipino hospitality. Ed and Nila are impacting their corner of the world for Christ through their hospitality and musical talent. They have been instrumental in turning many talented musicians into worshippers of God.

Mercedes, Ed and Nila, are good examples of diaspora Christians who are blooming where God has planted them. They are enterprising and have committed to build their community and reach their neighbors, and in so doing have attracted their adopted compatriots to them and their message. Because they are blooming where they are planted, Mercedes, Ed and Nila have many opportunities to share the Gospel of Jesus Christ.

Practicing Kingdom Ethics

Filipino Christians need to practice Kingdom ethics as described in the Beatitudes of Matthew chapter 5. The Filipinos described in the stories above are known by those around them including their employers and coworkers to be meek, merciful, and peacemakers. Godiva and Sarah are examples of Filipinos making Kingdom impact by practicing Kingdom ethics. Godiva cares for the women who are maltreated and abused, while Sarah is a true "good Samaritan" who sacrificed her own personal security during the war to stay behind and care for the wounded. They have touched many lives through their practice of Kingdom ethics.

Shepherding the Scattered — Godiva

Many Filipinos experience loneliness during their work period in Singapore. To many of the Filipina workers, particularly those who work as domestic helpers, Singapore is a mere work site, a desolate place where they are forced by circumstance to care for other people's children, while leaving their own children and husbands to the care of relatives back home in the Philippines. Godiva, a graduate student from the Philippines, is ministering to these runaway women. She encourages them, walks with them, and helps them in practical ways by acting as an advocate of the women. Godiva is making an impact by supporting and shepherding the scattered Filipino nannies in Singapore. As she touches them with Christ's love, they are also encouraged to share this love with their employers.

Under the Cloud of Fear — Sarah*

During the First Gulf War, thousands of temporary foreign workers were evacuated from Kuwait. They left in droves leaving their jobs in Kuwait for the safety of home. Many Filipino workers were also evacuated, but some chose to stay. One such person is Sarah, nurse who chose to stay under the cloud of fear. Sarah remembers bombs falling all around the hospital where she worked, and even the wounded Kuwaitis and Iraqis who were brought into the hospital. In the thick of war, Sarah chose to be there to comfort and nurse the wounded and displaced, reciting to them from Scripture. Because of her bravery and her loyalty to the hospital, Sarah won the respect of her employers and hosts. Like many Filipino believers who chose to stay during the war, Sarah demonstrated that her God enabled her to endure even in times of uncertainty and fear. She made an impact on many lives because she showed her faith in a sovereign God.

Godiva's and Sarah's stories illustrates how God can use negative situations to open doors and to reveal opportunities for presenting the Gospel. As diaspora Christians who practice Kingdom ethics and give of themselves to assist those in need, Godiva and Sarah demonstrated God's love to people.

The diaspora Filipinos described in the stories have acknowledged that God has providentially placed them where they are for His purposes. They are maximizing their God-given resources. They are blooming where they are planted by contributing to their host nation's development, and they are practicing Kingdom ethics. In these ways they are making Kingdom impact.

CONCLUSION

Advances in technology and travel have enabled people to move across the globe in hours. Millions of Filipinos are part of this migrating pool of people, and they can be found all over the world. They assemble computer parts in Taiwan, build ships in South Korea, entertain in Japan, and become therapists in Australia. They are bodyguards in Italy, dramatists and musicians in England, cooks in Romania, and journalists in France. They are dentists, nannies, drivers and nurses in Saudi Arabia, business executives in Kuwait, flight attendants on board Emirate flights. They construct roads in Qatar and work as salesclerks in Dubai. They care for young babies in Singapore and help grandmothers in Hong Kong. There are Filipinos digging for diamonds in Nunavut, and there are those working at the airports in Vancouver. There are computer programmers in Toronto, engineers in Ft. McMurray and nurses in Winnipeg. They are English teachers in Texas, students in Boston, and surgeons in Phoenix. Filipinos are everywhere!

The stories shared in this chapter are just examples of the countless stories of Filipino believers who have become all things to all people for the sake of the Gospel, and who are making an impact for the Kingdom in their communities and in the world. Their stories are real-life demonstrations of the impact diaspora Christians, particularly Filipino Christians, can have if they acknowledge their divine placement, maximize their God-given resources, contribute to their host nations, and practice Kingdom ethics.

REFERENCES

Agoncillo, Teodoro A. (1990). *History of the Filipino People.* Quezon City: Garotech Publishing.

Agoncillo, Teodoro A. "Filipino Traits and Custom." Accessed at (http://www.dock. net/rogers/filtraits.html) on March 28, 2004

Beltran, Ruby P. & Gloria F. Rodriguez. (1996). *Filipino Women Migrant Workers: At the Crossroads and Beyond Beijing.* Quezon City, Philippines: Giraffe Books.

Constable, Nicole. (1997). Maid to Order in Hong Kong: Stories of Filipino Workers. USA: Cornell University.

Iyer, Pico. (2000). *The Global Soul:* Jet Lag, Shopping Malls, and the Search for Home. United States: Vintage Books.

Jocano, Landa F. (1997). "Filipino Value System: A Cultural Definition" in the series *Anthropology of the Filipino People IV.* Quezon City, Philippines: Punlad Research House, Inc.

Jocano, Landa F. (1998). "Filipino Indigenous Ethnic Communities: Patterns, Variations and Typologies" in the series *Anthropology of the Filipino People II.* Quezon City, Philippines: Punlad Research House, inc.

Johnston, Patrick. (2001). Operation World 21st Century Edition. USA: Paternoster Lifestyle.

Kalaw-Tirol, Lorna ed. (2000). *From America to Africa: Voices of Filipino Women Overseas.* Makati City, Philippines: FAI Resource Management, Inc.

Miranda-Feliciano, Evelyn. (1990). Filipino Values and our Christian Faith. Philippines: OMF Literature.

Tendero, Efraim. (2002). "No Title." Sermon delivered to the FIN Global Consultation in Singapore, July 22-24, 2002.

Tira, Sadiri Joy B. (2001) "Tentmaking: A Missions Strategy for the Next Millennium." Speech presented at the Philippine National Tentmaking Conference in Manila, Philippines. March 17-23, 2001.

Zaide, Sonia M. (1999). *The Philippines: A Unique Nation.* Quezon City, Philippines: All Nations Publishing Co. Inc.

No Author Listed. (2001). "An Anthropology of Happiness" The Economist (December 20, 2001). Accessed at http://www.usuhs.mil/resday/eud28. html) March 18, 2003. WordNet 2.0 (2003). "Diaspora." New Jersey, USA: Princeton University.

MY JOURNEY AS A CHRISTIAN AMBASSADOR
Ambassador Rodolfo I. Dumapias

Jesus took the bread, gave thanks and broke it, and gave it to his disciples. Then He said, "This is my body, which is given for you. Eat this in remembrance of me." Thus, in the last supper, the moment that we now celebrate during our present-day communion, Christ enacted the process by which He gives out the bread: He takes it, prays over it, breaks it and then gives it.

The process by which my life was transformed followed the same pattern. Like many others whose spirits have been reborn, I first came to recognize and accept my desperate need for God. When I accepted Jesus as my personal savior and Lord, He took hold of me as I experienced an increasing desire to follow Him and to know and obey His will. When I invited the Holy Spirit to come into my life, He blessed me as He forgave me of my sins and through the Holy Spirit gave me the capacity to develop closer relationship with Him and to see the Kingdom of God. He broke me as my worldly desires, ambitions, plans and values died, and my material capabilities were crushed, when He allowed trials and crisis to befall me. And as my old self faded away and my spirit reborn, He gave me to the Church and the people for the unfolding of His plan in my life.

But what strikes me was the revelation that as Jesus set me in my journey as a Christian diplomat, I was confronted with one crisis after another in increasing difficulty. Through hindsight, however, I can now see that every crisis was a process that transformed my spirit, soul, and character and lifted me into the next level of faith as He unfolded His purpose for my life. As

He led me to the next phase of my journey, He never abandoned me. In fact, He opened new doors for me and through signs and wonders showed me His love and protection. In my years of serving in the Philippine diplomatic service, I have witnessed the omnipotence and faithfulness of God.

And I hereby attest to the reality and truth of His promise.

My Spiritual Rebirth

I was young, intelligent, and hard working and I thought that I had what it takes to assure a bright and secured future. Having passed the tough foreign service officer examination and earning college degree at UCLA and a master's degree from USC in Los Angeles, California, I thought I had the right to be proud of my personal abilities. Although my wife Eva and I were not irreligious, we were contented with just sitting in a Catholic mass or Methodist service, whichever fitted our schedule. We thought that the rosary, Santo Niño of various sizes and color, Sunday attendance, and being in good terms with others were enough to make us good Christians. Even after we spent years in various assignments in Peking, Kuala Lumpur, Hamburg, and Bucharest, and have met statesmen, dictators, Presidents, Princes and Kings, and brushed elbows with all kinds of people, we continued to think that our destiny was exclusively in our own hands and that we turn to God only when we need Him to get something more.

How wrong we were in all of those thoughts.

It was shortly after I assumed my posting as Minister Counselor and Consul General in Seoul, South Korea, that my views began to change dramatically. My career, the source of my pride and hope back then, was threatened by a high-ranking and powerful man in the Department of Foreign Affairs, Manila. He began to processed my transfer from Seoul, Korea to elsewhere after only ten months of my stay. A process that would discredit and humiliate me as acting Head of Mission (Charge d'Affaires, a.i.), and eventually impede my professional growth. He was a Goliath and to him I was just a small matchstick that he could easily break. All my appeals addressed to the Secretary of Foreign Affairs were screened by the powerful man, and my efforts to get the help of politicians were not answered. In desperation, I turned to God.

In the summer of 1991, my wife Eva and I accepted the Lord Jesus Christ as our personal savior. Prior to the aforementioned crisis, my sister Rebecca used to give my wife and me Bible and tracts every time we visited our folks in the U.S., but we quickly turned the pages and never really read them. This time, however, our prayers came from the heart and were intense, and I could now easily understand the Bible as my interest on the scriptures grew.

The Lord then led us to meet in Seoul the only daughter and the son-in-law (Ben and Tina Maynigo) of Foreign Secretary Raul Manglapus. Consequently, my letters reached the Secretary. Shortly thereafter, the threat was removed as the motion set by the high-ranking and powerful man was stopped and rendered null and void by the Secretary.

This experience awakened us to the reality that God is a living force, that He can be reached by us even if we are not priests or pastors, that He can listen directly to our pleas without us seeking the intercession of dead saints, and that in His own way and power He prevails over men and overrides their craftiness as He administers justice. It was during this time that Eva—as she was in tears—heard for the first time the voice of the Holy Spirit: "I know how you feel. If only I can embrace you, but let me do it in my own way, in my own time." We believe that our meeting with the Maynigos was not an accident. And several years later the powerful man became very nice to me and even asked that we include in our prayers the recovery of his wife who suffered a mild stroke—and we did.

SERVING GOD AND MAN

Amazed at the power of God that we have just witnessed, I was driven to give my first testimony before the congregation at the Filipino Christian Fellowship at Haebangchon, a humble district in Seoul. I thought it was going to be the first and last time I would speak before a church audience. What I did not know was that my presentation before a group of about fifteen people including my wife, my daughter Myra who was visiting from college, and our maid in a basement of a two-storey house would be the first step in my journey to serve God and man.

My wife and I and our maid Lita Mina joined FCF Pastor Tony San Buenaventura in visiting the Filipino workers in their living quarters where we also conducted Bible studies. To attract more workers to our visits, we announced in advance that the consul general was to come with the pastor to answer questions on the situation of undocumented workers. The various outreaches we conducted led us even to remotest corners of the city as well as to the isolated job sites and mud huts in the countryside.

Eva and I did not realize it but our attitude, taste, temper, and outlook in life began to change as we became more involved in bringing the Gospel to the Filipino workers. Our Mercedes Benz suddenly broke down and I could not afford the repair cost, so for several months through winter, we moved about for the first time without the convenience of a private car. At one time, we walked to the subway station with the pastor and elders carrying a guitar, portable keyboard, and a bag of gospel songs, clung to the strap onboard a crowded train, travelled for about an hour, then ran after a provincial bus and rode for another hour, then disembarked only to walk about two kilometers more from the highway. It was already dark, and as we struggled on a dirt road to reach an isolated factory a few miles from the border of North Korea, I began to see a new person in my wife and myself. We endured and enjoyed the long trek and the sleepless night in the workers quarters while we waited for the bus to operate again in the morning. Even the pit-toilet and icy cold water did not bother us. People asked us why, as a ranking embassy official, we attend worship service where workers, musicians, and housemaids are cramped in a small basement apartment-turned-mission house. The answer was simple: no longer did we look at only ourselves but to and at Christ.

The church outreach gave me the chance to see first hand the condition of the Filipino workers, documented and undocumented. I heard their life stories and experienced their lifestyle because we spent time with them in their places of work and in their homes. I understood and felt their anguish when they came to the embassy already disillusioned, mentally broken down, and raped. Some of them came to me with one eye blinded, fingers severed, and a foot amputated resulting from accidents at work.

Thus, the embassy's assistance-to-nationals function and consular services were carried out with added Christian compassion and direct personal knowledge on the plight of the Filipino overseas workers. Passport and documentation services were made quicker, and we wrote letters to immigration on behalf of anyone who needed reduction or exemption from penalty. The embassy basement was opened to accommodate the increasing number of stranded and victimized workers and we arranged with Filipino Catholic and evangelical churches, hotels, Filipino communities and the American base for the supply of food, medicine, blankets and cots. Priests, nuns and pastors such as Fr. Ray Sabio from Inchon, Sis. Maryann Terenal from Chayangdong, Fr. Eugene Docoy and Pastor Tony of FCF, came to give material support and share the gospel. Together with Catholic and evangelical churches, the host Ministry of Labor, the Lotte Welfare Foundation, and an NGO, the embassy assisted the victims of work accidents in getting their due compensation such as Bro. Guiller who lost four fingers and Bro. Abe who lost a foot.

The hunger for spiritual comfort among the Filipino workers became more evident in each problem that was brought to the embassy, and we discovered that sharing the Word of God made a difference to them in their moment of desperation. I recall one husband who was bent on going home to kill his wife and then himself because of her extramarital affair, but after I shared with him God's word and prayed with him, he cried and vowed to forgive her. From that time on, I always shared the Word, prayed and gave a Bible to any worker who came with a problem, even when Ambassador F. Benedicto and I visited the hundreds of OFWs in prison who were rounded up at the end of an amnesty period.

MASUK

Masuk is about two to three hours from Seoul by bus, and about an hour's drive by car. There were several furniture factories straddled on a cluster of hills in a mountain range, but their presence is hidden from the highway and they can be reached only through a narrow winding road. It was a perfect place for anyone to work and hide, and many Filipinos who were there indeed had reasons to hide: from immigration, spouses, creditors, gossips, or from the police as some have been accused of murder while others were reportedly involved in drugs.

While FCF and other Filipino evangelical groups had opened Bible studies in various places, nobody wanted to go to Masuk because of distance and other obvious reasons. But my wife and I decided to open a Bible study in Masuk in August 1994 in the midst of about 300 Filipino workers there. At first there was resistance and only four attended as other workers questioned the motives of a military general—a consul general, you see? We held the session every Saturday night inside the furniture factory where Rosie Abalos and Gina Loyola worked. My wife Eva led the singing of gospel songs backed up by Lita, Cerich Ponteres played the keyboard, while I shared the gospel. After a few weeks, the number of attendees increased, up to eighty men and women sometimes. Some of them even walked a few kilometers to join us despite the bitterly cold Korean winter. We would usually finish our fellowship at dawn and would drive back to Seoul at four in the morning.

Many of the Filipino workers have never read the Bible before, much less owned one, and the Bible study in Masuk changed their life. The story of Manong Ben, Sis. Rosie, Sis. Gina, Bro. Rommel, Bro. Ramir, Bro. Philip, Sis. Precy, Bro. Tony, Bro. Rodel, Sis. Josie, Bro. Bert, Bro. Vic, Bro. James, Sis. Daniela, Sis. Mary, Bro. Daniel, Bro. Lito, Sis. Ofie and many others are real life tales of painful childhood, broken dreams, and lost hope that were turned to a new dawn. Bro. Mac, for example, whose father died when he was very young and never finished beyond third grade, used to harbor deep hatred for his alcoholic mother for beating him and his younger sister and for forcing his hand to a pot of boiling water. At first, he used to escape through a window to avoid us and to be with his friends in drinking sessions. But after he joined and accepted the Lord, his heart changed and he gave up drinking, forgave his mother and reconciled with her.

Six months later, a Korean prayer mountain ministry learned about our Bible study and offered their facilities for us to start a regular Sunday worship service, free of charge. On 26 February 1995, the Filipino Christian Fellowship at Masuk was inaugurated at the chapel of the Sudong Prayer Mountain, which was headed by Rev. Pastor Lee Tae Hee and managed by Pastor Chun Young-Bum. Before the last snowfall of winter melted, about one thousand Filipino workers from five churches came by the busloads on that day. Our special guests were Sen. Blas Ople and Ambassador Francisco Benedicto. Thus, the Bible study grew and became a church, and I became its pastor.

A month later, the congregation in Masuk changed its name to Filipino Evangelical Christian Fellowship as it decided to be independent from the FCF in Seoul. Before my posting in Seoul ended in July 1996, I requested the help of Pastor Jaren Lapasaran of Jesus Our Hope in Cubao, Quezon City and he agreed to send Pastor Paul Pambid to take charge of the church. A year later, Pastor Paul was replaced by Pastor Charlie Pablo from the Jesus Our Life Ministry of Bishop Fred Magbanua.

EMFK

By 1994, the number of Filipino workers in South Korea had grown to more than 30,000. The thirst for the Word of God became more evident as workers even called the pastors to conduct Bible study for them at their place. Being the head of the Masuk Bible studies and an embassy official, I discussed the need for more aggressive and coordinated outreach with the evangelical pastors who, as it turned out, had the same idea. After a series of meetings, our group decided to set up the Evangelical Ministers Fellowship in Korea. I was elected chairman and Pastor Tereso Casiño of Touch International Christian Church as vice-chairman, and EMFK was inaugurated in October of that year. The other founding members who headed the committees were: Pastor Sammy Natividad of Soebuk Foreigners Church, Pastor Enrique Supsup of Philippine Body of Christ, Pastor Rey Castro of the FCF, Sis. Serlina Rufin of Freedom in Christ Church, Pastor Paula Koh of the Grace Full Gospel Church and joining us later was Pastor Jesse Arce. We received the support of associate Korean churches that had Filipino attendees, among them the Yoido Full Gospel Church under Rev. Pastor Paul/David Yonggi Cho but represented by Sis. Helen Byum. We were also blessed with the advise of Dr. Ho-Jin Jun of Asian Christian Theology School (ACTS), and Rev. Yung-Joon Kim of Somang Presbyterian Church, as well as the support of organizations such as The Lotte Welfare Foundation under Chairman Lho Shinyong and the Global Mission Fellowship. EMFK published its own periodical, *Vision*, in 1996.

The EMFK served as a catalyst in the evangelism process not only to Filipinos but also to other foreigners such as the Nigerians, Nepalese, and the Chinese. EMFK became the central network among the evangelical pastors for mutual support, coordination of their activities, and mapping out their respective strategies in their outreach program. It unified the Filipino evangelical ministries and linked them with the Korean body of Christ. To the workers, it provided an avenue by which they share information on immigration movements, job opportunities and mutual assistance for emergency or death.

EMFK was useful not only for the pursuit of the Great Commission but also to the work of the embassy. When the labor office was set up, Labor Attache Jun Sodusta utilized the EMFK churches as contact centers to reach the workers. Consular notices and embassy-issued IDs were also sent through the EMFK and other centers. Ambassador Benedicto called on the EMFK, the Filipino community and the Catholic churches to help implement his computer training program and other projects for the workers.

I was re-elected as chairman in October 1995. In the following year, God's plan for leading me into the EMFK and ministry work was revealed.

"FOR SUCH A TIME AS THIS"

The most ominous challenge that confronted me during my posting in Seoul was the threat to my life by the Unification Church, otherwise known as "the Moonies."

In the summer of 1995, the Moonies (official name: Holy Spirit Association for the Unification of World Christianity) held a mass wedding ceremony at the Philippine International Convention Center (PICC) in Manila. Several hundred Filipinas were "wed" to Korean men whom they were seeing for the first time, and in some cases the "groom" was not even present. Shortly thereafter, about 280 Filipina "brides" were boarded on the plane for Seoul where they were later brought to a Unification reception center, then to various churches for training before they were distributed to their respective "husbands."

Two events developed that brought me into the center of a gathering storm. First, the Department of Foreign Affairs in Manila became curious about a new batch of some 300 applicants for passport and asked me, being the CDA in Seoul at the time, to check on the background of the sponsor Unification Church. After consulting with various Korean church leaders through the EMFK network, I advised the Home Office to take "extreme caution." Succeeding reports on the system of the mass wedding reached then Immigration Chief Commissioner Hon. Leandro Verceles and he decided to disallow the departure of about 286 Filipina "brides."

Second, one of the "brides" who was brought to Korea, called the embassy asking to be rescued from the Moonies; but she did not know where she was. I took direct charge of the case, determined her location, and through the EMFK network arranged with a Korean pastor in that village for her escape. I then gave her a new identity—"Aida Santos, a run-away housemaid"—and told her to change into boy's clothing and a hat. I sent two embassy employees to pick her up and bring her to a safehouse in Seoul. Throughout the winter we brought Aida Santos from one safehouse to another, and one church to another, every time her real identity was about to be known to other Filipino workers or when suspicious Korean visitors and vehicles were nearby.

In January 1996, Aida Santos' identity became known to the Unification, and they began their search for her. Aida was afraid for her life and she called some politicians and the media in the Philippines about her plight. News stories about "Aida Santos" as an escapee from the Unification hit the front page of Philippine newspapers as well as the primetime news on television and radio. Stories revealing Unification link with top-ranking government officials including some senators, congressmen, military generals and the police were creating sensation and finger-pointing among some public personalities. Somehow, the media learned that I knew her whereabouts so I got long-distance calls from Noli de Castro and other broadcasters who interviewed me live via phone. I was told that the events were even reported in CNN. Pressure was building up in the media for in-depth investigation on the activities of the Unification in the Philippines. Meanwhile in Korea, the Unification was becoming restive and defensive to the news reports that the Filipina "brides" were treated as slaves and prostitutes.

Aida learned from the Filipina "brides" that the Unification had hired assassins from Latin America, and indeed a week later, two Latinos (they claimed to be workers but Latinos go to the US and not Korea for work) suddenly showed up during a church service asking the whereabouts of Dumapias and Aida. My family and I quickly but quietly picked up some of her belongings, rushed to the car and drove away to look for a new safehouse.

But a direct threat to my life came during a violent demonstration staged by the Unification at the embassy. In March, more than 300 Unification members gathered at the parking lot of the Philippine Embassy, beating drums and shouting and carrying placards with slogans such as "Dumapias Go Home!" and "Verceles and Dumapias, we are not prostitutes!" The demonstrators broke the glass front door of the embassy and a glass window, beat up our Korean janitor when they entered the lobby, and ran after our female staff and employees up to the second and third floors. Ambassador General (ret.) Ernesto Gidaya, who arrived two months before, allowed the leaders to come up where Unification and embassy officials held frank exchange of views. It was during this tense moment that the leader of the demonstration, a young Korean man in red jacket, said in front of the ambassador, the consul, military attache, and interpreter: "Dumapias, don't ever think that your life and that of your family is safe in Korea." I told him: "Don't threaten me while you are at the embassy. If anything happens to my family or anyone in the embassy I will hold you responsible!" After the event, we received anonymous and threatening phone calls at home.

The Korean police authorities later assigned armed officers to secure my apartment building even before the Philippine government filed an official protest note to the host government. Gen. Gidaya did not accept any police protection saying that he was safe. During the demonstration, four busloads of anti-riot troops were deployed while some remained to guard the embassy until the tension subsided two weeks later. But on the third demonstration, eight busloads of anti-riot forces arrived and this time the leaders including the young man in red jacket were chased, surrounded, handcuffed and boarded on the police wagon. I learned later from reliable sources that the demonstrations were staged to scare me into going home to the Philippines so that the plans of the Unification could proceed without any interruptions.

In the foregoing events, I began to understand why God led me to experience what I had gone through since I arrived in Seoul. It seems that the experiences built up to prepare me for the Unification crisis. In the 1991 crisis on my career, He frustrated the attempt to remove me from Seoul; He also taught me to be resolute and firm, yet calm and hardened. In the outreach and Masuk, He fine-tuned my sensitivity and compassion and led me to personally see the life condition that awaited the Filipina "brides"; He also led me to serve as a minister of the gospel and qualified me before the formation of EMFK. God's special purpose for the EMFK became more evident: it played an important role especially in the escape and safety of Aida Santos. Also, what many people did not know was that a Korean pastor offered a portion of his office located three blocks from the embassy as EMFK headquarters with free use of facilities; the EMFK office became a secured communication link with Manila at the height of the Unification crisis. Finally, in pursuing my official function of assisting Filipinos in distress even against strong pressure from powerful and wealthy parties, God led me to view the crisis not only from the legal and social angles but also on the basis of the Biblical truths. Had I not accepted Jesus beforehand, I probably would have taken the easy path of compromise and sacrificed what I believed was right.

It was also during the Unification crisis that I witnessed the protection of the Holy Spirit. At the start of the first demonstration, I came back to the office from lunch and walked in the middle of the shouting Moonies to get to the embassy. I came face-to-face with their leaders and the Filipinas who knew me, but they did not seem to see me. Again, after they broke into the embassy, the young man in red jacket ran to the second floor shouting: "Where is Dumapias?," "Where is Dumapias?" and as I blocked him I shouted back: "I am Dumapias!" But, as if he was blind and deaf, he turned around and went after the female staff who were then running to the third floor. Comforted by Divine protection, my family and I were not afraid and went on with the weekly evening Bible study at Masuk and still came home safely at dawn to the relief of the four armed policemen who were guarding our apartment 24 hours a day since the demonstration.

After the demonstrations, the Philippine government sent a team to Korea composed of an NBI inspector, immigration intelligence officer and a POEA lawyer who came with TV newscaster Julius Babao and a cameraman from ABS-CBN. The team spent a sleepless night finishing the affidavit of Aida Santos at my apartment and the next day we secretly boarded her with the team for her flight to Manila where her story was sensationalized. The DFA team led by Undersecretary Leonides Caday arrived later and took statements from the Filipina "brides." Amb. Gidaya and I were summoned to Manila and appeared at the Batasang Pambansa before the joint congressional hearing "in aid of legislation," amidst the shouting Filipino Moonies demonstrating on one side and Born Again prayer warriors on the other side. Thereafter, four members of Congress came to Seoul and discovered that other "brides" also wanted to escape. Weeks later, based on gathered evidence, a case was filed against the Unification for violation of mail-order bride law and other counts. Aida Santos was placed under witness protection program.

MEETING MEN OF GOD

When God directs us towards the fulfillment of his plan for our lives, He does not isolate us but surrounds us with people and events that would influence our outlook, values, and plans and therefore our future. Leading me to meet men such as Dr. Paul/David Yonggi Cho who has the biggest congregation in the world (more than 800,000), Bishop Eddie Villanueva, Bishop Fred Magbanua, Bishop Ef Tendero, Bishop Leo Alconga, Bishop Rolly Blas, Rev. Ptr. Butch Conde, Rev. Ptr. Eli Javier, Rev. Kim Bum-il of Canaan School, Rev. Pastor "Billy" Shin as well as the ministers mentioned earlier, God must have been leading me deeper into the ministry of Jesus Christ which I find to be basic as well as complementary to my work as a diplomat and a public servant.

It was therefore a logical sequence for me to continue on sharing the Gospel when I was assigned to the Home Office (DFA) in Manila in July 1996. I was invited to preach at Jesus our Life, BF Homes, once a month with Pastor Lito Gonzales, under the ministry of Bishop Magbanua. I shared the Word at the Baptist International Church under Rev. Pastor Tim Lardizabal, the PBTS in Baguio, and in several fellowships in Asingan, Pangasinan. At the Department of Foreign Affairs, I made sure that the Bible Study Group of the employees and staff had a permanent room with equal respectability as those of other religious groups. Also, jointly with the Catholic and Muslim groups, we in the BSG organized a Prayer and Value Formation Program at the main auditorium.

And in Bahrain, during my incumbency there as Philippine Ambassador, I preached on regular basis at the Word of Life under Pastor Bonny Villan-ueva and the Bahrain Christian Fellowship under Pastor Fred Cudiamat, and occasionally at Jesus is Alive under Pastor Ignacio Reyes, Shepherd's Flock under Pastor Jesse Cordova, and some other Filipino, Indian and mixed foreigners congregations.

THE JOSEPH IN US

When Jesus gave the bread that has been blessed and broken, it was for a purpose that was meant to be accomplished. In the same sense, God desires that the purpose in our life as followers of Jesus be accomplished. He allows us to encounter trials, sorrows, temptations, and pain so that we may become fit to serve for the fulfillment of His plans. Consider Joseph, the son of Jacob, whose life was broken as he was beaten, thrown into a deep well, sold by his brothers, taken away from his home, served as a slave, accused falsely and imprisoned for many years, and had therefore all the reasons to be bitter, unforgiving, and revengeful. However, his unyielding faith in God instead further refined his character through his trials and he became a completely new creation that even his own brothers did not recognize him. In addition to his God-given gift to interpret dreams, God gave him just the right degree of faith, wisdom, perseverance, self-control and compassion required to accomplish God's purpose for bringing him to Egypt. At the time he was made the prime minister of the land of his exile, he had the qualities of a prime minister. He was at the right place in the right office with the right attitude at the right time to fulfill the purpose of God to deliver the Israelites from famine.

In varying degrees and in one form or another, all of us—Filipino diplo-mats, officials, workers, housemaids, musicians, missionaries, professionals, and businessmen abroad—are like Joseph who had to undergo trials first in order for the Almighty to mold us into the jewels that He wants us to be. As God had planned for Joseph to have a role in rescuing His people from calamity, He also has a role for each one of us in the unfolding of His grand design to fulfill the Great Commission. Following Jesus and doing His will might cost us everything we own in this world, but His reward for those who do His will is much greater. As I served Him through one crisis after another, He never left me but instead protected me and strengthened me, and blessed me with miracles beyond my expectation. He would do the same for you if you allow Him to use you for His glory. And as He made Joseph into the most powerful man next only to the Pharaoh of Egypt, the Lord will also restore you and provide you with your needs as you serve Him.

In our present time when the signs point to the nearness of Christ's second coming, those who have not accepted Jesus as their personal savior should seize this moment and accept Him now for their eternal salvation. And those whose spirits have already been reborn should take up their role as the Joseph of our time.

Even ambassadors, I believe, are not exempted from His grand design. In the fall of 2002, the Lord allowed me and my family to experience the most painful period of our life. I was the Philippine Ambassador to Bahrain at the time, but I believe He started us into a new vista in our life. It is a long and sensitive story, and it deserves a separate narration in itself. But suffice it to say now that the Lord had shown us one miracle after another and brought me and my wife, as well as our daughter Myra and grandson Daniel Rudolf, to a higher level of faith. Now, our restoration has begun. Like Joseph, our hearts and spirits are ready to follow wherever He leads us next.

FROM THE URBAN JUNGLE OF TOKYO TO THE HINTERLAND OF MINDORO
Jocelyn Dino

I was standing at the very back of a jam-packed Filipino Jesus Is Lord church in Japan, watching and looking for a scoop their celebrity speaker might reveal that would be worth writing for my newspaper. Then my own story began.

That evening, November 25, 1998, Coney Reyes, a movie and television actress in the Philippines was invited to give her testimony. The actress was well known to have led a very 'colorful' and controversial life before becoming a 'Christian.'

I anxiously waited for Coney to begin her talk, hoping to catch all the dirty details of her now well-known colorful past. Then Coney began to speak. I wrote fast to catch every bit and morsel as Coney started to reveal details of her past. Then, Coney stopped talking about herself. Instead, she shifted her talk to a different story strand and started talking about this man "Jesus" who had come into her life.

I do not remember when I dropped my pen and stopped writing. All I know is that I was absolutely riveted to every word Coney Reyes was uttering each minute. In some strange and wonderful way, Coney's story seemed to be personally directed at me and I found myself no longer listening with my journalistic "ears." And a delightful conclusion to Coney's talk was the invitation to the audience to come and receive Christ as their personal Savior.

Coney invited anyone who want to accept Jesus Christ as their personal Lord and Savior. I found myself crying so hard and one of the four who stood up to accept Jesus as Lord and Savior of my life.

I came to that event looking for a murky past, for a dirty controversial story to headline my newspaper. I came looking for other people's story. Yet in God's grace and mercy, God rewrote my story.

Back in the Philippines, I grew up in a home that was wrecked by an affair my father had with another woman. My mom, believing in the value of education, took it upon herself to do all kinds of odd jobs, from selling cooked food to doing laundry for other people, just so she can support her seven children through school. My father believed in the same thing. Although he was living with the other woman, he continued to send us financial support for our schooling.

When I graduated from university, there was bitterness in my heart. An empty heart damaged by a broken family. But who cares, really?

I had a nice career, a supportive family and some good friends. What right do I have to complain? Others even have less than what I have.

I started my career as a reporter in a Filipino newspaper, first as a police reporter. Then I became a sportswriter and afterwards an entertainment journalist before I was assigned to write about Malacañang (the Philippine Presidential Palace) and the President. However, when a slot for an entertainment editor was vacated, I accepted the offer to take the position.

Then in 1997, an editor-in-chief position for a Filipino newspaper in Japan was presented to me. The offer came with free housing and transportation and a salary that was ten times higher than what I was earning in the Philippines. Hence, in February 1998, I landed in Tokyo, Japan, with great expectations. However, not long after, in this land they called the Rising Sun, my hopes dimmed and the vacuum in my heart continued to grow. While I seemingly got everything, the more I felt I had nothing.

So on that fateful evening of November 1998, when Coney Reyes spoke and issued the challenge, I invited Jesus to fill the hole in my heart. And as I started crying, God broke down the walls in my life for His light to shine through. Then Jesus started rewriting my story.

"Seek first His kingdom and righteousness and all these things will be provided to you as well."-a verse from the Book of Matthew 6:33 was given me.

I was introduced by a co-worker to a Filipino missionary and church worker in Japan. I tagged along this missionary friend wherever they conducted Bible studies.

Before long, I started one in my flat. Because of my position in the newspaper, I was also asked to be a liaison for the Filipinos having problems with their immigration papers. I acted as a labor coordinator for my fellow *kababayans* (countrymen) in Japan.

But God was not finished with me. In early 2000, I was convicted to go to a Bible school to further my study of God's Word. I wanted more head knowledge to sustain the fire that was already in my heart. All set to go to a Bible school, my missionary friend encouraged me to try joining the MV Doulos – a training and cross-cultural mission ship of the mission organization, Operation Mobilization.

"Seek first His kingdom and righteousness and all these things will be provided to you as well."

Shortly after, I quit my lucrative job in Japan and found myself in Taichung, Taiwan boarding the ship. For two consecutive years, I became a crew of the MV Doulos. The ship went around Asia, Pacific and Africa. With a crew of more than 300 people from 35 different nations, we travelled to over 18 countries. In all these places, I saw the same need for Jesus that people were looking for. Jesus is the answer! Be it in a very poor country like Tanzania, Africa or in a place as rich as Capetown, South Africa, *people need the Lord.*

In June 2001, while I was onboard the MV Doulos, my father died and I was greatly devastated. I went home for a few months and there God continued to work with my heart. It was during those times that the Lord delivered me from the bitterness I harbored for my father. He needed to renew my heart completely.

I finished my commitment with the MV Doulos in September 2002. Equipped with a more solid biblical foundation and training, I sensed that the Lord was leading me back to my homeland. But first I must complete the remaining year of my commitment to my ministry partner in Japan.

What? I wondered to myself. God took me out from the Philippines, brought me to Japan, in a land where they don't believe Jesus is Lord and Saviour, sailed me to 18 different countries, only to bring me back again to the Philippines? And also, why bring me back to Japan if I would be going back to my homeland?

"Seek first His kingdom and righteousness and all these things will be provided to you as well."

Back in Japan, God's intention became clear. As one of the missionaries of a Japan-based Filipino church planting mission agency, I learned more of the things God had been doing with Filipinos married to Japanese nationals. To these *kababayans*, I was able to minister and be a living witness of God's graciousness and mercy to them, and many were encouraged.

Again, God was not finished with me yet. I, together with the other missionaries and Filipino leaders in Japan, was also given the opportunity to receive a comprehensive training on evangelism and discipleship through the New Life Training Center (designed by Campus Crusade for Christ). The thrust of the program was to equip us with the vision and skill to be the Lord's effective multiplying disciples (as taken from 2 Timothy 2:2).

During these NLTC workshops in Japan (from March to November 2003), the Lord further demonstrated His gracious provisions. One of the trainers in the NLTC became not just a good friend in the Lord, but a ministry partner as well. She then invited me to meet their church in Canada and a partnership was forged in January 2004.

With the gracious prayer supports and ministry partnerships of our *kababayans* in Japan and Canada, I'm now back in the Philippines preparing for the next ministry the Lord wants me to be involved in.

My next dateline, 'Mangyan Tribe'- Mindoro, Philippines.

As the Lord continues to write His stories for my life, may it always testify to *"seek first His kingdom and righteousness and all these things will be provided to you as well."* And so my journey with Him continues.

19

ART IN A SHOWCASE
Luis L. Pantoja, Jr.

His name is Art Moreno – a quintessential Filipino immigrant with an unusually colorful set of life experiences. Ask any of those who know Art and they will say mostly positive comments about him to the extent that even when they criticize him, they do it with respect.

From the time I met him in 1982 in Vancouver, British Columbia, Canada, I have concluded that Art reflects best the magnificence of God's grace in a person's life. That is what makes the title of this vignette on him appropriate because as Paul remarked to the Ephesians, "we are God's work of art created in Christ Jesus to do good works which God has programmed in us before-hand to characterize our life and witness" (Eph. 2:10 free translation). We are forgiven of our sins and given the assurance of eternal life by God's favor extended to us (Eph. 2:8-9). Salvation is not a reward for our good works but the moment the Spirit of God comes to live in us, He produces good works, as evidences that we are Christians whom God showcases before the observing world. Thus, let me present Art in a showcase.

In 1974, when he was barely nineteen years old, Art left Muntinlupa, Rizal and began his adventures as a seaman working for a Danish shipping enterprise. Like most Filipino seafarers, part of his salary was sent back to the Philippines to augment his parents' livelihood and to help send his school-age siblings to college. What he kept for himself went to his savings. Although he lived a very frugal existence, the oil tankers and cruise ships for which he worked took him to most of the European and North American ports as well as to numerous other parts of the globe.

Upon the close of one of his work contracts in October 1979, Art decided to remain in Vancouver, BC on a limited tourist visa. With a substantial amount of savings to show the Canadian immigration authorities, he was able to obtain extensions of his temporary stay. At that time, he discovered that he could have an arranged marriage to a Canadian citizen in order to ensure that he acquires a landed immigrant status. In such an arrangement, the "couple" does not have to live together but simply be married on paper. Yet as a Christian, Art felt uncomfortable with the situation and decided to be a dutiful husband to the woman. She, however, stuck with the "marriage" transaction and divorced him after the purpose of the deal was achieved and materialized. Art acquired his landed immigrant status in Canada.

When I first arrived in Vancouver in July 1982, Art was part of the Filipino Baptist Church delegation that met me at the airport and welcomed me as pastor of the congregation of about 40 people. Later, I found out that Art always takes time to meet new Filipino immigrants, whether known or foreign to him, as his standard practice of hospitality. Because his personal vehicle is a delivery truck which he uses for his newspaper distribution brokering business, it becomes a convenient vehicle too for transporting goods for families on the move. Furthermore, since his job requires him to work very early, he finds plenty of time during the day to help people in any way. Art was showcased before the world as a hardworking, good-natured, fun-loving, generous, hospitable, down-to-earth Christian young man. Many new Filipino immigrants have found their way to God and to the church because of Art's Spirit-given gift of Christian hospitality. But he was stigmatized, howbeit mildly, by the unfortunate experience of his divorce.

In 1982, Art Moreno met Leila Sison in one of the church functions and was attracted to her simple lifestyle complemented with profound Christian values. Compared to her upbringing and family background, Art was circumstantially and economically humble as he was indeed genuinely so in spirit. Then after a few months of getting to know each other, Art decided to propose marriage. But how does a young man observe the Filipino tradition of formally asking the woman's parents for the privilege of marrying their daughter (*pamamanhikan*)? Along with three respected Filipino elders, I represented Art's family and served as his pastor at the same time.

On the way down to Seattle, U.S.A. for that special evening, Art and I stopped by a jewelry store in Bellingham to purchase the appropriate engagement and wedding rings. Because that called for a substantial amount of money, I went ahead and paid for it with my credit card and Art paid me the cash upon our return to Vancouver. Obviously, our mission was successful. Shortly thereafter, on August 11, 1984, I pronounced Art and Leila husband and wife in a simple ceremony in a church in Bellevue, Washington. Then the groom took his new wife to Canada and purchased a house just down the road from where my family and I lived in Burnaby, BC.

Being knowledgeable and burdened about the plight of Filipino and other seafarers, Art committed his efforts and funds to ministering to them by joining the volunteer staff of the Lighthouse Harbor Ministries. On a weekly basis, Art visits seamen on dock, shares the gospel with them by word of mouth or literature or film, and in many situations, counsels with them and assists those having employment-related and personal concerns. That has been his main ministry since 1986.

Leila and Art have three children: Eliezer, 17; Liza, 15; and Jeremiah, 12; and the family resides in Coquitlam, BC. After an interstate trucking business venture that proved too demanding, Art went into the ship chandler's trade and now owns the Boatswain Bazaar near the Vancouver port area. He has since arranged for the immigration of his parents and all of his siblings and other family members from the Philippines into Canada.

Often heard from his lips are the words "Praise the Lord" because truly God has been good to Art Moreno. This vignette may sound like a eulogy and, well, it might as well be while he could still hear it. Art is very much alive and well running his business and serving His Master. In fact, we are scheduled to tee off and hit the greens immediately after I finish writing this. Subsequently, when he reads this brief, he just might swing harder, putt better and maybe score lower than usual.

IN THE SERVICE OF THE KING: THE STORY OF A MODERN DAY NEHEMIAH
Sadiri Joy B. Tira

M y doctors have declared cakes and other good-tasting things anathema to my diet. But in the fall of 2002, I found myself in a kingdom island, in one of the world's Limited Access Regions (LAR), eating cakes and pastries of a quality I had never tasted before, and to my stomach's delight.

This unique situation presented itself one night after a worship service of Filipino believers working on the island. The pastor had just pronounced the benediction after a rather lengthy service. Having just preached I was quite tired of the excellent buffet service there. But then I was invited to stay late for the evening meal and fellowship with the congregation members. As usual the Filipinos were punctuating the worship service with a time of extended fellowship over a potluck feast. The ensuing meal is almost a requisite in Filipino gatherings, so I decided to stay and was content to eat whatever vegetarian dishes were available (and might I say, in Filipino gatherings, the vegetarian selection is few and far between). While the others were eating great rich dishes of meats, I finished off my plate of steamed rice and *pinakbet*, a Filipino vegetable stew.

For dessert I started to look around for a banana, the one sweet thing my doctors have deemed safe for me to eat, but I was stopped by the pastor and his wife who had a dish of pastries in hand. "Try this, Pastor Joy," they said. To which I replied my well-practiced, "I pass. A banana is enough. It is good for me. I'm fine, thank you." Again, they insisted, "No, Pastor Joy. You must try this. Even a little bit of it. It is the best in the kingdom." "I can't," I protested. Seconds later they returned with a shy middle-aged man with a boyish face, still with pastry plate in tow.

"Pastor Joy, you must try the pastries. Our friend here, baked them. This guy here is the King's baker, and these goodies are from the King's very own palace. These pastries are the best, Pastor Joy. You must try them now or we, and he, will be offended."

There was no way I could back out now, so out went the doctors' orders. It was a good thing that my ever-watchful wife was not there to stop me. The pastries were indeed delicious! So I had one of each type of pastry that night, and seconds and thirds too! I even took some back to my hotel. It really was the best in the land! I left the Filipino shindig with the impressive thought: "That guy was really the King's baker! How he is like Nehemiah, the Jewish cupbearer for a Babylonian king, serving in a modern king's palace!"

Two years later in May 2004, I would return to that island kingdom to preach in the same church. This time I planned to sit down with the king's baker and I planned to ask how he came from a little town in the Philippines to the palace of a king. In response to my invitation he arrived at my hotel with his niece and a bag of scrumptious banana bread. The story that he would share with me is described in this writing with his permission.

JOURNEY TO THE PALACE

Luis was born in the summer of 1950 in Toledo, Aklan, in the central Philippines. He lived in his hometown for 17 years before moving to Cubao, Metro Manila. He was not embarrassed to tell me that before he moved to Manila he was a "no read, no write," finishing only the First Grade in elementary and not completing any formal education. Luis, however, gained his training in pastry-making when his cousin hired him to apprentice in his Cubao bakeshop. In retrospect, Luis sees God's goodness in allowing him to start off as a baker. He worked for his cousin for eight years then moved to the upper-class city of Makati, where he worked from 1975 to 1990. When the Makati bakery closed, it became necessary for Luis to find work abroad. He applied through a Philippine Overseas Employment Administration-endorsed agency.

In 1992, after patiently waiting four years for an overseas position, Luis set out for the island kingdom to work in the palace. As a palace baker, Luis was responsible for making delicious baked delights for the royal family. Over the years Luis gained more valuable experience in baking. His royal employers even sent him to study culinary arts with the Sheraton Hotels. He was mentored by "the best" baker in the region.

Luis' service through the years is rewarded with many benefits. He earns a handsome salary, accommodation on the palace compounds, one month paid vacation including airfare every year. His employers are extremely generous and kind to him. During their festivals Luis is showered with monetary bonuses and assorted gifts such as jewelry and clothing. They treat him with respect and even respect his Christian faith.

In our time together, Luis tells of when his employers tried to persuade him to forsake his Christian faith. They offered him extra benefits if he would denounce his faith in Jesus Christ. With gentle but firm response, Luis refused their offers. From that time, Luis says, his employers have treated him with "greater respect" and even openly dialogue with him regarding Christianity. They do not restrict his religious activities, including late night Bible studies and prayer meetings outside the palace. They also encourage Luis to share food from the palace with the Filipino congregation on the island, such as the goodies that I indulged in at the Filipino church potluck dinner. There are many different expatriates working at the palace. There are workers from Pakistan, Sri Lanka, and India, and Luis' humble disposition and kindness has won him many "international" friends among his palace coworkers.

Luis is an extremely generous man. Though officially separated from his wife, and is without children, Luis' life extends back to his homeland, the Philippines, as he continues to support his family. He pays for the tuition of his nephews and nieces, and has invested his resources in property and real estate in order to assist his extended family in the Philippines.

IN THE SERVICE OF THE KING OF KINGS

It is interesting to note that Luis decided to follow Jesus Christ in the year 2000, during his stay in the island kingdom. He was introduced to Jesus

Christ by his countrymen who had been trained in FIN-initiated evangelism and discipleship seminars (New Life Training Curriculum or NLTC). After he decided to follow Christ, Luis became consistent in attending Bible studies and became an active member of the Christian community. Luis, himself, has gone through NLTC training. Now, he regularly invites his co-workers at the palace to fellowship and worship gatherings with the Filipino Christians.

Luis humbly states: "I feel that I don't give much and I have nothing to contribute because I am just a simple man, and my English is not very good." But I assured him that his contribution is significant for the building of the Kingdom. I reminded him that his shared baking with the Filipino Christians, his invitation to his friends to learn more about Jesus Christ in Church and Bible studies, and his financial support to his relatives in the Philippines are not overlooked by the Heavenly Father.

As we finished our cup of tea and concluded our time together, I opened my New Testament and read to him Hebrews 6:10, "God is not unjust. He will not forget your work and the love that you have shown to him as you have helped his people and as you continue to help them." He nodded and grinned, his face brightening up with joy. I then prayed for him and his niece and moved from the restaurant to the lobby to take pictures.

My time with Luis and his niece was inspiring. I was challenged and encouraged to continue praying that God would raise more modern-day Nehemiahs — Filipinos who would serve God, and who would become trust-worthy "servants" to modern-day masters, and in so doing demonstrate Christ-likeness to their community.

In retrospect, Luis could see the providence of God in his life. It is amazing how a Filipino boy from a remote village in the Philippines was trained to be a baker in a little Cubao-corner bakery, a head baker in Makati, and from there became the baker in a king's service. Now with 33 years of baking experience under his belt, Luis recognizes how God led him from his hometown and providentially brought him to the island kingdom where he has decided to follow and serve the King of Kings. He looks back with understanding at the circumstances God has brought him through, including how he had to wait four years for a reply to his job application and the processing of his documents with the Philippine government. Had he not waited, he may have ended up abroad in a far less favorable job, perhaps in another corner bakeshop, but certainly not in a palace.

It encourages me to see God's foreknowledge and day-to-day control in Luis' life. To think that Luis could have denounced his faith in exchange for more material fortune, and how God used that situation instead to soften his employers' hearts toward him. It is possible that Luis could have been dismissed and deported for refusing his employers' offer, as is the reported case of many other expatriate workers. But instead, Luis gained his employers' respect. Certainly, Luis is like Nehemiah who gained the favor of the Babylonian king.

I started this story with me tasting Luis' baking at the Filipino potluck after their worship service, so I will go back to the subject of Luis' baked goodies. Luis and I met again a couple of months ago, and he left me carrying a bag of banana bread to my hotel room. For two days I feasted on the banana bread. It was like a gift that kept on giving, because in two days, I still had so much of it that I gave some of it to the Pakistani man who cleaned out my hotel room, and I gave even more of it to Luis' pastor. Then just before I left that island kingdom, Luis came to give me about 10 kilos of dried dates. He said, "Pastor take these dates home to your wife and family in Canada." I could not carry all 10 kilos of dates, so again I gave some away. The banana bread and the dates are an example of how generous Luis is.

To end, let me tell you what Luis once said to me: "Today, the little children I used to feed are princes and princesses. I have been baking for them for 12 years and they are grown up now." As I look at Luis and his generous service, I cannot help but wonder what impact his witness has had on the royal family whom he serves, and on his group of international co-workers and friends. I wonder how God has used Luis to plant seeds of hope and "a gift that keeps on giving" in the lives of those around him. Like with the story of Nehemiah, I am certain that only eternity will tell.

FILIPINO-NEPALI CONNECTIONS
Philip Pacle

S tock markets since the latter part of the '80s were mixed with good and bad news due to a general lack of direction and the uncertainty ahead of a number of political upheavals in the Asian region. With the situation continuing to bring investors in doubt, affected countries such as Nepal, India, Bangladesh, Sri Lanka, and the Philippines experienced heavy economic losses and an increased unemployment rate. Citizens from these nations ventured out in search for a better living. Among the number of those who left their homeland for a brighter future were some Christians.

Many job seekers landed in regions where there were high-paying jobs at that time. However, this also meant having to work and live in countries where governments practiced religious intolerance.

In the late 1996, three Nepali Christians found their way to a country with religious intolerance. Hungry and longing for the Word of God to feed their soul, these Nepalese searched for Christian fellowship. They came to know Jay, who offered a room at his place for them to have fellowship. Later their group increased in number so that the tiny room could no longer accommodate them. They moved to another room in Street No.1. There were eight who studied the Bible and fellowshipped with one another.

The name QICM at that time was already a byword from the Christian community as a large group composed of about 70% Filipinos and 30% from different nationalities that had been around for quite sometime. When the evangelism group of QICM extended into the industrial area, they met another Nepalese named Sanji. It was at this meeting that the Filipino – Nepalese fellowship became a reality.

Sanji, Jay and George, had found a growing fellowship of believers, most of whom were Filipinos in this part of the world. Other Nepali believers came to Christ and were baptized at this Fellowship on Street No.1. However, there were many adversities and trials to be experienced. The tiny group was evicted from Street No.1, and so it became difficult to meet as a group. But this handful of faithful servants of the Lord did not stop. They moved out towards "wilderness" and exercised their faith in the "open field," hiding behind sand dunes and avoiding getting caught by the authorities. They memorized verses in their meetings as they opted not to bring Bible for security reasons. They prayed quietly and did so as if they were whispering with each other so that they won't be suspected of doing anything "illegal."

The Lord continued to teach and build these Nepalese. The Holy Spirit continued to move and show signs that they had to do something for harvest. It was early in 1997 when some of these Nepali brothers came forward to seek the helping hand and fellowship from QICM.

The Nepali brothers were praying for a larger place for worship and God answered their prayers. God touched the heart of QICM leaders to allow them to use the adjacent place which was built just a few weeks earlier. There they met weekly. It was during this time that the name "QICM Nepal Chapter" was formed and became part of the church (QICM).

As the number of believers grew and some brothers missed the chance to join the weekly fellowship due to the distance of their accommodation and work place from their new meeting place, the Lord allowed them to move back to Street No.1 with a bigger place of worship. On August 13, 1997, the Nepali Christian congregation, QNCF, was born. In the following year, a bi-monthly newsletter of QNCF (in collaboration with the newsletter of QICM) intended for Nepali brothers came off the press which contained relevant information about the internal and external activities of the group. It also focuses on the testimonies of Nepali brothers.

After a few months, QICM was blessed with a new fellowship service for Filipino Christians residing outside the neighborhood. The new worship house was located in the industrial area, Street No.2. It was also decided by

QICM leadership that QNCF must also use the 6x8 square meter well-ventilated room to save on rental expenses. During the opening message in the dedication of the new edifice, Pastor G said, "Work together hand-in-hand so the theme will work well." He continued to challenge everyone not to be mere listeners but a worker indeed. "You must be an expert builder in building your church because the rock who is Jesus Christ has given you grace to lay a foundation which must be strong and firm so that if the times of testing come and you survive, you will receive a reward."

The Filipinos use the place in the morning while the Nepali brothers meet in the afternoon. QNCF celebrated their second anniversary in this place with much gusto. Later, the lot where the fellowship was housed was acquired by a new owner to develop it into a bigger business enterprise. The congregation had to move again. Both fellowships, the Filipino and Nepali, became temporarily relocated for six months.

The Lord provided another place for fellowship in Street No.3 for almost a year. Since the owner took advantage of increasing the rent every month (he had observed that a big crowd would always gather there), leaders of both QNCF and QICM had no choice but to look for another place.

QICM and QNCF finally got its new worship house on Street No.4 which was offered for lease with a minimal fee by a Korean businessman. A new 4x4 van was later provided by QICM for its continued support to QNCF evangelism and for other ministry purposes. The Lord is blessing QNCF. It has produced very faithful servants who are instrumental in nurturing QNCF leaders and members as well as making the church a strong foundation. Some members have gone on to seminary for theological training.

At present, there are close to 200 believers worshiping with QNCF. Six departments have been established such as Music, Education, Transportation, Catering and Cleaning who work together for the establishment of God's Kingdom. Seminars have also been conducted to teach leaders and members such as the EE seminar, NLTC, and other basic training seminars in evangelism.

While our host country sets a good example for fast-growing industrial countries, QNCF on the other hand, with strong support from the Filipino congregation, maintains its position to lead in the area of evangelism which caters mostly to our Nepali brothers who dream of searching for fortune and happiness for themselves and loved ones but find a greater prize – that of meeting Jesus Christ as their Lord and personal Savior. Many are saved, and each new believer continues to grow and teach the Word of God to their friends and co-workers as well as to their families and relatives in Nepal. God used the uncertainty of events so that a fellowship for Nepali brothers would exist in our city.

22

LAURA, A SHEER GIFT OF GRACE:
FILIPINO SENIORS DIASPORA

Idrenne Lim-Alparaque

*"Stories go in circles, They don't go in straight lines.
So it helps if you listen in a circle because there are stories inside
stories and stories between stories."* (Metzer, 1985)

Someone once said that nothing is unnoticed as that which is self-evident. Subtly tucked away within the circle of stories about the Filipino diaspora or scattering around the globe, are the stories of our senior Filipinos.

One such story is that of Laura Lim's. Just like the many other Filipino seniors diaspora stories, it is easy to overlook Laura's story because it is self-evident in the fabric of the closely knit Filipino family. I chose to tell Laura's story to represent the many other seniors' stories that play out everyday in Filipino diaspora families all over North America. I feel it is Laura's story I can tell best, because I have witnessed Laura's story rather closely. I am Laura's daughter.

Laura's story took place some twenty years ago when my husband and I invited her to come to Canada. I told her, "Mama, how'd you like to do a PhD with me?" Laura, a former educator, loved the idea and my sisters also thought that a brief stay in Canada would be a refreshing change of scenery for our widowed mother. Of course, she knew that the practical reality of her coming to Canada was so that my husband and I could pursue our careers without having to worry about hiring a nanny for our three young children.

Actually, inviting Laura to come and stay with us in Canada was really quite a tall order. We were in a way asking her to give up the leisurely life of comfort and security she was enjoying as a retired teacher administrator. Like many retired Filipino professionals, Laura had already earned her place of honor in her church and wider community. Like other seniors, she continued to draw energy and delight in serving and helping people. She was the President of the Women's Missionary Society, the Interfaith Association. She led Bible studies and served on advisory boards for Christian schools and organizations, among other responsibilities. She was leading an active, meaningful life among her loved ones, friends and family. Our invitation meant asking her to give this all up to come help us out in Canada. And of course, this would mean for her leaving the warm and invigorating climate of Malaybalay, Bukidnon to come to live in a place many of us in Canada amusingly referred to as having only two seasons "Winter and July." Laura knew this would not be an easy transition for her at her age. But she came to Canada as a rather reluctant part of the Filipino senior diaspora.

Laura's first few months in Canada must have been quite a bitter-sweet experience for her. There was the awe-inspiring trip through the Canadian Rockies, her first "taste" of snow, access to books and titles she could only dream of in the Philippines. And many other delightful discoveries of convenience in the Canadian lifestyle which we just take for granted in North America.

Like most senior Filipinos in North America, Laura found herself confined most of the time at home alone. But the Lord had given Laura a gentle humility of personality, an insatiable love for learning, and most of all a quiet countenance of a vibrant faith in Jesus Christ. Thus, even in the stark loneliness of a northern Alberta winter, she turned to her strongest refuge: Her Lord. Laura turned to the Word and continued consistently in her posture of prayer. she utilized the 'luxury' of time she had to read and meditate on His Word. If you read Laura's old Bible today, you will find the almost tattered pages and pages with her meticulous margin notes and comments on the verses she read each day. There are thick reams of notes she had written down in notepads, reams of thoughts and insights she gleaned from her daily extended devotions. And always these notes were punctuated with specific prayers (and names of individuals) she brought before her Lord sometimes in worship or in thanks for blessings received, and at times in supplication and intercession for others.

Sundays were the only days Laura could actually go out because she had our hectic schedules to adjust to. It must have been quite a culture shock for her, to have a drastically limited social life and participation in the church and the community. We introduced her to people in church, and because they knew nothing of her background, I don't think it ever occurred to any of them to invite her to be actively involved in the church activities.

However, as I am now able to reflect upon Laura's life as I write this, I remember that when Rev. Ed Carlson, our pastor, announced in church a Personal Evangelism class, Laura was one of the first who signed up for the course. She basked in this new opportunity to learn more about how to share her faith. And to have this in Canada was something she considered an honor and a unique learning experience.

There were now several books to read – books catering to her voracious appetite for good Christian literature. There were classes to attend, prayer sessions and practical door-to-door cold-calling in personal evangelism. There were Bible verses to learn by heart, study guides, and homework assignments. And like the ideal diligent student every teacher wants in her class, Laura poured herself prayerfully with sensitivity and quiet enthusiasm into the course. This course opened up what for Laura was an exciting arena of a teaching-learning event. Never mind that this all took place in the midst of the usual -35°C of a Ft. McMurray winter!

Laura didn't wait for her home church to connect with her. She took the initiative to continue her ministry with the women. She prayed for them consistently, corresponding with them regularly and sharing the new ideas she was learning from the course and her readings. She used to copy by hand pages and pages of devotional books, (sometimes an entire book she had read) and wrote down her personal notes and comments on each book. She sent these copies to the women who each took turns copying them (by hand) so that they too could read and learn more about growth in their daily Christian walk and witnessing for Christ. (Note: printers were not readily accessible in Laura's hometown)

Laura's women friends in her home church also delighted in these readings because they now had the privilege of reading excerpts and books by contemporary authors. Most of the Christian books, if not the only ones these women had access to, were the books at the local Baptist Mission Library. A bulk of the Mission's collection consisted of discarded copies of the Grace Livingstone Hill book series, Paul Anderson's so-called Christian romance novels, other uninteresting titles that someone in America figured he'd donate to a third world country inasmuch as it would go to the garbage bin anyway. Or there were the musty dark-green hardcover volumes in theology, eschatology, or some obscure doctrine way too abstract for the average Christian lay person's reading fare. Thus, Laura's letters came as a breath of fresh air in their literary scene. This was obviously before the advent of e-mail and the internet. This was Laura's version of Distance Learning ministry.

Laura also continued to support Filipino students from her home church with her prayers and she even managed to send a few US dollars regularly to help nursing students with their school expenses. Two of those student nurses immigrated to the US after graduation and are currently administrators in their respective California teaching hospitals. Cheryl and Nonita continue to serve the Lord with their families and in turn are helping support Filipino students and missionaries in the nursing profession.

A year later, we moved to Michener Park in Edmonton, a graduate student housing complex. Praise the Lord for leading Laura to meet Frisco and Vangie Consolacion, a Filipino couple doing their post graduate studies at the University of Alberta. Laura was soon involved leading Bible studies and prayer group meetings at the Consolacion residence. This tiny fellowship of Filipino believers, most of whom were graduate students, became the core founding group that started the First Filipino Alliance Church (FFAC).

At the FFAC fellowship, the Lord blessed Laura as she served and ministered to others in her own unassuming ways. I'd like to call it Laura's Ministry of Care. She directed the choir, taught Sunday school and trained the Sunday school teachers at the FFAC. She worked closely with another Senior lady, Letty Tuason, who made sure the students and other young people made it to these Bible study groups and prayer meetings. Everyone in the church loved "Grandma Lim" as they fondly called Laura. Her personal ministry found her mentoring many young people and collaborating with Letty in prayerful support of the FFAC members. With a "gentle and mindful regard for others," she allowed them to confide in her as they shared their difficulties and dreams. She was a great listener who listened with apt attention as the leaders in church spoke of their vicissitudes and vision. She prayed with them through trauma and rejoiced with them in their triumphs. And always she listened humbly. And always Laura prayed.

Meantime, Laura was taking care of her three grandchildren Suiram Dale, Ian Patrick and Mizella Laura. Here, the story takes me back a few months before Laura's arrival in Canada. My husband's parents had come for a brief visit in their tour of the US and Canada.

I told the kids that their Grandpa and Grandma Alparaque were coming to visit. And that's all I said. I distinctly remember that morning when we introduced the children to their grandparents in our living room. The two younger children said "hi," and promptly ran off to resume their playing, But our eldest son Dale stood shyly and just kept looking at his grandparents even as I prodded him to greet them with a hug. But Dale continued to stand quietly, almost staring at them with a quizzical look on his face. Dale motioned me to come close as if to tell me something was amiss. I asked him if there was anything wrong, and with a look that suggested a serious gravity of situation, our six-year-old son. Asks in hushed tones: "But Mommy, how come they're brown?"

I then understood the context of Dale's question, because it promptly reminded me that up to this point in our children's lived experiences, we had asked them to always politely address our senior friends as "Grandpa and Grandma" instead of by their first names which was a usual practice among our Canadian friends. But of course Dale had a very valid question for his 6-year-old mind because all of our senior friends happened to be white!

After that incident and other stories we heard about Filipino grandparents and their Canadian grandchildren, my husband and I decided to make sure that our children had a better understanding and appreciation of our family and its multi-layered contexts of culture, the blend of their Filipino and Canadian identities, our grounding in the Christian faith and the intricacies of kinship inherent in their inter-generational familial relationships.

And so we turned to stories. Stories and storytelling helped prepare our children for Laura's coming to our home in Canada. Months before Laura's arrival, we told stories and narrated vignettes from our childhood so they could better understand what "grandma" really meant. We told "tuck-in" stories at bedtime about me and my mother. We described childhood photographs of their Mommy and her Mom – their grandmother. Through the weave of memories came more stories reminiscing their Dad's childhood and these stories reminded them and re-connected them with their happy and concrete experiences during that first visit with their grandparents. In a big way, the concept of grandparents started to impress our children in a much more personal way.

Gradually, our children came to have a more intimate understanding of their relation to Laura. For instance, their comments about letters or photos from the Philippines started to reveal a more personal attachment of kinship. The boys no longer referred to Laura's letters as in "Hey Mom, you've got mail from your country." Instead, Dale or Ian would say, "Mom you have a letter from Grandma."

In the spring of 1982, our children welcomed their grandmother Laura into our home. The children treated her with the same respect they accorded us as parents. And a bit more. They also treated Laura as a guest in our home. Years later Dale, Ian and Mizella described those first few years with Laura:

Ian: "I think my brother and sister and I knew that Grandma was family. We understood that she was not just a casual friend from the Philippines. However, the first time I realized that Grandma was more than a just a guest was by the way she talked to my mother. For the first time I witnessed my mother in the role of a child as Grandma talked to her in a motherly way. Then later there were times when she'd chide my Mom, or task my mother's remarks away. And I knew even at 7 that only mothers talk that way to their children.

Grandma asserted her parental authority with us from the very start. I remember how frustrated she was with us one day. So she basically summoned all three of us to the bathroom. Then taking a piece of toilet paper, she says, "Dale, Ian, Mizzy this is a roll of toilet paper. This is a section of this roll of toilet paper. You take two sections, one, and two sections of the toilet paper, you fold it this way, then use the folded two sections of the toilet paper, drop it into the bowl, flush the toilet and then wash your hands. You use only two sections of the toilet paper at a time, not clumps and clumps of toilet tissue like you do."

Of course I thought to myself at that time, "What's the big deal, this is not the Philippines. We always have a roll of toilet paper when one roll is used up. We never run out of toilet paper! And I looked up at the rolls of toilet paper on the shelf, but was scared to say anything to Grandma. You just obeyed her I guess, because she would ask you only once and then just expect you to do it. So you did it."

Mizella: "Grandma was just like our Mom, always reading and studying! She actually loved studying . She helped us with our homework everyday. And she always wanted me to get a perfect score on my tests. When I was in Grade Two I remember her asking me why I only got 17 points out of 20 points in my spelling test. I told her that I misspelled the words on purpose on Wednesdays so that the teacher would not give me a new spelling list to study. I always got a perfect 20/20 on Fridays. But Grandma was also not like our Mom. Once, I was crying because I hurt my knee. I wanted Grandma to make it better but she never looked at my bruised knee. She just continued folding the laundry quietly."

Dale: "Grandma was always praying and reading her Bible in her room. She was always writing down notes when she was reading. But Grandma didn't know how to cook. Sometimes she tried to copy our Dad's recipe and the food sort of looked like Dad's cooking. But it sure didn't taste like it. So my Mom taught me how to cook chicken adobo. For a week I cooked chicken adobo until my brother and sister begged my mother to teach me another recipe. I learned how to do spaghetti and lasagna after that."

Laura also extended her witness to those around her in the neighborhood. At the Graduate Student Housing Complex, she was the most popular babysitter especially among the Asian students. Laura took in children to care for because many of them were the neighborhood friends of her own three grandchildren. The parents always felt comfortable and secure with her taking care of their kids. There were many a time when parents could not afford to pay Laura for babysitting because their scholarship or grant monies had not come through. Laura simply said that a " thank you" would be more than sufficient compensation. One couple I know could not afford to pay Laura for an entire year and she accepted their thanks just as sincerely. Perhaps as a former teacher and a Christian, she knew that the fruits of her work and witness would be evident years and years later.

When Laura took other children in her care she always told them about the Lord she loved. She cared for a 4- and 5-year old teaching them Christian songs and Bible verses. She spent time telling stories of Zaccheus, David and Goliath, Noah's ark and the baby Jesus. One Buddhist parent used to tell me how grateful she was of Laura teaching their child to speak English! They apparently didn't mind that their child often recited John 3: 16 and narrated stories about this man Jesus. This child is now a university medical student doing her residency in the States. And if asked about Canada, she will tell you about a woman named "Grandma Lim" and the wonderful Bible stories and Christian songs she learned. And yes even though she is not a Christian she still knows John 3: 16 by heart. I claim the promise in the Scriptures that His Word will never return to Him void.

In 1992, our family moved to Vancouver and Laura, who was then 80 years old maintained the same energy in her work for the Lord. Once again she was actively serving in a Filipino church, now pastored by one of the former members of the core group that met at Michener Park. Laura joined the choir and was the Sunday School Superintendent for the joint Sunday school groups of the Filipino church and their host Canadian church.

In this fellowship, those who knew Laura, among them Carmen, Cynthia, Beth and Emma gave Laura the inspiration to continue to use her gifts of teaching, mentoring, and prayer as they sought her spiritual counsel and loving support like a second mother.

Perhaps Laura's story may have ended shortly thereafter. On August 8, 1999, back home in the Philippines Laura passed away to be with her Lord and Savior Jesus Christ.

But Laura's story does not have to end here. Hers is only one story that narrate the lived – experiences of many Seniors in the Filipino diaspora.

Laura's story is told over and over again by the many senior Filipinos scattered in North America. We find sterling examples of these senior Filipinos and their personal ministry of caring for their family and others. There's Virginia Benzon, in Edmonton, whose narrative life reads like a ride on the roughest, toughest side of survival. When you meet this petite 75-year-old lady and ask her how she stayed steady and strong through the currents of difficulties and dire times, she beams radiant joy in her eyes and replies, "I didn't do anything, I just held back and the Lord gave me all the blessings with my children." Virginia's seven children are all successful professionals in North America and Europe. And they all actively support global missions.

There is Letty Tuazon who, in spite of a life-long debilitating illness, cared for and "mothered" many university students and the young people in her church, facilitating their needs so that they could in turn serve the Lord. Letty ministered to these young people through the excruciating physical pain her arthritis inflicted on her body. She always gave the students a ride to church, Bible studies, and prayer meetings in the blistering cold of Alberta winters that naturally wreaked havoc on her withering arthritic nerves. Nanay Letty, as everyone called her, opened her home to a Ministry of Care for others. Her living room and basement were constant venues for prayer meetings, Bible study, leadership and discipleship seminars. She cared for many a Visa university and college student, feeding them, giving them shelter at desperate times so that they could complete their studies on their very limited if not non-existent student budget. And Letty prayed for them!

I want to wind up the threads of my story about Laura's story with tentative thoughts – questions really, to remind us of the importance of the Senior's role in the diaspora, the Filipino global presence, and its relevant connections in our work in global missions. We may ask the following questions for a start:

- Why is it noteworthy to listen to Laura's story and the stories of the many Filipino seniors in the diaspora?

- How can we approach our work in global missions from the perspective of the seniors' strategic place of pedagogic parental responsibility – taking care of our Filipino Canadian/American children.?

- What insights and implications can we derive from the lives of Filipino seniors as it relates to the Great Commission and our obedience?

Thanks be to our Lord Jesus Christ for the sheer gift of Grace: the seniors in the Filipino diaspora.

UNDER HIS WINGS: INCREDIBLE STORIES OF DIVINE PROTECTION

Sadiri Joy B. Tira

The Psalmist, as recorded in Psalm 91, is so assured of the Most High's protection that he compared God's protection to that of a mother bird, securing her young beneath her encompassing wings. It is proclaimed, "He who dwells in the shelter of the Most High will rest in the shadows of the Almighty... He will cover [him] with His feathers and under His wings [he] will find refuge." (verse 4)

Some of the greatest examples I have seen of this "wing-like refuge" are demonstrated in the lives of two OFWs who I met while visiting Kuwait and the United Arab Emirates. Their respective stories are "high-profile," having attracted international press coverage (e.g. CNN, BBC, CBC, etc.) in the last couple of years, and while many journalists have already told their stories, I approach them from a divine perspective. Their stories told here with their permission, are illustrative of the protection of God as proclaimed by the ancient Psalmist.

JIMMY: ACCUSED BUT VINDICATED

In the Fall of 2002, while on my sabbatical leave from the daily duties of my parish, I had the opportunity to again visit Kuwait. After speaking in one of the many church services at the National Evangelical Church of Kuwait (NECK), I was introduced to Jimmy who came from the province of Bulacan, Philippines.

Unmarried, Jimmy came to Kuwait in the summer of 2001 in hopes of finding a high-paying job and greater economic opportunity. He was a new Believer when he left the Philippines, and when he arrived in Kuwait he soon found a group of other Filipinos who befriended him during his first days in a new but foreign land. Soon after Jimmy arrived in Kuwait, the tragedy of 9/11 (the destruction of the World Trade Towers in New York) set off a powder keg of anti-American sentiment among some Arab Muslims in Kuwait. In the aftermath of 9/11, American nationals living in Kuwait were instructed by their government to "keep a low profile." A Canadian who was American-looking man (and married to a Filipina) working inside Camp Doha, a U.S. military base outside Kuwait City, risked taking a walk outside the base and was shot dead by a then unknown assailant. Seven Filipinos were taken into custody by local police as suspects of the brutal murder. Several other OFWs in Kuwait were summoned for interrogation.

One of these Filipinos was Jimmy. On October 10, 2001, Jimmy, along with the other six Filipinos were arrested and detained for several weeks. At the height of the investigation, six of the seven Filipinos who could no longer bear the stress of the situation, decided to admit to the charges. Jimmy, however, maintained his stance and insisted on his innocence, saying that he had no part in the shooting of the Canadian national. He said *"Kahit patayin nila ako dito, hindi ako aamin."* (Even if they kill me, I will not admit to that crime!)

Jimmy's sisters who were working at Camp Doha came to his help and provided money to hire a Kuwaiti lawyer to defend their brother. They spent more than 2,000 Kuwaiti Dinars (approximately US$6,700) for Jimmy's legal expenses. In the summer of 2003, Jimmy was acquitted of the crime and was considered a free man. Wanting to counter charge and seek justice in order to recover the financial loss, the Philippine diplomats in Kuwait advised Jimmy to return to the Philippines. And he did.

These days, Jimmy drives his own passenger jeepney for his living. He is now happily married and has a newborn son. He married another OFW whom he met during his turbulent years in Kuwait. A blessing in disguise is that they met while they were detained by the police.

At the height of the investigation and interrogation, and in the uncertainty of the Kuwait jail, Jimmy says he had nowhere to turn but to God. He prayed earnestly for courage and strength. He was blessed by the support of his family and the community of believers in Kuwait, and he witnessed the intercession of the Filipino Christians for wisdom for his Kuwait lawyer, and justice and mercy from the Kuwaiti courts. In those turbulent months in a foreign land, Jimmy's young faith was tested and strengthened. "I learned to fix my eyes on Jesus Christ who alone is my burden bearer!" he exclaims.

One of the greatest blessings in all these is the change of heart of his devoutly religious mother coming to personal relationship with Jesus Christ. His mother who was living in the Philippines, while separated from her son also experienced God's comfort through the believers in their community in Bulacan. According to Jimmy, his pastor in the Philippines visited his parents regularly and prayed for them and shared the message of hope found in Jesus Christ with them. When I asked him if his father also came to a personal relationship with Jesus Christ, Jimmy said, "I am sorry to say but he is not yet a believer, and I will appreciate your prayers for this PJ."

In July 2004, Jimmy and I reconnected again, but this time we had an hour to chat. Over the phone told me all about his experiences in Kuwait, and his triumphal journey through trials, his happy marriage, the joy of being a father, and his evident success as a new entrepreneur in his hometown. He is now more than ever aware of his security "under His wings."

GEORGE: CRASHED BUT NOT CRUSHED

In February 2004, I was in Dubai, UAE for a few days. A Filipino friend asked if I was willing to go with him and his wife to pray for a Filipino patient confined in one of the hospitals. Having just come off a long-haul flight, I hesitated, but was overcome with obligation. Just before arriving at the hospital, this friend told me, "PJ, I want you to pray for this couple. The husband's name is George, and the wife's name is Maritess." I responded: "George and Maritess who?" My friend explained to me that George is a survivor of a horrible plane crash and his wife, Maritess, has just arrived from the Philippines to be with him, leaving behind their one and only child in the care of their relatives. George was one of the three survivors of what was referred to in the *Sunday, February 22, 2004 Gulf News*, as "the worst [airline accident] in UAE's aviation history since the country's federation in 1971."

Like Jimmy, George was a new believer who came to the UAE looking for a job. While waiting for job opportunities, he needed to renew his visa. This brought him to exit Dubai to the Iranian island of Kish. His return flight to Dubai would be the Kish Airline's ill-fated Fokker 50 that crashed before landing at the Sharjah International Airport, killing 46 out of 49 passengers and crew.

At the Al Qasimi Hospital, I read Psalm 91 to the couple before asking the Creator-God to prolong George's life. I prayed that the Father gently touch and heal George's wounds and burned skins; that Christ will be exalted in this situation; that the doctors and hospital staff may know the power of the unseen but present Healer; that someday George and his wife will find courage to stand before the crowd testifying God's goodness and loving-kindness; and that this couple will experience the peace of God and the comfort of the Holy Spirit. While my time with them was very brief, it was one of the most tender moments that I have had with a patient. In the following months, stories of George's miraculous survival and recovery would be recounted in newspapers and on television news segments. These press releases would become a wonderful way for George and his wife to share to the world how God has been faithful to them.

In March 2004, I received a letter from Maritess updating me about George's situation. At the time of writing, George was undergoing extensive medical treatment, mainly debridement and skin grafting. Maritess wrote: "Day by day George is improving... Medical staff who assist him always say that he's the best patient they've ever had... Day by day, God shows His miracles to us." Maritess wrote about how George was being called "the luckiest among the lucky ones" and how many different people were visiting them "to find out the truth about [George]." She wrote that they (George and herself) are happy that when people pray for George's situation, they (the people) remember "that there is still God who could listen and answer such prayers."

I was again in Dubai in June 2004. This time I was invited by the same friend to preach to his Filipino congregation at the United Christian Church of Dubai (UCCD). Again, because of the tight schedule, I was hesitant to take this invitation, but he twisted my arm.

"PJ, you must come to preach. Guess who will be there at the service? George and Maritess will be there to celebrate their anniversary. This is the first time George is allowed to leave the hospital. George and Maritess are going to thank all the people who prayed for them, especially for George. He will also share his testimony for the first time in public."

This was a very convincing invitation and I decided that I could not miss the opportunity. I was going to preach from Psalm 23, but as I listened to George's testimony, I decided to preach instead from Psalm 91 – the Scripture that I had read to George and Maritess during our first meeting in the hospital. I believe that George and many other OFWs in the crowd need to hear the message of God' protection and tender loving care. I preached from this passage before and so, as the service was going on, I quickly wrote my sermon outline and trusted the Holy Spirit to direct and guide me during my sermon delivery (I normally don't change my sermons at the last minute, certainly not during the service, but this time I did for the glory of God). As I was preaching, I made eye contact with George who was in tears. I believe that those tears were of joy and triumph over his tragic accident. His wife was also in tears.

When George and Maritess shared their testimony with the congregation, it was an emotional moment for everyone. George broke into tears as he thanked the congregation for their prayers and support in many ways. Encouraged by God's goodness to George and Maritess and moved by God's faithfulness, many in the congregation also broke out in tears.

God knows our tears. The Psalmist wrote that God keeps our tears in a "bottle" (Psalm 56:8).

After the service, the congregation not only celebrated George's new lease on life, but they also celebrated the couple's wedding anniversary with a big feast. Many people who followed the story of George Cruz say that his survival is miraculous. I agree.

The lives of Jimmy and George are similar in many ways. Both were OFWs but without jobs at the time of their great challenges in life. Both were young believers who were surrounded by a loving and praying congregation. Both called on God to intervene in their respective and very difficult situation. Both experienced God's mercy and grace.

With this profound security, Jimmy and George have had many opportunities to share others their faith in God who is their refuge. Like Jimmy and George, other OFWs may be exposed to tragedies and misfortunes in life, but like Jimmy and George, their trials and hardships may introduce them to the God who hides them under His wings.

From these stories we see God's protection and deliverance. In moments like these when we are under His wings, we may be engulfed by darkness. William O. Cushing penned the hymn *Under His Wings* which eloquently expresses God's protection and security:

> *Under His wings I am safely abiding;*
> *Though the night deepens and tempests are wild, Still I can trust Him, I know He*
> *will keep me; He has redeemed me, and I am His child.*

> *Under His wings — what a refuge in sorrow! How the heart yearningly turns to*
> *His rest! Often when earth has no balm for my healing, There I find comfort, and*
> *there I am blest.*

> *Under His wings — oh, what precious enjoyment! There will I hide till life's trials*
> *are o'er; Sheltered, protected, no evil can harm me; Resting in Jesus I'm safe ever*
> *more.*

> *Under His wings, under His wings, Who from His love can sever? Under His*
> *wings my soul shall abide, Safely abide forever.*

Note:
- For Press Release published by Department of Foreign Affairs, Republic of the Philippines, regarding Jimmy's case, see Press Release No.235-02 28 October 2002 at http://www.dfa.gov.ph/news/pr/pr2002/oct/pr235.htm (accessed June 20, 2004).
- To read more about George's story, see article published by Jay Hilotin Staff Reporter of Gulf News, Sunday, February 22, 2004.

CONCLUSION

❦

A s documented in this volume, a multitude of Filipinos have been scattered abroad as part of the eschatological schema of in-gathering for the new order (Revelation 7:9; 21:1-3). In this volume, it is shown that the sovereign grace of the Father (Jeremiah 29, Romans 8:28) had made the FIN movement possible for His Kingdom through the plight and flight of Filipinos from their homeland (see Chapter 4 and Postscript). The lordship of the Son (Philippians 2:5-11) in the lives of Filipino Christians abroad had turned these suffering and struggling sojourners into a mighty army for world missions (see Chapters 7 to 15). The empowering of individual Filipino Christians by the Holy Spirit (Acts 1:8) enabled them to become fruitful and powerful witnesses, even in difficult situations and dire circumstances (see Chapters 16 to 23).

The significance of this volume goes beyond the historical account of FIN as a missions movement at a global scale through the scattering of the Filipinos:

Theological significance:

- Anybody interested in the theme of diaspora will find the biblical and lexical survey of the uses of the word diaspora and its cognates in biblical and comparative extra-biblical literature in Chapter 3 to be very informative;

- The five theses and the fifteen theological propositions on diaspora in Chapter 4 are relevant to many diaspora groups; not only Filipinos.

Missiological significance:

- The mere fact of increased frequency and explosive scale of diaspora worldwide will require mission-minded Christians to examine the phenomenon of diaspora missiologically, and Chapter 5 is a valuable study of this type;

- "Is diaspora missions valid?" is a legitimate missiological question that deserves much research, while Chapter 6 is very relevant in the context of the on-going debate on "What is Christian missions?" and "How many types of Christian missions are there?"

- The "glocal missions paradigm" (i.e. thinking and acting locally and globally simultaneously" (Chapter 7) as modeled by the First Filipino Alliance Church in Alberta, Canada, leading to the emergence of FIN movement may be duplicated elsewhere in the context of a local congregation participating in world missions.

- The nine chapters of Part IV on "global strategy" and the Postscript (include case studies in different continents and diverse contexts) surely have multiple implications for the practice of Christian missions by other ethnic groups.

- The many personal stories (Part V) are inspiring and telling as to how God works in mysterious ways in spite of human feebleness, suffering and injustice.

The twenty-three chapters of this volume are intended to be informative and insightful to all mission-minded and action-oriented world Christians and practitioners.

The missions movement of FIN is a testimony to God's grace and provision incorporating the scattered and suffering Filipino diaspora into the process of Kingdom expansion.

Invitation is hereby extended to organizations such as LCWE (http://www.gospelcom.net/lcwe/index.html), CCCOWE (the first ethnic group with global network for world evangelization http://www.cccowe.org/cccowe_e.asp – among Chinese diaspora) and other sister organizations to partner with FIN (http://www.fin-online.org) for global missions.

Postcript

THE CHALLENGE OF DIASPORA LEADERS FOR WORLD EVANGELISM
Tom Houston

⚜

THE DIASPORAS IN THE BIBLE

Does the scattering of peoples have a place in the purposes of God? We know that the Israelites were exiled to Assyria (721 BCE) (2Ki.17:18). The Jews were deported to Babylon (721 BCE) (2Ki.25:11). The narrative shows that some also went to Egypt and in time to other places also.

Jeremiah and Ezekiel lived through this and forecast the return under Ezra and Nehemiah and others (Eze.36:19, 24 Jer.29:10). Ezekiel and other prophets also spoke of other people being scattered by God. It was not just the Jews whom God dispersed to achieve his purposes. The Egyptians were scattered and gathered (Ezek.29:12-16, 30:23). Isaiah spoke of God scattering all the nations and ultimately gathering them again (Isaiah 24:1, 66:18). Diaspora, then, would seem to be one of the ways that God works and not just one historical event.

You sense this also in the New Testament. The Dispersion has become a technical term for the Jews scattered throughout the world (Jas. l: l, 1 Pet. l: l, Jn.11:25-52). On a smaller scale, the early church continued in that same framework, advancing through compulsory scattering from persecution in Jerusalem, to Antioch and beyond (Ac.8:4, 11:19).

After the fall of man in Genesis 3 and its consequences in the scattering of the peoples from the Tower of Babel (Gen.11:1-10), God's historic purpose was to bring the whole world back to himself. He began with a promise to Abraham, "In you shall all the families of the earth be blessed" (Gen.12:3).

Later, God sent the 70-person family of Jacob down into Egypt, while he worked some things out with the people of the land (Gen. 15:16). Four hundred years later, Moses and Joshua brought them out of Egypt to Palestine.

Moses foresaw this on the eve of their entry into the promised land. They were to worship only God and keep his law. If they did not, God said, "I will scatter you in foreign lands" (Lev.26.33). When they came to their senses, God would bring them back (Dt.30:3). This was clearly to be a scattering for a divine purpose.

First they divided along tribal lines. In the ninth century BC, ten tribes became Israel, the northern kingdom. Two became Judah, the southern kingdom. The northern tribes of Israel were deported to Assyria in 721 BC. (2Ki.17:23). They never came back. They are the lost ten tribes.

More than a century later it was Judah's turn. They were exiled to Babylon, but they came back after 70 years (Nehemiah and Ezra). They came back a changed and chastened people.

Jesus came and restored the vision of the good news to all nations (Mk.13:10). In spite of that the early Christians had a hard time shaking off their Jewish cultural straight jacket, until Diaspora did it again. It took the push of persecution, added to the pull of God's call, to send them out to reach Gentiles. This was where the widespread Diaspora communities of Jews became the bridgehead for the planting of new city churches. By the time Paul reached the very pagan Athens in Greece, he began to articulate the missiological purpose of history including migration (Ac.17: 26-27).

Spasmodic persecution keeps dogging the churches, sometimes with unbelievable ferocity. Yet it did not destroy the vision of the ultimate universal spread of the gospel. John wrote about the city of God at the end of the New Testament (Rev.21:24, 26).

MIGRATION IN CHURCH HISTORY

The movement of Christian people throughout the Roman Empire which started in Acts continued throughout the first three centuries of the church. When Constantine made Christianity the faith of the Roman Empire, this lay movement accelerated its spread with official help. Eventually Rome fell to invading, migrating hordes from the East–Huns, Goths, Visigoths, Ostrogoths, etc. The remarkable result was the conversion of the invading migrants.

In the 15th century, the gospel followed the traders and explorers and the maritime empires came in to being. The Portuguese came to Brazil and Goa, the Spanish to Latin America and the Philippines, the French to Indochina, the Germans to East Africa and the British all over the world. The greater success of the British is attributed to the fact that they sent people who settled. There was much tragedy in this, especially in the ten million Africans who were involuntarily transported as slaves to America, the Caribbean, and Brazil over four centuries.[1] It has not, however, been without its effect in the expansion of Christianity as has been noted above. This brings us back to the question of the significance of the current massive Diasporas. There are two distinct cases.

THE EFFECT OF MIGRATIONS TO THE NORTH FROM MAJORITY CHRISTIAN NATIONS

Christian churches in Europe have been in serious decline for most of the 20th century. This decline continues in the main line churches with a few exceptions that do not affect the trend. Immigrant congregations, however, are growing. The largest churches in London are immigrant churches, mostly of African but also of Caribbean origin.[2]

In America, the injection of Hispanic migrants into the population has boosted the fortunes of the Roman Catholic Church.[3] The Mosaic of Migrant churches in the US has led a recent author to argue that a book by Diana Eck, *How a Christian Country Has Become the World's Most religiously Diverse Nation,* should better be titled, *How Mass Immigration Ensured That a Christian Country Has Become an Even More Christian Country.*[4] Observers are beginning to suggest that the Pacific Rim countries, in addition to its economic potential, could become also a Christian arc.[5]

This is not just a demographic phenomenon. The immigrants from the churches of the South are more biblical in their beliefs and theology. This was illustrated in the Lambeth Conference of Bishops from the Anglican Communion in 1998. The biblical view on homosexuality was enshrined in Anglican policy by a ten to one vote of the 736 bishops present, most of whom were from churches in the South. In the 2003 controversies on the same issue, the weight of the churches of the South was still heavily against the liberalizing tendencies in the USA and UK. Some are even beginning to wonder if it will be the churches of the South that will eventually turn the tide against the secularizing tendencies in Western Theology.

THE SIGNIFICANCE OF MIGRATIONS TO THE NORTH FROM MINORITY CHRISTIAN NATIONS

Many of the migrants to the North are from minority Christian nations. Even here, the trend seems to be that the proportion of Christians in such Diasporas is higher than in their country of origin. This is true of the people from the Middle East – Arabs and Iranians. This is partly because the Christians have fled discrimination or persecution. It may also be that they are the better educated in their country of origin because of the contribution of the Mission Schools. When there is less pressure from their fellow citizens in their new country, even the non-Christians have the chance to consider the gospel in a more congenial climate. In France, where the majority of the immigrants are Muslims from North Africa, it is the immigrant churches that are growing while the French churches are static or declining.

The proportion of Christians in the Chinese Diaspora in North America is higher that in China itself. On the other hand, this is not true in several other countries where there is a significant Chinese Diaspora. This leads to the question of the challenge to Diaspora Christian leaders.

THE DIRECTIVES TO DIASPORA CHRISTIAN LEADERS

There are two kinds of migrant leaders. Some are voluntary migrants, some had no choice but to leave home. The voluntary migrants are often frowned upon by the people back home. They are seen as having been materialistically motivated to leave in the first place. Even if they were not, they are often more prosperous now and their Christian authority is seen to be compromised. They are seen to have deprived the work of God in their home country of the gifts and experience that they have taken out with them.

Even those who felt they had no choice but to leave are still open to the temptations of materialism. Their first goal is to survive and they have to bend all their efforts to do that. They want to prosper and when and if they do, it gets into their blood but not without a tinge of guilt about how well they are doing compared to those left behind at home. This can be masked by developing a critical spirit of the people back home. Where this is so, they do not easily develop a practical concern to make a sacrificial contribution to the evangelization of their mother land.

When this is the case — and they are part of a Diaspora church—it tends to become an ethnic ghetto, with varying degrees of internal strife. They do not make much of an impact either on the host population or on their country of origin.

How can it be different?

There is an answer in Jeremiah 29. This is a letter from Jeremiah in Jerusalem to the first generation of deportees to Babylon. We may summarize what he says in this way:

- **See it as in God's plan!** (29:11) and believe it has a positive purpose.

- **Take the long view!**

  Count on seventy years, not two years (29:10). Do not be susceptible either to triumphalist or doom-mongering prophets (28:2, 29:8-9). Get property and become self sufficient in food (29:5). Have healthy families (29:6).

- **Make a social, spiritual and economic contribution to your host city!** (29:7). Take advantage of the administrative opportunities presented to you like Nehemiah, Daniel and his companions, or the public relations openings like Esther.

- **Making a new and deeper covenant start in knowing God!** (29:12-13) Having escaped the ruts of your previous life, seek God whole heartedly and discover him in new ways. Plumb the depths of the word of God like Ezra. Much of the truth that we take for granted emerged from this period. There is much we would not have known if the people of God had not been scattered. The concept of the New Covenant came out of the Diaspora (Jer.31). The Messiah as the suffering servant, as in Isaiah 53, came from this period. The suffering servant was discriminated against and rejected. This is what happens when one is in exile. Eschatology developed comprehensively during the exile and the return. The Day of the Lord, the New Jerusalem all come out of the Diaspora. The promises we love so much come from this period. "They that wait on the Lord shall renew their strength." When the Jews left home, they were driven from Judah to Babylon like slaves. They needed to learn to run and not be weary, to walk and not faint, and even dream of mounting up on wings like eagles!

- **Keep hope alive!** (29:14). There is a future and a hope. It may not be in your generation. If the exile was to last seventy years (i.e. two or more generations), and those who got the letter would not live to see the return, they could leave that to their faithful God.

There is evidence that some Diaspora churches are following Jeremiah's guidelines, and the contribution to world evangelization is remarkable.

ENDNOTES

[1] Philip Jenkins, "The Next Christendom" p.98-99

[2] Ibid. pp. 100-101

[3] Ibid. pp. 105-106

[4] Ibid pp.102.

[5] Figures from the Chinese Coordinating Committee for World Evangelisation

"¹⁹Go therefore and make disciples of all the nations, baptizing them in the name of the Father and of the Son and of the Holy Spirit, ²⁰teaching them to observe all things that I have commanded you; and lo, I am with you always, *even* to the end of the age." Amen.

Matthew 28:19-20 (NIV)

CONTRIBUTORS

CONTRIBUTORS

RONALD ADHIKARI (D. Min., Fuller Theological Seminary; M.Th., Presbyterian Theological Seminary, Seoul; B.A., St. Edmund's College, Gauhati University; Diploma in Theology, Singapore Bible College) has been a missionary with SEND International since 1989. He is involved in church planting, training tentmakers, and teaching in seminaries. He was also involved with InterVarsity Christian Fellowship (IVCF) and OMS International for a number of years.

IDRENNE LIM-ALPARAQUE (Ph.D.–Education, University of Alberta; M.Ed.–Literacy & Language, University of Alberta; M.A. ed., TESL, Silliman University; B.S.E., Philippine Normal College) has been a professor in Education at Central Washington University, National University, the University of British Columbia & San Diego State University. She teaches Qualitative Research Methodology, Critical Pedagogy, Action Research, Language Acquisition & Development, Thesis & Dissertation Writing. She is the Executive Director for Academic Research, PRAXIS Research Seminars Inc.

ROSALINDA DIMAPILIS-BALDOZ (MNSA, National Defense College of the Philippines; LL.B., Manuel Luis Quezon University; B.A., Manuel Luis Quezon University) is currently the Administrator of Philippine Overseas Employment Administration (POEA). She was former Undersecretary of Labor and Employment, Republic of the Philippines; the first Filipino and the first Asian woman to be elected as Chair of the International Labor Committee (ILC) on the application and standards, 87th Session of the International Labor Conference, Geneva, Switzerland, June 1999.

TERESO C. CASIÑO (Ph.D.–Missiology/Contextualization, ACTS/ Asia United Theological University; Th.D.–Systematic Theology, Asia Baptist Graduate Theological Seminary; M.Div., Asia-Pacific Nazarene Theological Seminary; B.Th., Luzon Nazarene Bible College) is Associate Professor of Systematic Theology & Missiology and Dean of Continuing Education Center at Torch Trinity Graduate School of Theology in Seoul, South Korea. He was Dean and Professor of Theology & Missiology at the Asia Baptist Graduate Theological Seminary. A member of the British *Society for the Study of Theology* (SST), Dr. Casiño edits the *Asia-Pacific Journal of Interdisciplinary Studies* and serves among the diaspora communities in Korea.

LORAJOY TIRA DIMANGONDAYAO (B.Th., Canadian Bible College) is Editor of Filipino International Network's (FIN) quarterly newsletter, and serves with the editorial committee for the missions E-Journal www.GlobalMissiology.net. She was a member of the International Fellowship of Alliance Professionals (IFAP) while teaching Primary English in Ulsan, South Korea.

JOCELYN DINO (B.A. Journalism, Polytechnic University of the Philippines) is now working among the Mangyan tribes in the Hinterland of Mindoro, Philippines. She was Editor-in-Chief of Pinoy Gazzette, a Filipino newspaper in Japan. Ms. Dino also served as missionary with Operation Mobilization assigned onboard the ship MV Doulos.

RODOLFO I. DUMAPIAS (Master in International Relations, University of Southern California; AB International Relations and Political Science, University of California, Los Angeles) is currently serving as Philippine Deputy Chief of Mission and Consul General to Mexico. He was Philippine Ambassador to Bahrain (1999-2002). He also served as Philippines' Chargé d'Affaires to Malaysia, Romania, and South Korea, and as Consul to China and Germany. He was Professor of Political Science and History at Lyceum of the Philippines and Far Eastern University, and lecturer at the National Defense College of the Philippines. He attended Haggai Institute, Singapore, in 2003.

BRIAN FARGHER (Ph.D.–History of Missions, University of Aberdeen; M.Th., Northwest Theological Seminary; B. Div., University of London) is Executive Director of the Urban Missionaries Association of Canada. He served more than 25 years as missionary with Sudan Interior Missions (SIM) in Ethiopia.

RODRIGO C. FELOMINO, JR. (D. Min. Cand., Lutheran Theological Seminary; M.Div., Alliance Biblical Seminary; M.A.–Socio-Political Studies, University of the Philippines; B. Min. S., Ebenezer Bible College; Bachelor of Arts–Political Science, King's College) has been a pastor, and Bible teacher with the Christian and Missionary Alliance of the Philippines (CAMACOP). He is currently an Associate Pastor of Kowloon Tong International Congregation in Hong Kong.

VENUS HANNAH GALVEZ (M.A.–Mass Com., University of the Philippines; B.A.–Social Sciences, University of the Philippines) is President of the Filipino Christian Ministry Network (FCMN), and International Coordinator for the Japan Educational and Mission Exposure (JEME) Program. She served on board the Operation Mobilization ship MV Doulos.

TOM HOUSTON has been a pastor in Scotland and Kenya. He has served as the Chief Executive Officer with The British and Foreign Bible Society (1971-1983), as President of World Vision International (1983-1988), and as International Director for The Lausanne Committee for World Evangelization (1989-1994).

ROBERT FERDINAND K. LOPEZ (B. Sc. Econ., University of the Philippines) is currently the National Director of Philippine Missions Association. He is also serving as Board Member of the Tentmakers International Exchange (TIE), Asian School of Development and Cross-Cultural Studies (ASDECS). He was Chief Operating Officer of Asian Center for Missions (ACM) in Manila.

CHARLIE H. MANCE (M. Div., Tyndale Seminary, Toronto; M.Sc.–Zoology, University of Alberta; Graduate studies at Osaka University of Foreign Studies and Kyushu University; B. Sc., University of the Philippines) is Senior Pastor of the River of Life Alliance Church in Calgary, Alberta (Canada). He is also serving as Associate Coordinator for the Conference of Filipino Alliance Ministries (CFAM), and member of the Christian and Missionary Alliance (C&MA) Western Canadian District Ordaining Council.

PHILIP PACLE (B.F.A., Philippine Women's University) is employed as an Art Director for an advertising agency in a Limited Access Nation. A cartoonist and a freelance photographer for newspapers. Currently serves as a lay leader of his local church (QICM).

LUIS PANTOJA, JR. (Th.D., Dallas Theological Seminary; S.T.M., Dallas Theological Seminary; M.Div., Denver Conservative Baptist Seminary; B.Th., Febias College) is Senior Pastor of Greenhills Christian Fellowship (Pasig, Metro Manila); President of Conservative Baptist Association of the Philippines; Executive Secretary for Theological Commission of the Evangelical Fellowship of Asia.

AMADOR A. REMIGIO, JR. (Ph.D.–Geography, Imperial College of Science and Technology at Wye, University of London; M.Sc.–Rural Resources and Environmental Policy, Imperial College of Science and Technology at Wye, University of London; B.S. Pol. Sci., University of the Philippines) has worked in various capacities for various governments, the academe, the private sector and several international organizations in the last 20 years. He was a Research Fellow at the School of Resource and Environmental Management of Simon Fraser University, and currently is on the faculty of the Department of Geography, History / Politics and International Studies at Trinity Western University, B.C.

NARRY F. SANTOS (Ph.D.–New Testament, Dallas Theological Seminary; S.T.M.–New Testament, Dallas Theological Seminary; M.Div., International School of Theology-Asia; B.S. in Civil Engineering, University of Philippines) is Associate Pastor of Greenhills Christian Fellowship (Alabang, Metro Manila). He is also Adjunct Faculty Member at International School of Theology-Asia.

REYNALDO SOLANO (M.Div., Asia Pacific Theological Seminary, Baguio; M.A.–Biblical Studies, Asia Pacific Theological Seminary; B.C.M., Immanuel Bible College, Cebu City) is currently serving as Pastor of Filipino Ministry at Victory Family Centre in Singapore and has served as President of Kapatiran ng mga Simbahang Pilipino sa Singapore (KSPS) in Singapore.

HENRY H. TAN (Ed.D.–Educational Leadership, University of San Diego; M.Div., International School of Theology, San Bernardino; M.B.M.,

Asian Institute of Management, Manila; B.S. Chem., University of Malaya) is currently the CEO of GlobaLead Inc. He served as National Director of Campus Crusade for Christ in the Philippines, and as President of International School of Theology-Asia.

SADIRI JOY B. TIRA (D. Min.–InterCultural Studies, Reformed Theological Seminary, Jackson, Mississippi; M.T.S., Edmonton Baptist Seminary; M. Mis., Canadian Theological Seminary; B.S.I.E., FEATI University; Marine Engineering, FEATI University) is Senior Pastor of First Filipino Alliance Church (Edmonton, Alberta, Canada) and the International Coordinator for Filipino International Network. He has served on the General Council of the Evangelical Fellowship of Canada (EFC).

ENOCH WAN (Ph.D.–Anthropology, State University of New York; M.A., State University of New York; M.T.S., Gordon-Conwell Theological Seminary; B.A., Nyack College, New York) is Professor of Intercultural Studies, Director of Doctor of Missiology Program, and Chair for Division of Intercultural Studies at Western Seminary. He has served on the Board of Directors of the American Society of Missiology, as Vice-President of Evangelical Missiological Society (EMS-SE), and the editor of the e-journal www.GlobalMissiology.net.

GODIVA D. YSIP (M.A.–Education & Intercultural Studies, Singapore Bible College; B.S. Geology, Mapua Institute of Technology, Manila) has been serving full-time with the Pastoral Staff of Faith Methodist Church in Singapore since 1996. She serves as Parish Leader for Small Groups, and as Ministry Staff for the Women's Ministry. She served in the staff of Christ for Greater Manila and as a missionary with Operation Mobilisation (England).

LIFECHANGE™
Publishing, Inc.

96-B Panay Avenue, Brgy. South Triangle, Quezon City 1103 Philippines
Phone: (632) 374-5996 • Fax: (632) 374-5997
E-mail: lifechange@i-manila.com.ph

Filipino International Network

10115-79 Street, Edmonton, Alberta, Canada T6A 3G4
Phone: (780) 468-7004 • Fax: (780) 469-1002
www.fin-online.org